ABOUT THE ARTIST

Born in 1936, Kazuo Umezu is Japan's most respected and influential horror manga artist. Umezu began his artistic career at the age of 18, creating stories for both *shōjo* (girls) and *shonen* (boys) manga magazines, and working in an amazingly diverse range of genres. In Japan he is most famous for the gag manga *Makoto-chan* (1971), but his most ambitious works are horror and science fiction, including *The Drifting Classroom* (1972-1974), *My Name is Shingo* (1982-1986), *The Left Hand of God, the Right Hand of the Devil* (1986-1989) and *Fourteen* (1990-1995). His works have been adapted into anime and live-action films.

THE DRIFTING CLASSROOM
Vol. 2

STORY AND ART BY KAZUO UMEZU

Translation/Yuji Oniki
Touch-up Art & Lettering/Kelle Han
Design/Izumi Evers
Editor/Jason Thompson

Editor in Chief, Books/Alvin Lu
Editor in Chief, Magazines/Marc Weidenbaum
VP of Publishing Licensing/Rika Inouye
VP of Sales/Gonzalo Ferreyra
Sr. VP of Marketing/Liza Coppola
Publisher/Hyoe Narita

Printed in the U.S.A.

Published by VIZ Media, LLC
P.O. Box 77010
San Francisco, CA 94107

10 9 8 7 6 5 4 3 2
First printing, October 2006
Second printing, May 2008

www.viz.com
store.viz.com

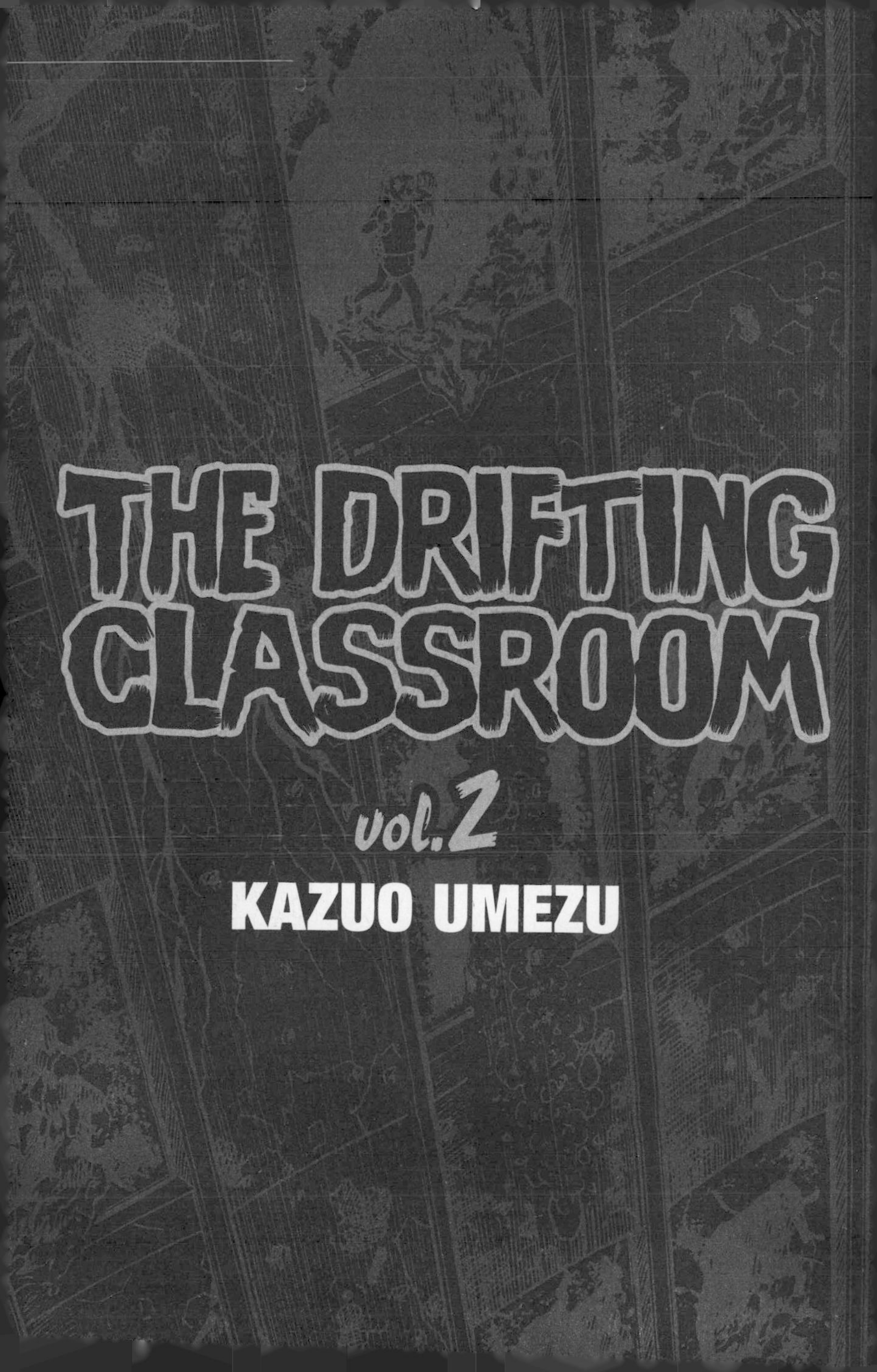

THE DRIFTING CLASSROOM

vol. 2

KAZUO UMEZU

CONTENTS

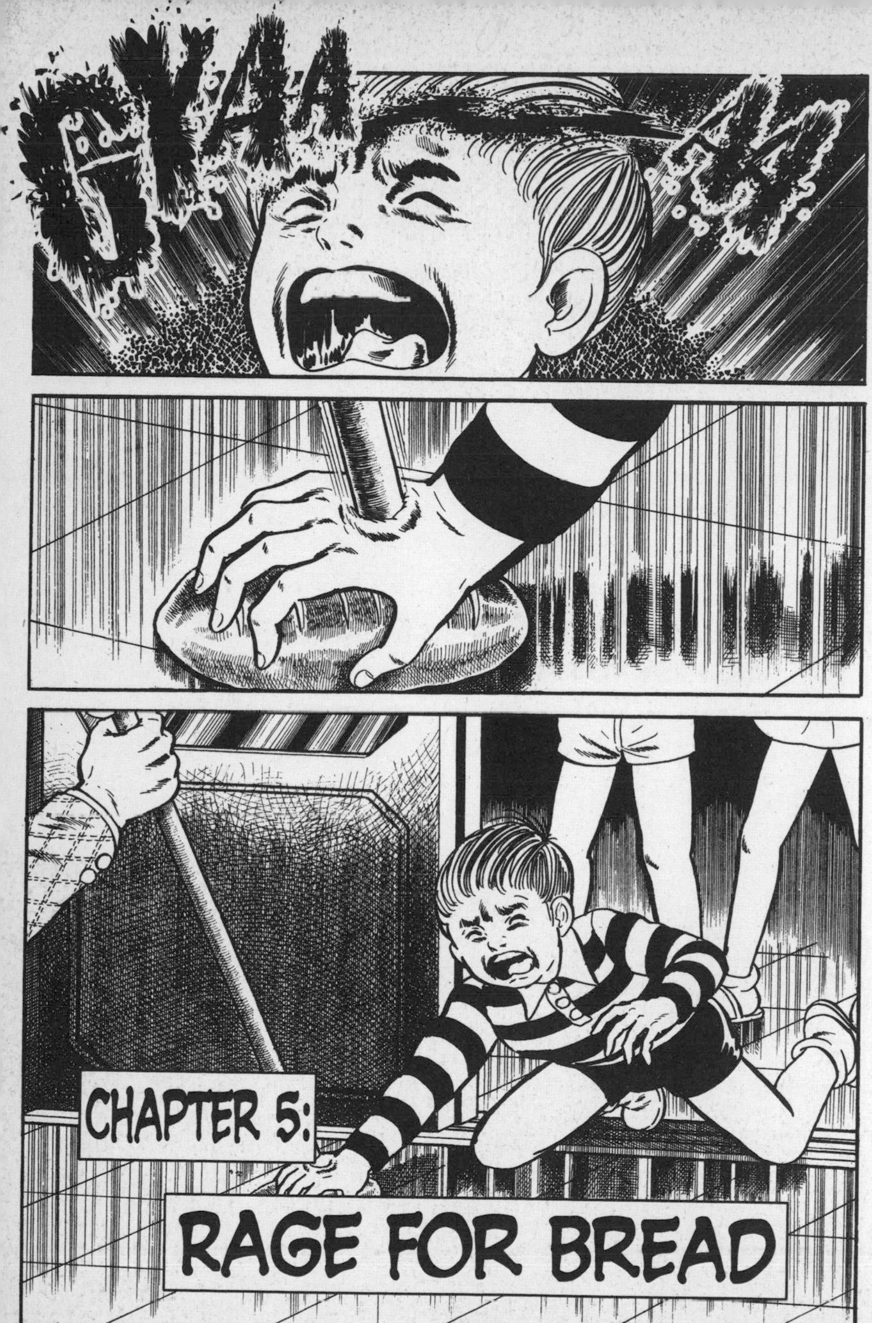
GYAA
AA!
CHAPTER 5:
RAGE FOR BREAD

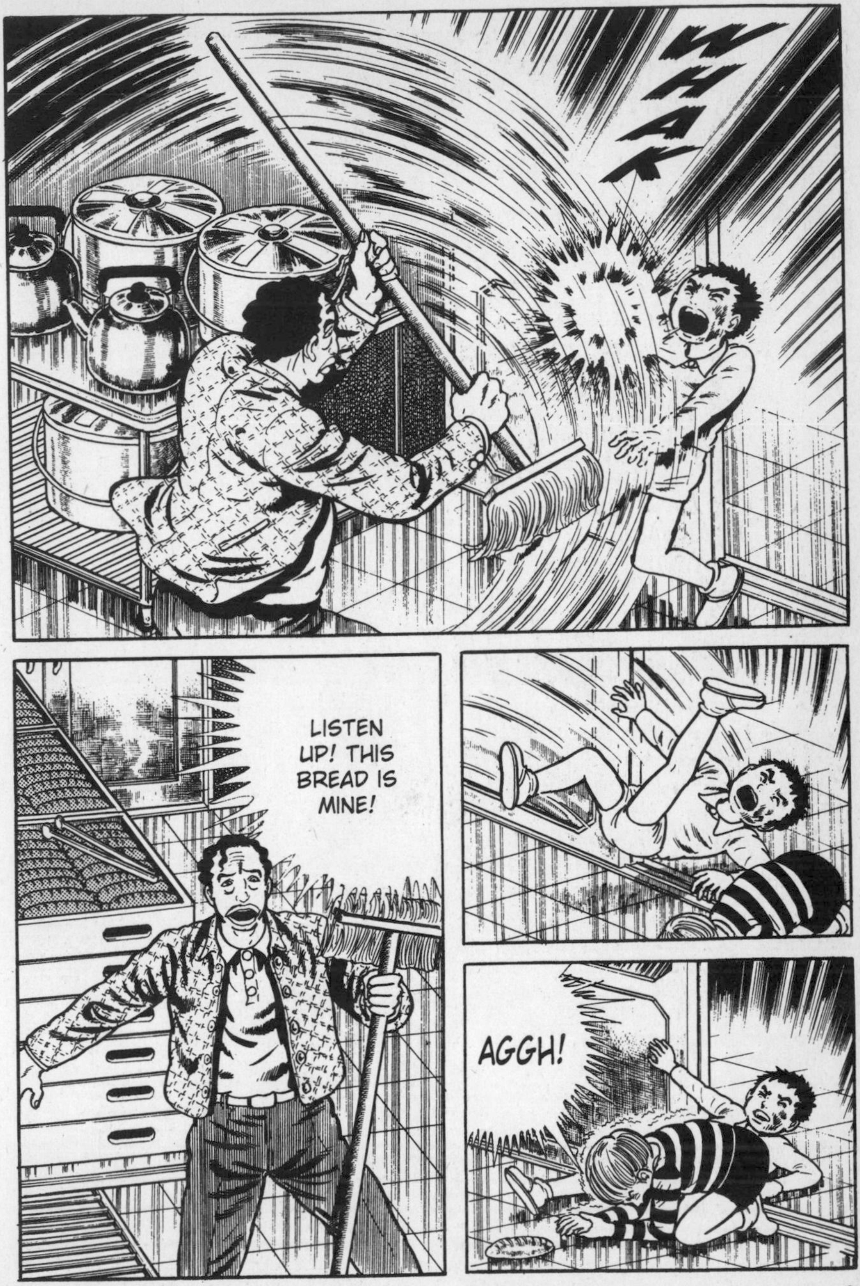
WHAK
AGGH!
LISTEN UP! THIS BREAD IS MINE!

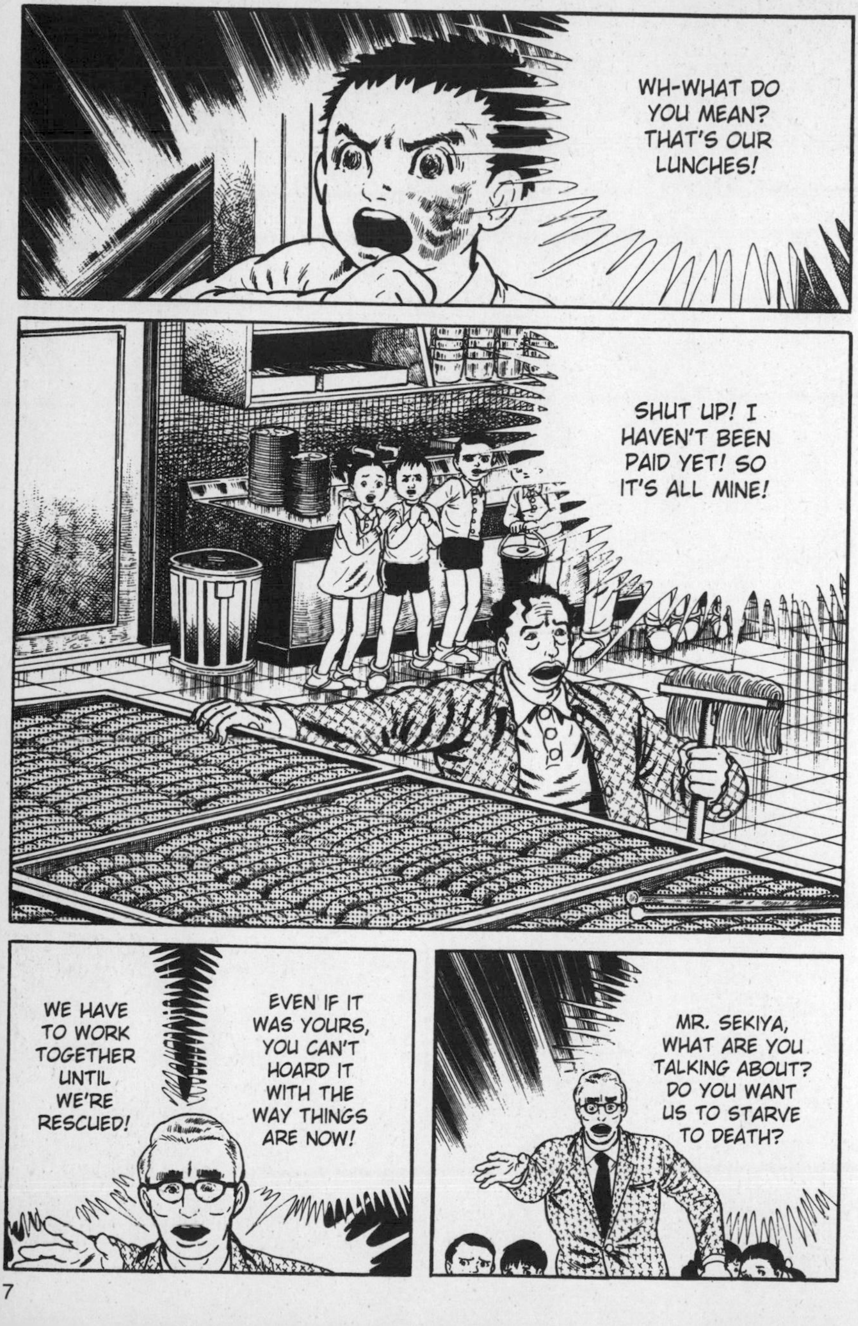
WH-WHAT DO YOU MEAN? THAT'S OUR LUNCHES!
SHUT UP! I HAVEN'T BEEN PAID YET! SO IT'S ALL MINE!
MR. SEKIYA, WHAT ARE YOU TALKING ABOUT? DO YOU WANT US TO STARVE TO DEATH?
EVEN IF IT WAS YOURS, YOU CAN'T HOARD IT WITH THE WAY THINGS ARE NOW!
WE HAVE TO WORK TOGETHER UNTIL WE'RE RESCUED!

I WON'T EVEN GIVE YOU A CRUMB!

SHUT UP!

W S S H

AGH!

KRAK

"WORK TOGETHER TILL WE'RE RESCUED"?

HA HA HA HA

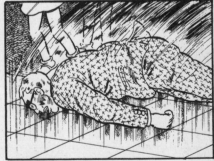

MR. YAMASHINA!

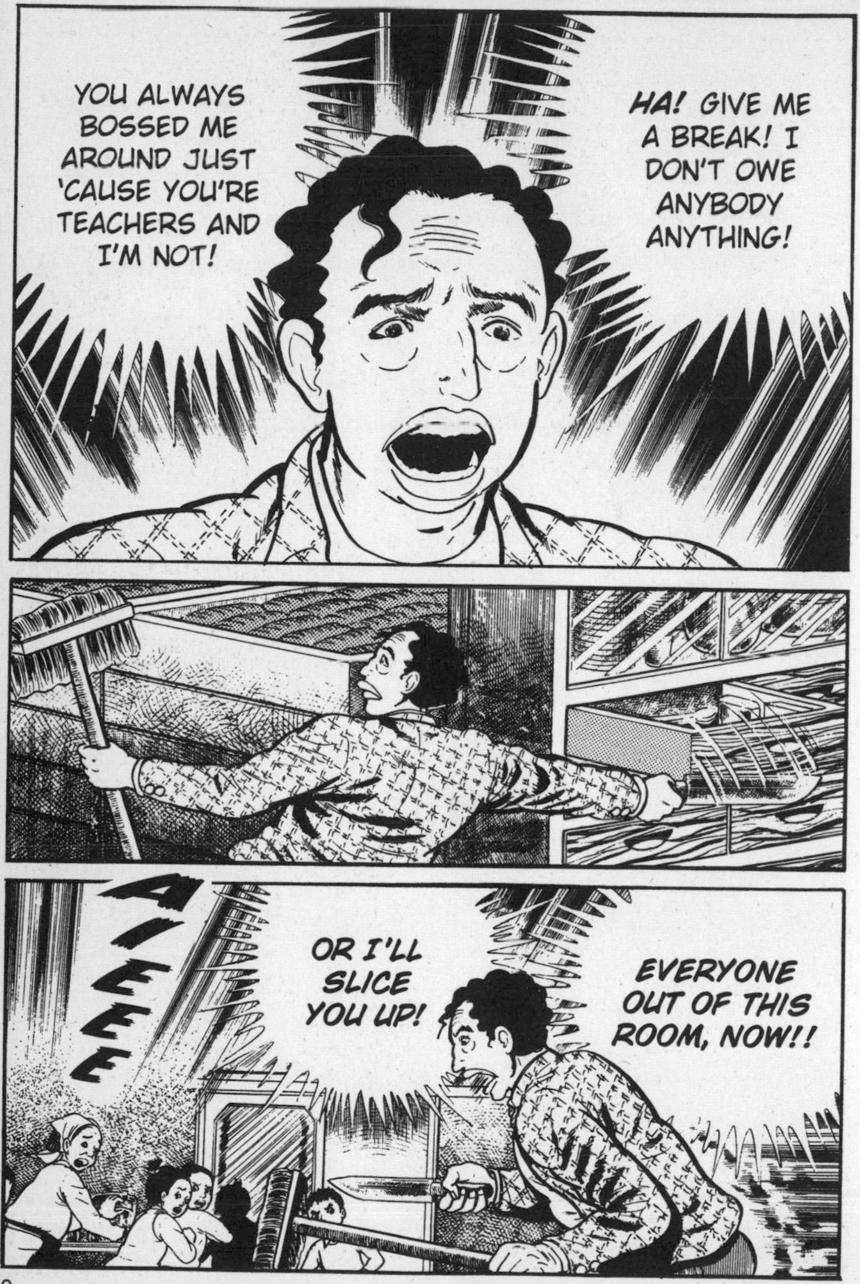
HA! GIVE ME A BREAK! I DON'T OWE ANYBODY ANYTHING!
YOU ALWAYS BOSSED ME AROUND JUST 'CAUSE YOU'RE TEACHERS AND I'M NOT!
EVERYONE OUT OF THIS ROOM, NOW!!
OR I'LL SLICE YOU UP!
AIEEE

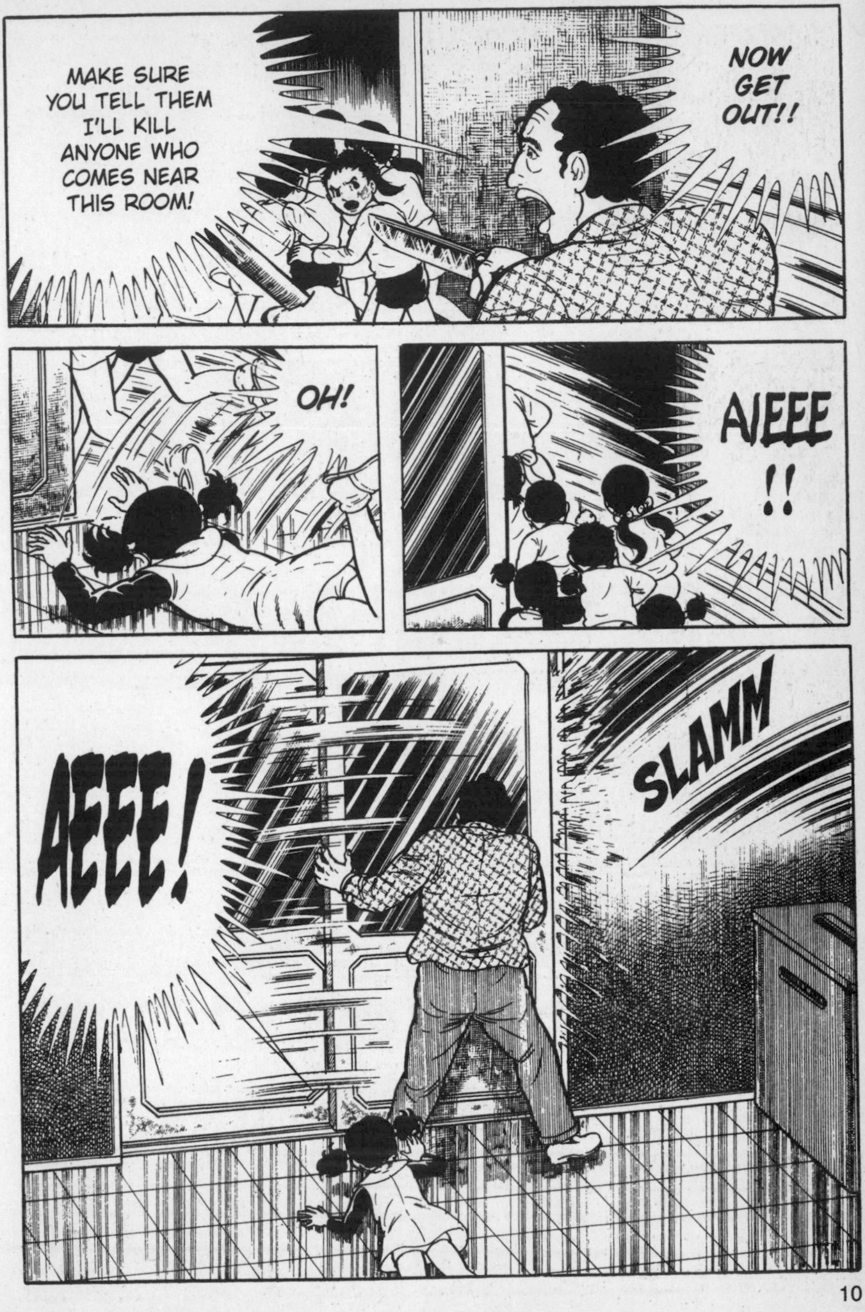
NOW GET OUT!!
MAKE SURE YOU TELL THEM I'LL KILL ANYONE WHO COMES NEAR THIS ROOM!
AIEEE !!
OH!
SLAMM
AEEE!

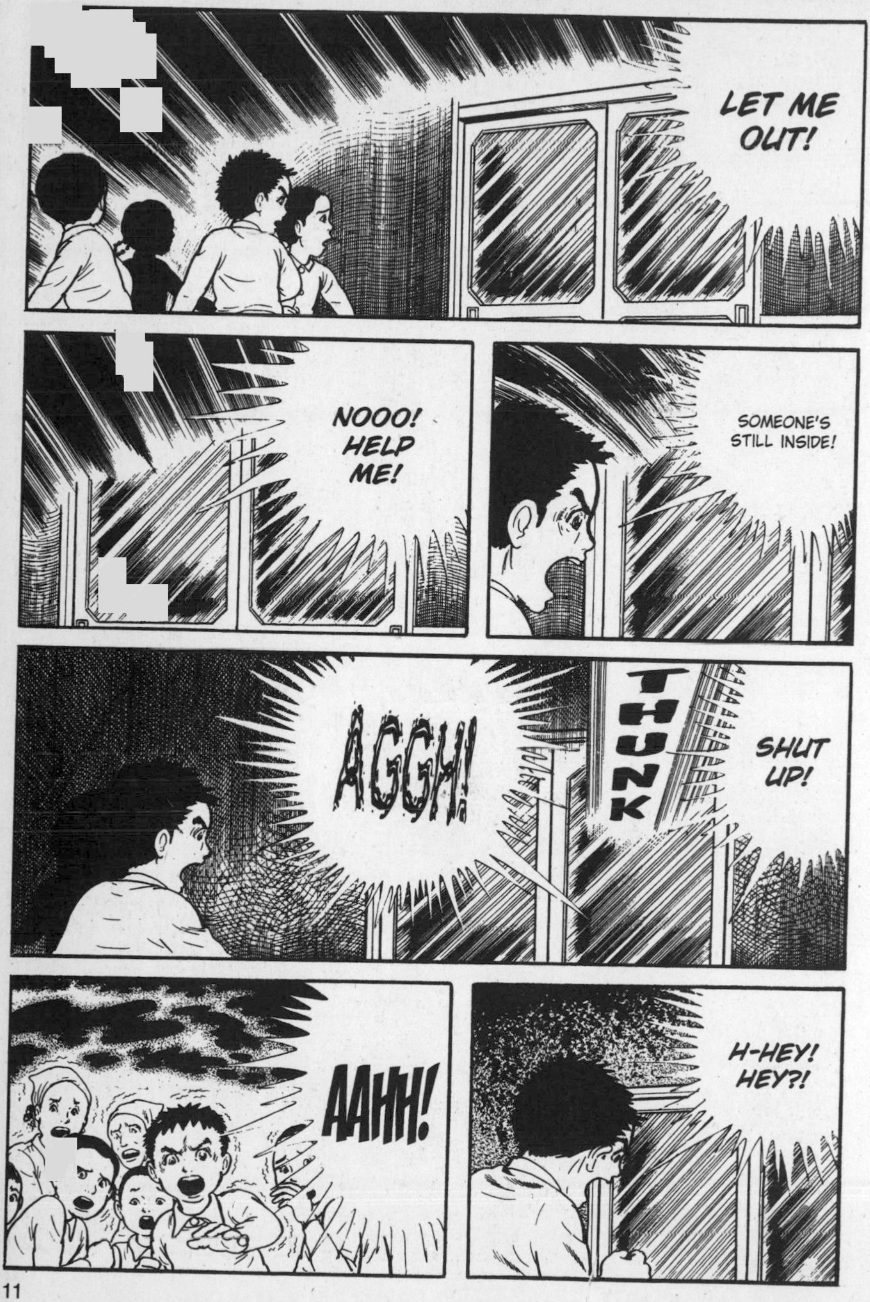
LET ME OUT!
SOMEONE'S STILL INSIDE!
NOOO! HELP ME!
SHUT UP!
THUNK
AGGH!
H-HEY! HEY?!
AAHH!

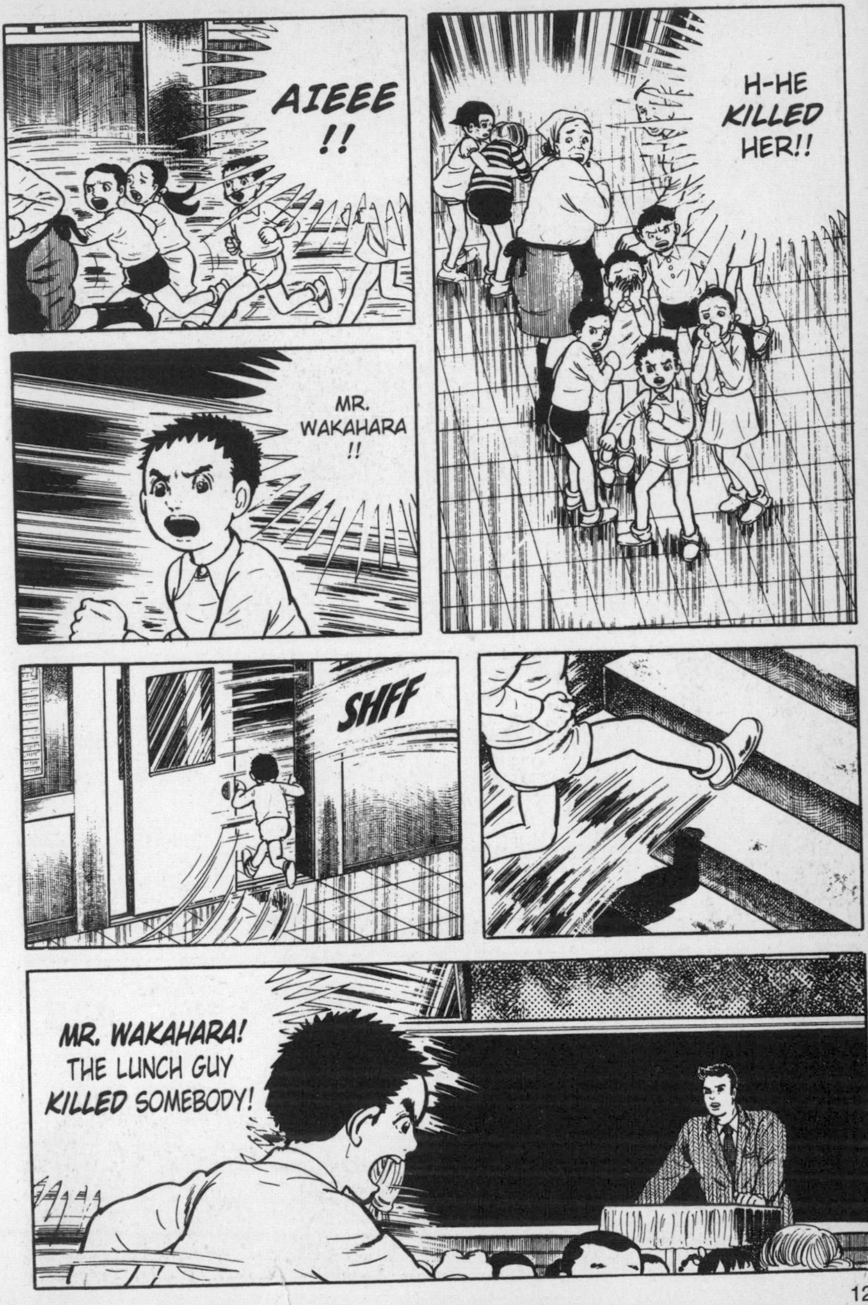
H-HE KILLED HER!!
AIEEE !!
MR. WAKAHARA !!
SHFF
MR. WAKAHARA! THE LUNCH GUY KILLED SOMEBODY!

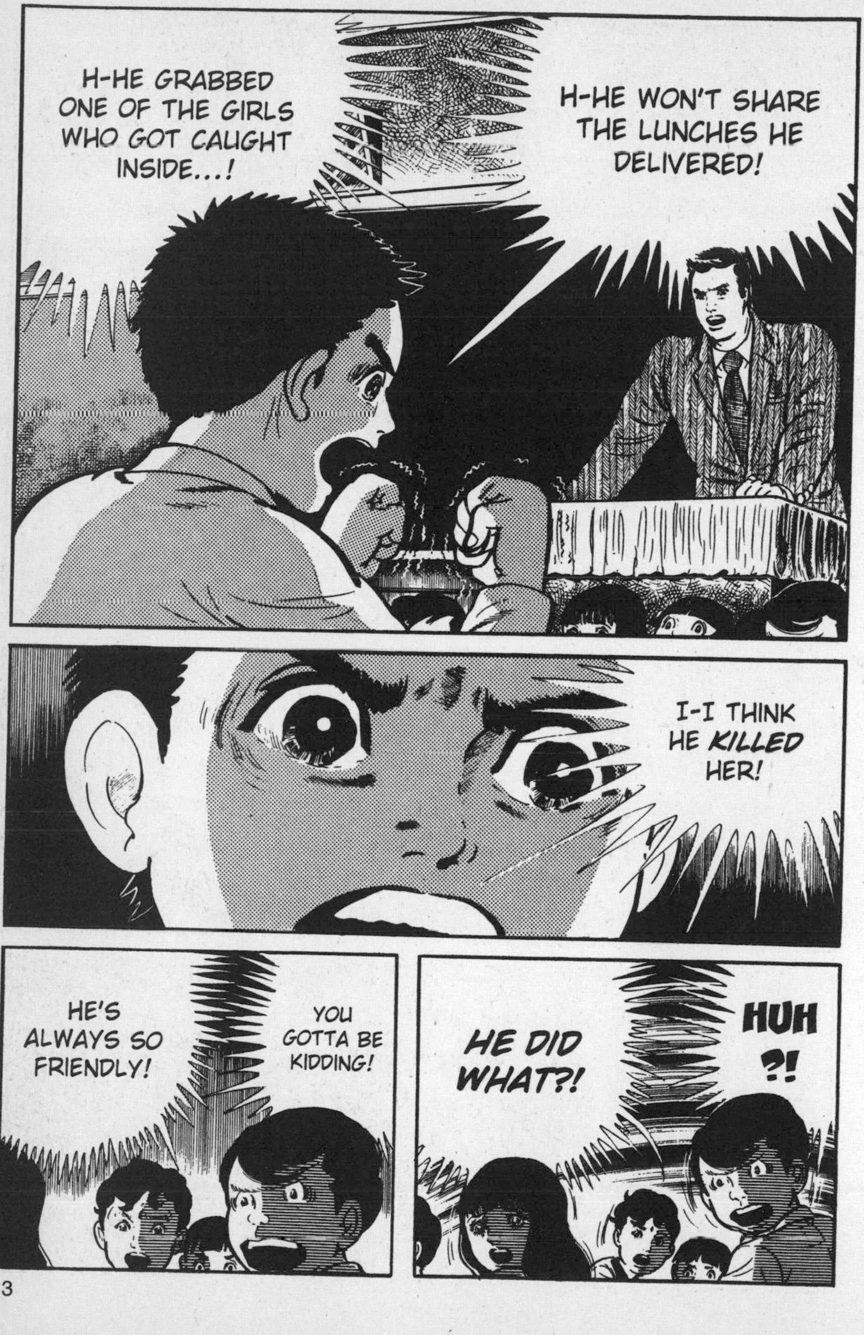
H-HE WON'T SHARE THE LUNCHES HE DELIVERED!
H-HE GRABBED ONE OF THE GIRLS WHO GOT CAUGHT INSIDE...!
I-I THINK HE *KILLED* HER!
HUH ?!
HE DID WHAT?!
YOU GOTTA BE KIDDING!
HE'S ALWAYS SO FRIENDLY!

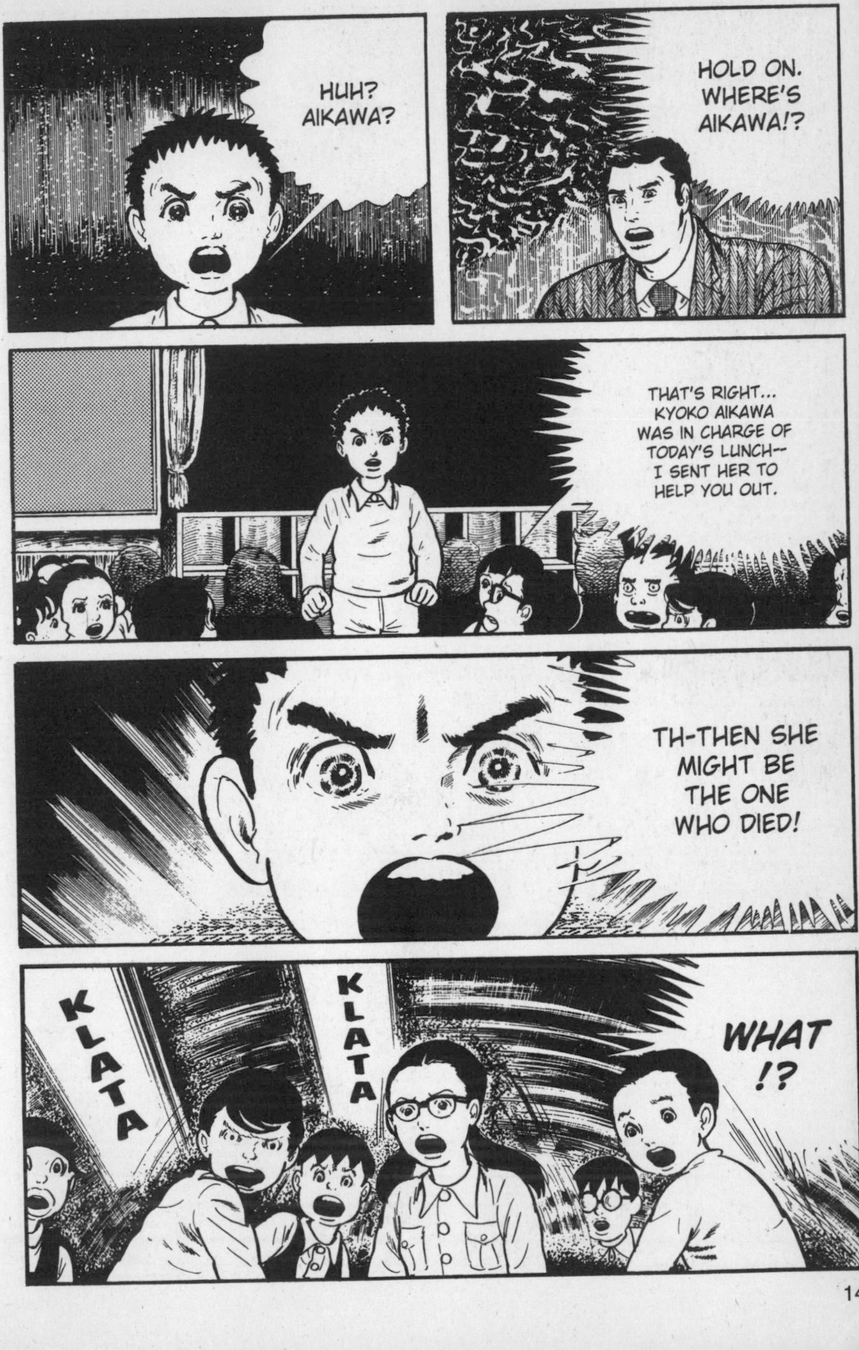
HOLD ON. WHERE'S AIKAWA!?
HUH? AIKAWA?
THAT'S RIGHT... KYOKO AIKAWA WAS IN CHARGE OF TODAY'S LUNCH-- I SENT HER TO HELP YOU OUT.
TH-THEN SHE MIGHT BE THE ONE WHO DIED!
WHAT !?
KLATA
KLATA

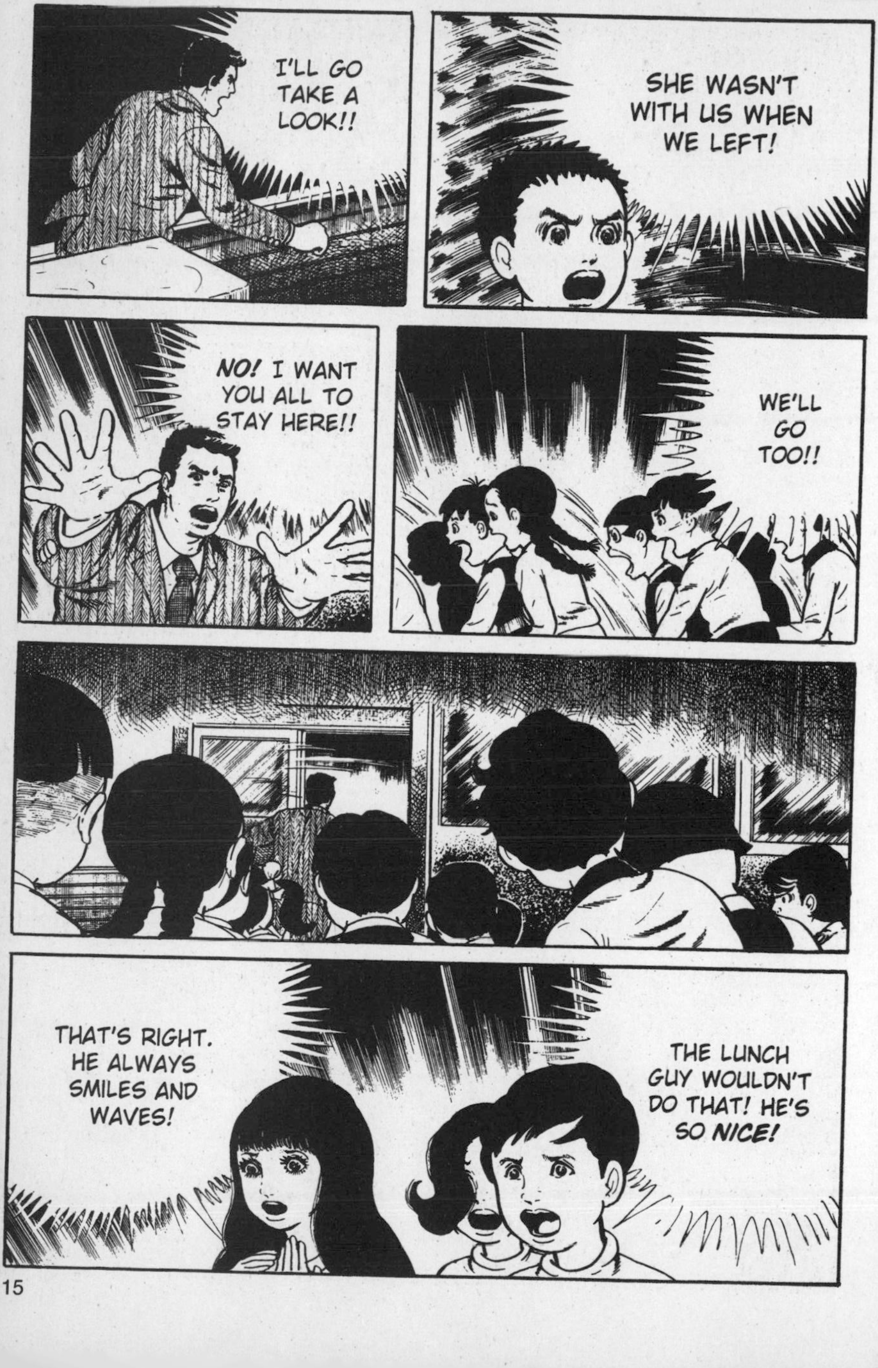
SHE WASN'T WITH US WHEN WE LEFT!
I'LL GO TAKE A LOOK!!
WE'LL GO TOO!!
NO! I WANT YOU ALL TO STAY HERE!!
THE LUNCH GUY WOULDN'T DO THAT! HE'S SO NICE!
THAT'S RIGHT. HE ALWAYS SMILES AND WAVES!

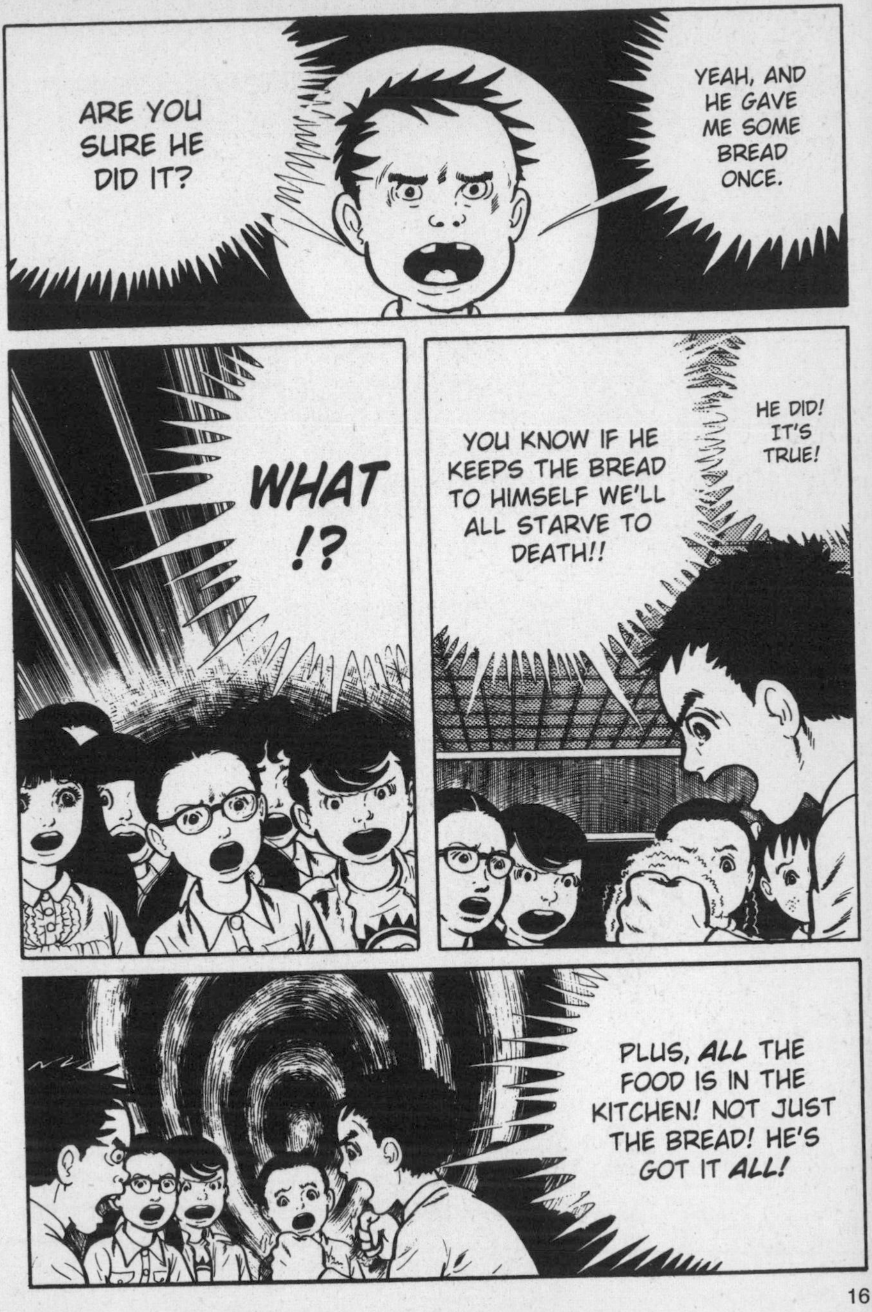
YEAH, AND HE GAVE ME SOME BREAD ONCE.
ARE YOU SURE HE DID IT?
HE DID! IT'S TRUE!
YOU KNOW IF HE KEEPS THE BREAD TO HIMSELF WE'LL ALL STARVE TO DEATH!!
WHAT !?
PLUS, ALL THE FOOD IS IN THE KITCHEN! NOT JUST THE BREAD! HE'S GOT IT ALL!

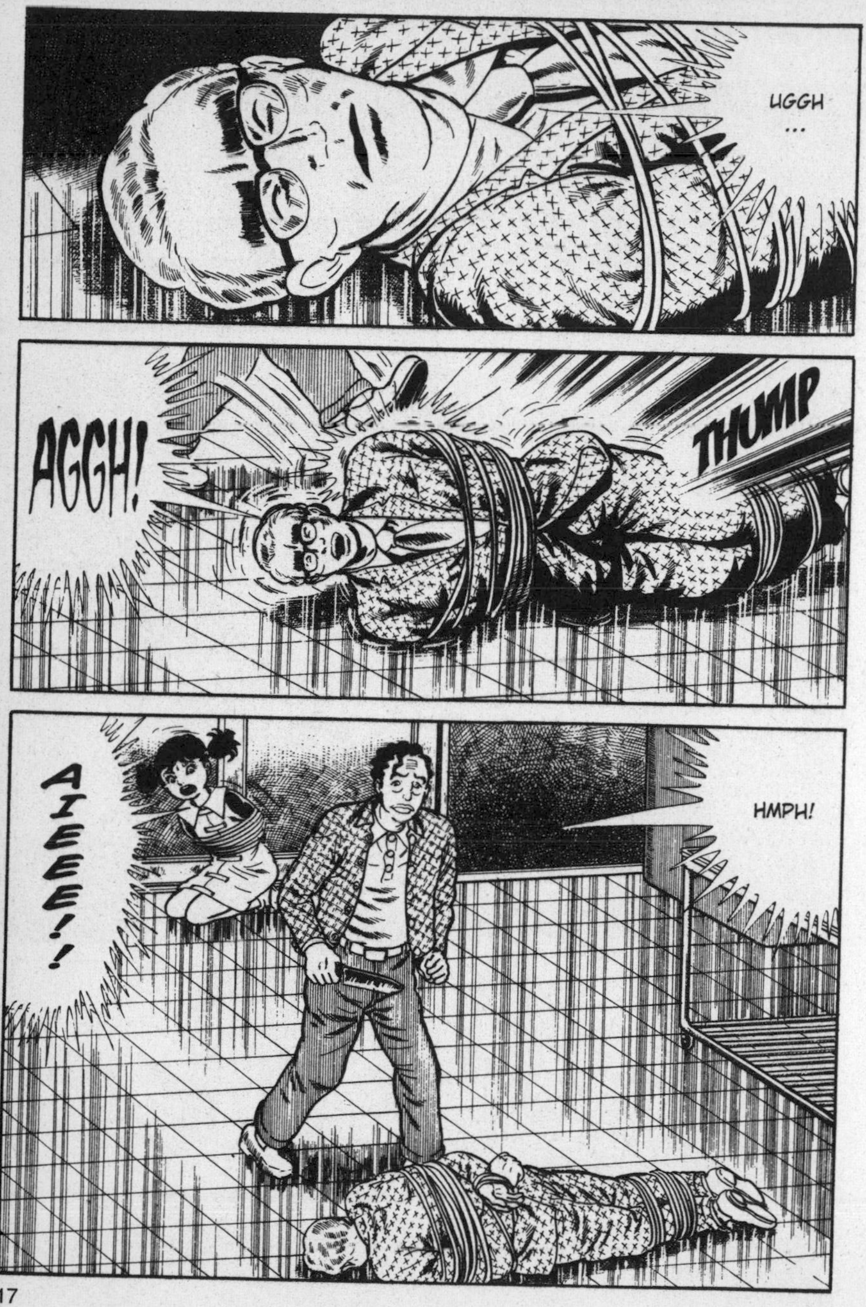
UGGH
...
THUMP
AGGH!
HMPH!
AIEEEE!!

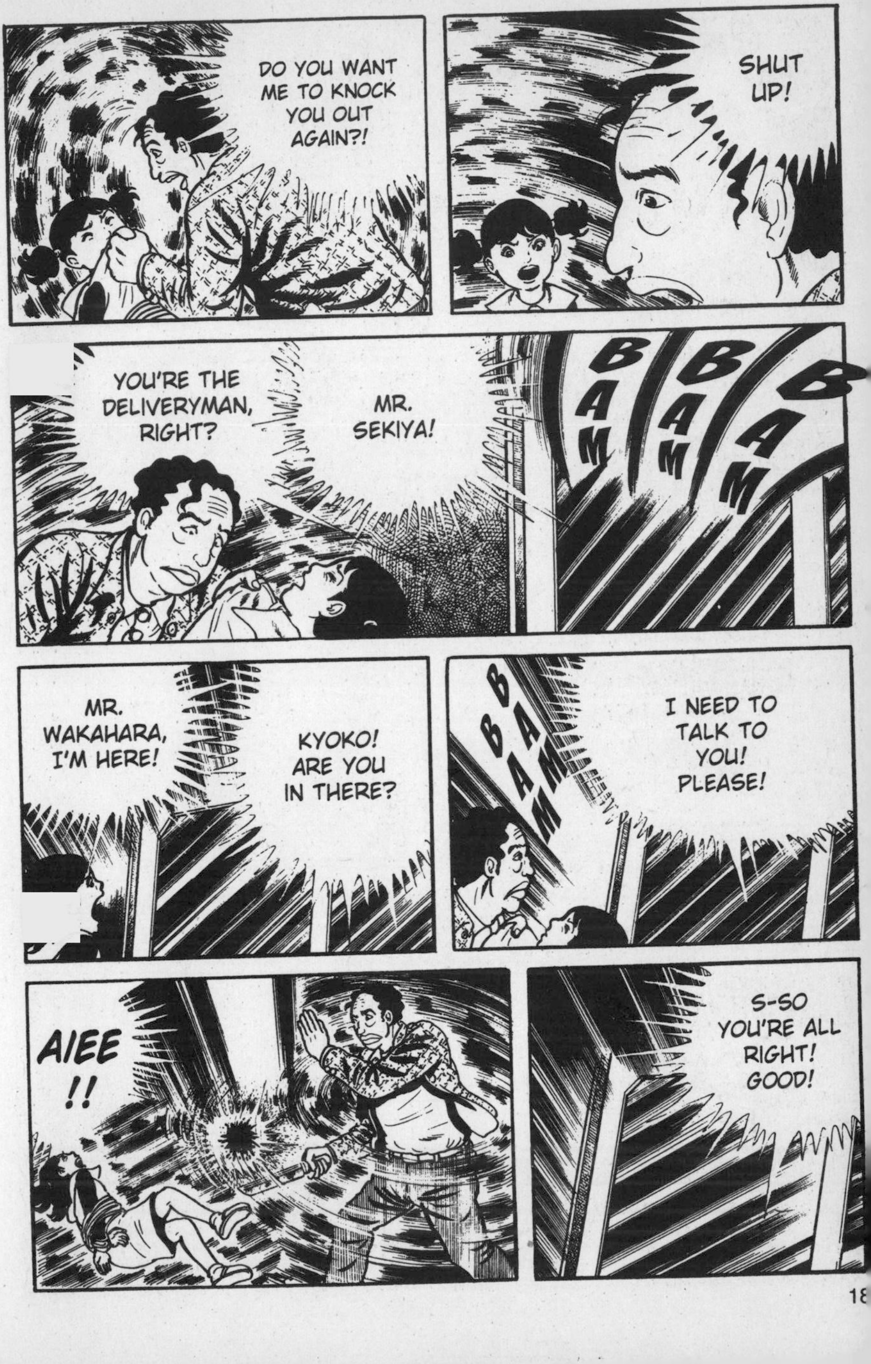
SHUT UP!
DO YOU WANT ME TO KNOCK YOU OUT AGAIN?!
BAM
BAM
BAM
MR. SEKIYA!
YOU'RE THE DELIVERYMAN, RIGHT?
I NEED TO TALK TO YOU! PLEASE!
BAM
BAM
KYOKO! ARE YOU IN THERE?
MR. WAKAHARA, I'M HERE!
S-SO YOU'RE ALL RIGHT! GOOD!
AIEE !!

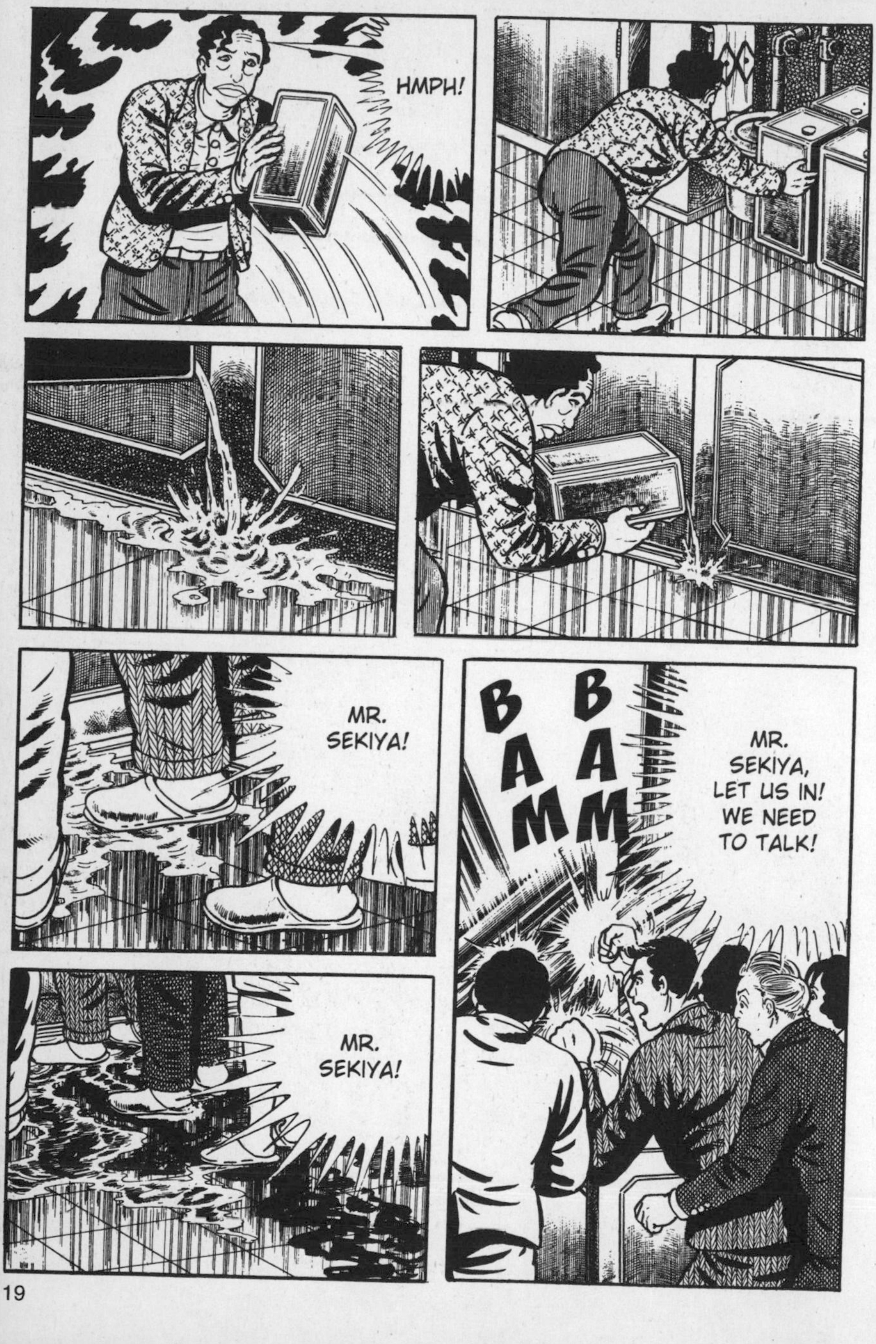
HMPH!
BAMM BAMM
MR. SEKIYA, LET US IN! WE NEED TO TALK!
MR. SEKIYA!
MR. SEKIYA!

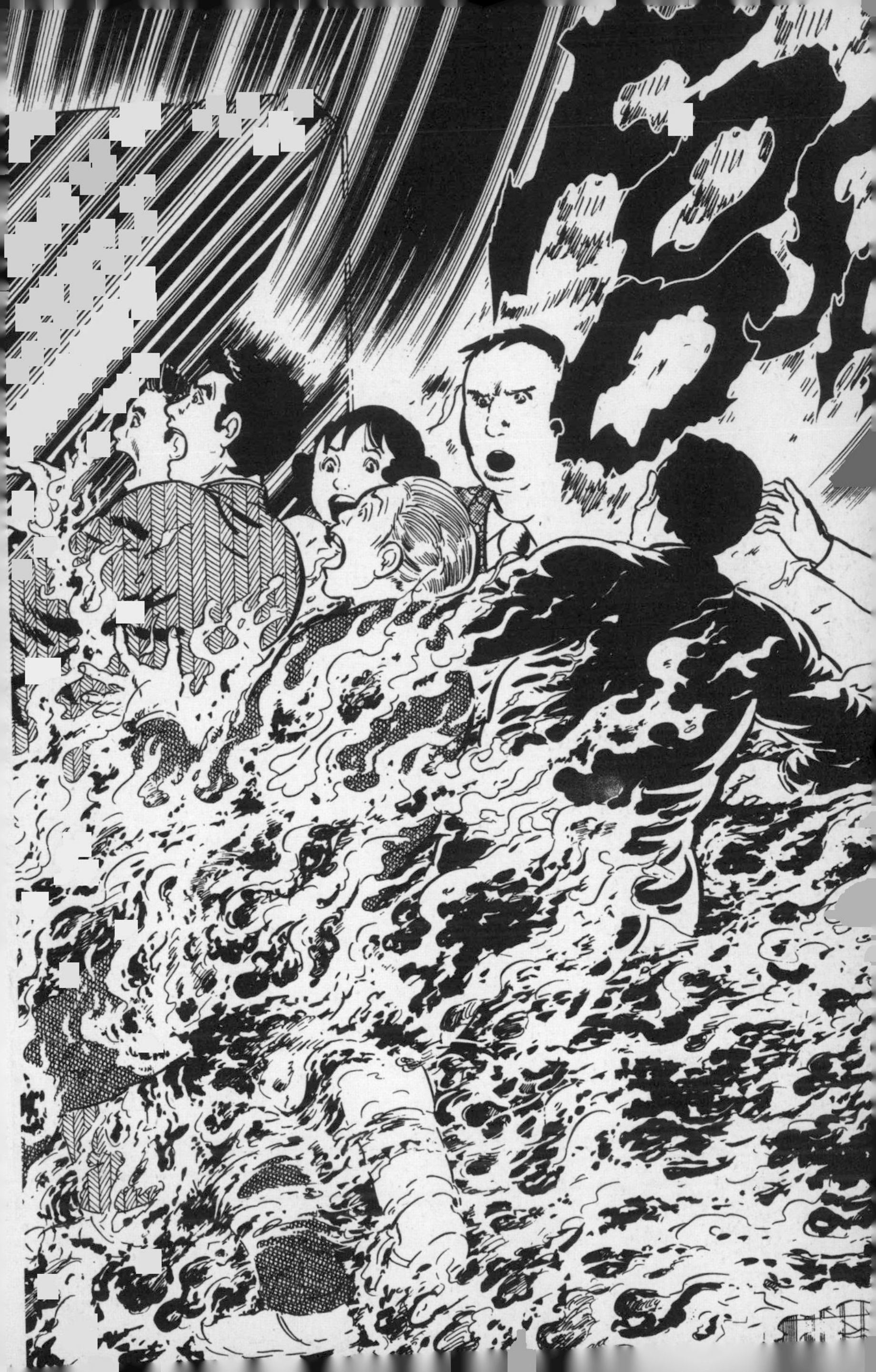

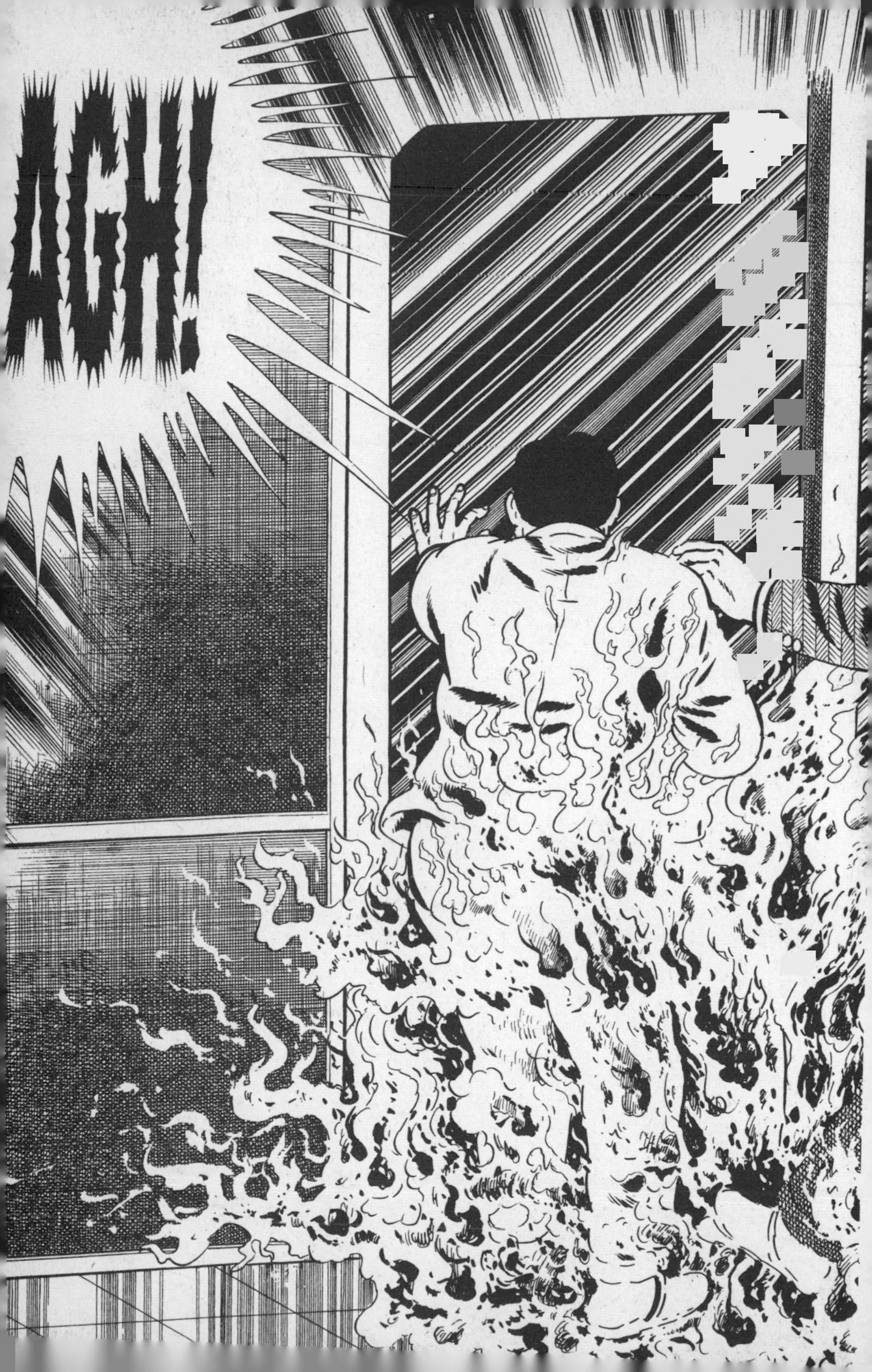
AGH!

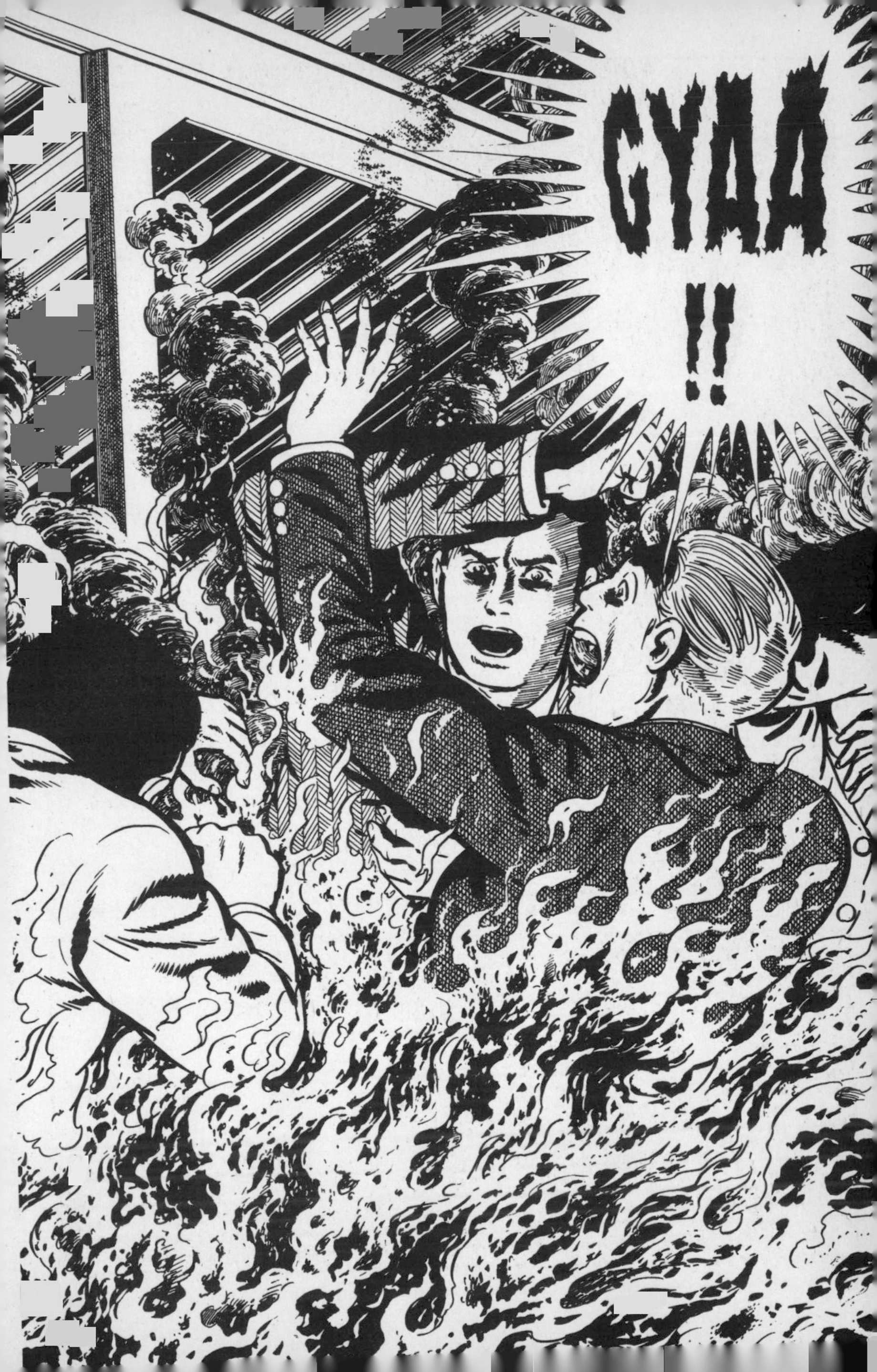
GYAA !!

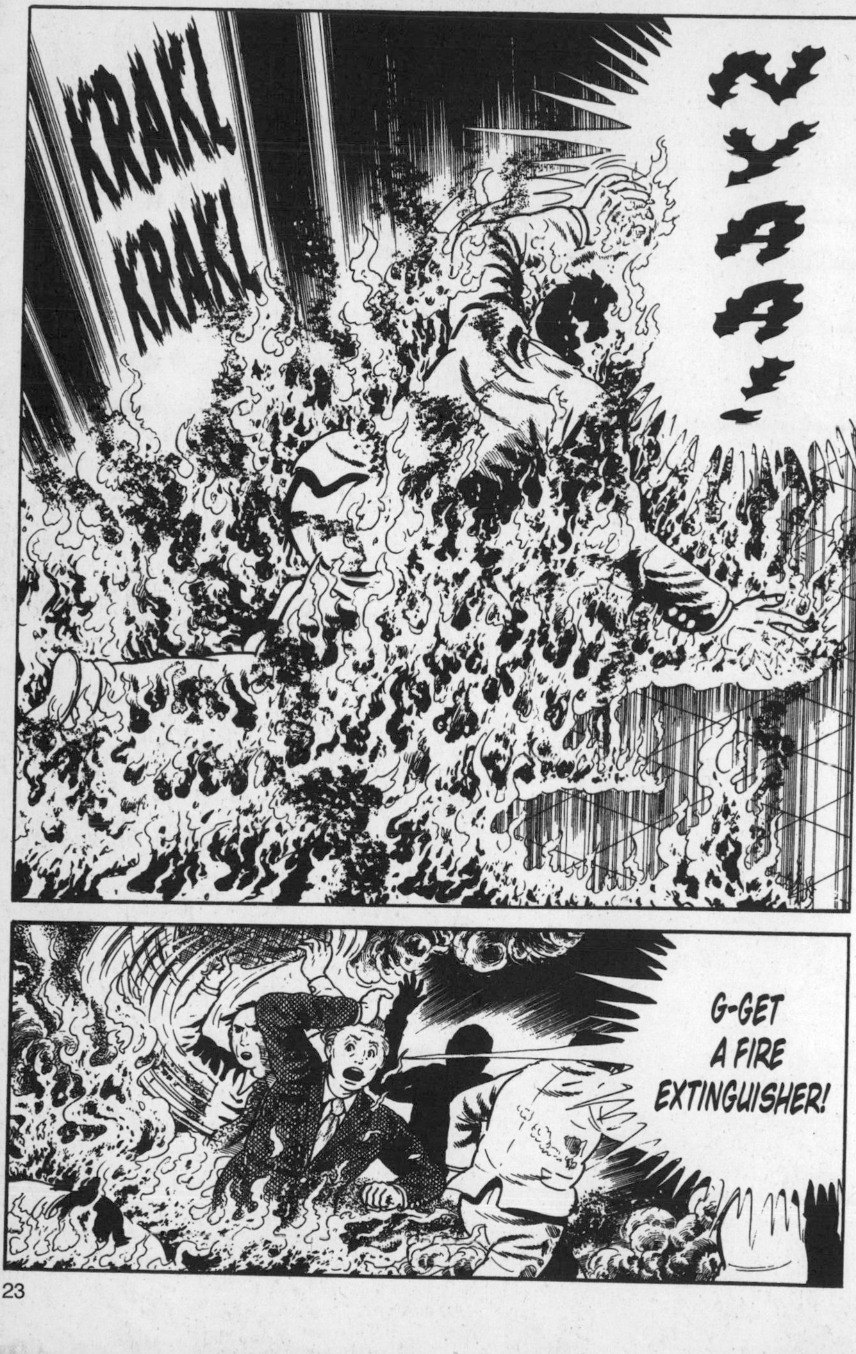
NYAAA!
KRAKL KRAKL
G-GET A FIRE EXTINGUISHER!

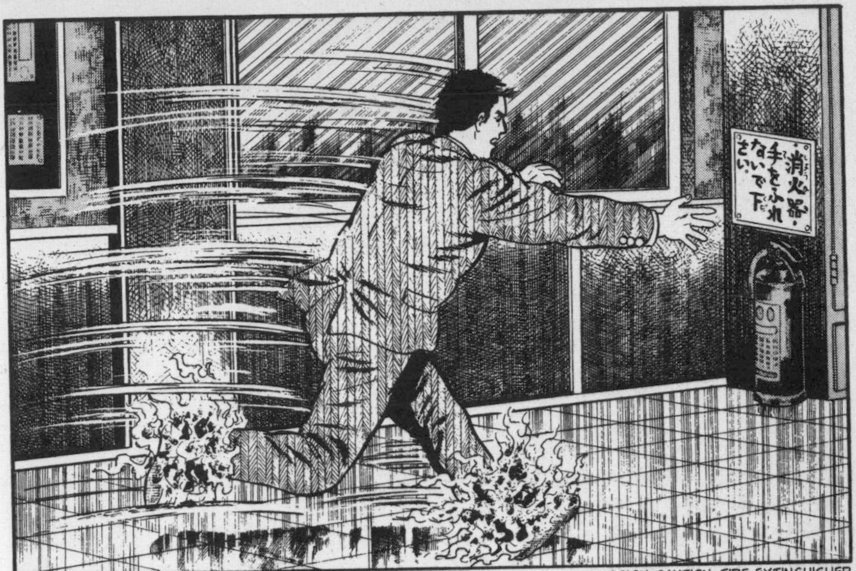
消火器・手をふれないで下さい。

*SIGN=CAUTION: FIRE EXTINGUISHER

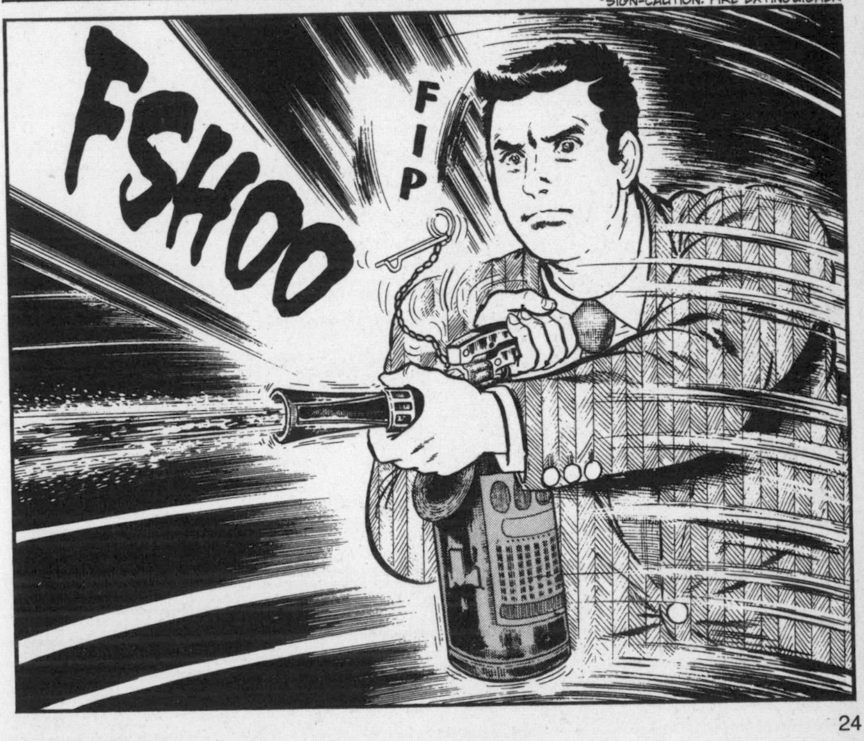
FIP
FSHOO

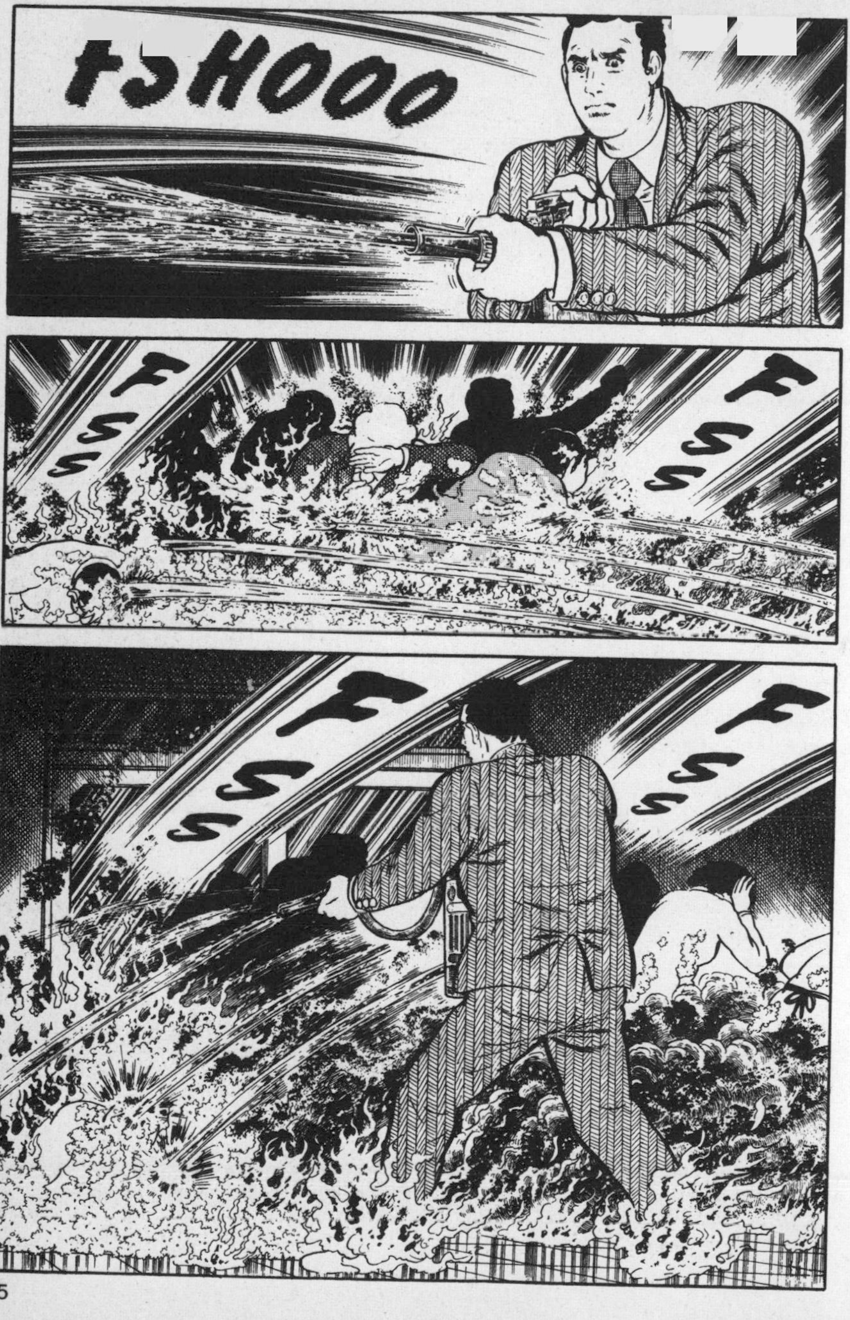
TSHOOO
FSSS
FSSS
FSSS
FSSS

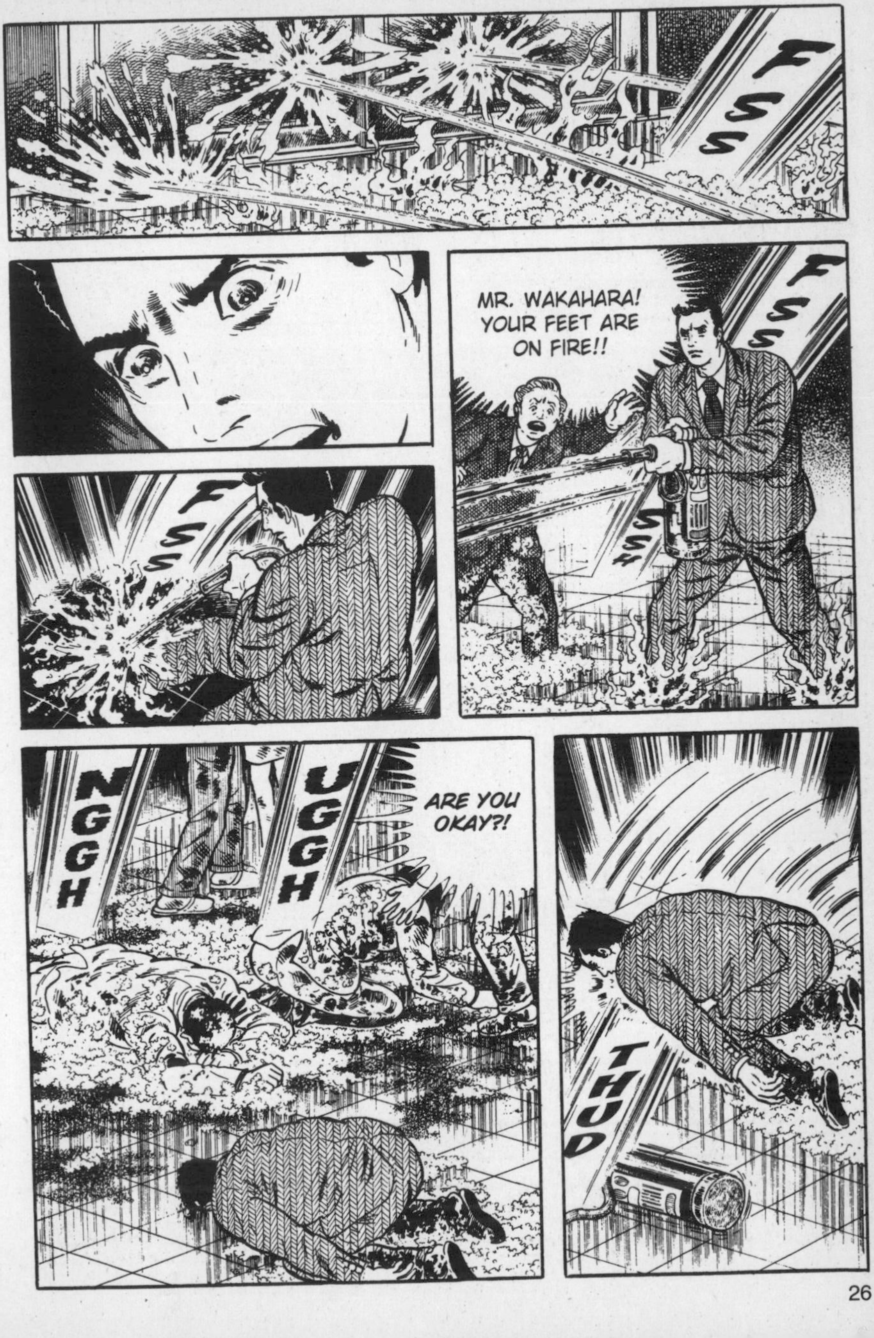
FSSS
FSS
MR. WAKAHARA! YOUR FEET ARE ON FIRE!!
FSS
THUD
ARE YOU OKAY?!
UGGH
NGGH

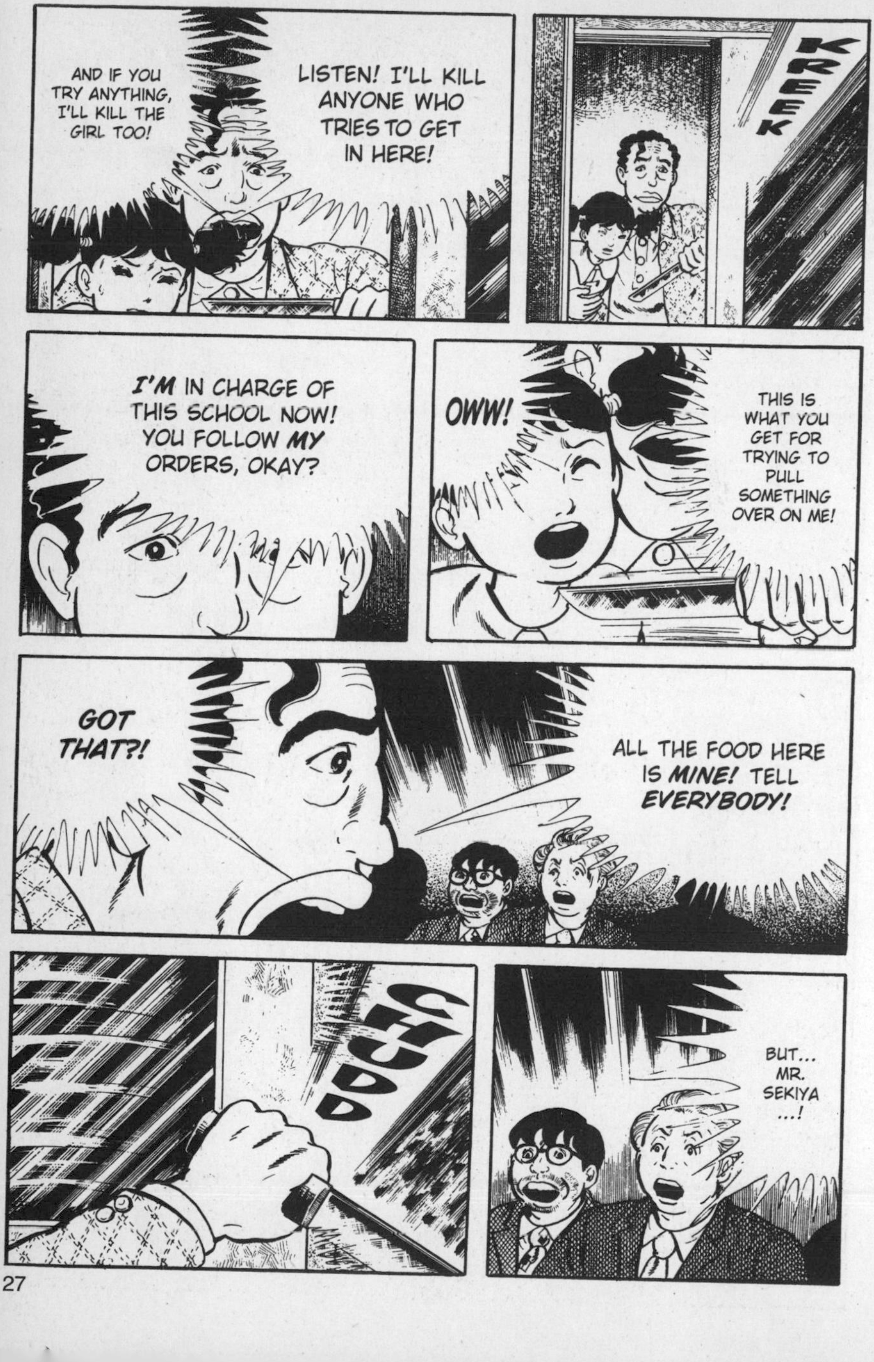
KREEK
LISTEN! I'LL KILL ANYONE WHO TRIES TO GET IN HERE!
AND IF YOU TRY ANYTHING, I'LL KILL THE GIRL TOO!
THIS IS WHAT YOU GET FOR TRYING TO PULL SOMETHING OVER ON ME!
OWW!
I'M IN CHARGE OF THIS SCHOOL NOW! YOU FOLLOW *MY* ORDERS, OKAY?
ALL THE FOOD HERE IS *MINE!* TELL *EVERYBODY!*
GOT THAT?!
BUT... MR. SEKIYA ...!
CHUDD

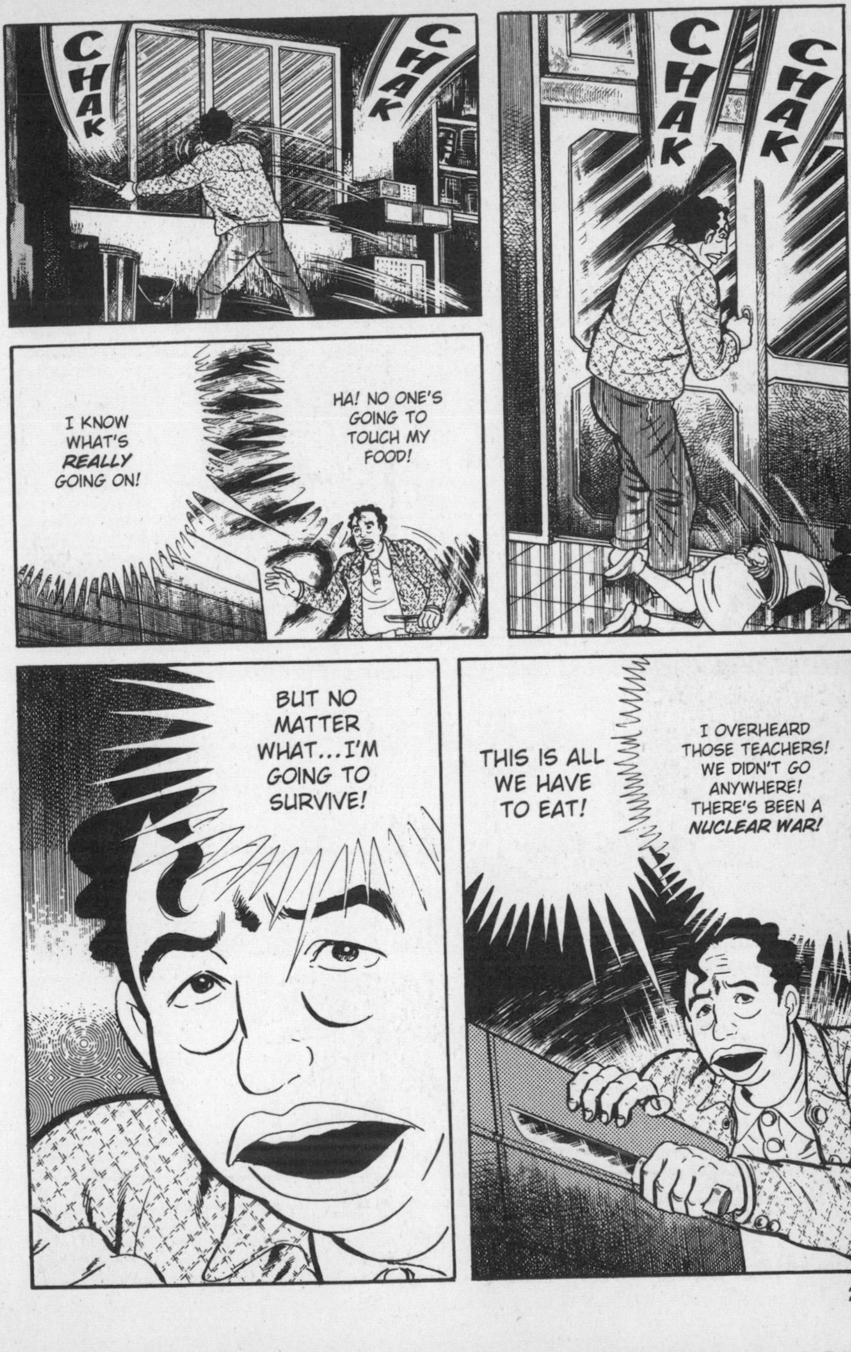
CHAK
CHAK
CHAK
CHAK
HA! NO ONE'S GOING TO TOUCH MY FOOD!
I KNOW WHAT'S *REALLY* GOING ON!
I OVERHEARD THOSE TEACHERS! WE DIDN'T GO ANYWHERE! THERE'S BEEN A *NUCLEAR WAR!*
THIS IS ALL WE HAVE TO EAT!
BUT NO MATTER WHAT...I'M GOING TO SURVIVE!

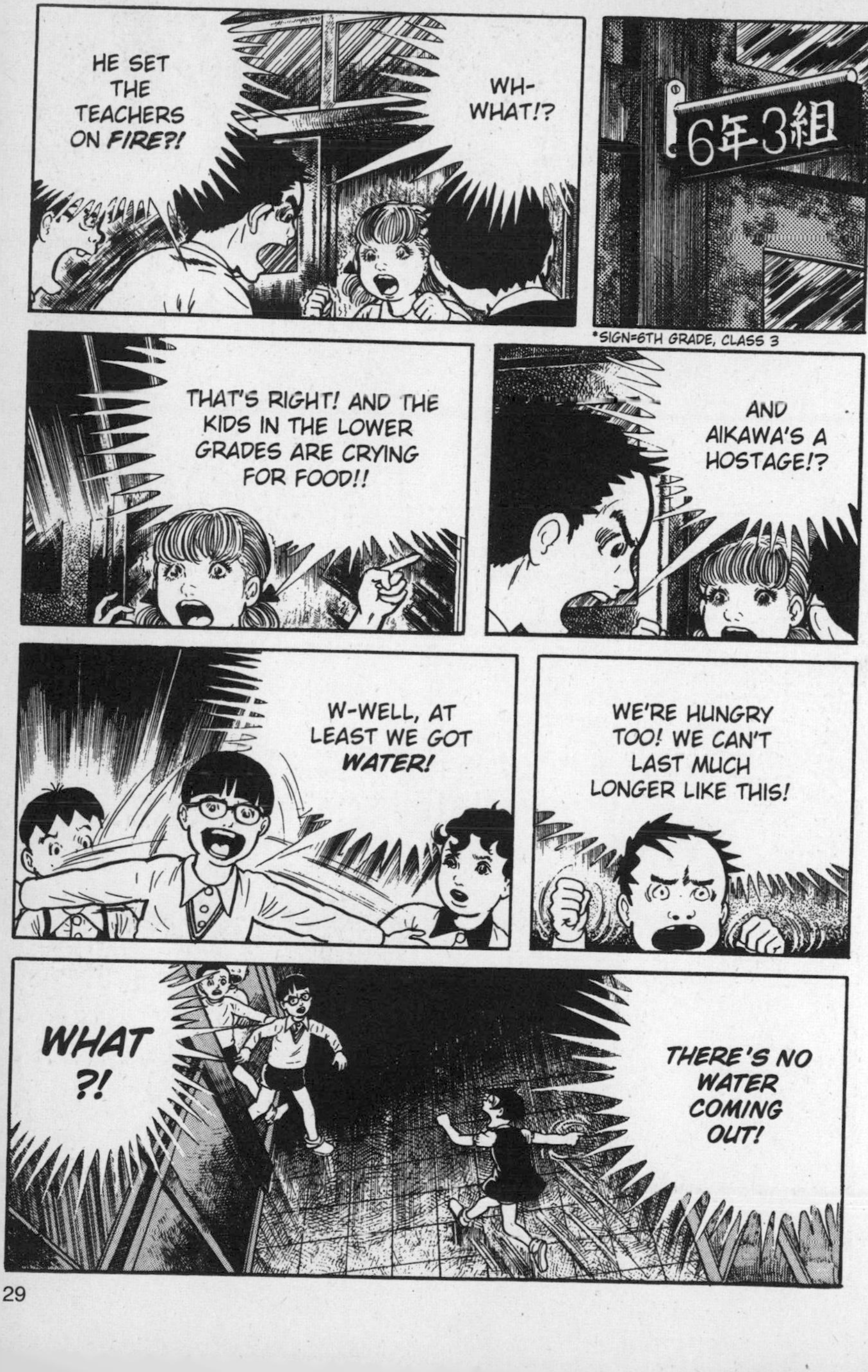
6年3組
*SIGN=6TH GRADE, CLASS 3
WH-WHAT!?
HE SET THE TEACHERS ON FIRE?!
AND AIKAWA'S A HOSTAGE!?
THAT'S RIGHT! AND THE KIDS IN THE LOWER GRADES ARE CRYING FOR FOOD!!
WE'RE HUNGRY TOO! WE CAN'T LAST MUCH LONGER LIKE THIS!
W-WELL, AT LEAST WE GOT WATER!
THERE'S NO WATER COMING OUT!
WHAT ?!

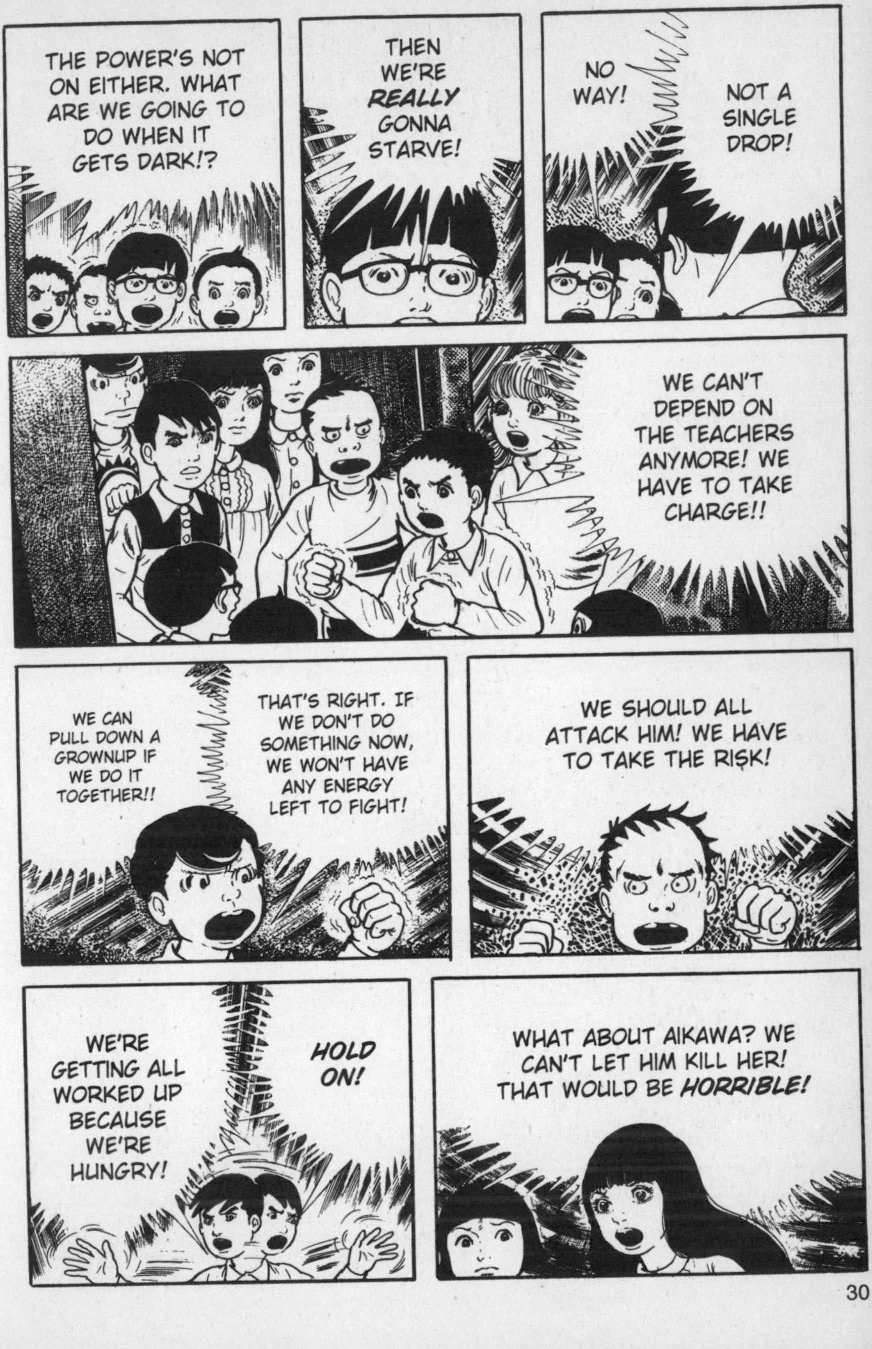
NOT A SINGLE DROP!
NO WAY!
THEN WE'RE *REALLY* GONNA STARVE!
THE POWER'S NOT ON EITHER. WHAT ARE WE GOING TO DO WHEN IT GETS DARK!?
WE CAN'T DEPEND ON THE TEACHERS ANYMORE! WE HAVE TO TAKE CHARGE!!
WE SHOULD ALL ATTACK HIM! WE HAVE TO TAKE THE RISK!
THAT'S RIGHT. IF WE DON'T DO SOMETHING NOW, WE WON'T HAVE ANY ENERGY LEFT TO FIGHT!
WE CAN PULL DOWN A GROWNUP IF WE DO IT TOGETHER!!
WHAT ABOUT AIKAWA? WE CAN'T LET HIM KILL HER! THAT WOULD BE *HORRIBLE!*
HOLD ON!
WE'RE GETTING ALL WORKED UP BECAUSE WE'RE HUNGRY!

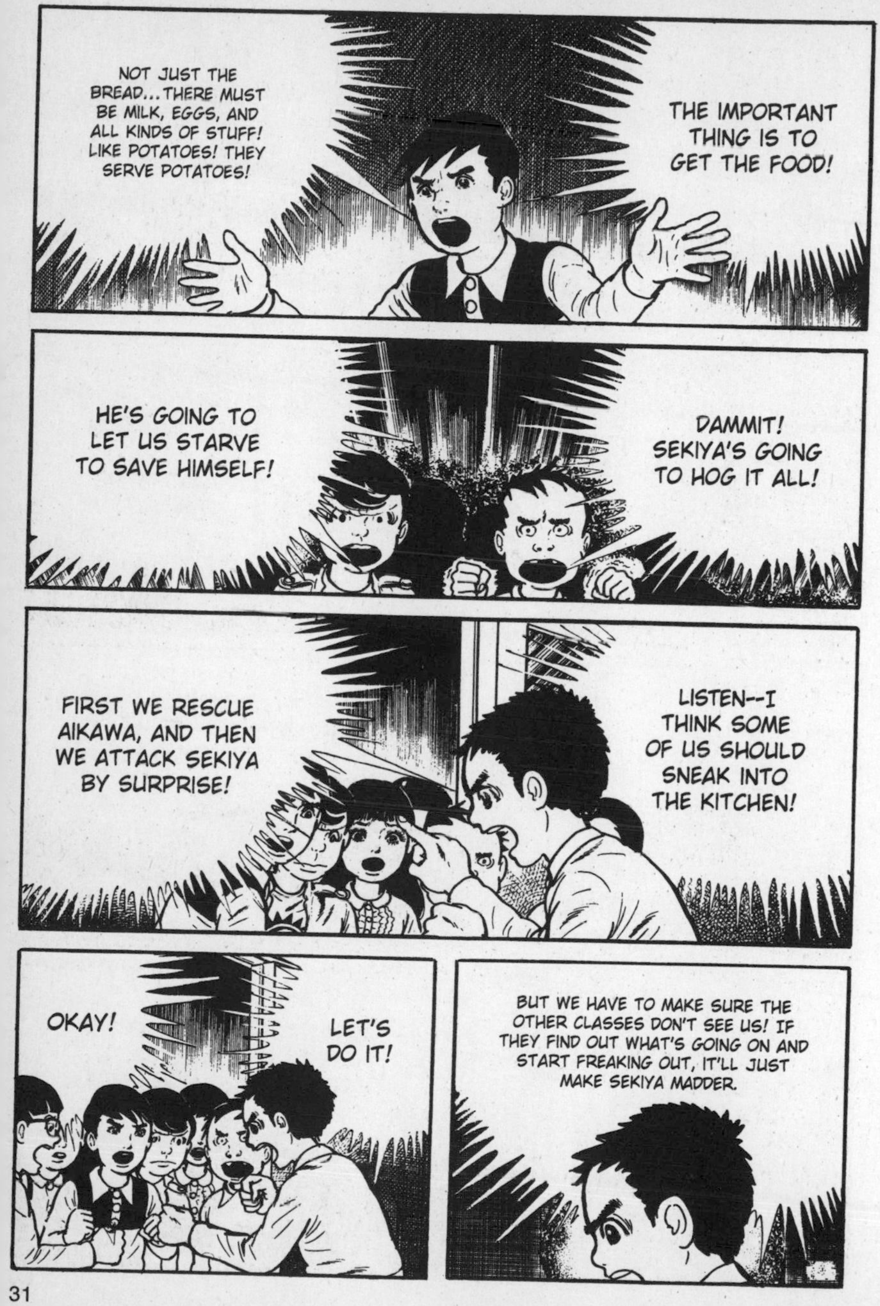
THE IMPORTANT THING IS TO GET THE FOOD!
NOT JUST THE BREAD...THERE MUST BE MILK, EGGS, AND ALL KINDS OF STUFF! LIKE POTATOES! THEY SERVE POTATOES!
DAMMIT! SEKIYA'S GOING TO HOG IT ALL!
HE'S GOING TO LET US STARVE TO SAVE HIMSELF!
LISTEN--I THINK SOME OF US SHOULD SNEAK INTO THE KITCHEN!
FIRST WE RESCUE AIKAWA, AND THEN WE ATTACK SEKIYA BY SURPRISE!
BUT WE HAVE TO MAKE SURE THE OTHER CLASSES DON'T SEE US! IF THEY FIND OUT WHAT'S GOING ON AND START FREAKING OUT, IT'LL JUST MAKE SEKIYA MADDER.
LET'S DO IT!
OKAY!

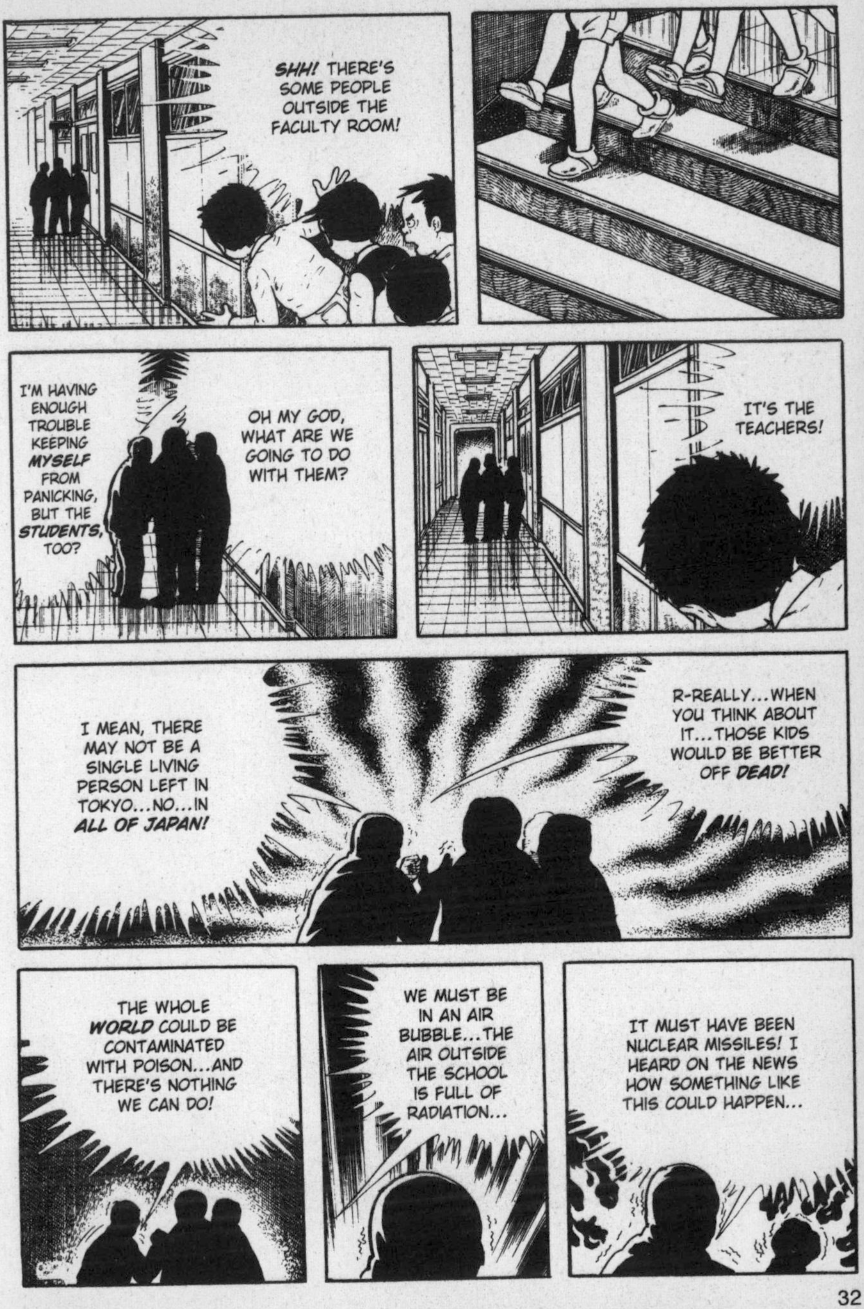
SHH! THERE'S SOME PEOPLE OUTSIDE THE FACULTY ROOM!
IT'S THE TEACHERS!
OH MY GOD, WHAT ARE WE GOING TO DO WITH THEM?
I'M HAVING ENOUGH TROUBLE KEEPING MYSELF FROM PANICKING, BUT THE STUDENTS, TOO?
R-REALLY...WHEN YOU THINK ABOUT IT...THOSE KIDS WOULD BE BETTER OFF DEAD!
I MEAN, THERE MAY NOT BE A SINGLE LIVING PERSON LEFT IN TOKYO...NO...IN ALL OF JAPAN!
IT MUST HAVE BEEN NUCLEAR MISSILES! I HEARD ON THE NEWS HOW SOMETHING LIKE THIS COULD HAPPEN...
WE MUST BE IN AN AIR BUBBLE...THE AIR OUTSIDE THE SCHOOL IS FULL OF RADIATION...
THE WHOLE WORLD COULD BE CONTAMINATED WITH POISON...AND THERE'S NOTHING WE CAN DO!

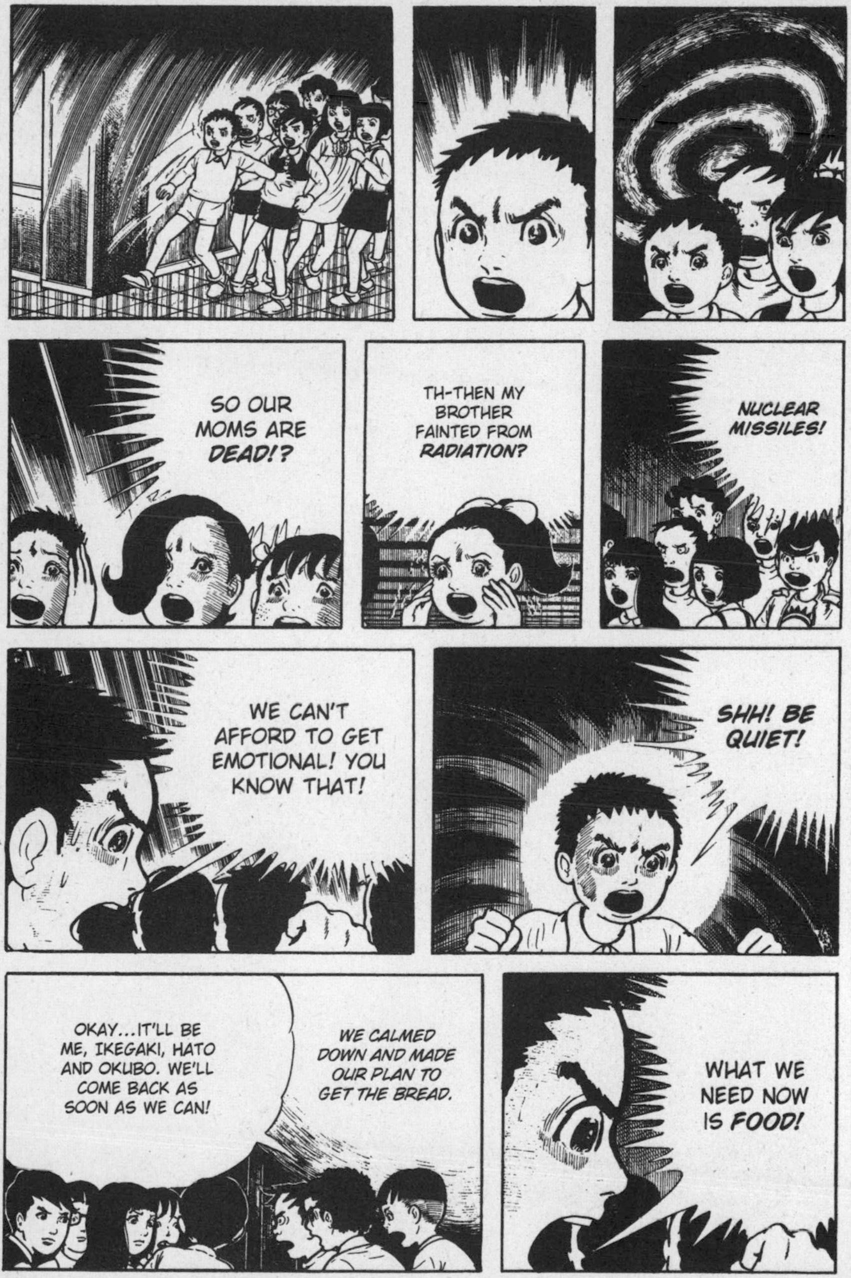
NUCLEAR MISSILES!
TH-THEN MY BROTHER FAINTED FROM *RADIATION?*
SO OUR MOMS ARE *DEAD!?*
SHH! BE QUIET!
WE CAN'T AFFORD TO GET EMOTIONAL! YOU KNOW THAT!
WHAT WE NEED NOW IS *FOOD!*
WE CALMED DOWN AND MADE OUR PLAN TO GET THE BREAD.
OKAY...IT'LL BE ME, IKEGAKI, HATO AND OKUBO. WE'LL COME BACK AS SOON AS WE CAN!

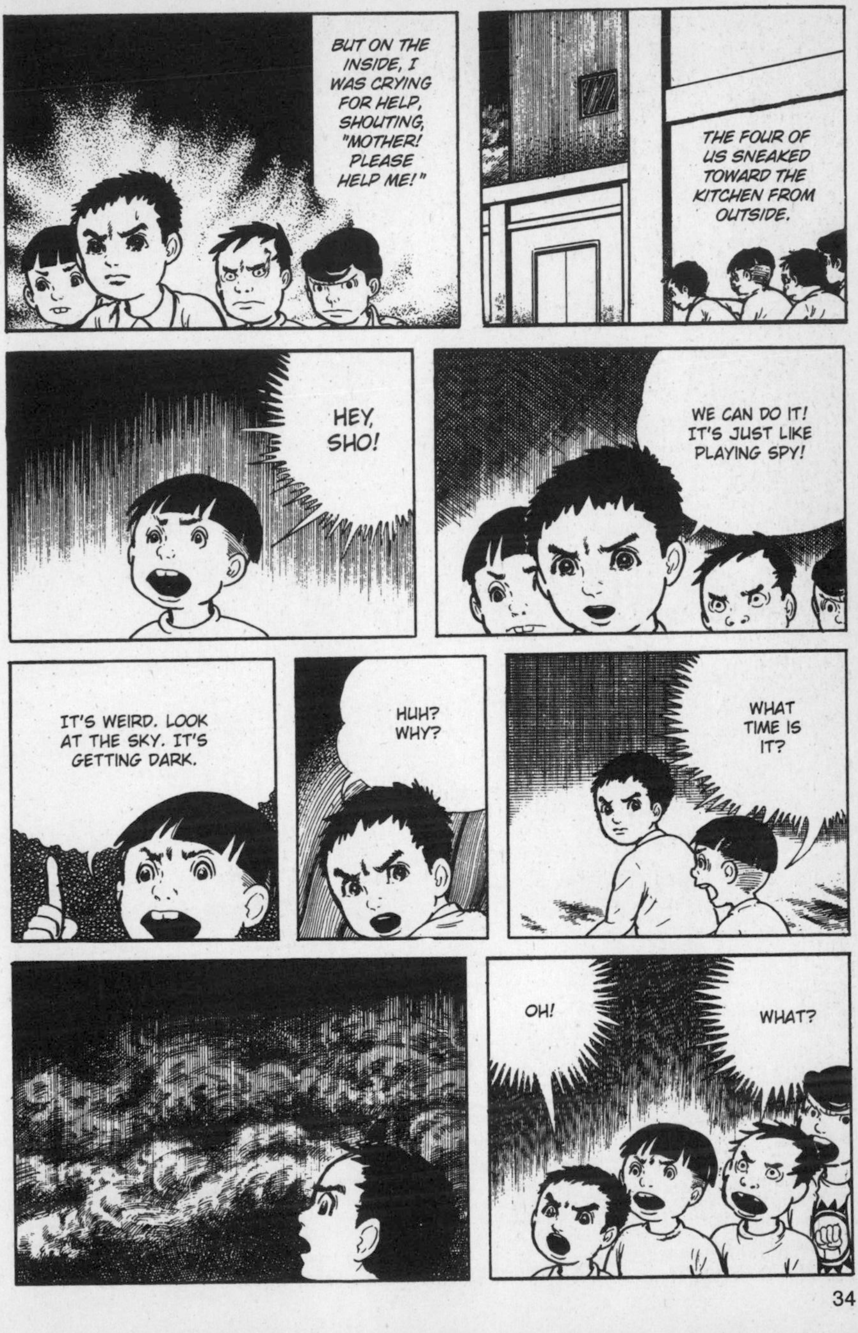
BUT ON THE INSIDE, I WAS CRYING FOR HELP, SHOUTING, "MOTHER! PLEASE HELP ME!"
THE FOUR OF US SNEAKED TOWARD THE KITCHEN FROM OUTSIDE.
HEY, SHO!
WE CAN DO IT! IT'S JUST LIKE PLAYING SPY!
IT'S WEIRD. LOOK AT THE SKY. IT'S GETTING DARK.
HUH? WHY?
WHAT TIME IS IT?
OH!
WHAT?

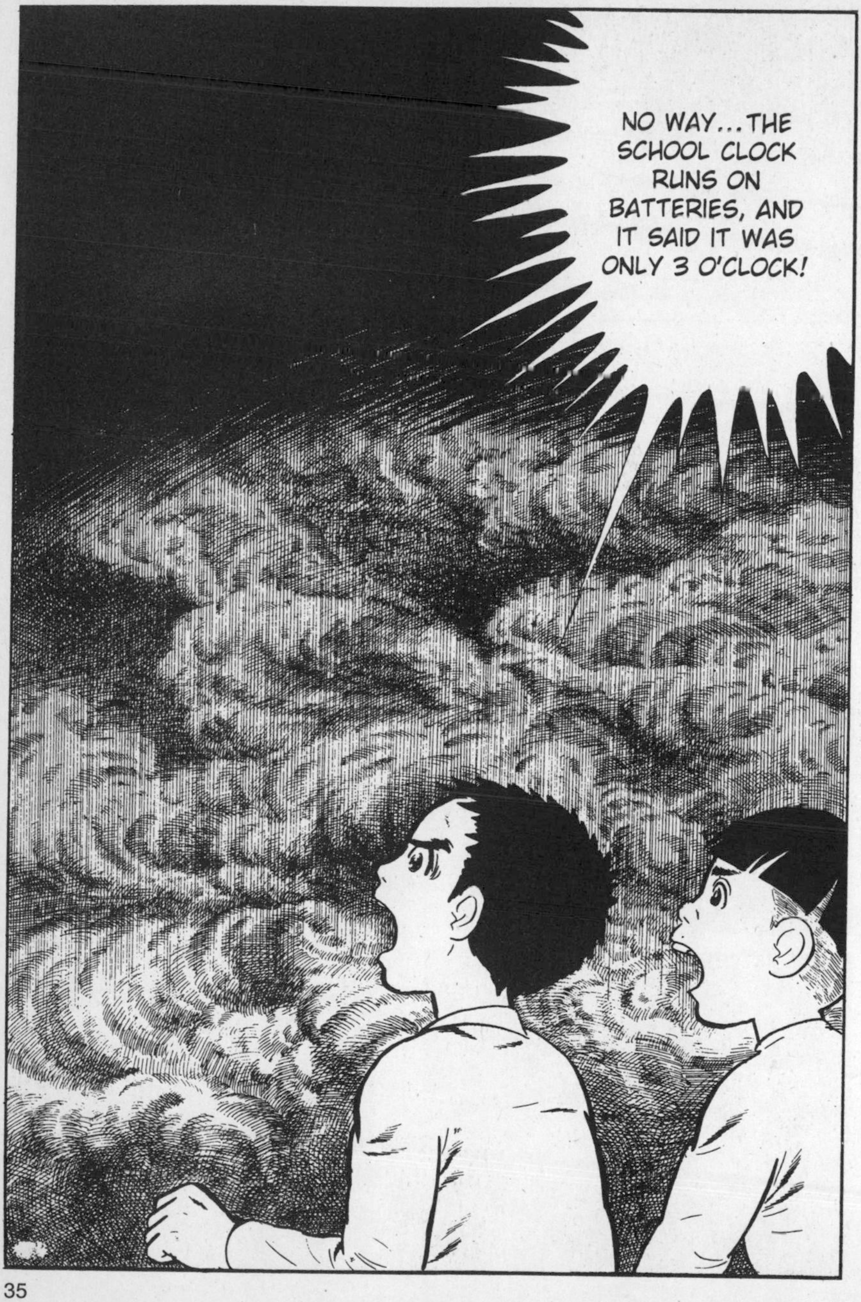
NO WAY...THE SCHOOL CLOCK RUNS ON BATTERIES, AND IT SAID IT WAS ONLY 3 O'CLOCK!

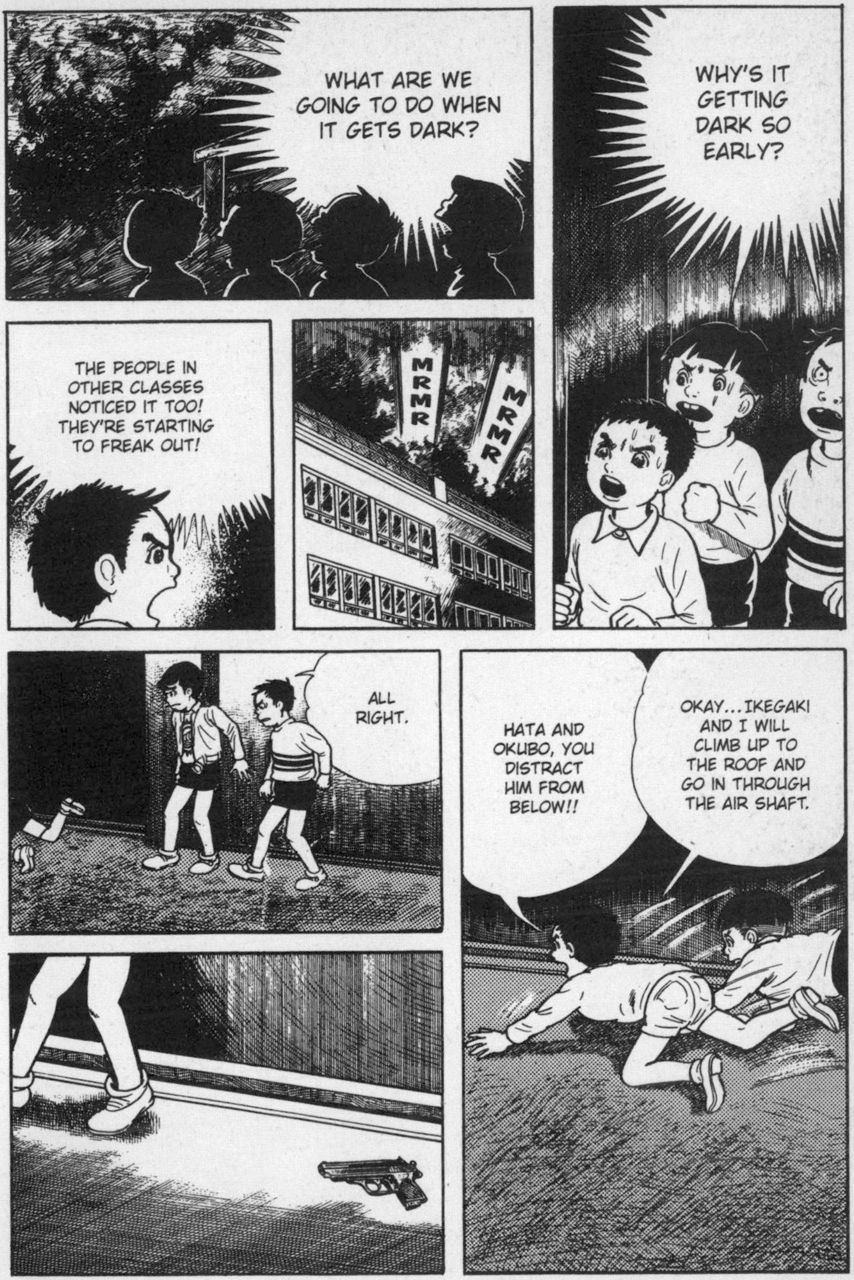
WHY'S IT GETTING DARK SO EARLY?
WHAT ARE WE GOING TO DO WHEN IT GETS DARK?
MRMR
MRMR
THE PEOPLE IN OTHER CLASSES NOTICED IT TOO! THEY'RE STARTING TO FREAK OUT!
OKAY...IKEGAKI AND I WILL CLIMB UP TO THE ROOF AND GO IN THROUGH THE AIR SHAFT.
HATA AND OKUBO, YOU DISTRACT HIM FROM BELOW!!
ALL RIGHT.

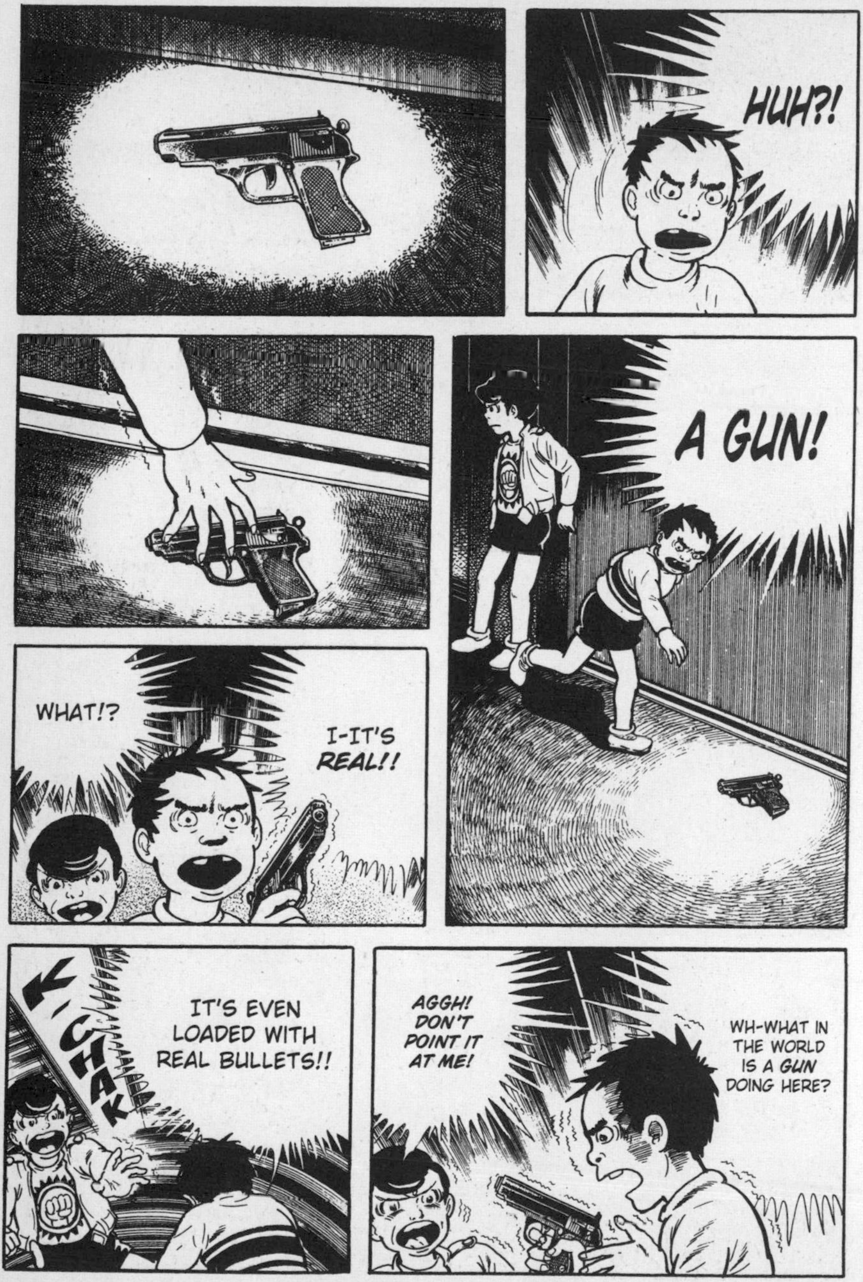
HUH?!
A GUN!
I-IT'S REAL!!
WHAT!?
WH-WHAT IN THE WORLD IS A GUN DOING HERE?
AGGH! DON'T POINT IT AT ME!
IT'S EVEN LOADED WITH REAL BULLETS!!
K-CHAK

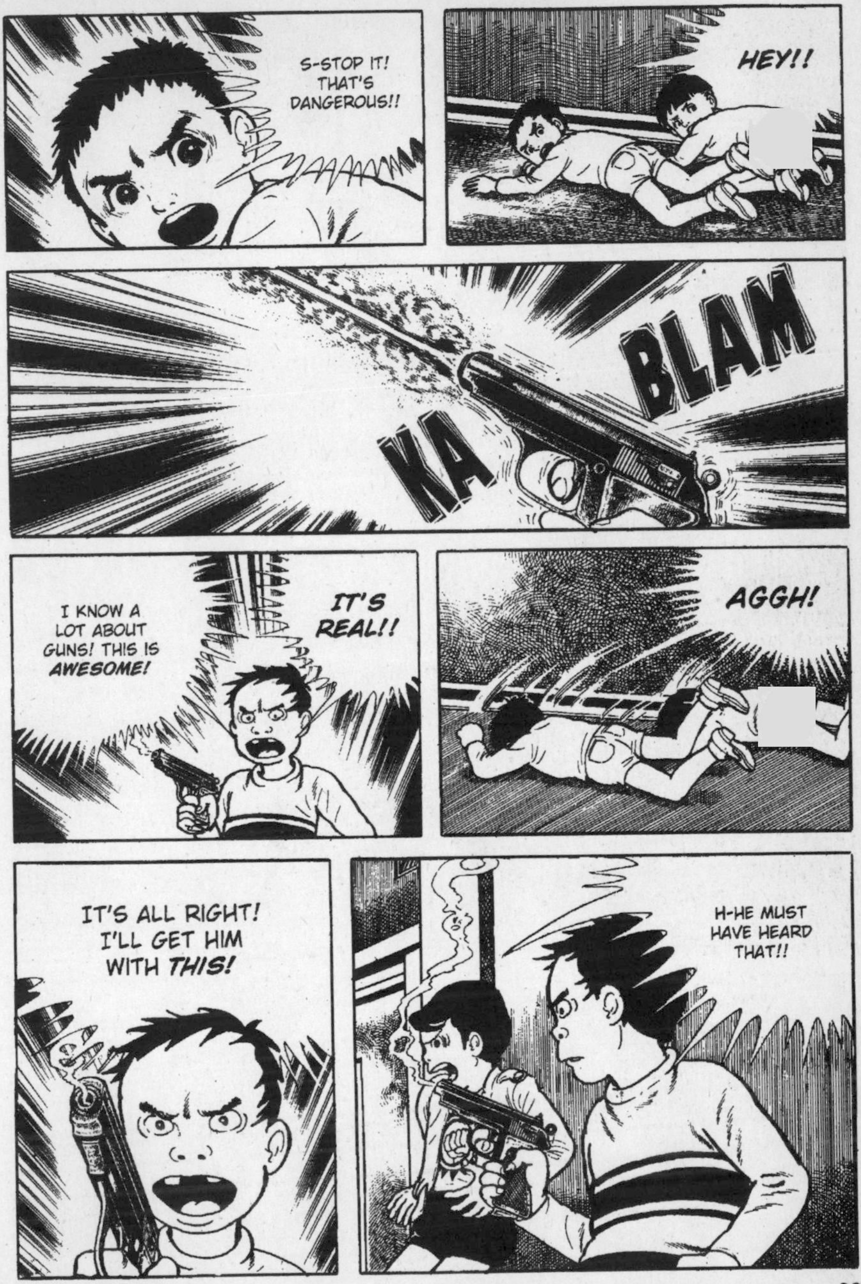
HEY!!
S-STOP IT! THAT'S DANGEROUS!!
KA BLAM
AGGH!
IT'S REAL!!
I KNOW A LOT ABOUT GUNS! THIS IS AWESOME!
H-HE MUST HAVE HEARD THAT!!
IT'S ALL RIGHT! I'LL GET HIM WITH THIS!

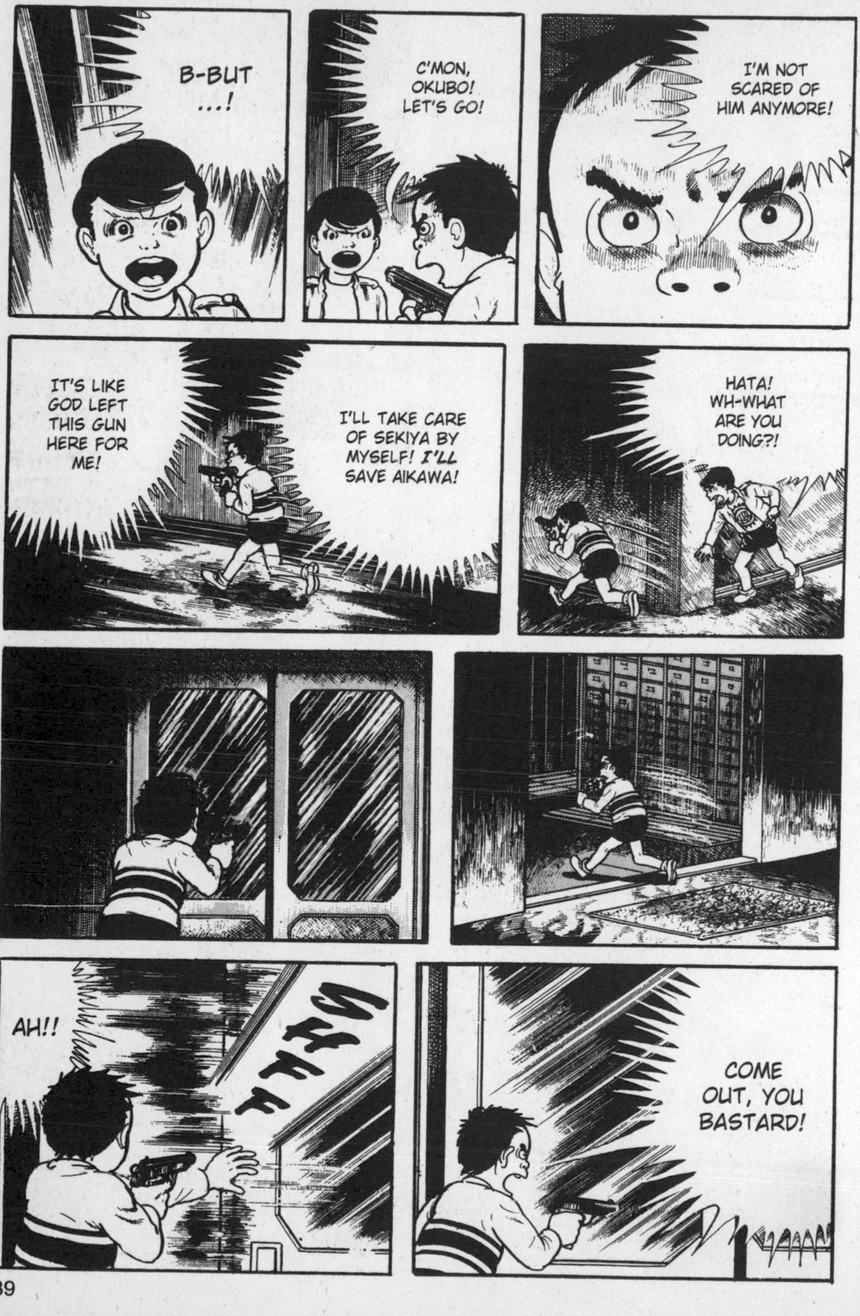
I'M NOT SCARED OF HIM ANYMORE!
C'MON, OKUBO! LET'S GO!
B-BUT ...!
HATA! WH-WHAT ARE YOU DOING?!
IT'S LIKE GOD LEFT THIS GUN HERE FOR ME!
I'LL TAKE CARE OF SEKIYA BY MYSELF! *I'LL* SAVE AIKAWA!
COME OUT, YOU BASTARD!
SHFF
AH!!

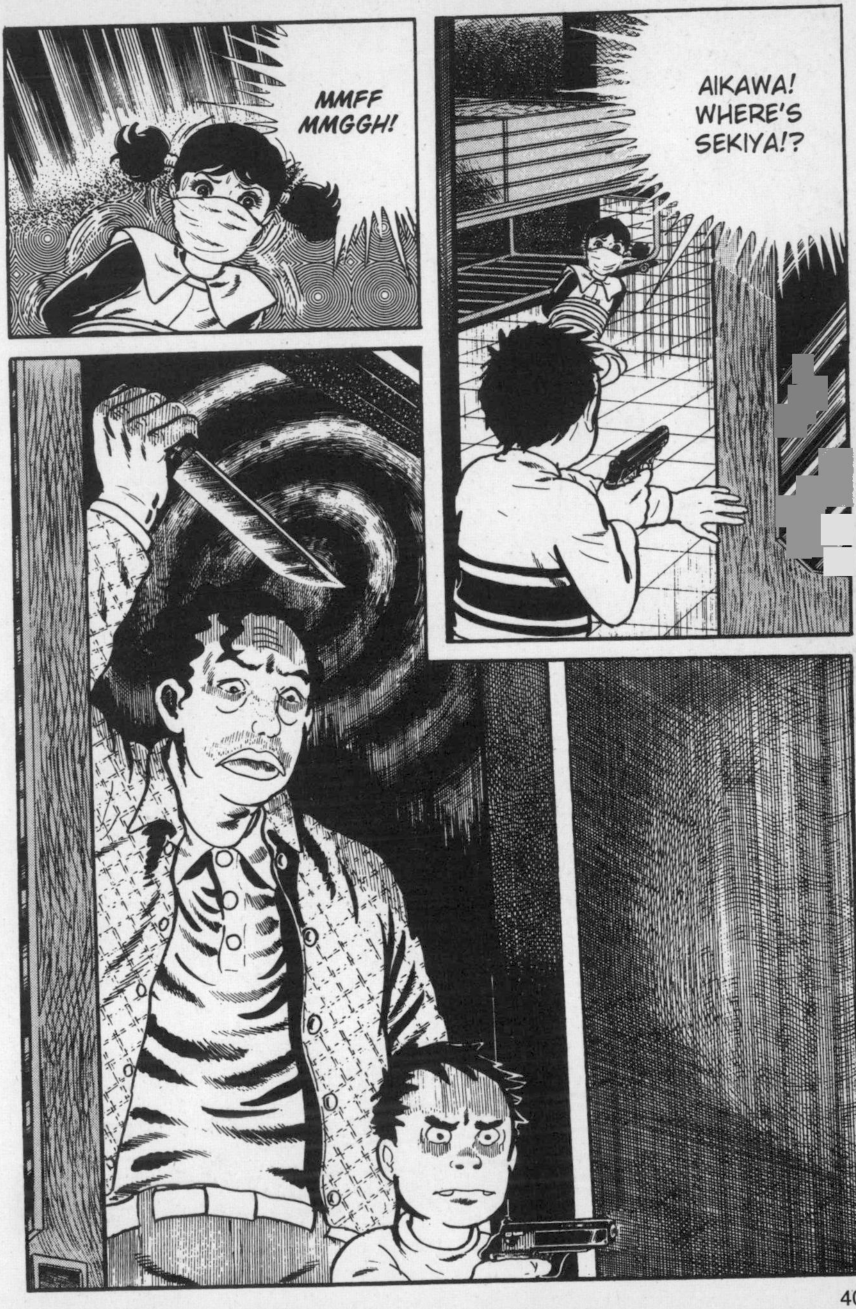
AIKAWA! WHERE'S SEKIYA!?
MMFF MMGGH!

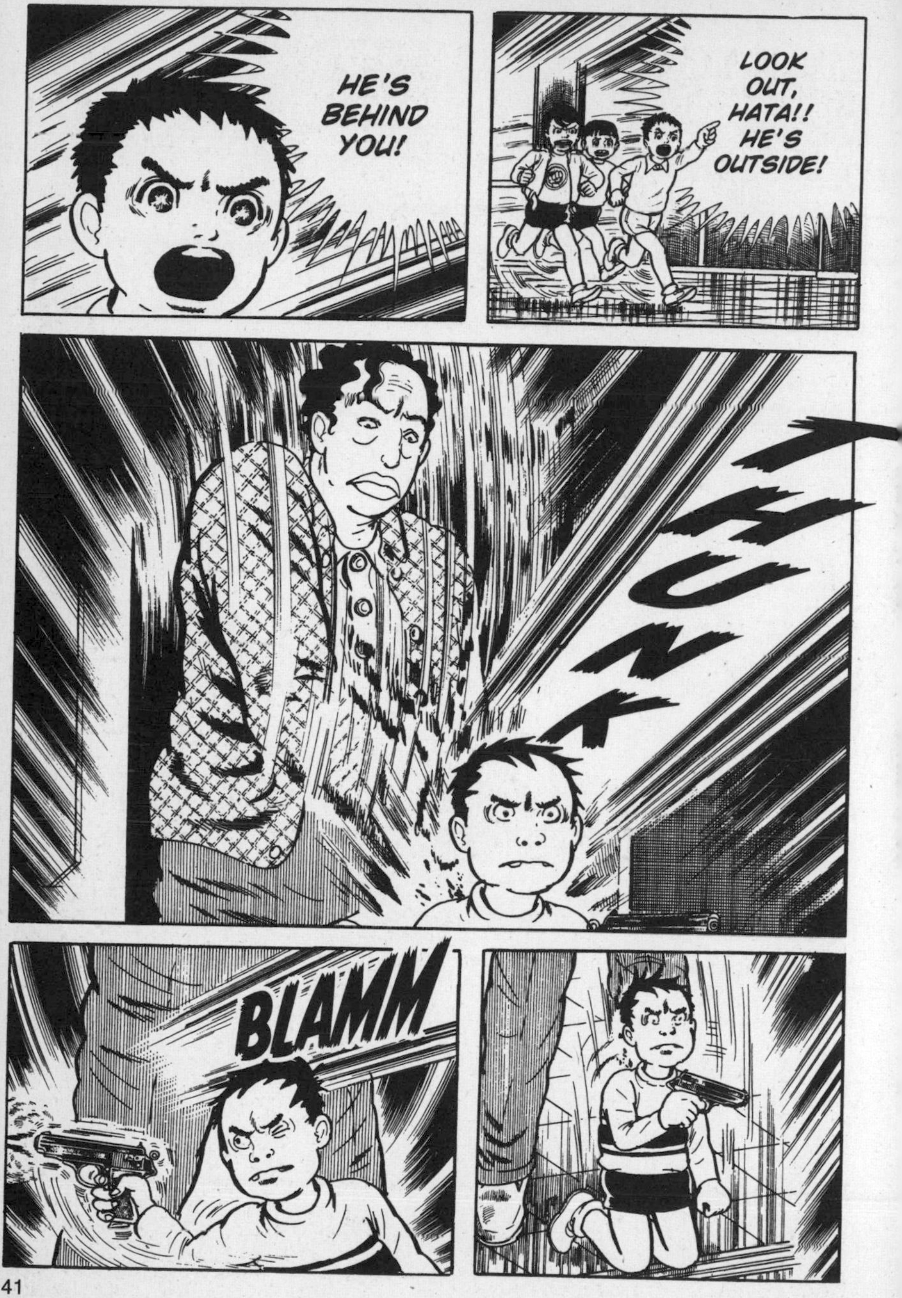
LOOK OUT, HATA!! HE'S OUTSIDE!
HE'S BEHIND YOU!
THUNK
BLAMM

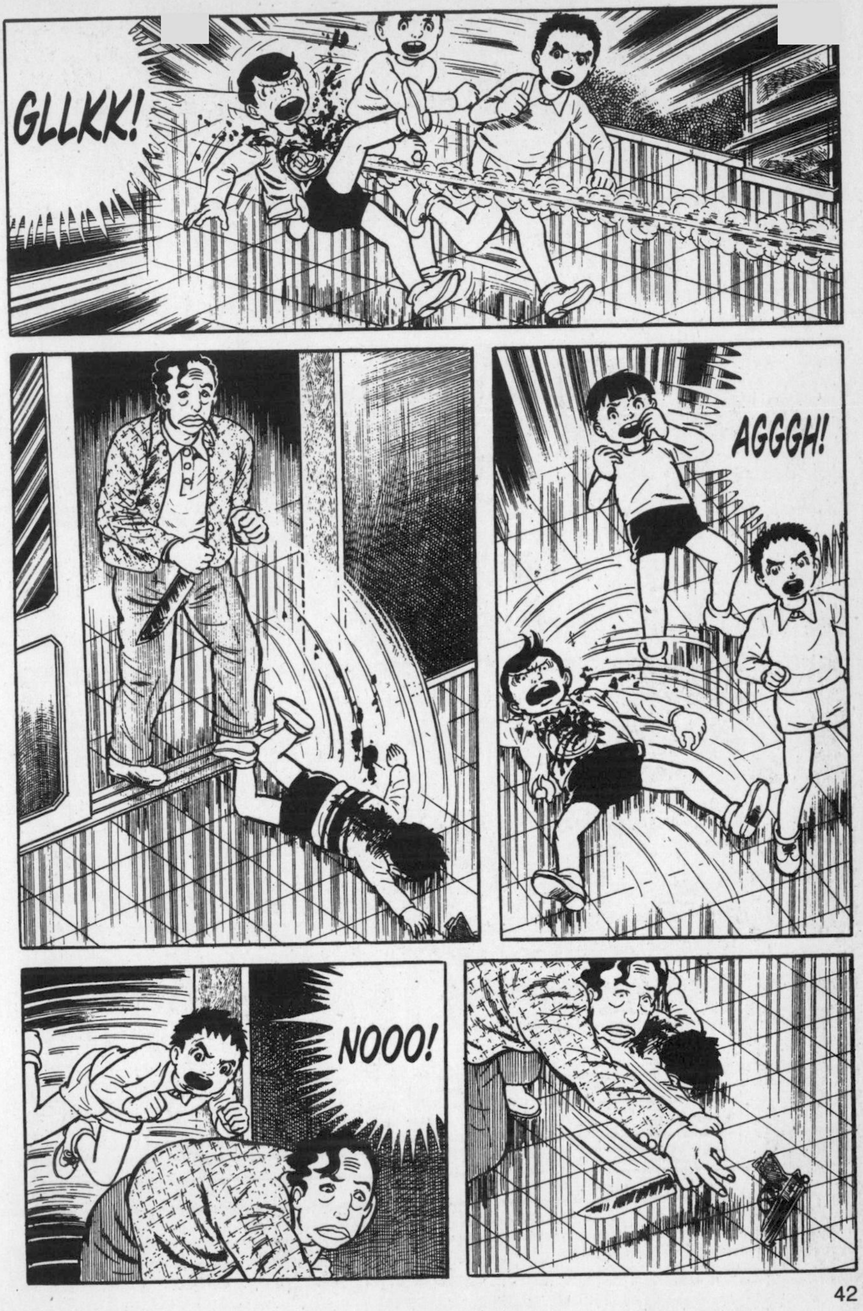
GLLKK!
AGGGH!
NOOO!

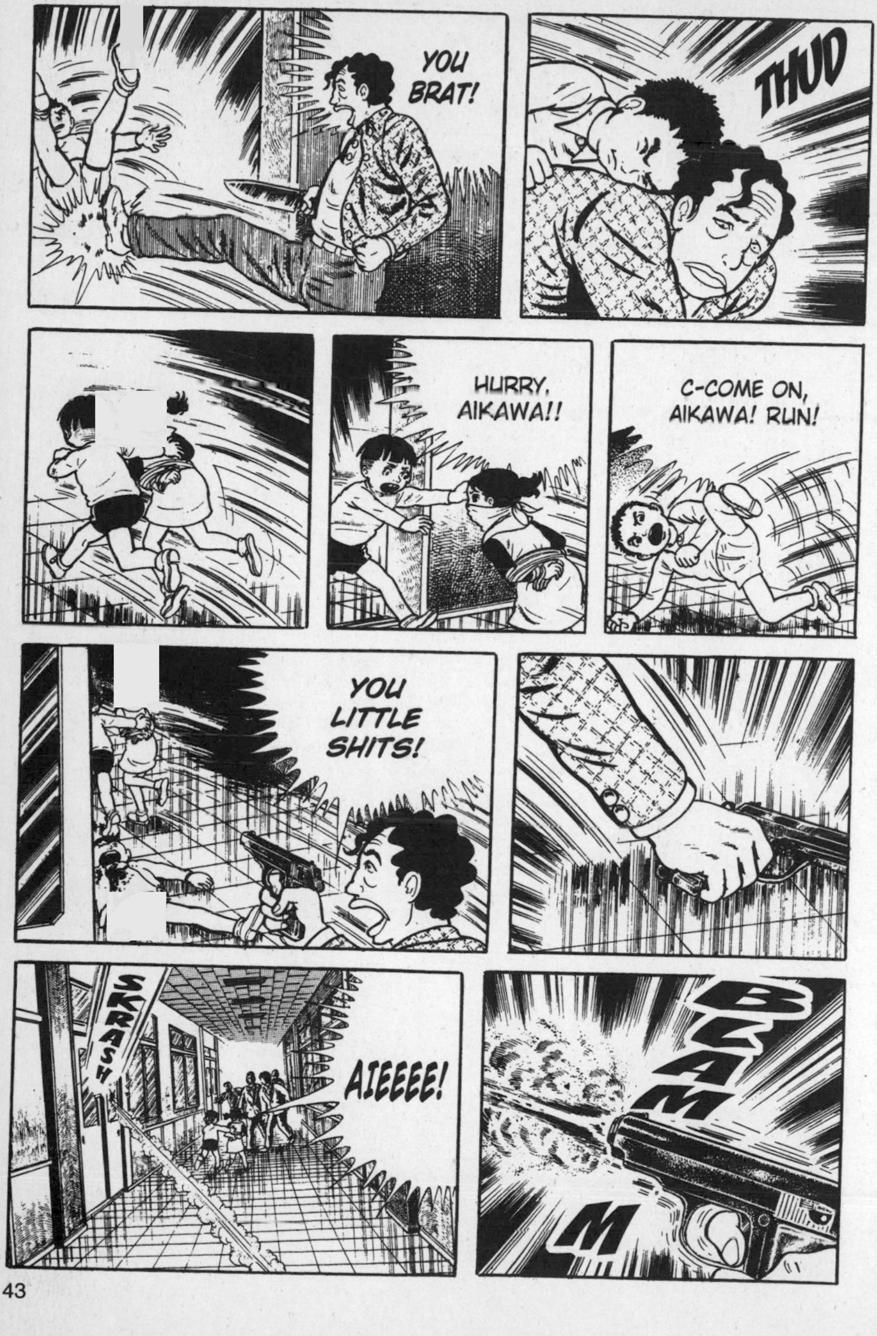
THUD
YOU BRAT!
C-COME ON, AIKAWA! RUN!
HURRY, AIKAWA!!
YOU LITTLE SHITS!
BLAMM
SKRASH
AIEEEE!

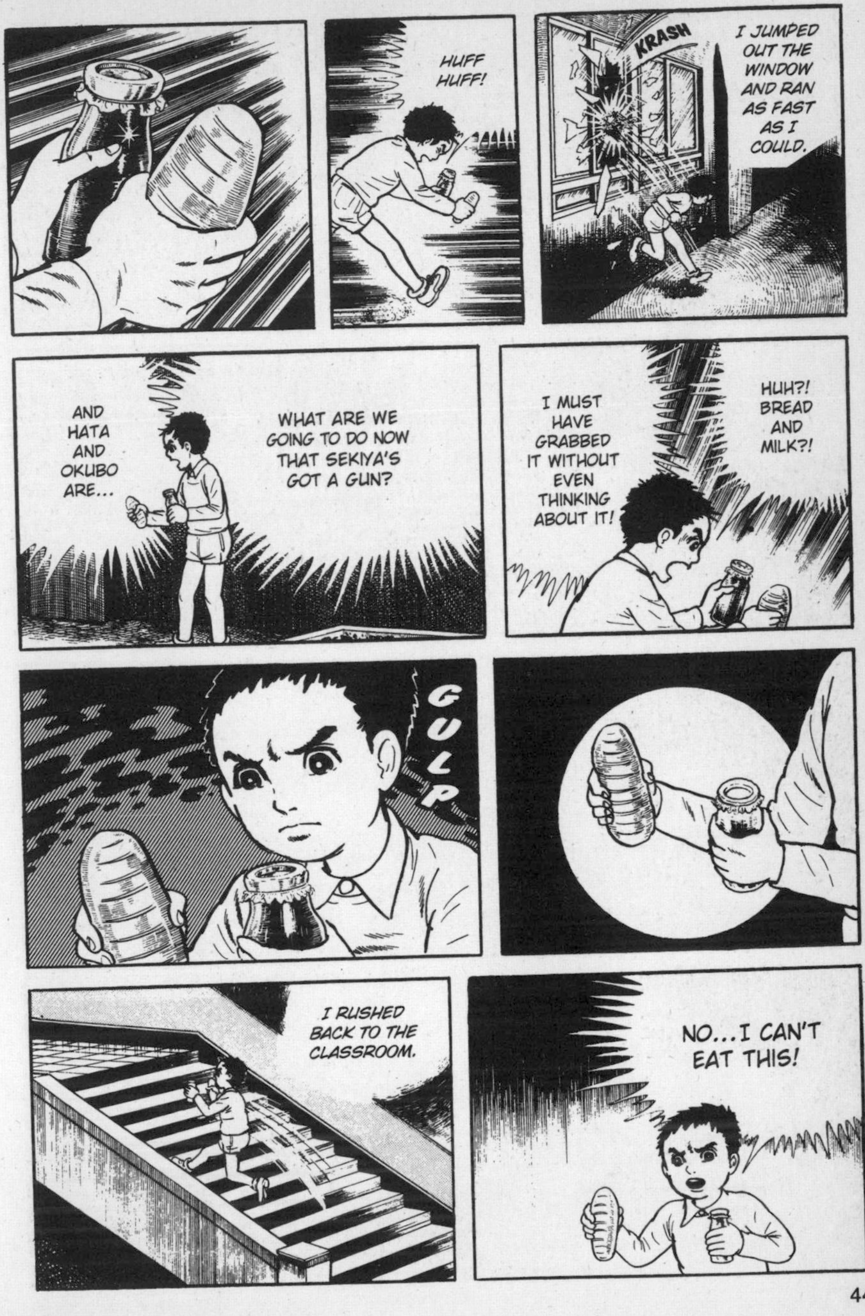
I JUMPED OUT THE WINDOW AND RAN AS FAST AS I COULD.
KRASH
HUFF HUFF!
HUH?! BREAD AND MILK?!
I MUST HAVE GRABBED IT WITHOUT EVEN THINKING ABOUT IT!
WHAT ARE WE GOING TO DO NOW THAT SEKIYA'S GOT A GUN?
AND HATA AND OKUBO ARE...
GULP
NO...I CAN'T EAT THIS!
I RUSHED BACK TO THE CLASSROOM.

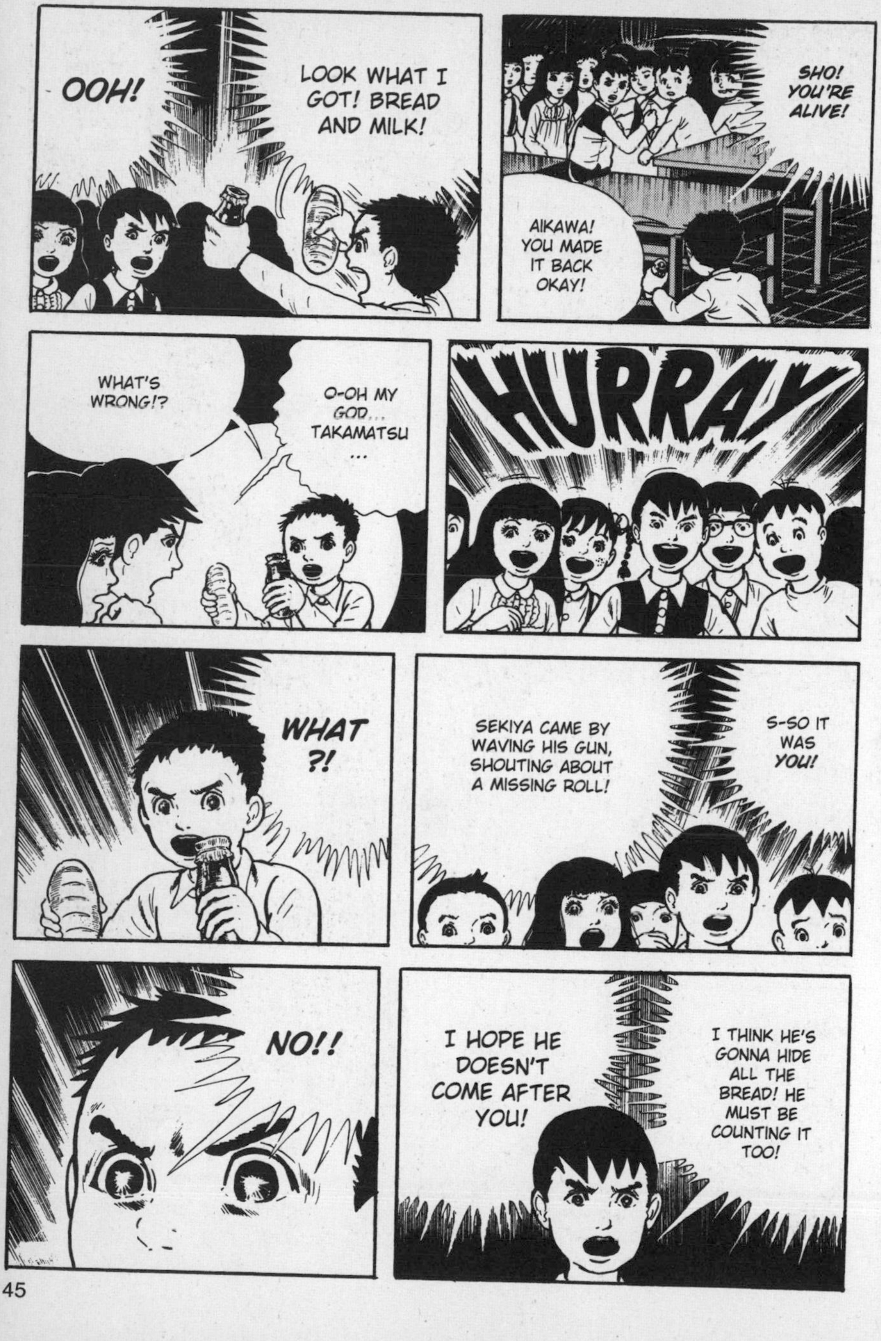
SHO! YOU'RE ALIVE!
AIKAWA! YOU MADE IT BACK OKAY!
LOOK WHAT I GOT! BREAD AND MILK!
OOH!
HURRAY
O-OH MY GOD... TAKAMATSU ...
WHAT'S WRONG!?
S-SO IT WAS YOU!
SEKIYA CAME BY WAVING HIS GUN, SHOUTING ABOUT A MISSING ROLL!
WHAT ?!
I THINK HE'S GONNA HIDE ALL THE BREAD! HE MUST BE COUNTING IT TOO!
I HOPE HE DOESN'T COME AFTER YOU!
NO!!

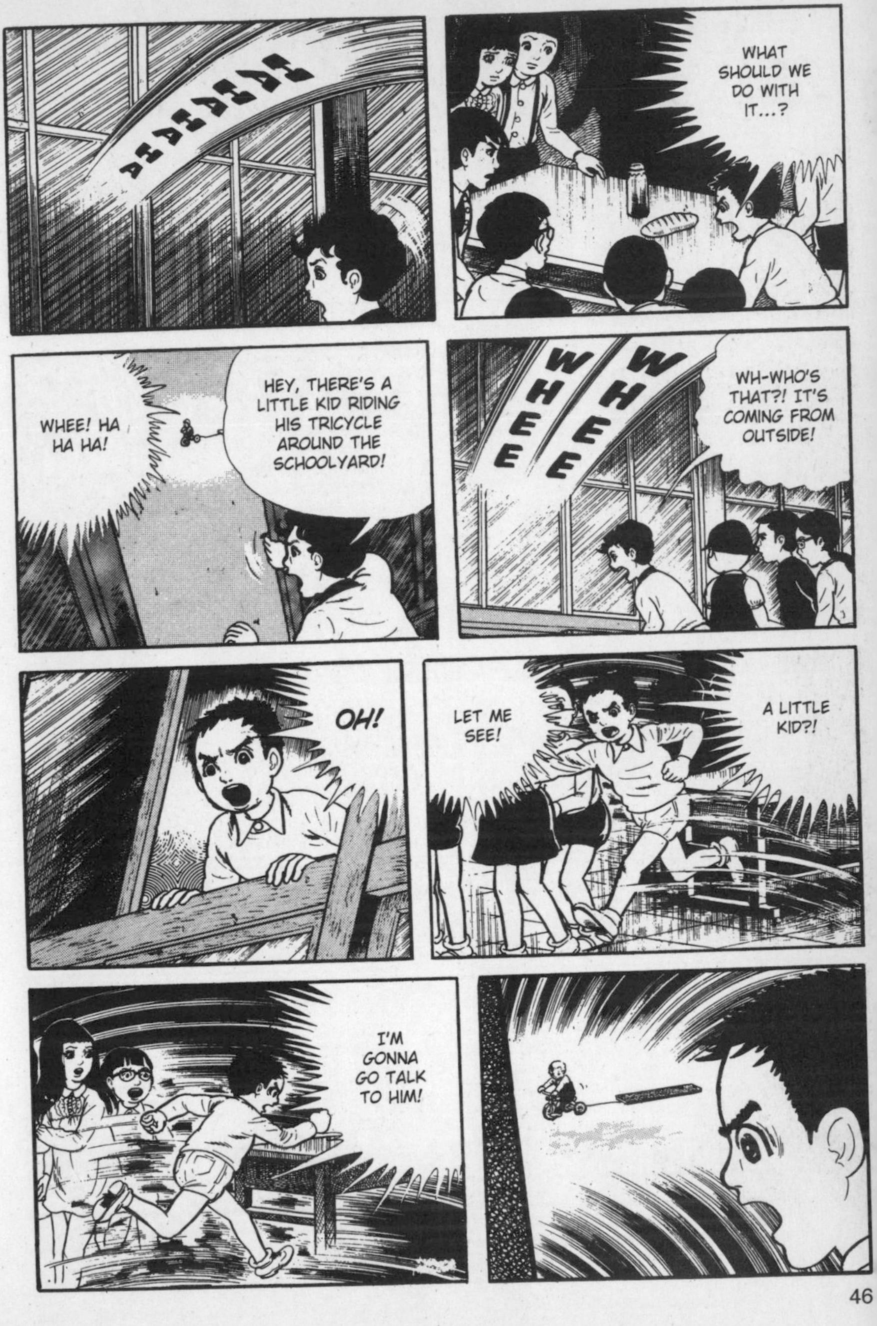

WHAT SHOULD WE DO WITH IT...?
HAHAHAHA
WHEE
WHEE
WH-WHO'S THAT?! IT'S COMING FROM OUTSIDE!
HEY, THERE'S A LITTLE KID RIDING HIS TRICYCLE AROUND THE SCHOOLYARD!
WHEE! HA HA HA!
A LITTLE KID?!
LET ME SEE!
OH!
I'M GONNA GO TALK TO HIM!

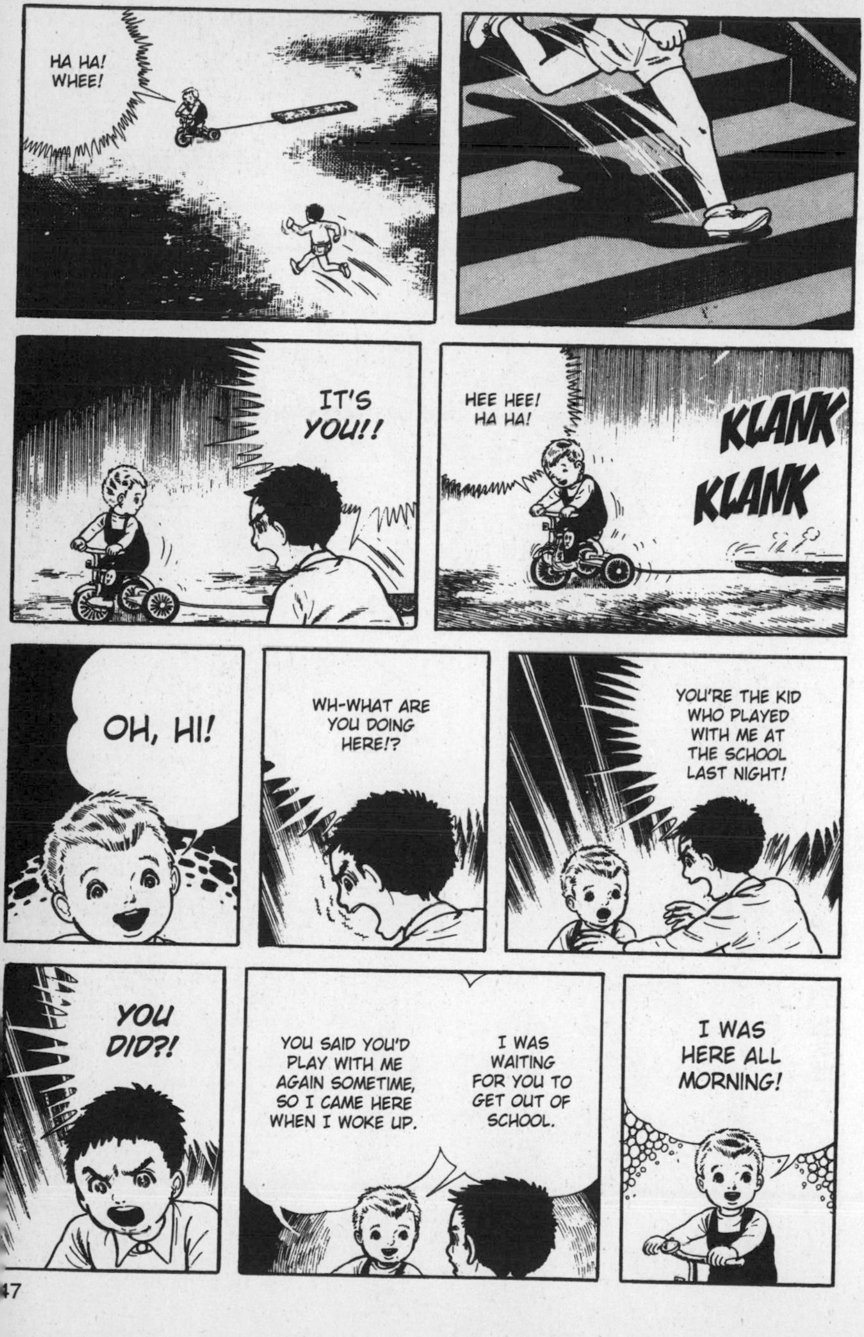
HA HA!
WHEE!
HEE HEE!
HA HA!
KLANK
KLANK
IT'S YOU!!
YOU'RE THE KID WHO PLAYED WITH ME AT THE SCHOOL LAST NIGHT!
WH-WHAT ARE YOU DOING HERE!?
OH, HI!
I WAS HERE ALL MORNING!
I WAS WAITING FOR YOU TO GET OUT OF SCHOOL.
YOU SAID YOU'D PLAY WITH ME AGAIN SOMETIME, SO I CAME HERE WHEN I WOKE UP.
YOU DID?!

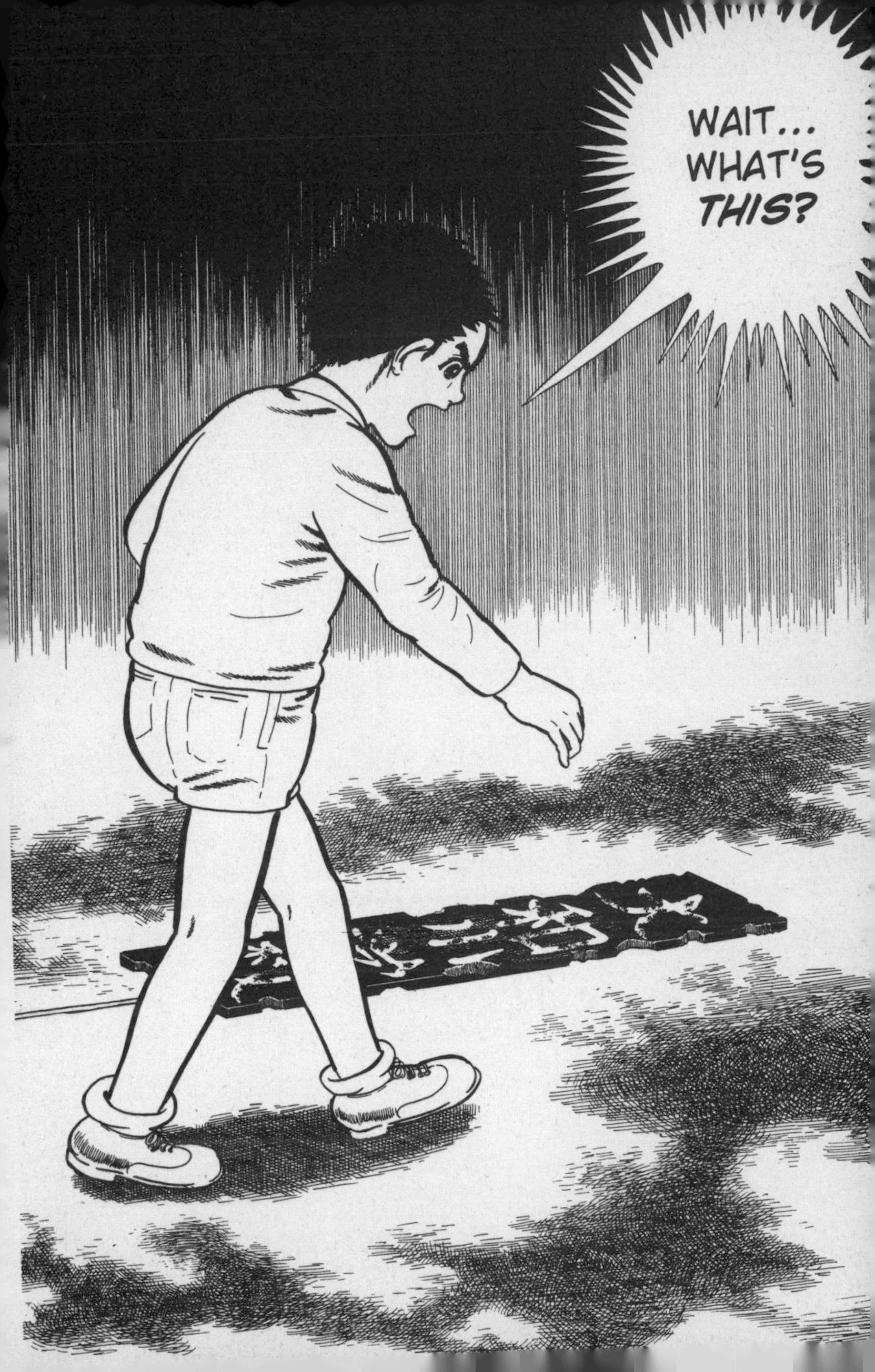
WAIT... WHAT'S *THIS?*

CHAPTER 6: THE BATTLE OF THE 6TH GRADERS

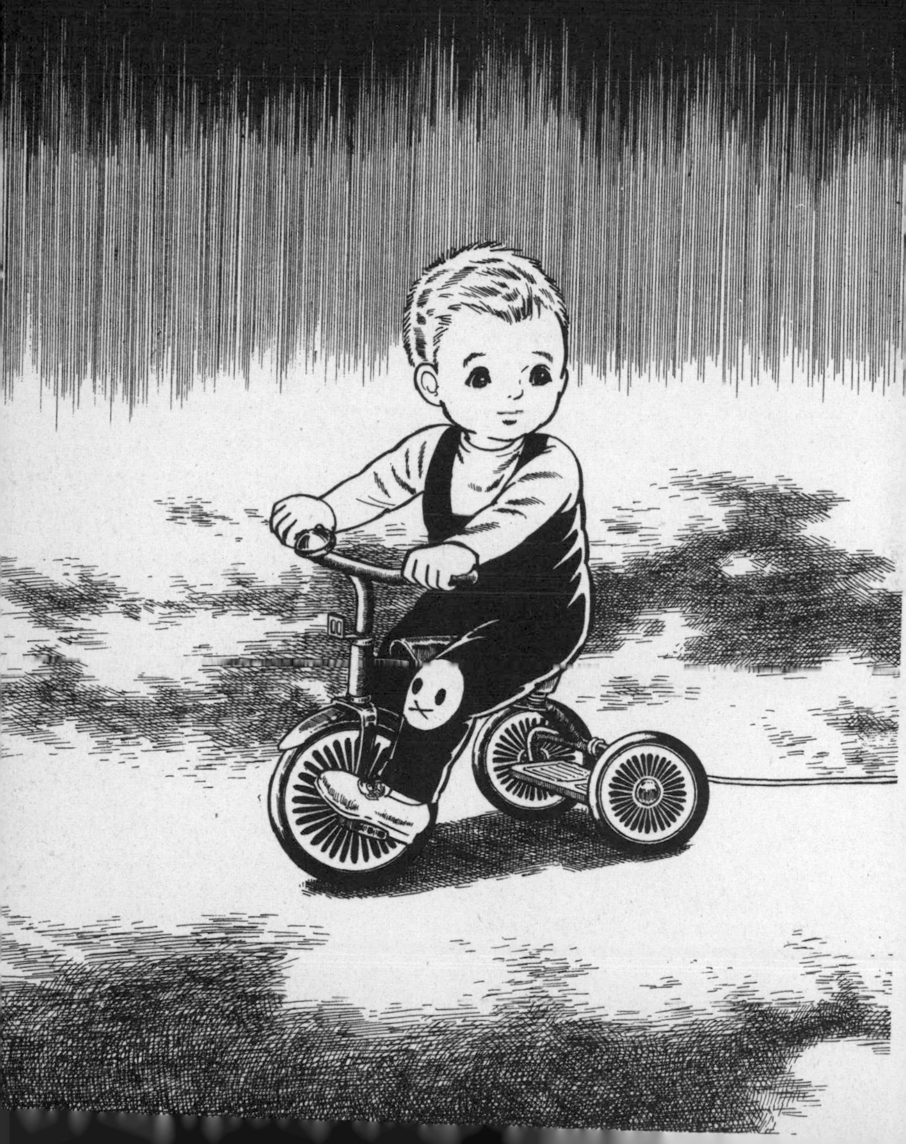

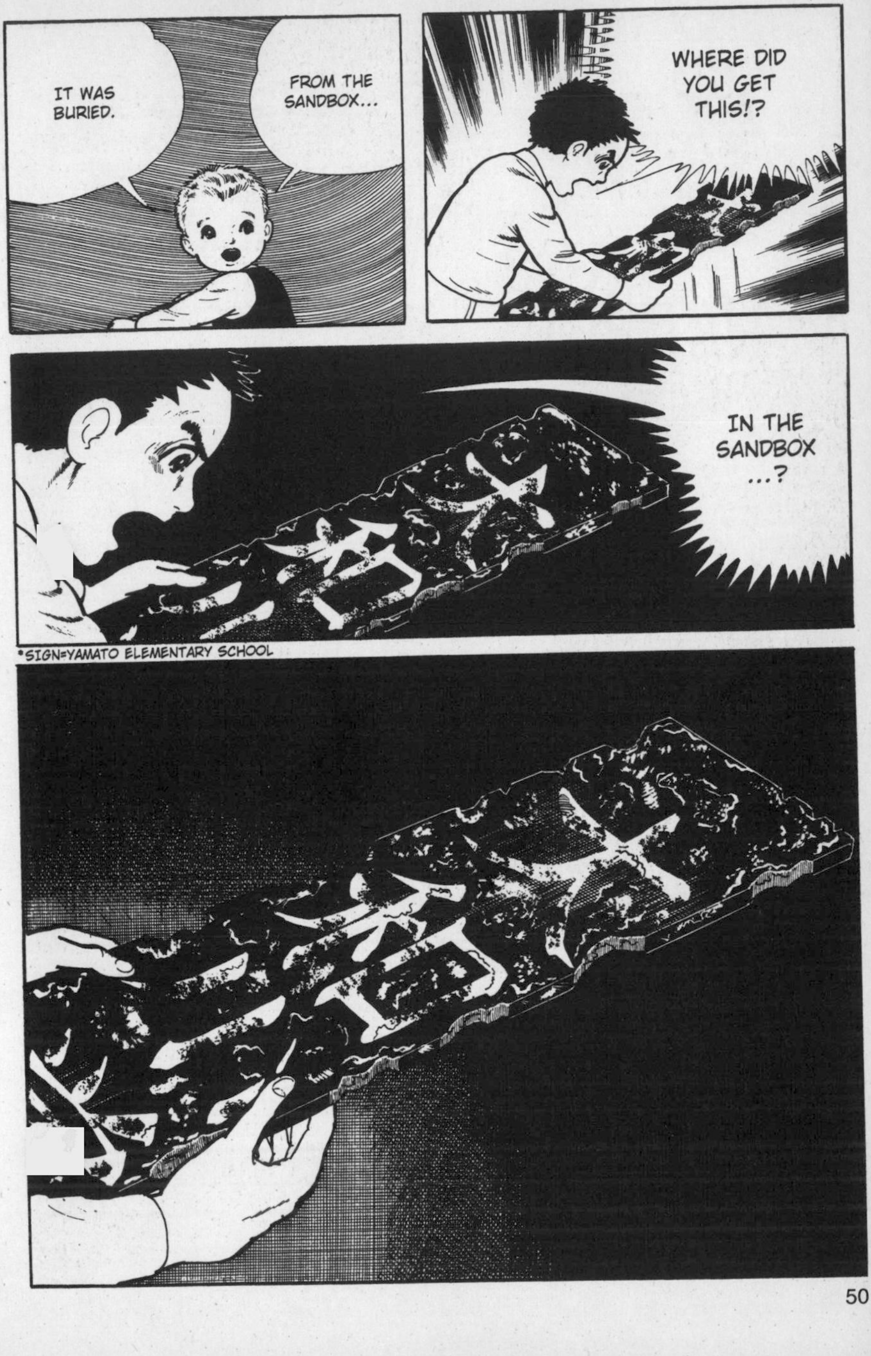
WHERE DID YOU GET THIS!?
FROM THE SANDBOX...
IT WAS BURIED.
IN THE SANDBOX ...?
*SIGN=YAMATO ELEMENTARY SCHOOL

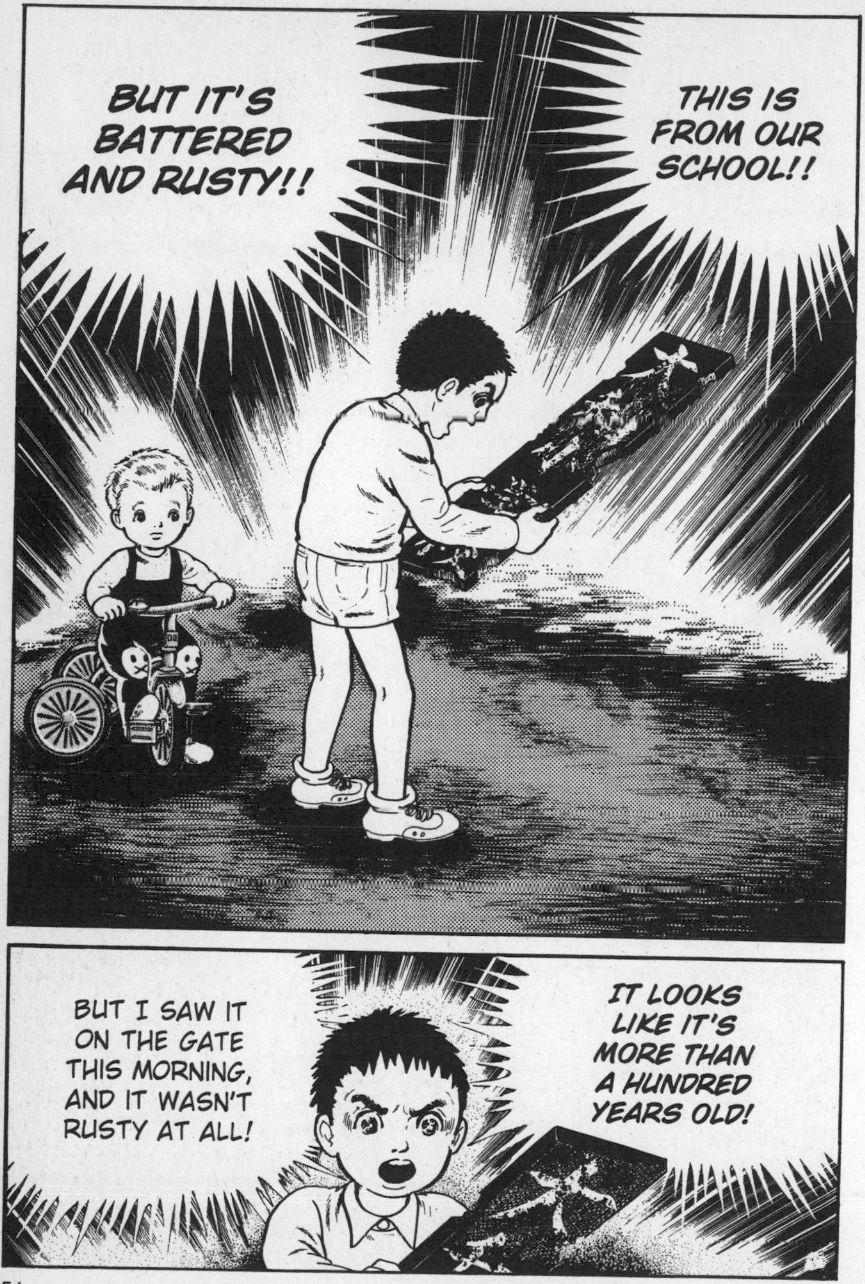
THIS IS FROM OUR SCHOOL!!
BUT IT'S BATTERED AND RUSTY!!
IT LOOKS LIKE IT'S MORE THAN A HUNDRED YEARS OLD!
BUT I SAW IT ON THE GATE THIS MORNING, AND IT WASN'T RUSTY AT ALL!

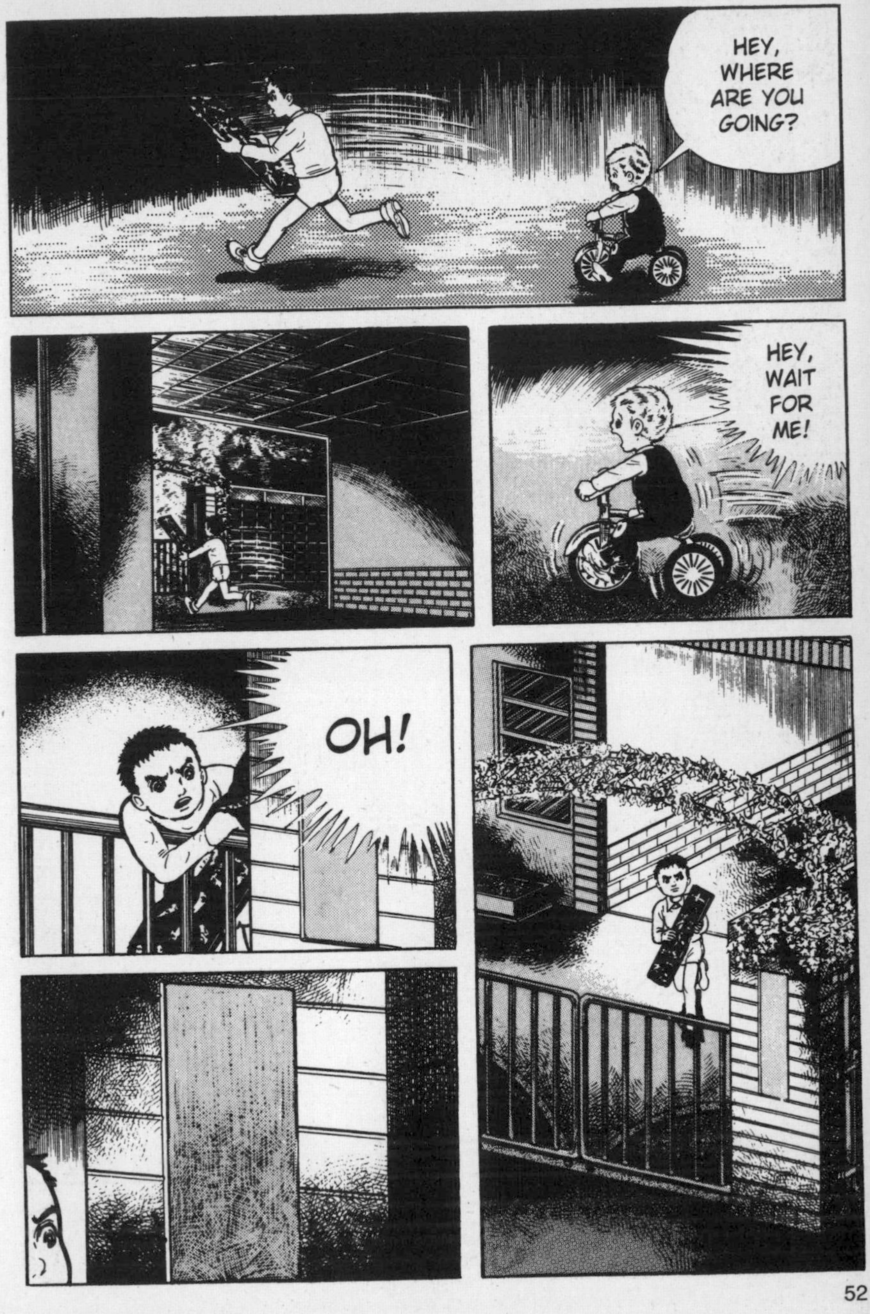
HEY, WHERE ARE YOU GOING?
HEY, WAIT FOR ME!
OH!

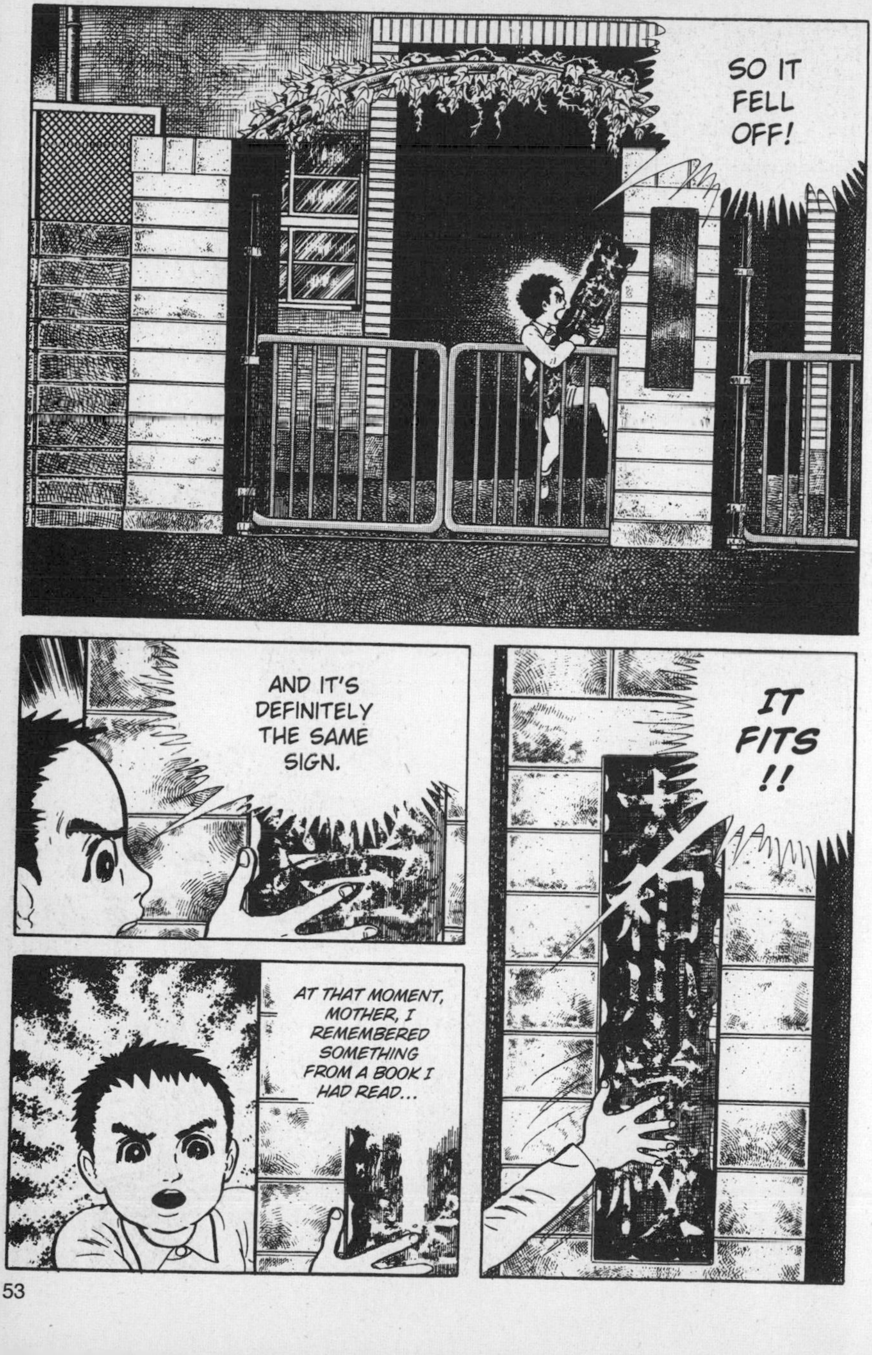
SO IT FELL OFF!
IT FITS !!
AND IT'S DEFINITELY THE SAME SIGN.
AT THAT MOMENT, MOTHER, I REMEMBERED SOMETHING FROM A BOOK I HAD READ...

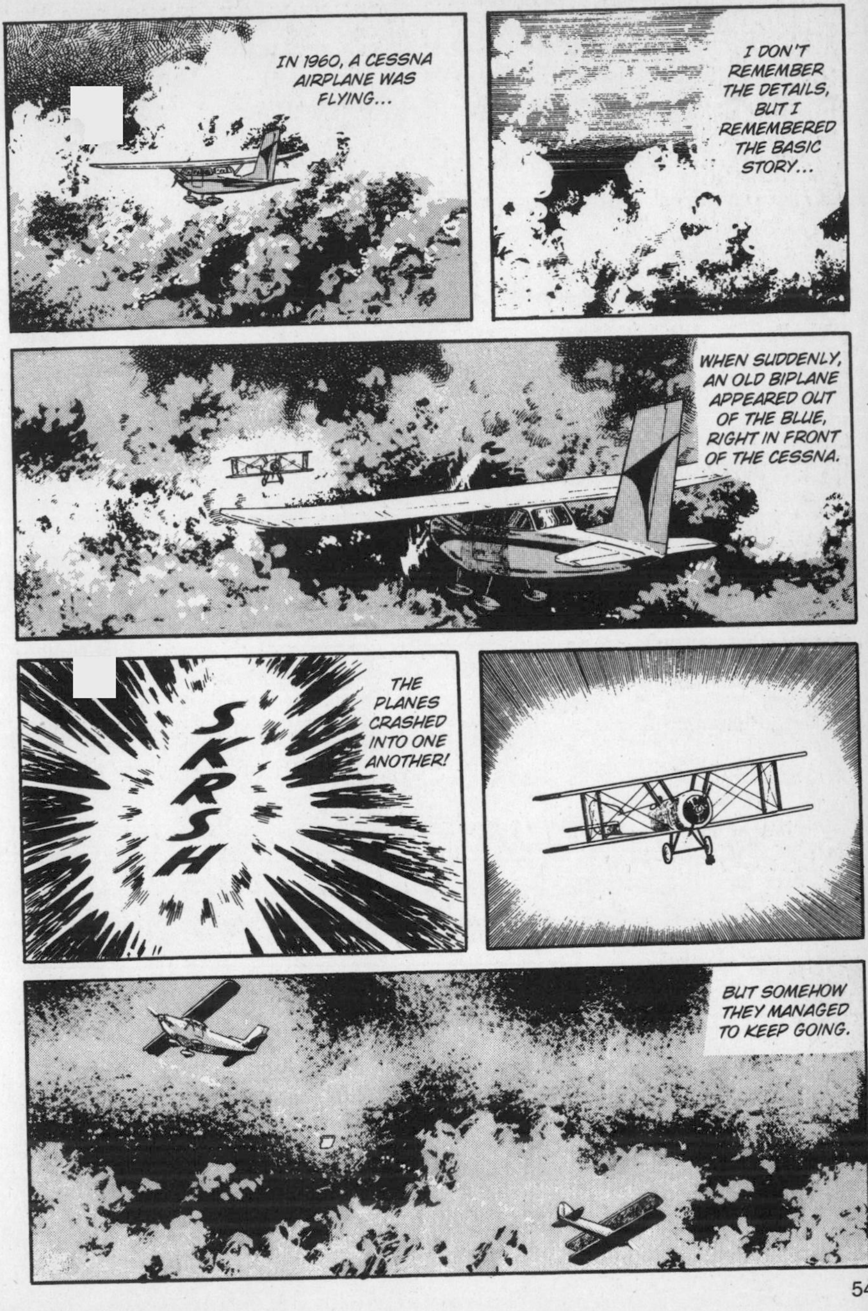
I DON'T REMEMBER THE DETAILS, BUT I REMEMBERED THE BASIC STORY...
IN 1960, A CESSNA AIRPLANE WAS FLYING...
WHEN SUDDENLY, AN OLD BIPLANE APPEARED OUT OF THE BLUE, RIGHT IN FRONT OF THE CESSNA.
THE PLANES CRASHED INTO ONE ANOTHER!
SKRSH
BUT SOMEHOW THEY MANAGED TO KEEP GOING.

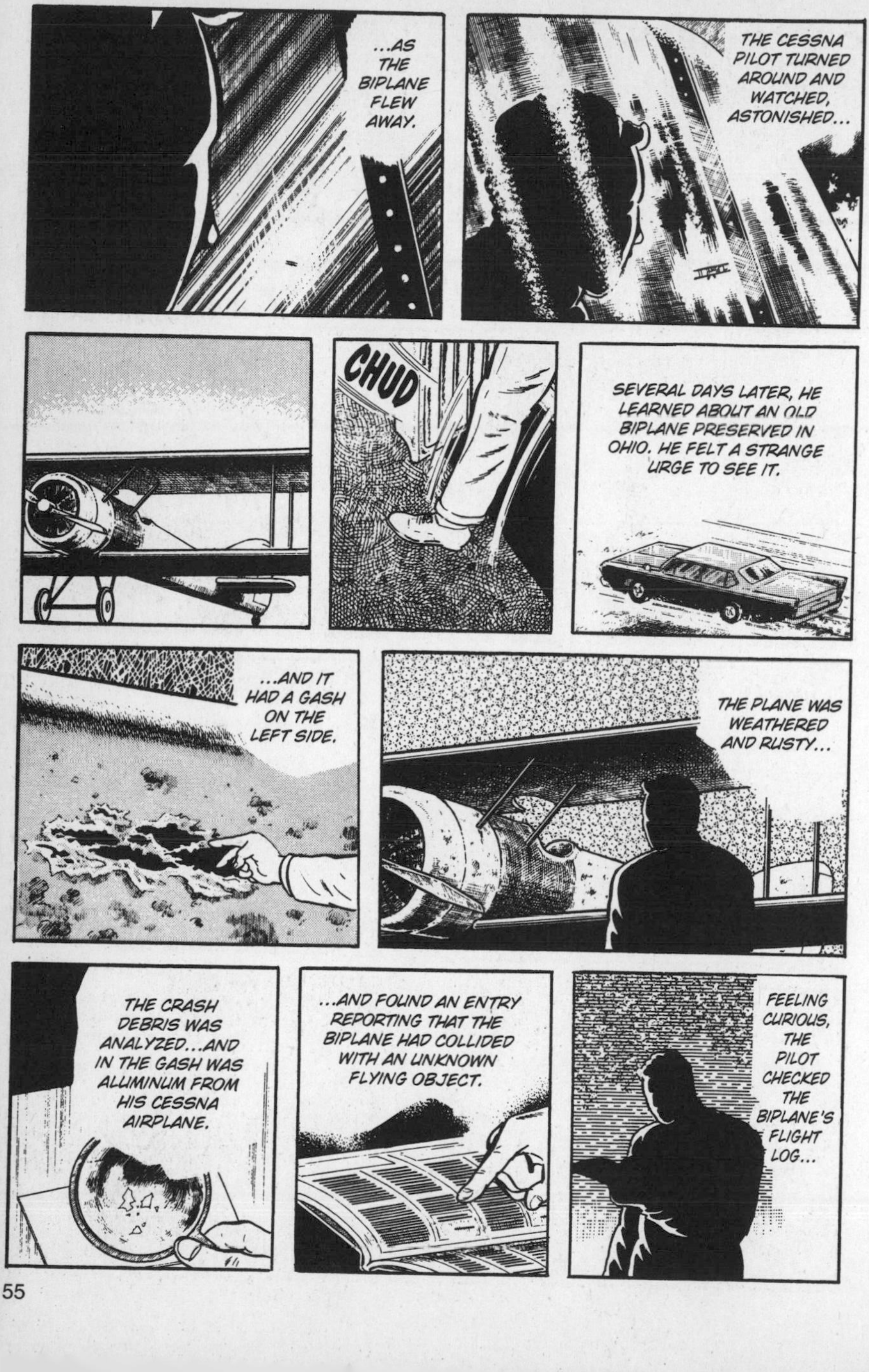
THE CESSNA PILOT TURNED AROUND AND WATCHED, ASTONISHED...
...AS THE BIPLANE FLEW AWAY.
SEVERAL DAYS LATER, HE LEARNED ABOUT AN OLD BIPLANE PRESERVED IN OHIO. HE FELT A STRANGE URGE TO SEE IT.
CHUD
THE PLANE WAS WEATHERED AND RUSTY...
...AND IT HAD A GASH ON THE LEFT SIDE.
FEELING CURIOUS, THE PILOT CHECKED THE BIPLANE'S FLIGHT LOG...
...AND FOUND AN ENTRY REPORTING THAT THE BIPLANE HAD COLLIDED WITH AN UNKNOWN FLYING OBJECT.
THE CRASH DEBRIS WAS ANALYZED...AND IN THE GASH WAS ALUMINUM FROM HIS CESSNA AIRPLANE.

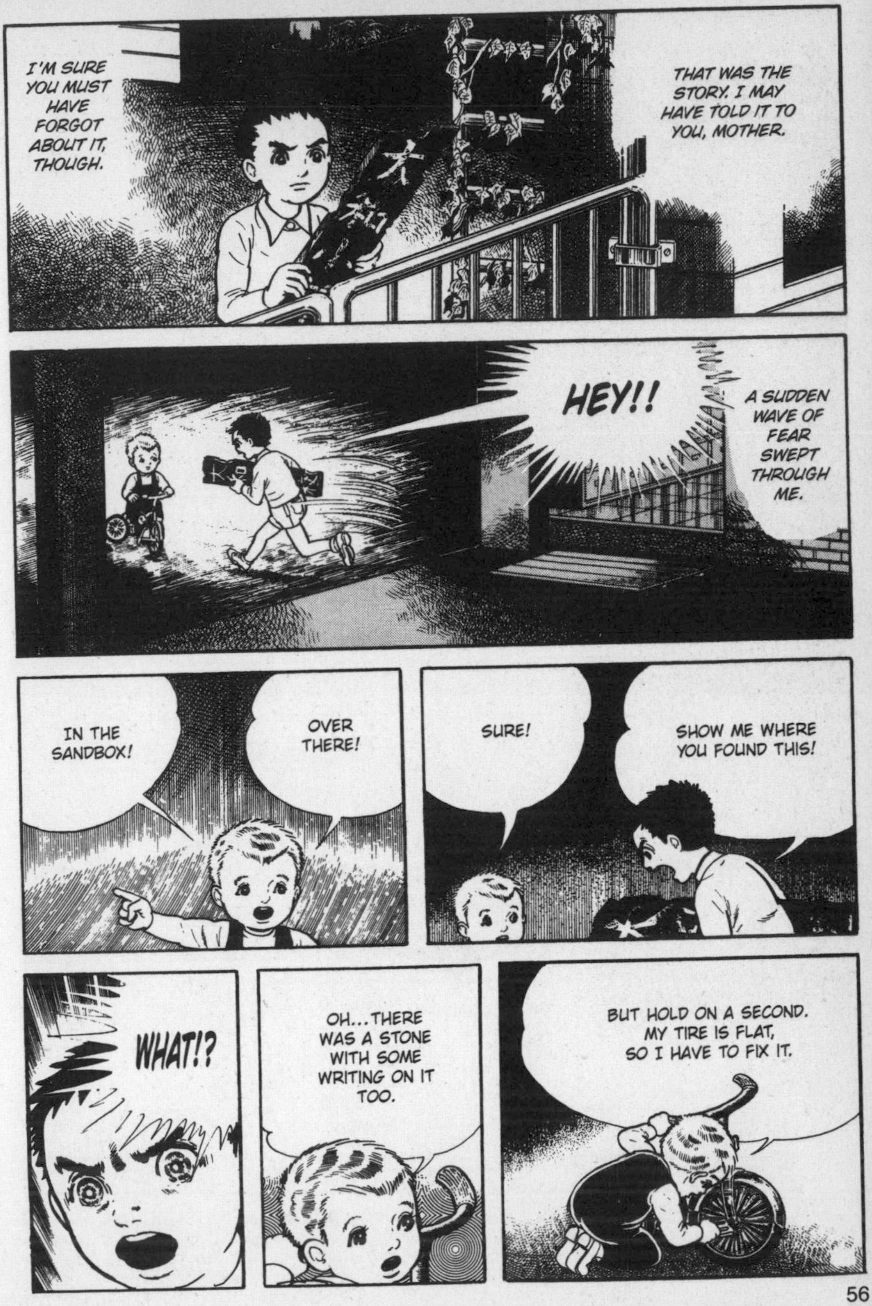
THAT WAS THE STORY. I MAY HAVE TOLD IT TO YOU, MOTHER.
I'M SURE YOU MUST HAVE FORGOT ABOUT IT, THOUGH.
A SUDDEN WAVE OF FEAR SWEPT THROUGH ME.
HEY!!
SHOW ME WHERE YOU FOUND THIS!
SURE!
OVER THERE!
IN THE SANDBOX!
BUT HOLD ON A SECOND. MY TIRE IS FLAT, SO I HAVE TO FIX IT.
OH...THERE WAS A STONE WITH SOME WRITING ON IT TOO.
WHAT!?

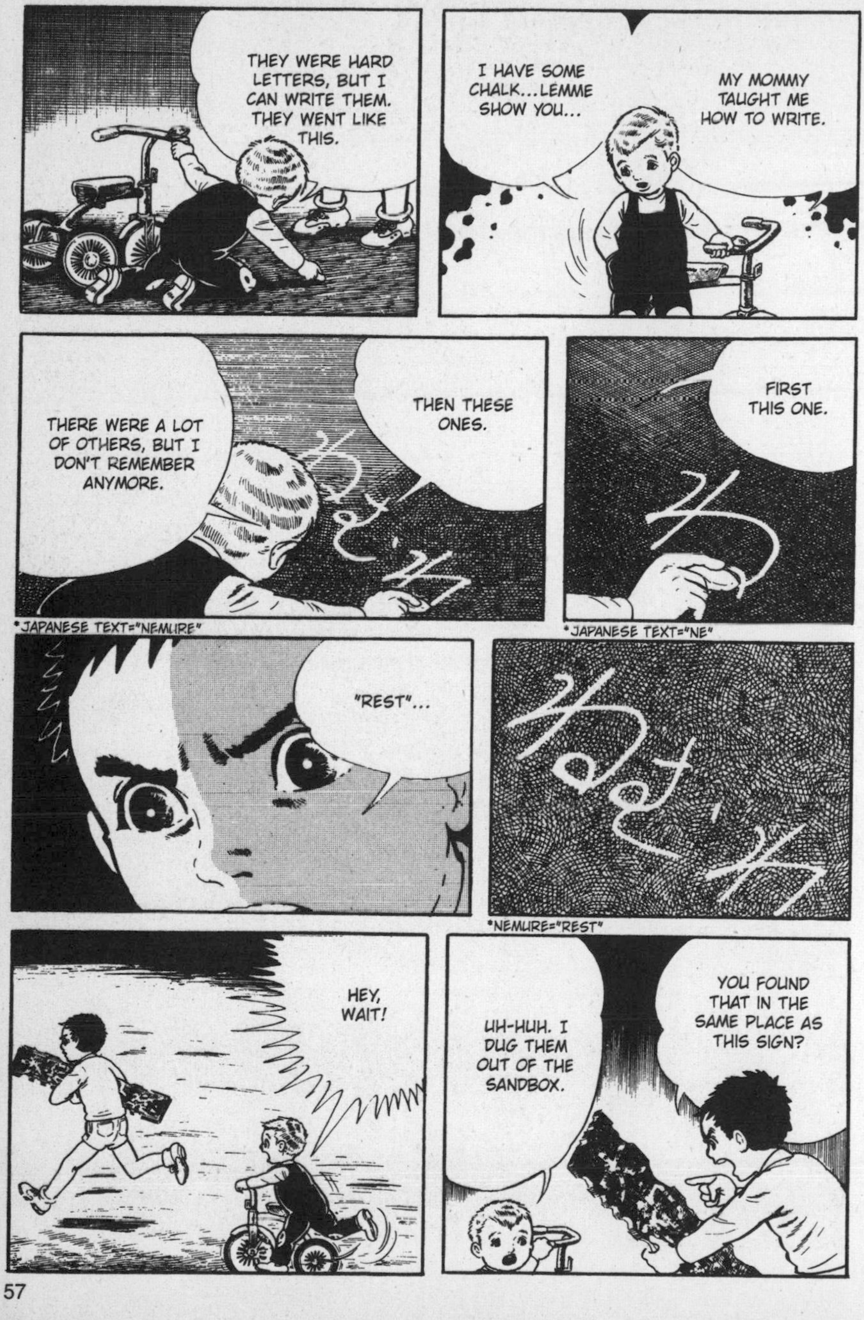
MY MOMMY TAUGHT ME HOW TO WRITE.
I HAVE SOME CHALK...LEMME SHOW YOU...
THEY WERE HARD LETTERS, BUT I CAN WRITE THEM. THEY WENT LIKE THIS.
FIRST THIS ONE.
*JAPANESE TEXT="NE"
THEN THESE ONES.
THERE WERE A LOT OF OTHERS, BUT I DON'T REMEMBER ANYMORE.
*JAPANESE TEXT="NEMURE"
*NEMURE="REST"
"REST"...
YOU FOUND THAT IN THE SAME PLACE AS THIS SIGN?
UH-HUH. I DUG THEM OUT OF THE SANDBOX.
HEY, WAIT!

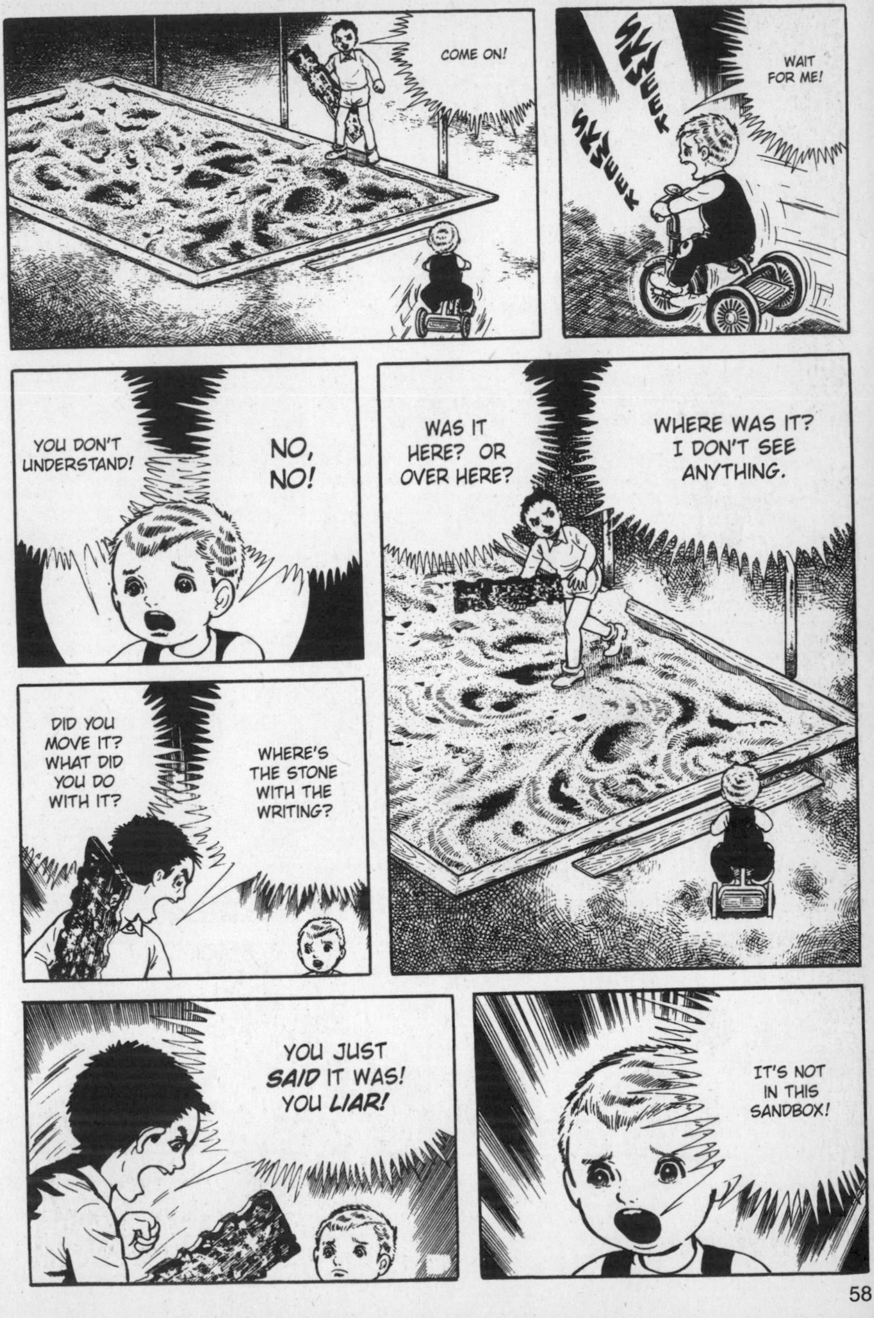
WAIT FOR ME!
SKWEEK
SKWEEK
COME ON!
WHERE WAS IT? I DON'T SEE ANYTHING.
WAS IT HERE? OR OVER HERE?
NO, NO!
YOU DON'T UNDERSTAND!
WHERE'S THE STONE WITH THE WRITING?
DID YOU MOVE IT? WHAT DID YOU DO WITH IT?
IT'S NOT IN THIS SANDBOX!
YOU JUST SAID IT WAS! YOU LIAR!

WAAH!!!

I'M NOT LYING!

NOT *THIS* SANDBOX! *THE OTHER* SANDBOX!

I'M GOING HOME. MY MOMMY IS WAITING FOR ME.

NO! YOU GET ANGRY SO I'M NOT GOING TO TELL YOU!!

I APOLOGIZE. LOOK...COULD YOU EXPLAIN IT TO ME ONE MORE TIME? PLEASE?

HEY, I'M SORRY.

LOOK, IT'S ALREADY DARK. YOU HAVE TO SPEND THE NIGHT HERE WITH ME.

UH...NO! *NO!* YOU CAN'T GO HOME.

I CARRIED THE CHILD TO OUR CLASSROOM.

I DON'T *WANT* TO! I'M *HUNGRY!*

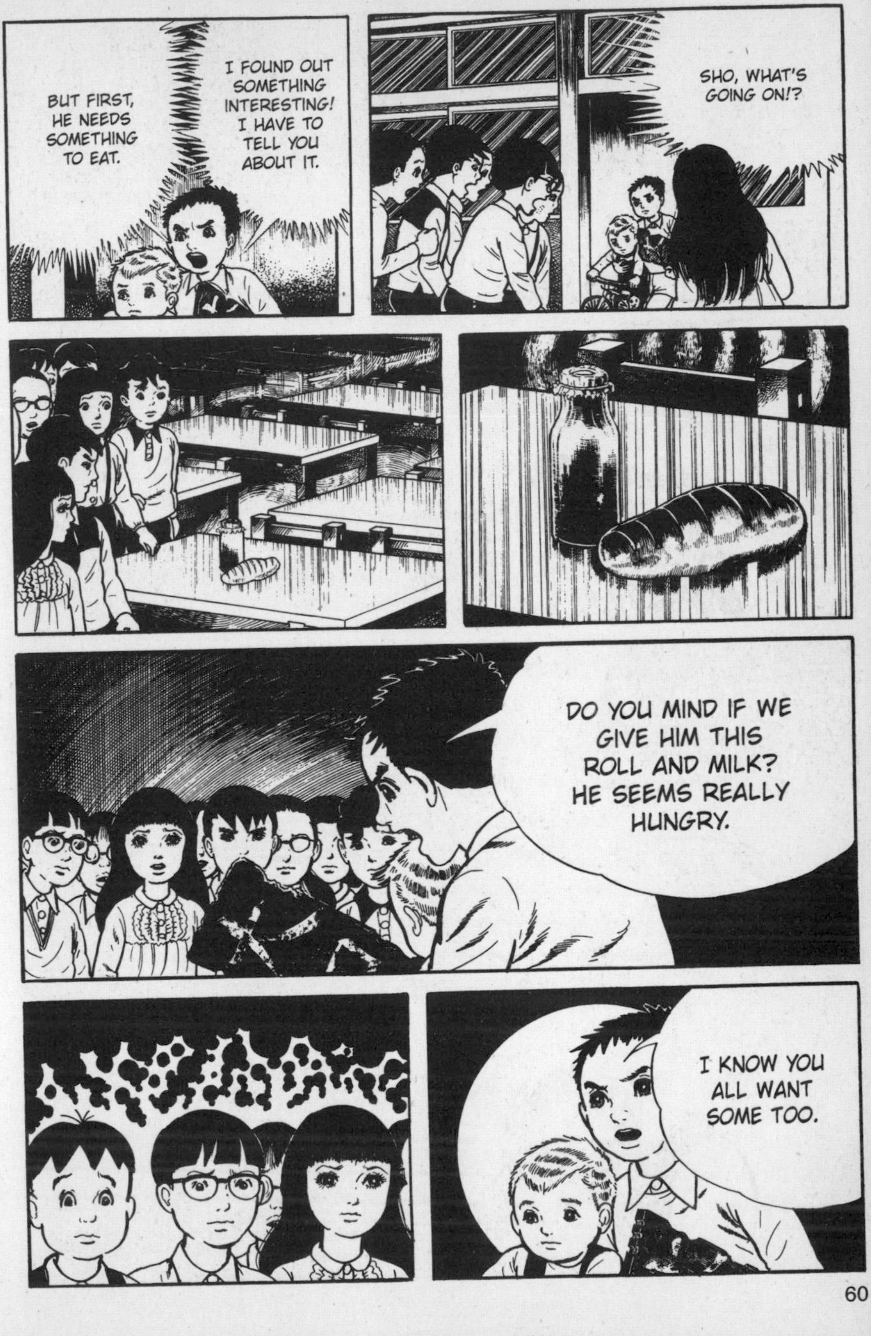
SHO, WHAT'S GOING ON!?
I FOUND OUT SOMETHING INTERESTING! I HAVE TO TELL YOU ABOUT IT.
BUT FIRST, HE NEEDS SOMETHING TO EAT.
DO YOU MIND IF WE GIVE HIM THIS ROLL AND MILK? HE SEEMS REALLY HUNGRY.
I KNOW YOU ALL WANT SOME TOO.

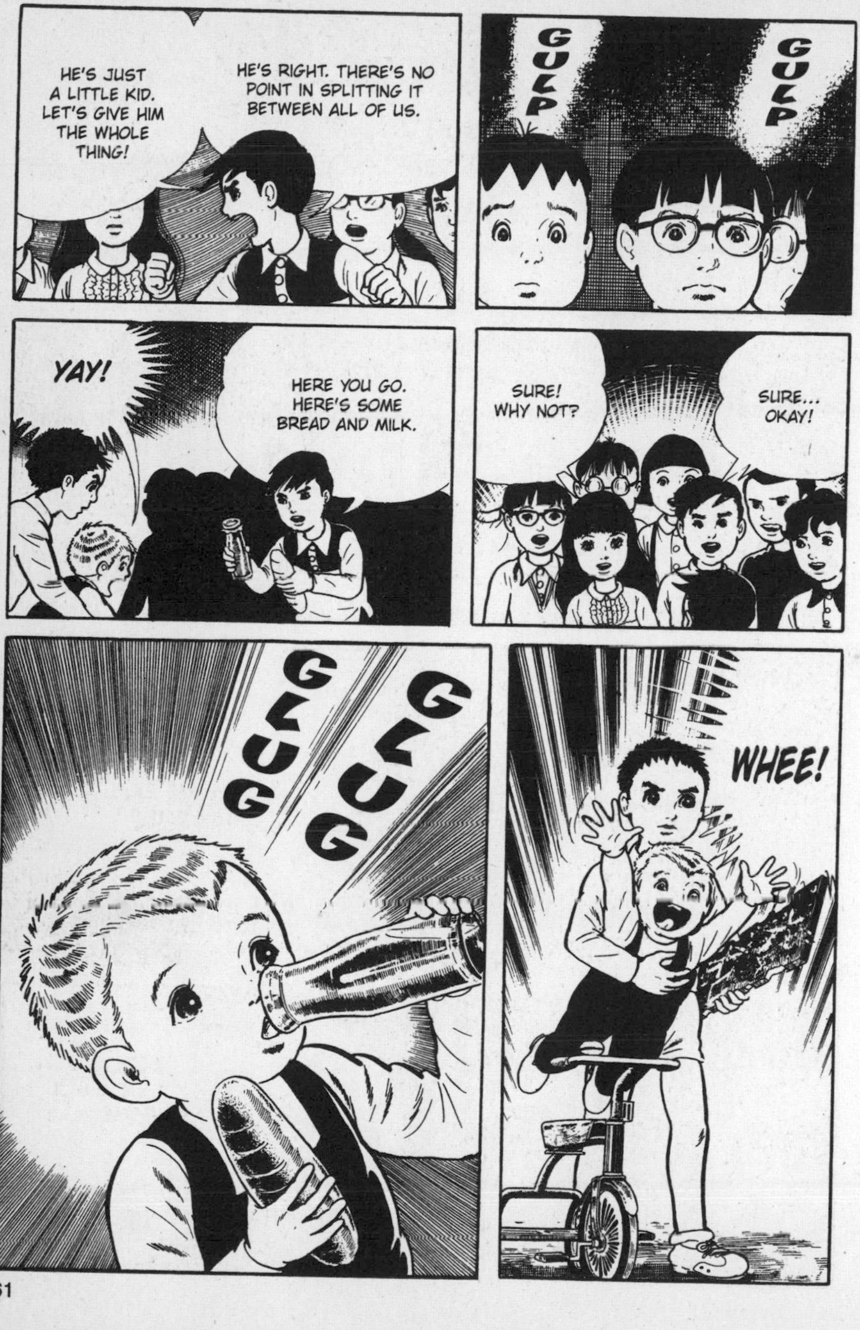
GULP
GULP
HE'S RIGHT. THERE'S NO POINT IN SPLITTING IT BETWEEN ALL OF US.
HE'S JUST A LITTLE KID. LET'S GIVE HIM THE WHOLE THING!
SURE... OKAY!
SURE! WHY NOT?
HERE YOU GO. HERE'S SOME BREAD AND MILK.
YAY!
WHEE!
GLUG
GLUG

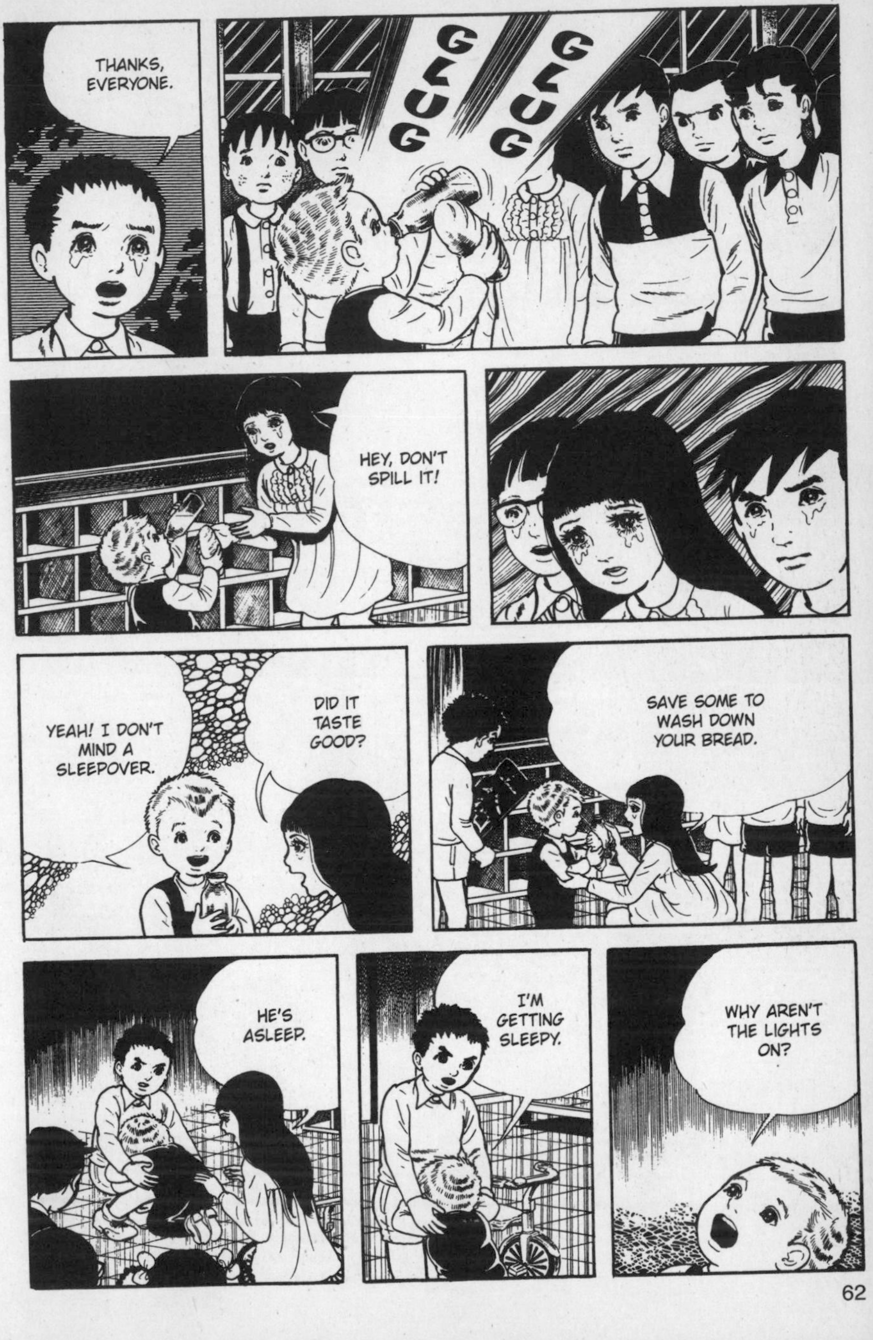
GLUG
GLUG
THANKS, EVERYONE.
HEY, DON'T SPILL IT!
SAVE SOME TO WASH DOWN YOUR BREAD.
DID IT TASTE GOOD?
YEAH! I DON'T MIND A SLEEPOVER.
WHY AREN'T THE LIGHTS ON?
I'M GETTING SLEEPY.
HE'S ASLEEP.

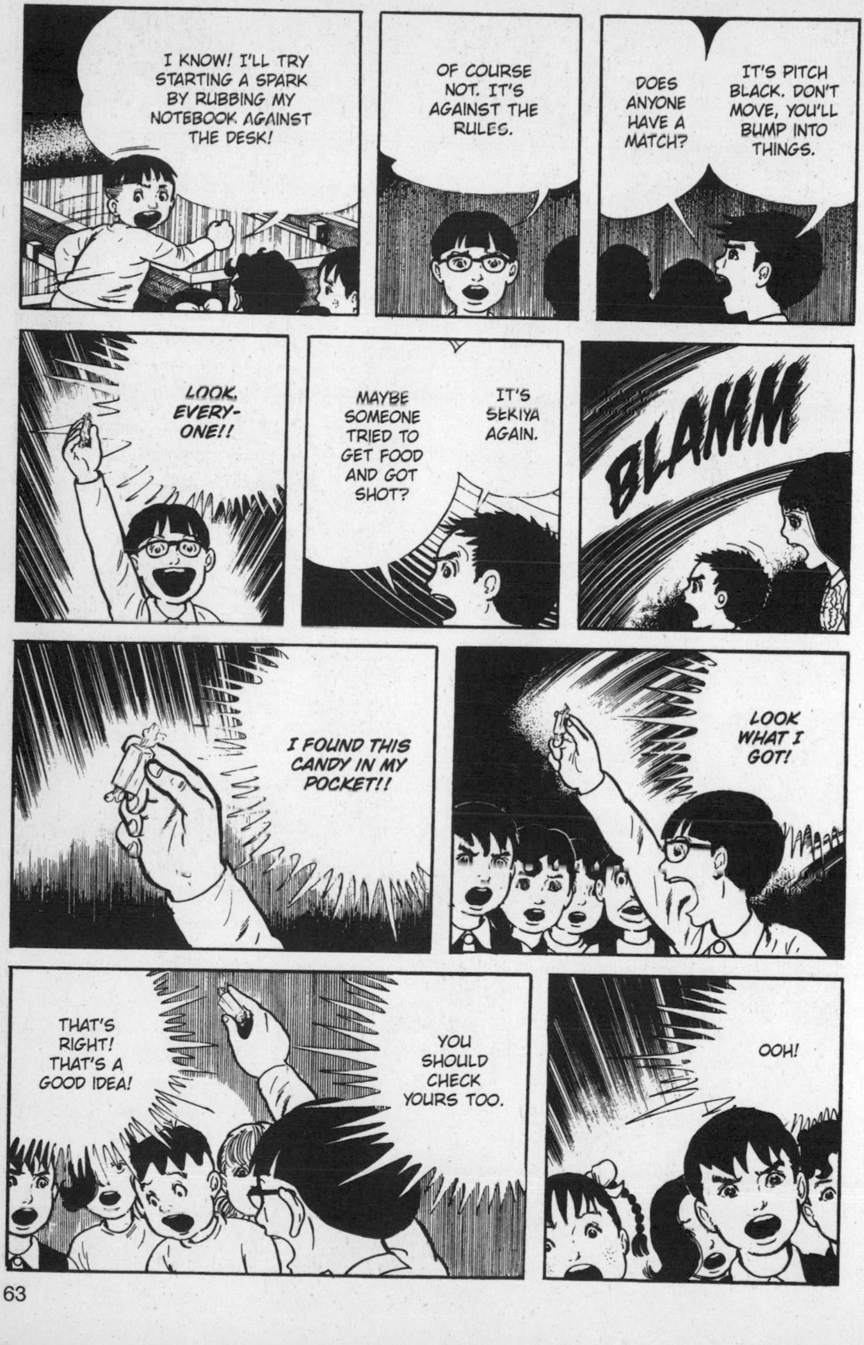
IT'S PITCH BLACK. DON'T MOVE, YOU'LL BUMP INTO THINGS.
DOES ANYONE HAVE A MATCH?
OF COURSE NOT. IT'S AGAINST THE RULES.
I KNOW! I'LL TRY STARTING A SPARK BY RUBBING MY NOTEBOOK AGAINST THE DESK!
BLAMM
IT'S SEKIYA AGAIN.
MAYBE SOMEONE TRIED TO GET FOOD AND GOT SHOT?
LOOK, EVERYONE!!
LOOK WHAT I GOT!
I FOUND THIS CANDY IN MY POCKET!!
OOH!
YOU SHOULD CHECK YOURS TOO.
THAT'S RIGHT! THAT'S A GOOD IDEA!

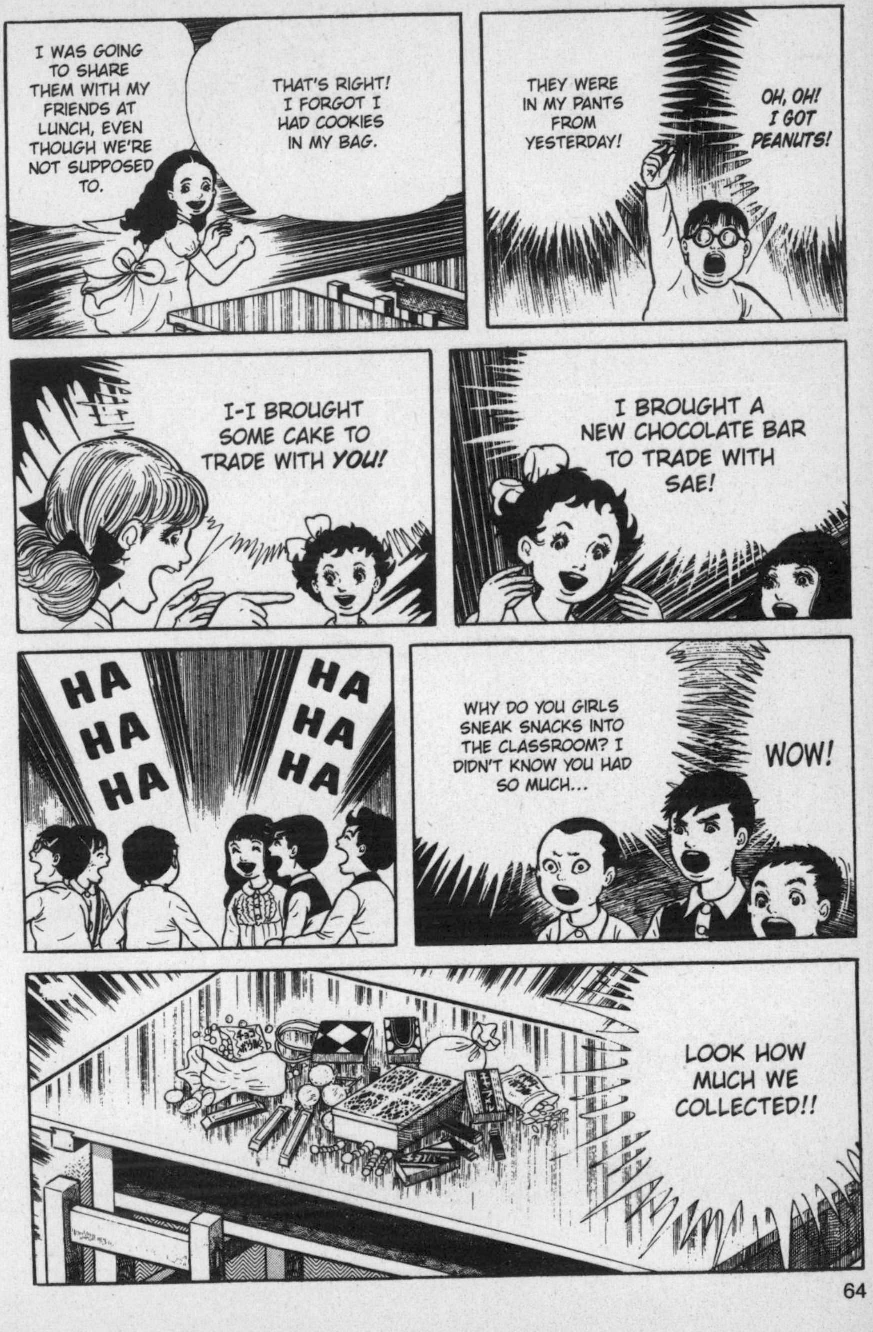
OH, OH! I GOT PEANUTS!
THEY WERE IN MY PANTS FROM YESTERDAY!
THAT'S RIGHT! I FORGOT I HAD COOKIES IN MY BAG.
I WAS GOING TO SHARE THEM WITH MY FRIENDS AT LUNCH, EVEN THOUGH WE'RE NOT SUPPOSED TO.
I BROUGHT A NEW CHOCOLATE BAR TO TRADE WITH SAE!
I-I BROUGHT SOME CAKE TO TRADE WITH *YOU!*
WOW!
WHY DO YOU GIRLS SNEAK SNACKS INTO THE CLASSROOM? I DIDN'T KNOW YOU HAD SO MUCH...
HA HA HA
HA HA HA
LOOK HOW MUCH WE COLLECTED!!

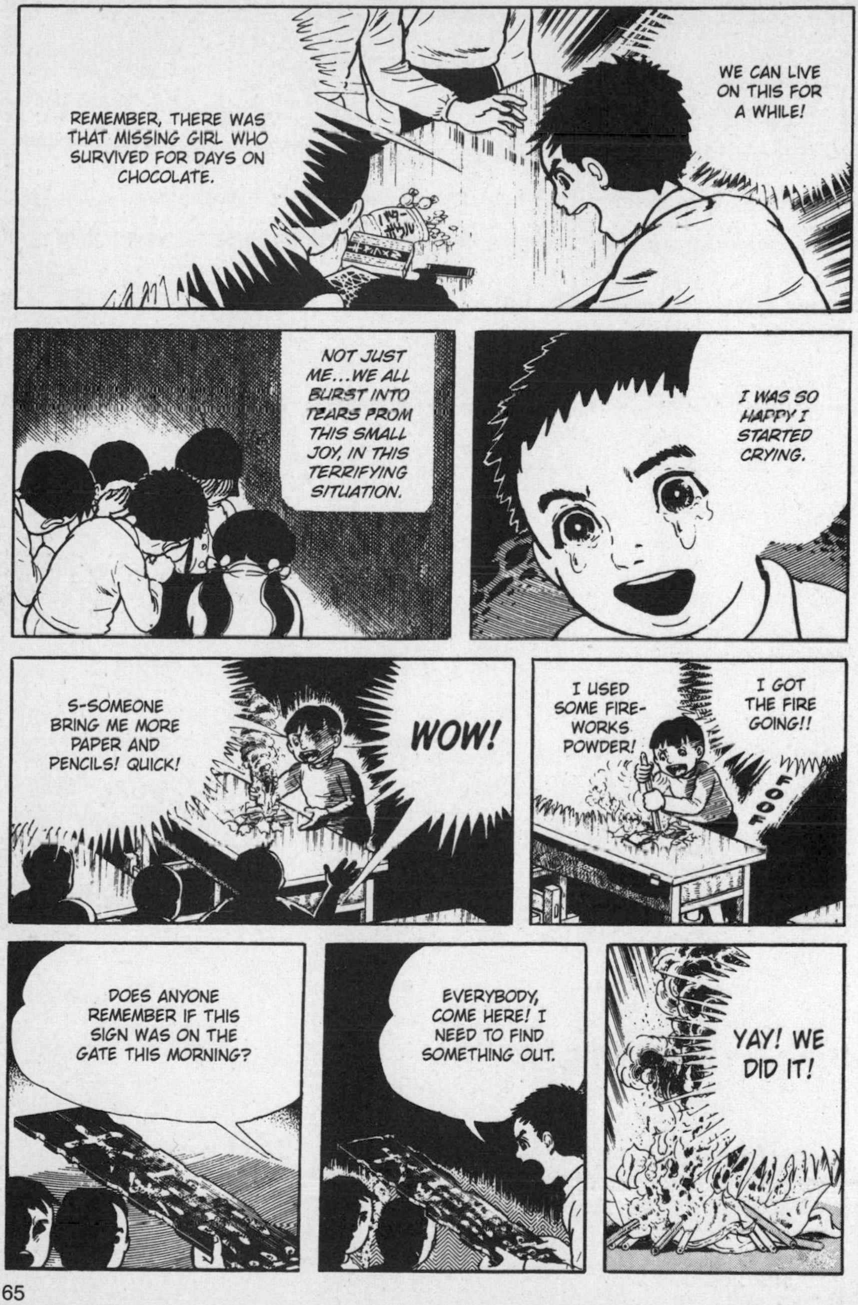
WE CAN LIVE ON THIS FOR A WHILE!
REMEMBER, THERE WAS THAT MISSING GIRL WHO SURVIVED FOR DAYS ON CHOCOLATE.
I WAS SO HAPPY I STARTED CRYING.
NOT JUST ME...WE ALL BURST INTO TEARS FROM THIS SMALL JOY, IN THIS TERRIFYING SITUATION.
I GOT THE FIRE GOING!!
I USED SOME FIRE-WORKS POWDER!
FOOF
WOW!
S-SOMEONE BRING ME MORE PAPER AND PENCILS! QUICK!
YAY! WE DID IT!
EVERYBODY, COME HERE! I NEED TO FIND SOMETHING OUT.
DOES ANYONE REMEMBER IF THIS SIGN WAS ON THE GATE THIS MORNING?

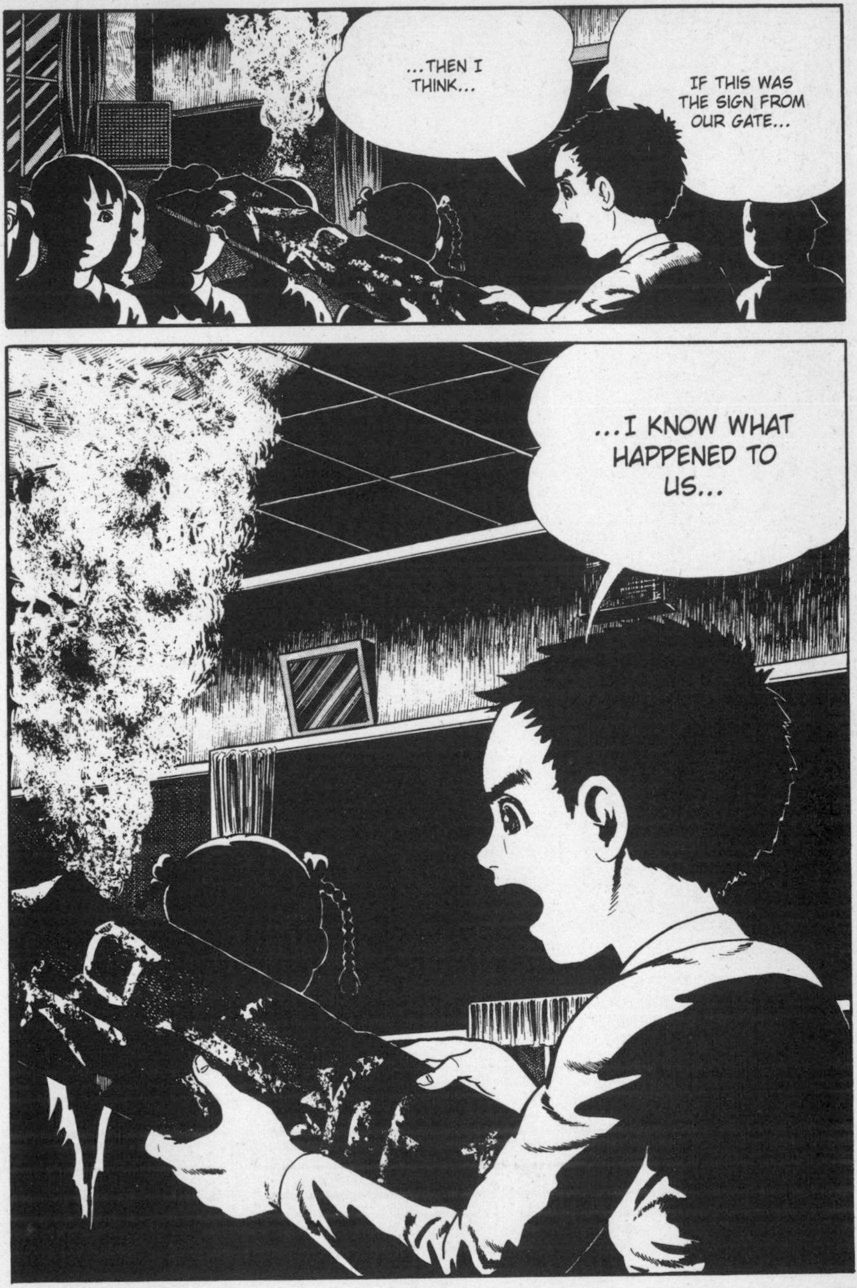
IF THIS WAS THE SIGN FROM OUR GATE...
...THEN I THINK...
...I KNOW WHAT HAPPENED TO US...

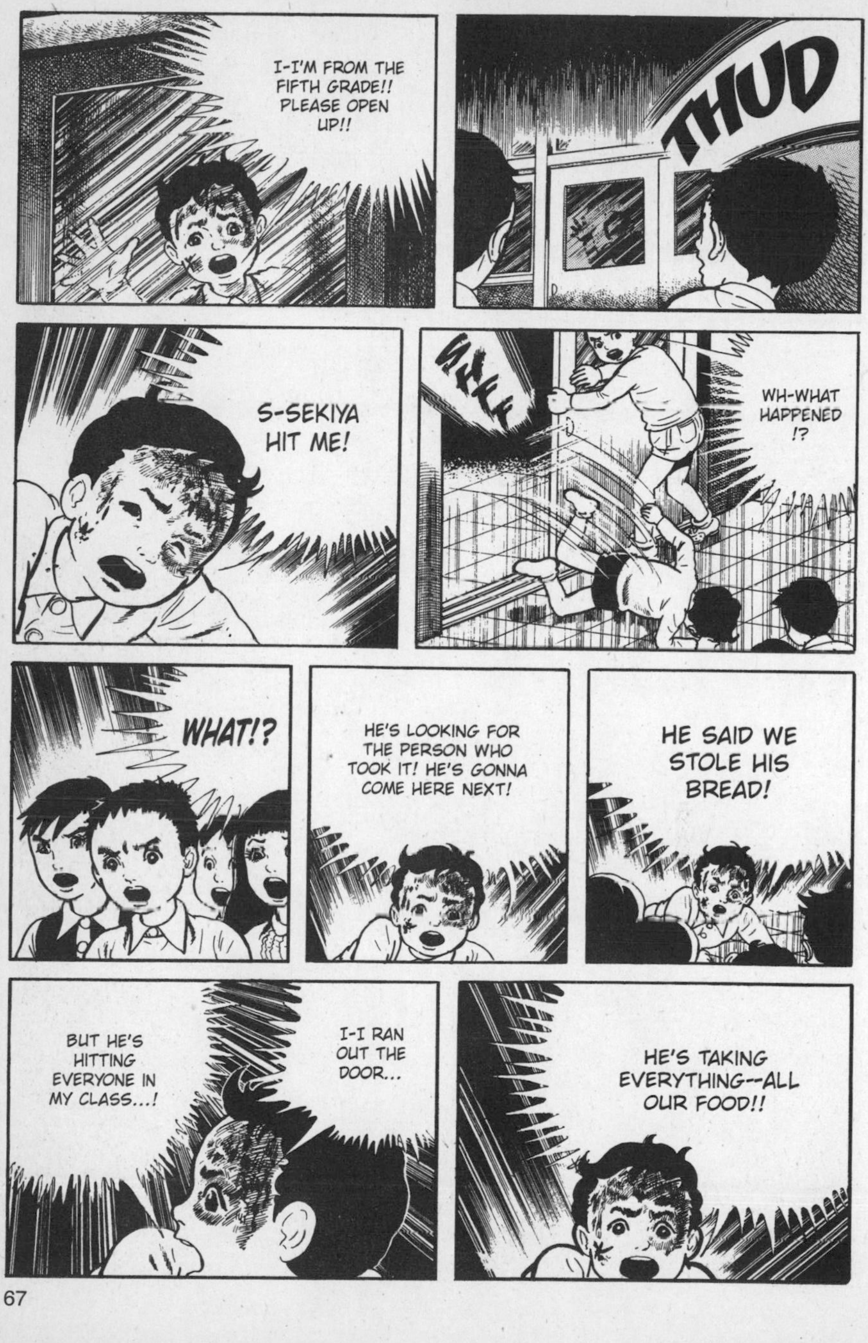
THUD
I-I'M FROM THE FIFTH GRADE!! PLEASE OPEN UP!!
SHFF
WH-WHAT HAPPENED !?
S-SEKIYA HIT ME!
HE SAID WE STOLE HIS BREAD!
HE'S LOOKING FOR THE PERSON WHO TOOK IT! HE'S GONNA COME HERE NEXT!
WHAT!?
HE'S TAKING EVERYTHING--ALL OUR FOOD!!
I-I RAN OUT THE DOOR...
BUT HE'S HITTING EVERYONE IN MY CLASS...!

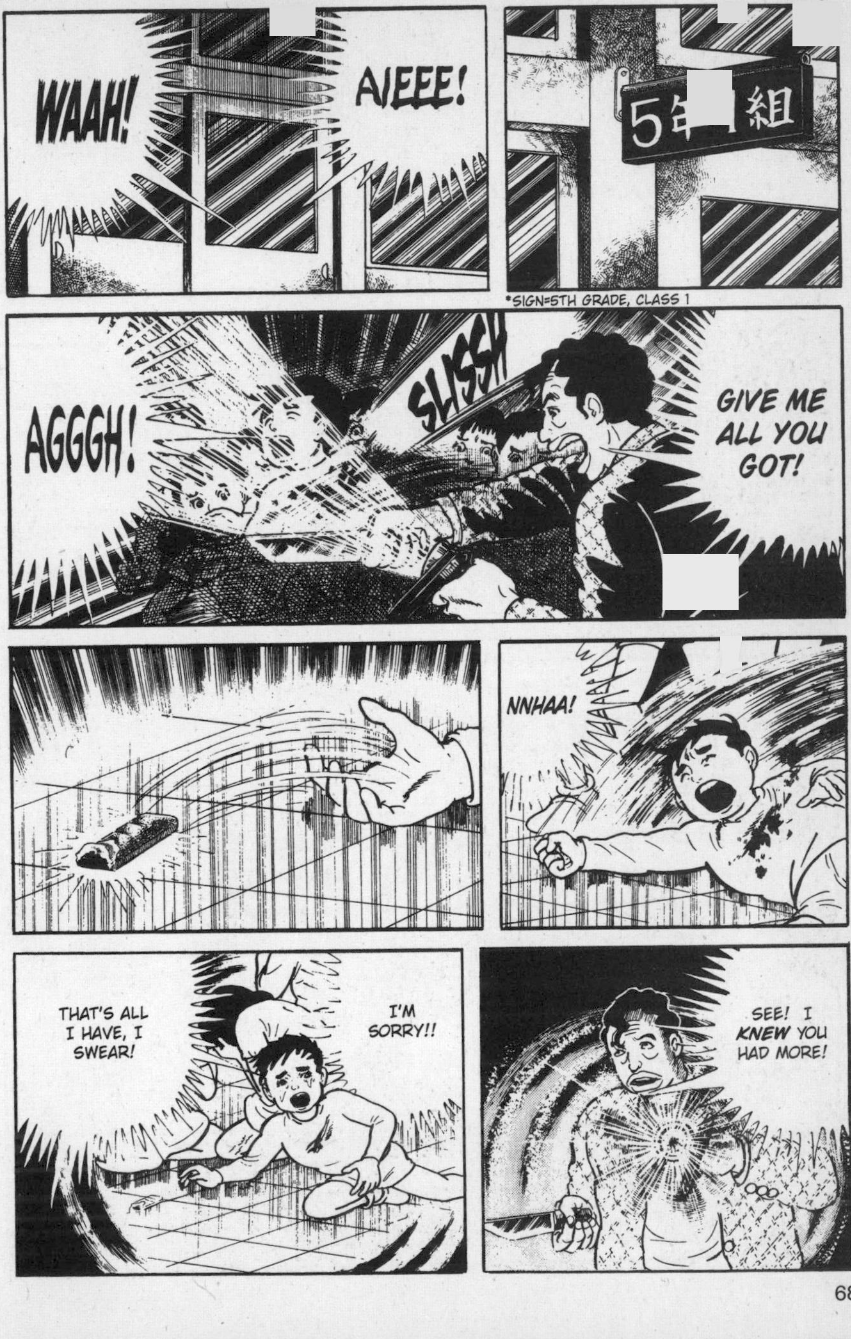
5年
組
*SIGN=5TH GRADE, CLASS 1
AIEEE!
WAAH!
GIVE ME ALL YOU GOT!
SLISSH
AGGGH!
NNHAA!
SEE! I KNEW YOU HAD MORE!
I'M SORRY!!
THAT'S ALL I HAVE, I SWEAR!

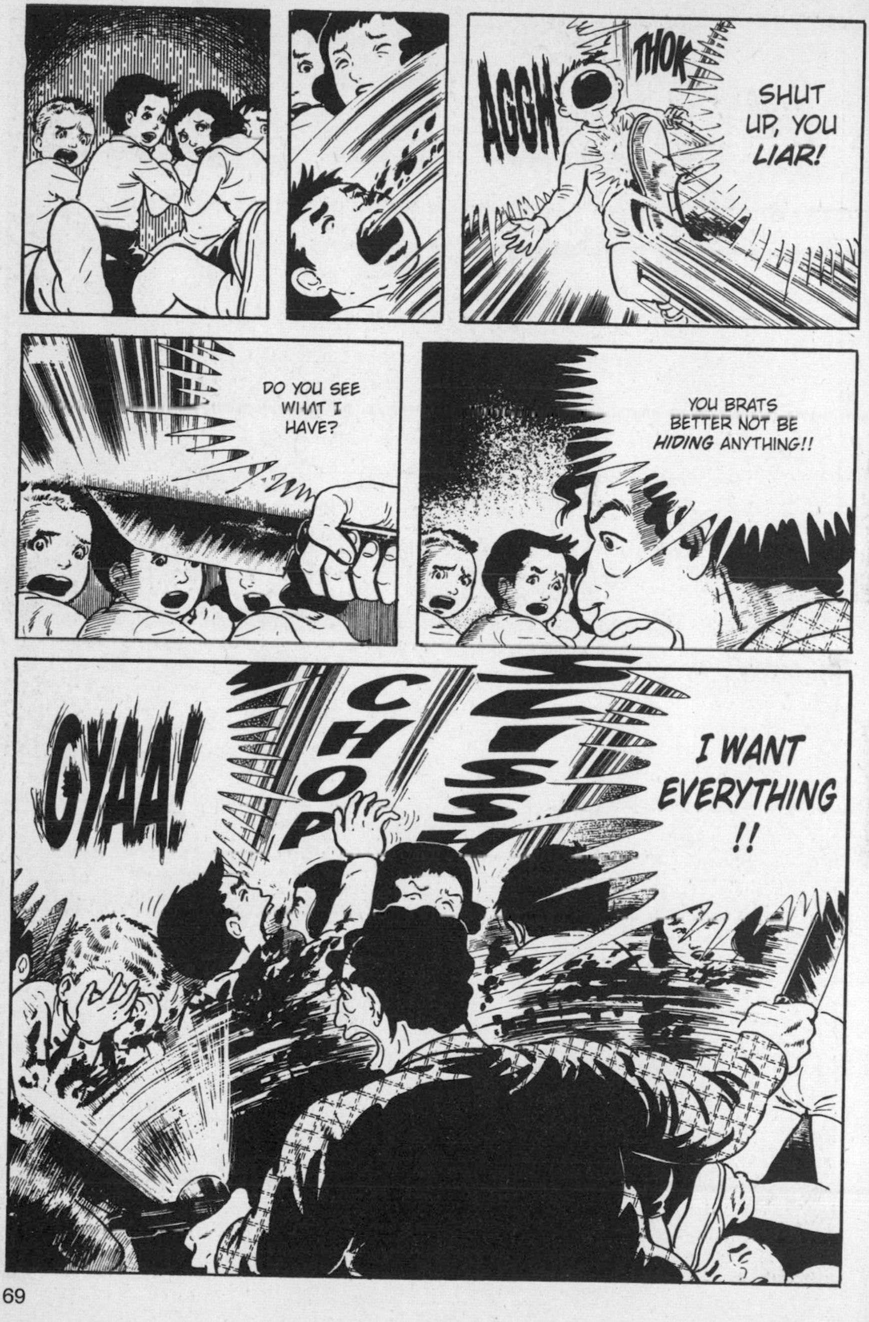
SHUT UP, YOU LIAR!
THOK
AGGH
YOU BRATS BETTER NOT BE HIDING ANYTHING!!
DO YOU SEE WHAT I HAVE?
I WANT EVERYTHING !!
CHOP
GYAA!

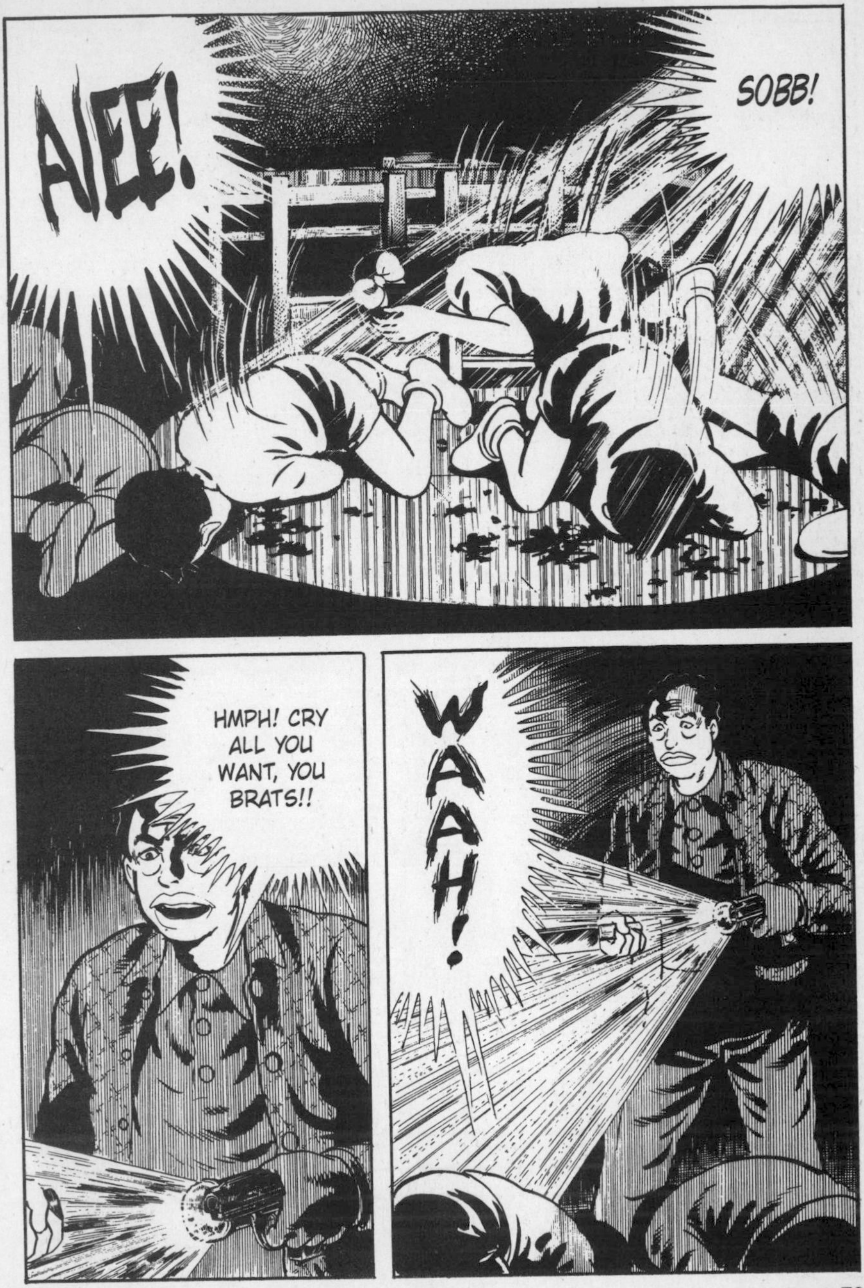
SOBB!
AIEE!
WAAH!
HMPH! CRY ALL YOU WANT, YOU BRATS!!

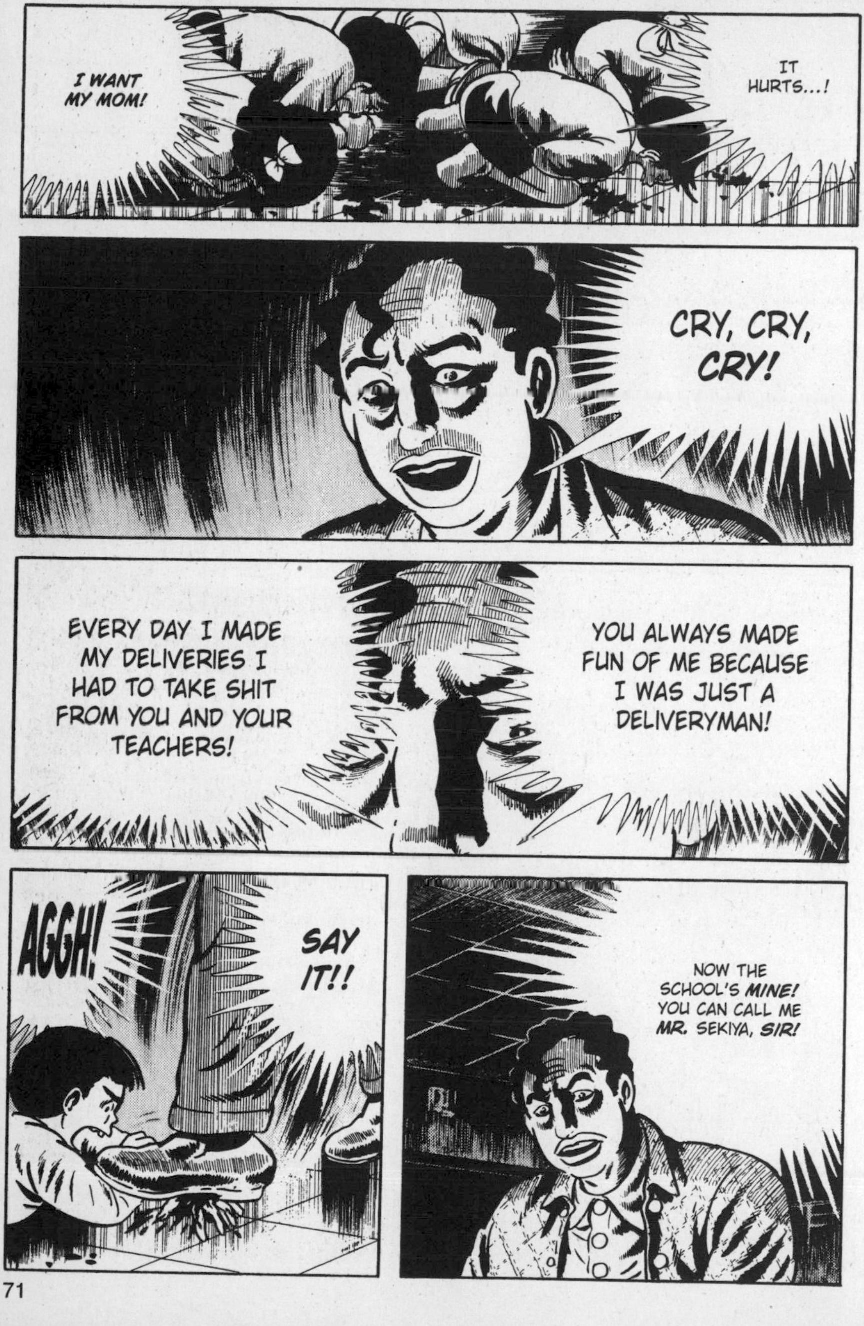
IT HURTS...!
I WANT MY MOM!
CRY, CRY, CRY!
YOU ALWAYS MADE FUN OF ME BECAUSE I WAS JUST A DELIVERYMAN!
EVERY DAY I MADE MY DELIVERIES I HAD TO TAKE SHIT FROM YOU AND YOUR TEACHERS!
NOW THE SCHOOL'S *MINE!* YOU CAN CALL ME *MR.* SEKIYA, *SIR!*
SAY IT!!
AGGH!

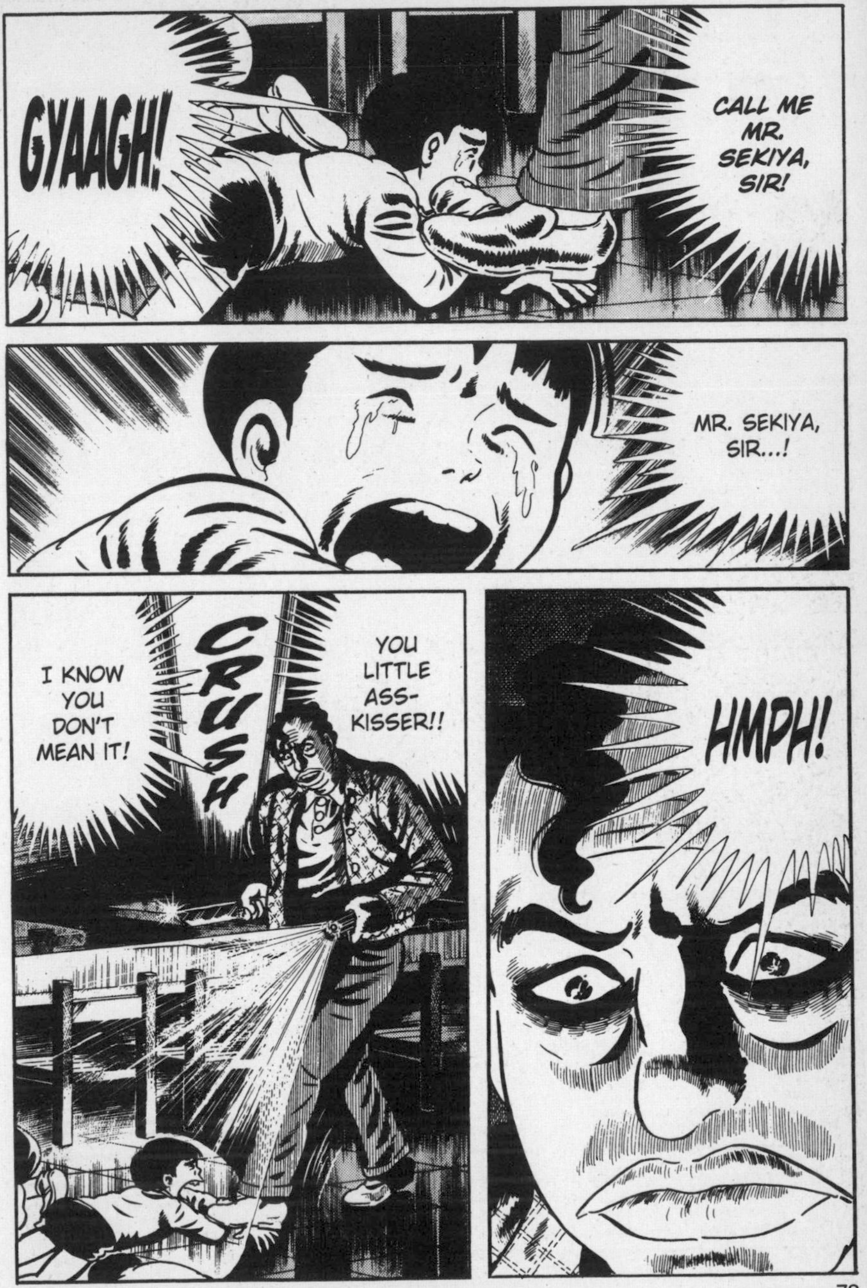
CALL ME MR. SEKIYA, SIR!
GYAAGH!
MR. SEKIYA, SIR...!
HMPH!
YOU LITTLE ASS-KISSER!!
CRUSH
I KNOW YOU DON'T MEAN IT!

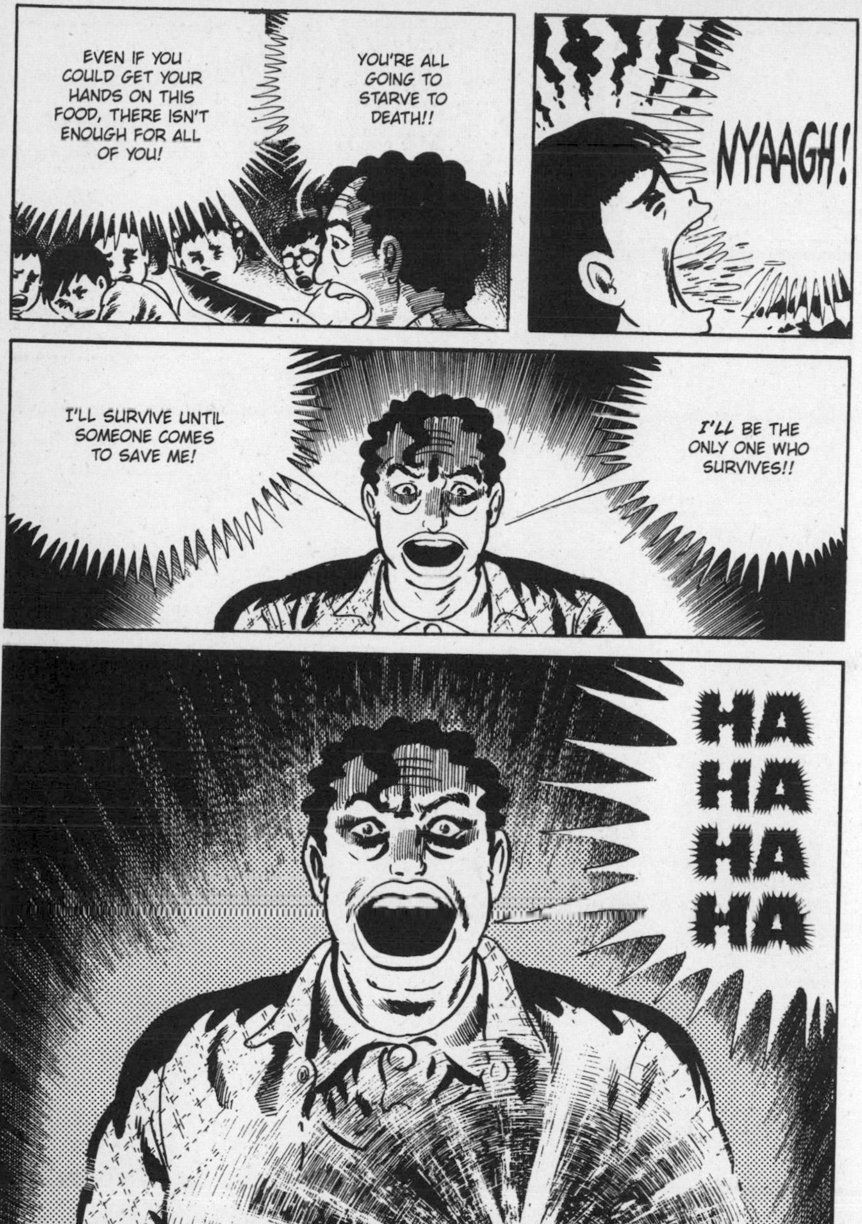
NYAAGH!
AAAGH!
YOU'RE ALL GOING TO STARVE TO DEATH!!
EVEN IF YOU COULD GET YOUR HANDS ON THIS FOOD, THERE ISN'T ENOUGH FOR ALL OF YOU!
I'LL BE THE ONLY ONE WHO SURVIVES!!
I'LL SURVIVE UNTIL SOMEONE COMES TO SAVE ME!
HA HA HA HA

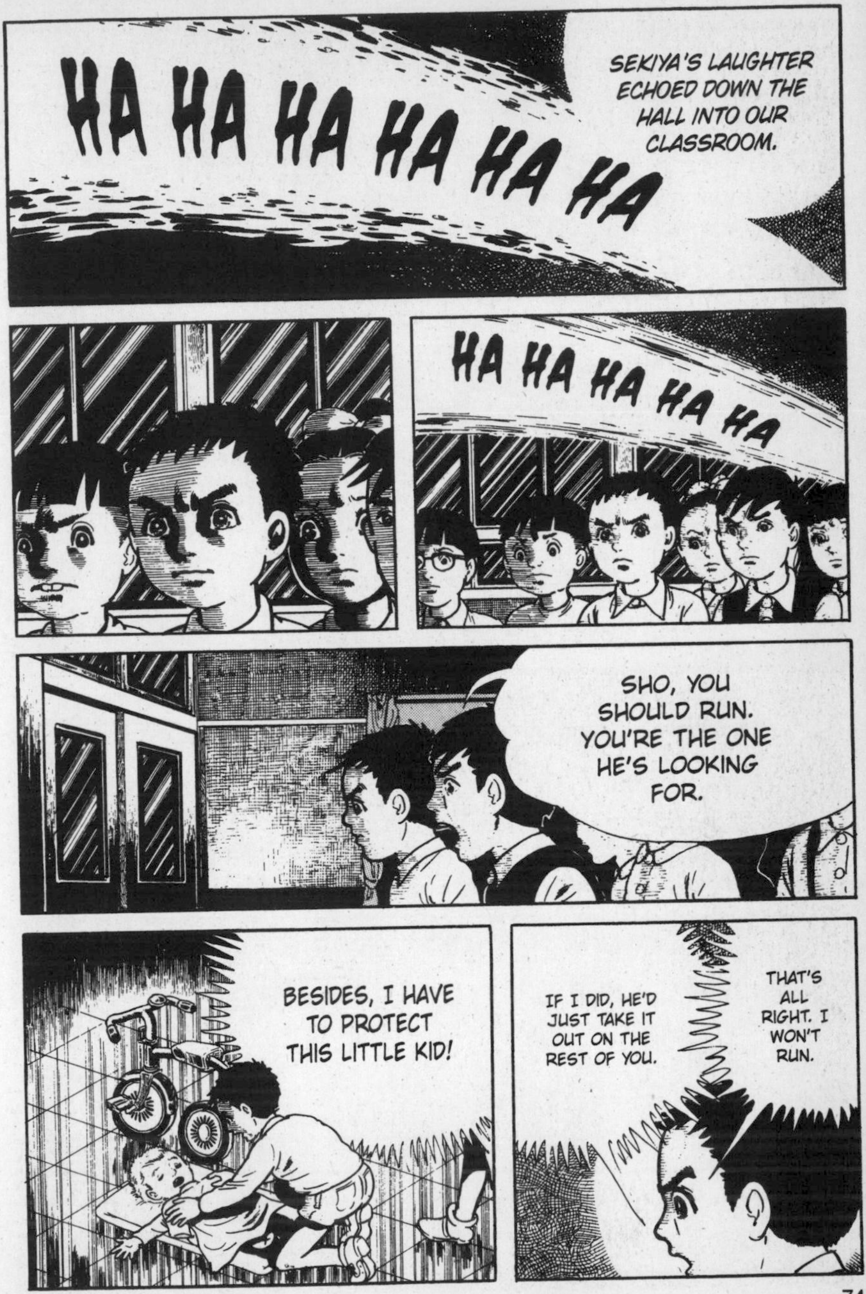
SEKIYA'S LAUGHTER ECHOED DOWN THE HALL INTO OUR CLASSROOM.
HA HA HA HA HA HA HA
HA HA HA HA HA
SHO, YOU SHOULD RUN. YOU'RE THE ONE HE'S LOOKING FOR.
THAT'S ALL RIGHT. I WON'T RUN.
IF I DID, HE'D JUST TAKE IT OUT ON THE REST OF YOU.
BESIDES, I HAVE TO PROTECT THIS LITTLE KID!

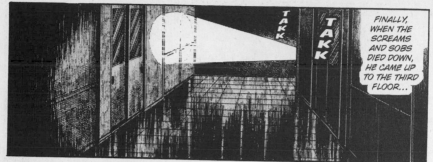

FINALLY,
WHEN THE
SCREAMS
AND SOBS
DIED DOWN,
HE CAME UP
TO THE THIRD
FLOOR...

TAKK   TAKK

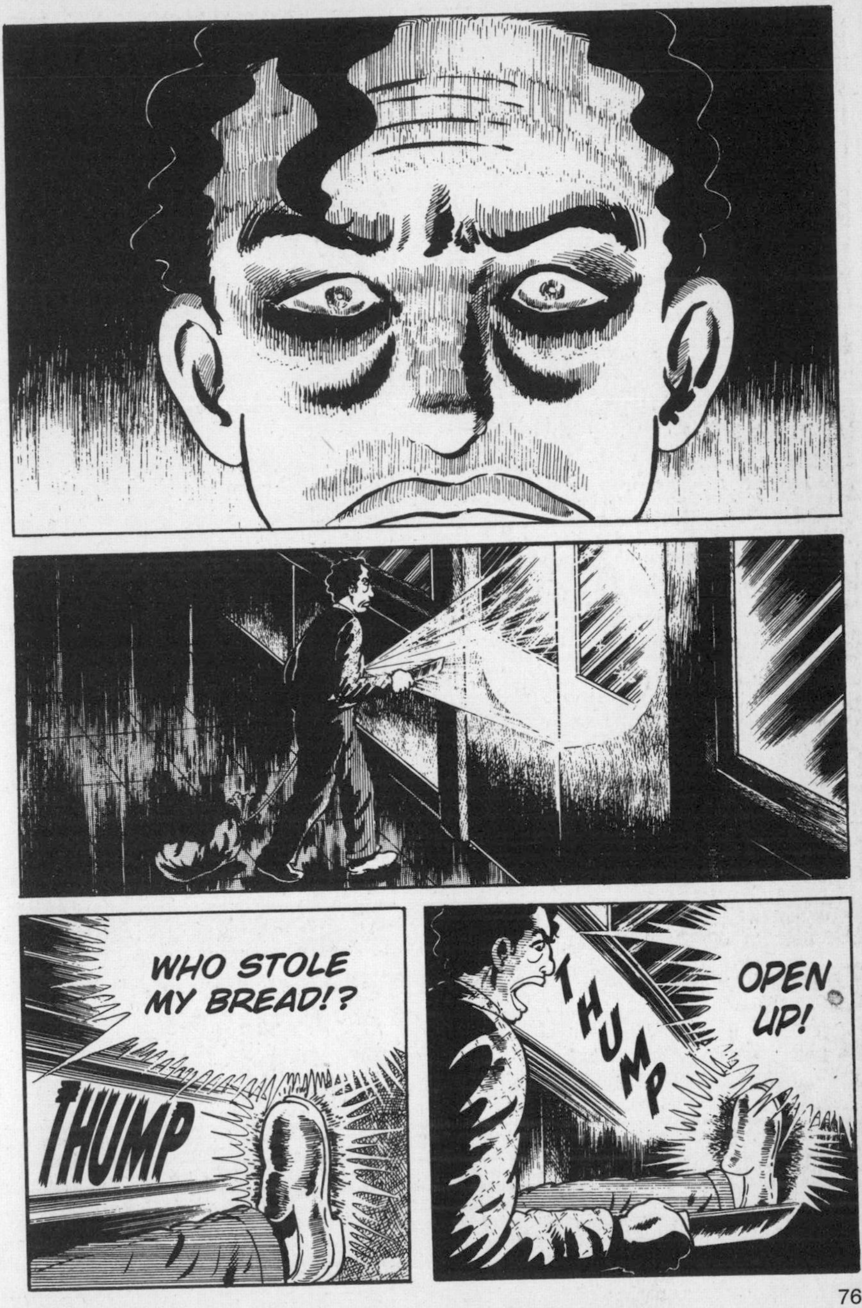
OPEN UP!
THUMP
WHO STOLE MY BREAD!?
THUMP

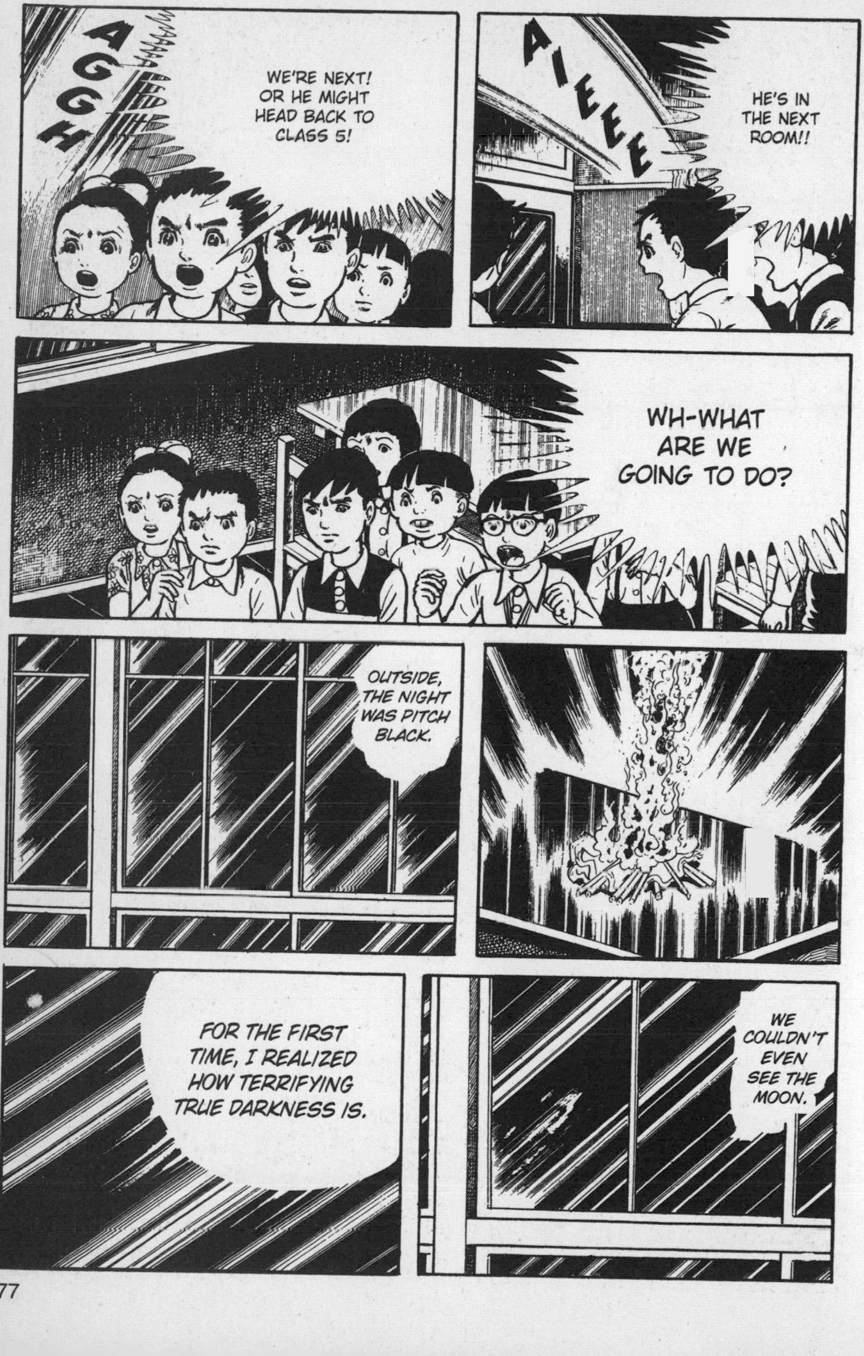
AIEEE
HE'S IN THE NEXT ROOM!!
AGGH
WE'RE NEXT! OR HE MIGHT HEAD BACK TO CLASS 5!
WH-WHAT ARE WE GOING TO DO?
OUTSIDE, THE NIGHT WAS PITCH BLACK.
WE COULDN'T EVEN SEE THE MOON.
FOR THE FIRST TIME, I REALIZED HOW TERRIFYING TRUE DARKNESS IS.

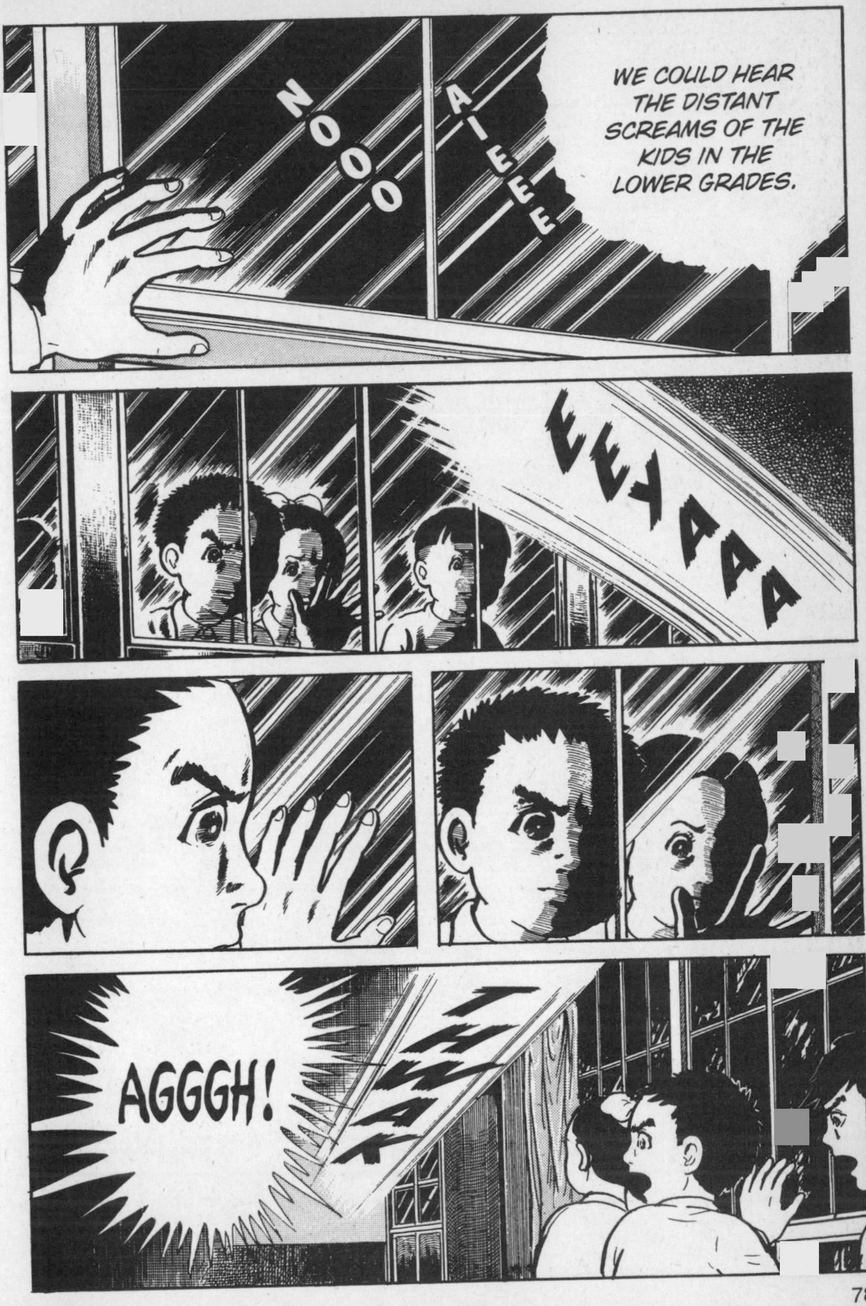
WE COULD HEAR THE DISTANT SCREAMS OF THE KIDS IN THE LOWER GRADES.
AIEEE
NOOO
EEYAAA
THWAT
AGGGH!

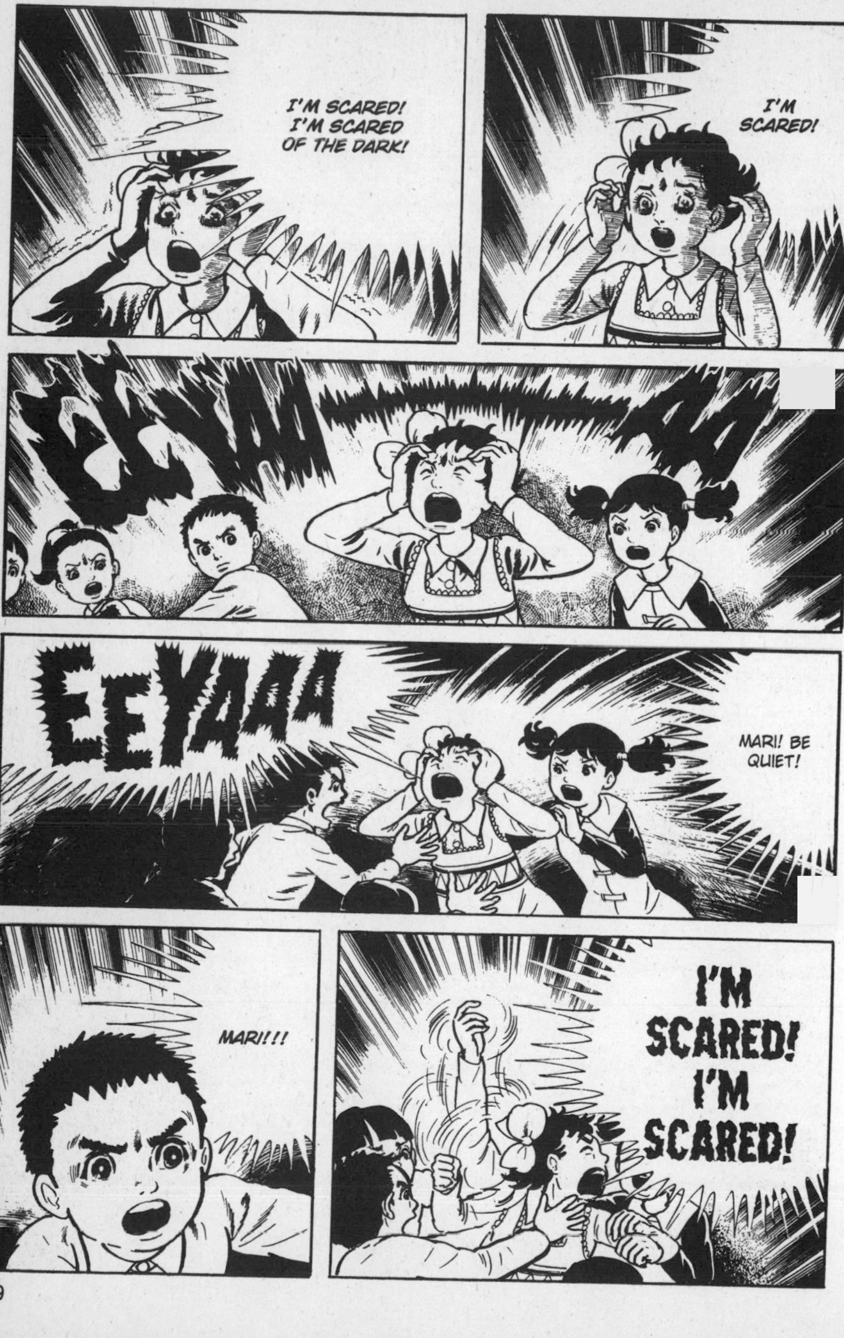
I'M SCARED!
I'M SCARED! I'M SCARED OF THE DARK!
EEYAAA
MARI! BE QUIET!
I'M SCARED! I'M SCARED!
MARI!!!

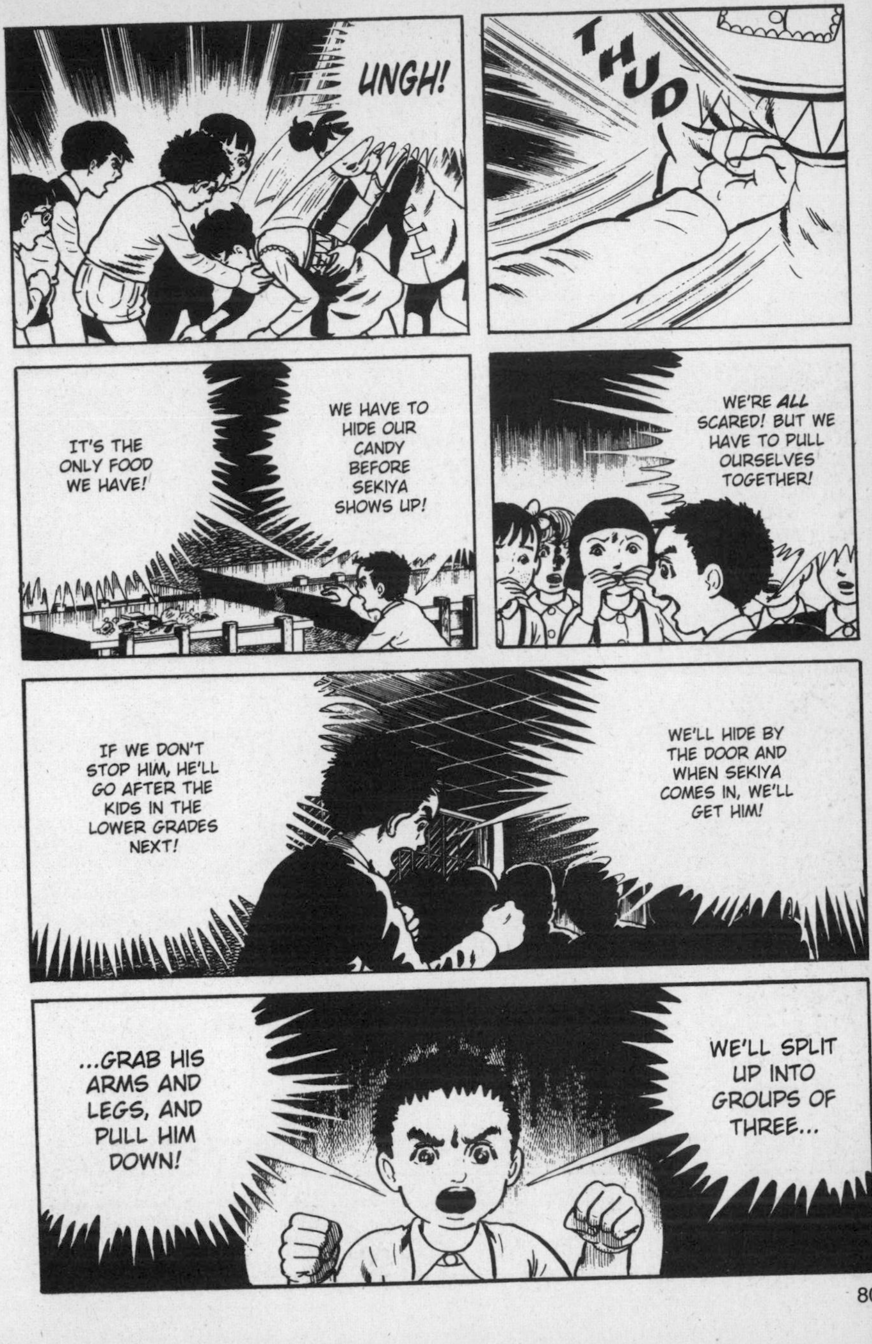
THUD
UNGH!
WE'RE ALL SCARED! BUT WE HAVE TO PULL OURSELVES TOGETHER!
WE HAVE TO HIDE OUR CANDY BEFORE SEKIYA SHOWS UP!
IT'S THE ONLY FOOD WE HAVE!
WE'LL HIDE BY THE DOOR AND WHEN SEKIYA COMES IN, WE'LL GET HIM!
IF WE DON'T STOP HIM, HE'LL GO AFTER THE KIDS IN THE LOWER GRADES NEXT!
WE'LL SPLIT UP INTO GROUPS OF THREE...
...GRAB HIS ARMS AND LEGS, AND PULL HIM DOWN!

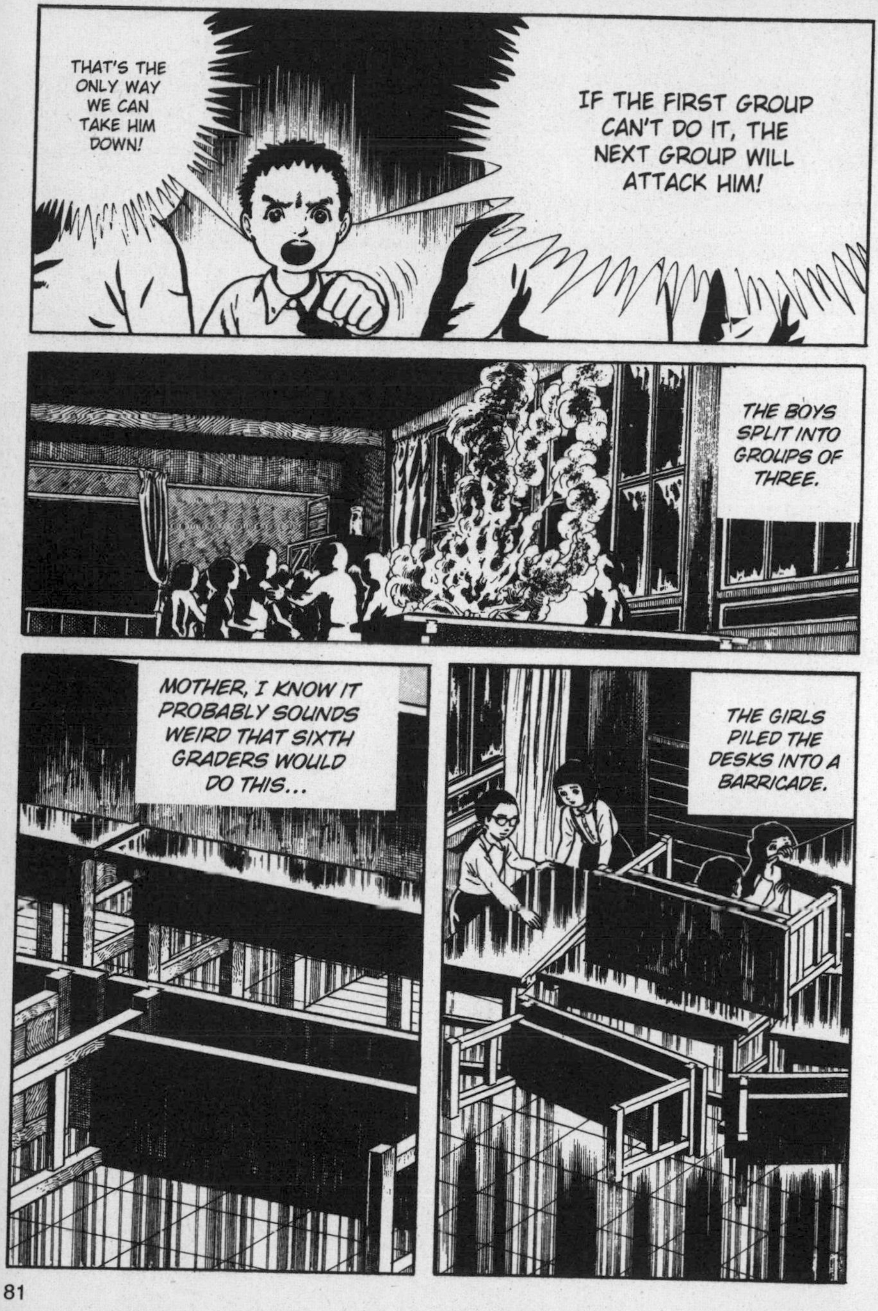
IF THE FIRST GROUP CAN'T DO IT, THE NEXT GROUP WILL ATTACK HIM!
THAT'S THE ONLY WAY WE CAN TAKE HIM DOWN!
THE BOYS SPLIT INTO GROUPS OF THREE.
THE GIRLS PILED THE DESKS INTO A BARRICADE.
MOTHER, I KNOW IT PROBABLY SOUNDS WEIRD THAT SIXTH GRADERS WOULD DO THIS...

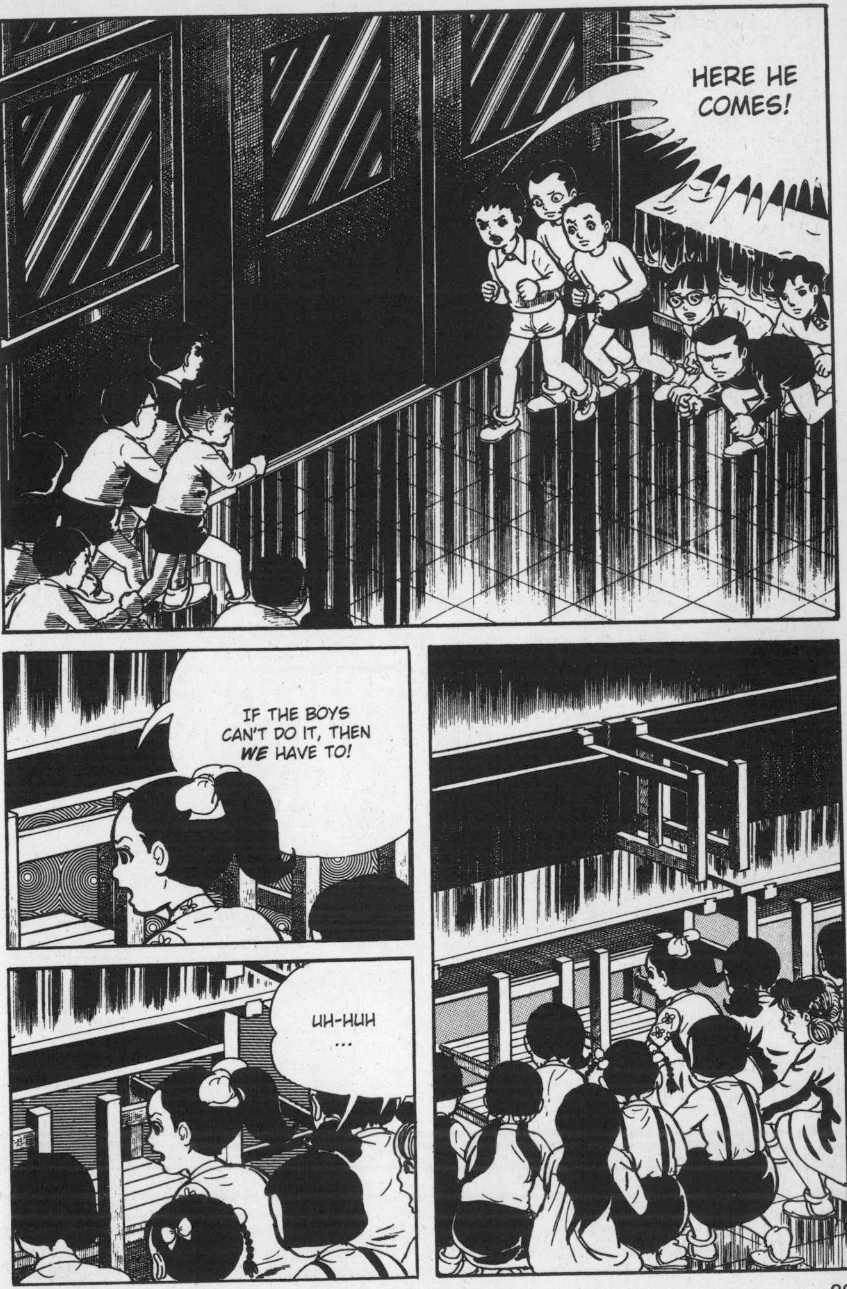
HERE HE COMES!
IF THE BOYS CAN'T DO IT, THEN WE HAVE TO!
UH-HUH ...

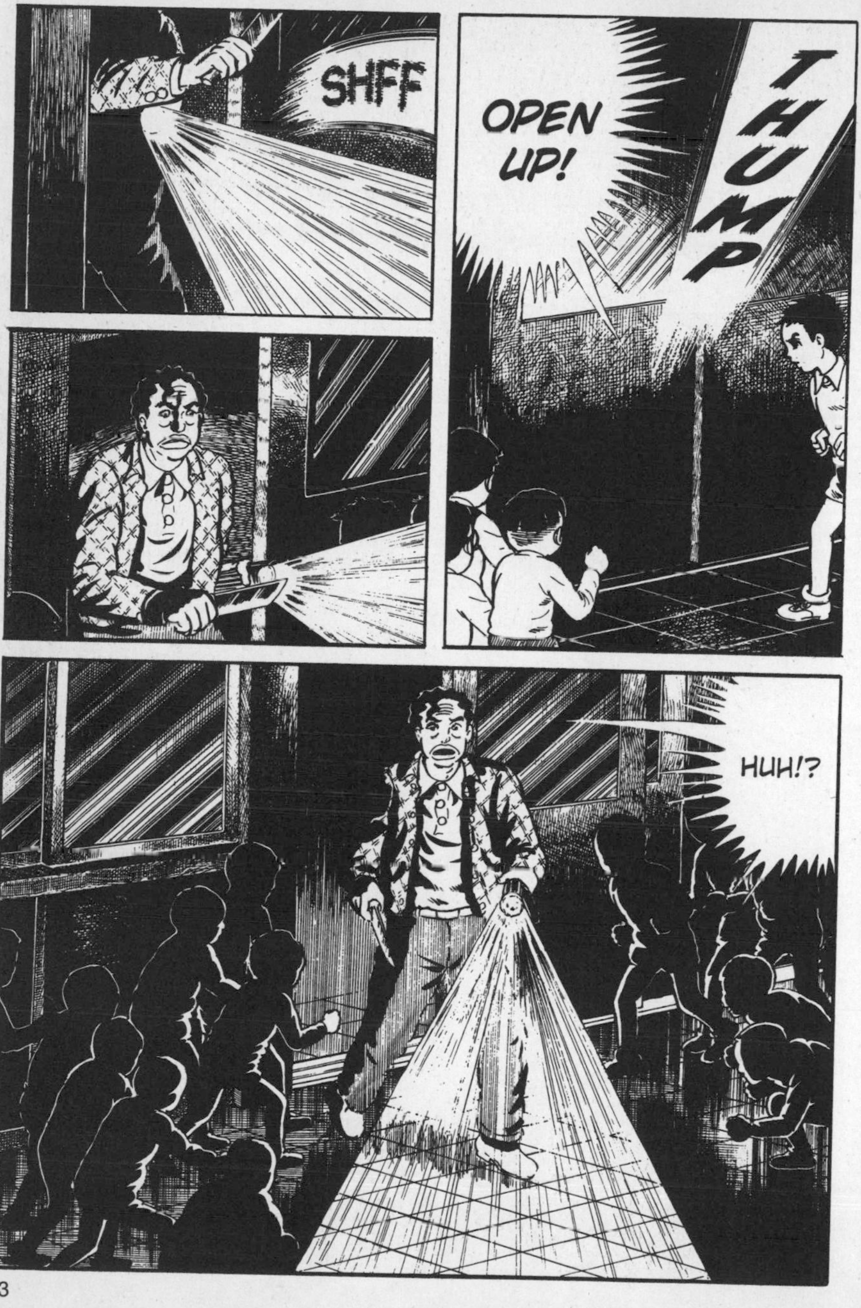
OPEN UP!
THUMP
SHFF
HUH!?

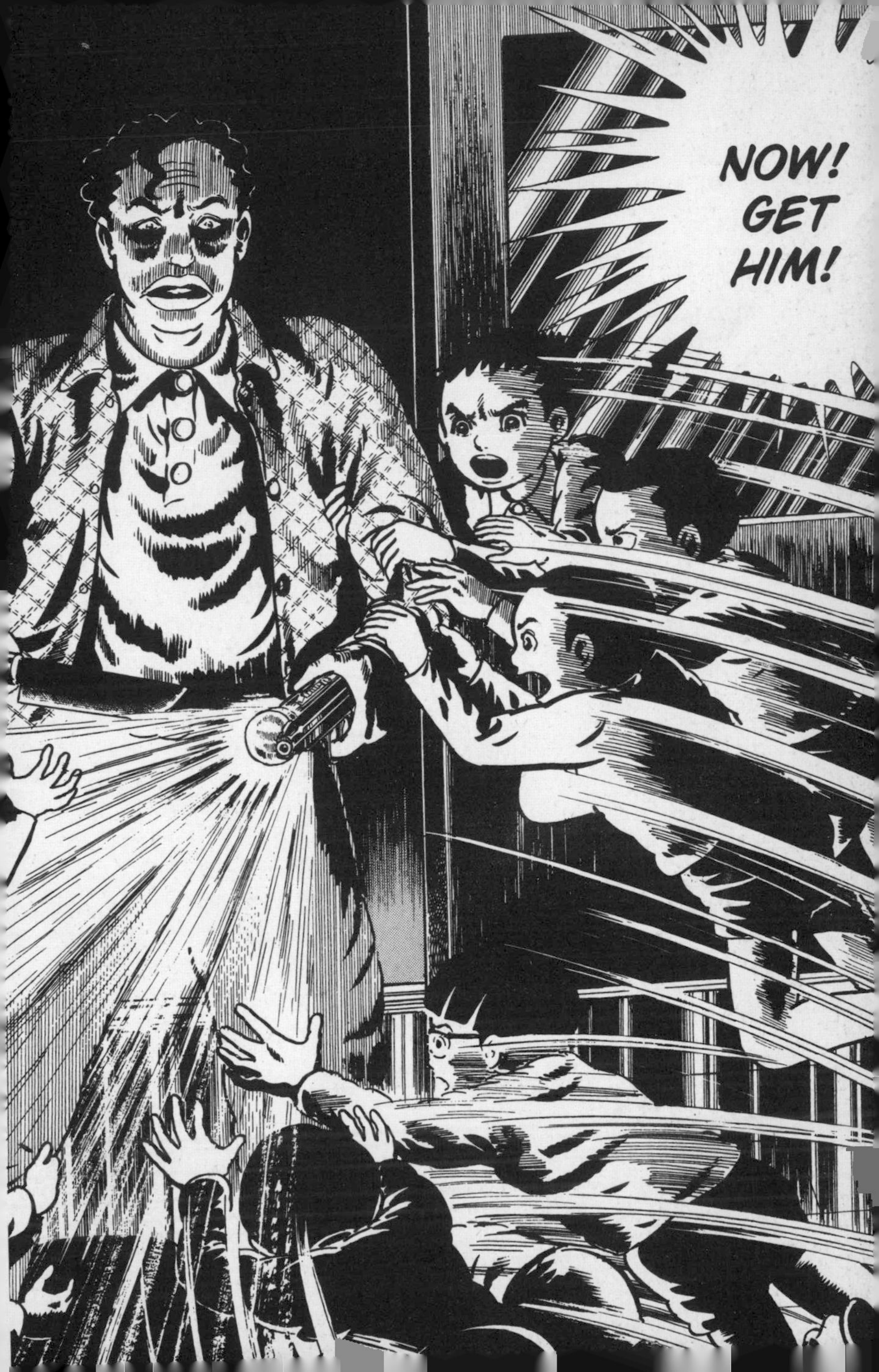
NOW! GET HIM!

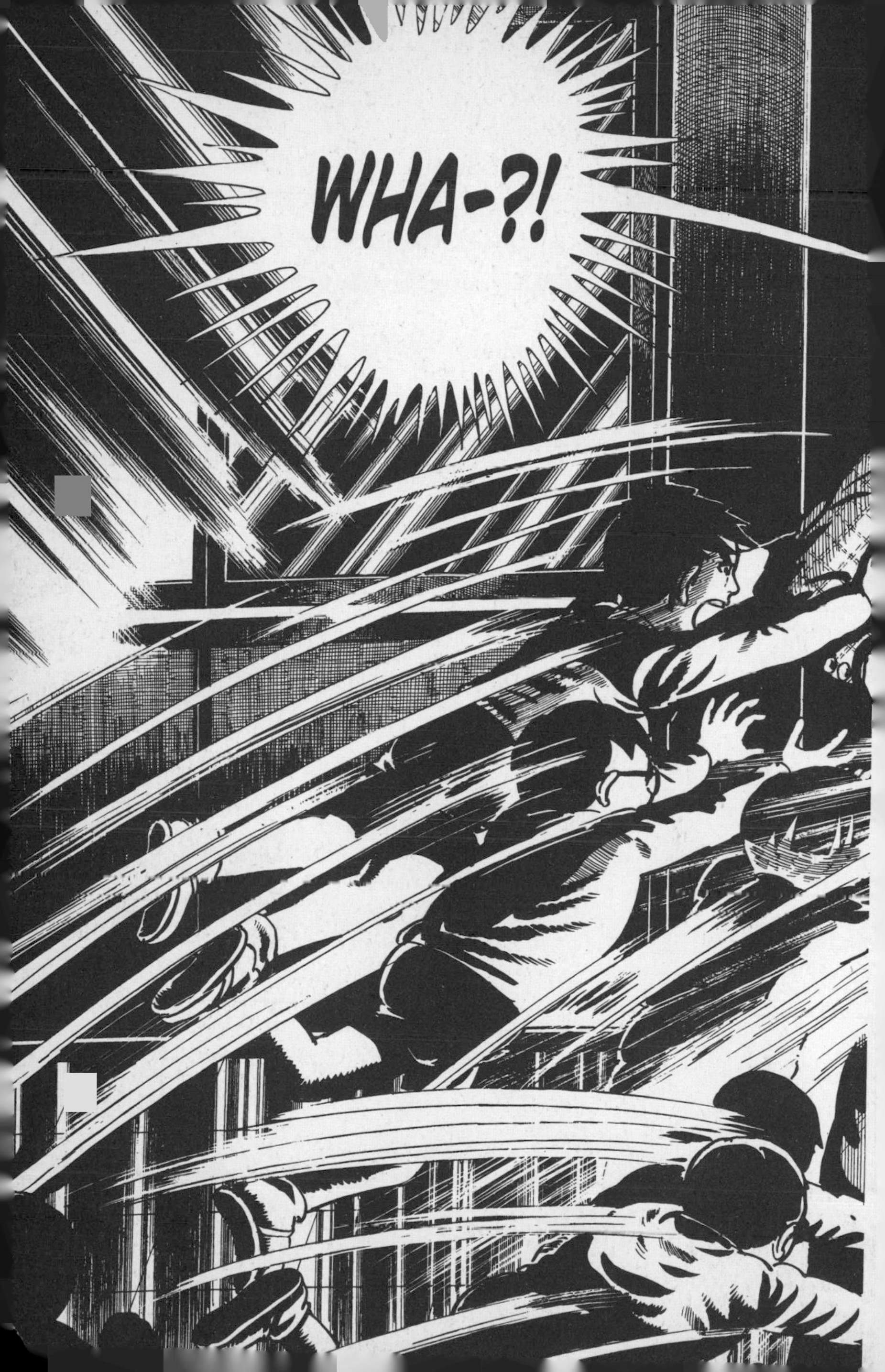
WHA-?!

LET GO!!

WH-WHAT'S GOING ON HERE?!

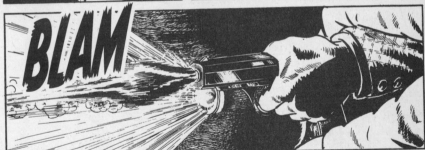

BLAM

AIEEE!

VEEN

WAAH!

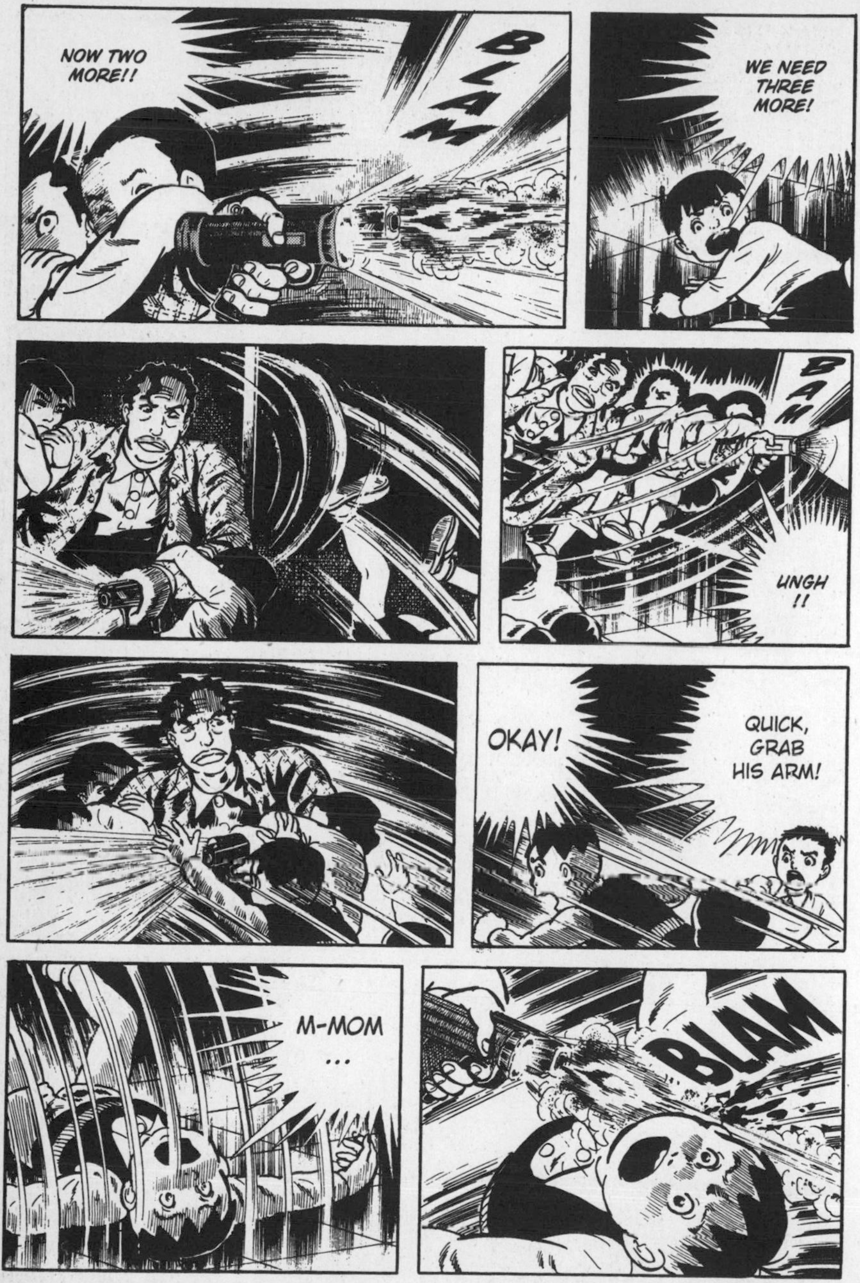
WE NEED THREE MORE!
BLAM
NOW TWO MORE!!
BAM
UNGH !!
QUICK, GRAB HIS ARM!
OKAY!
BLAM
M-MOM ...

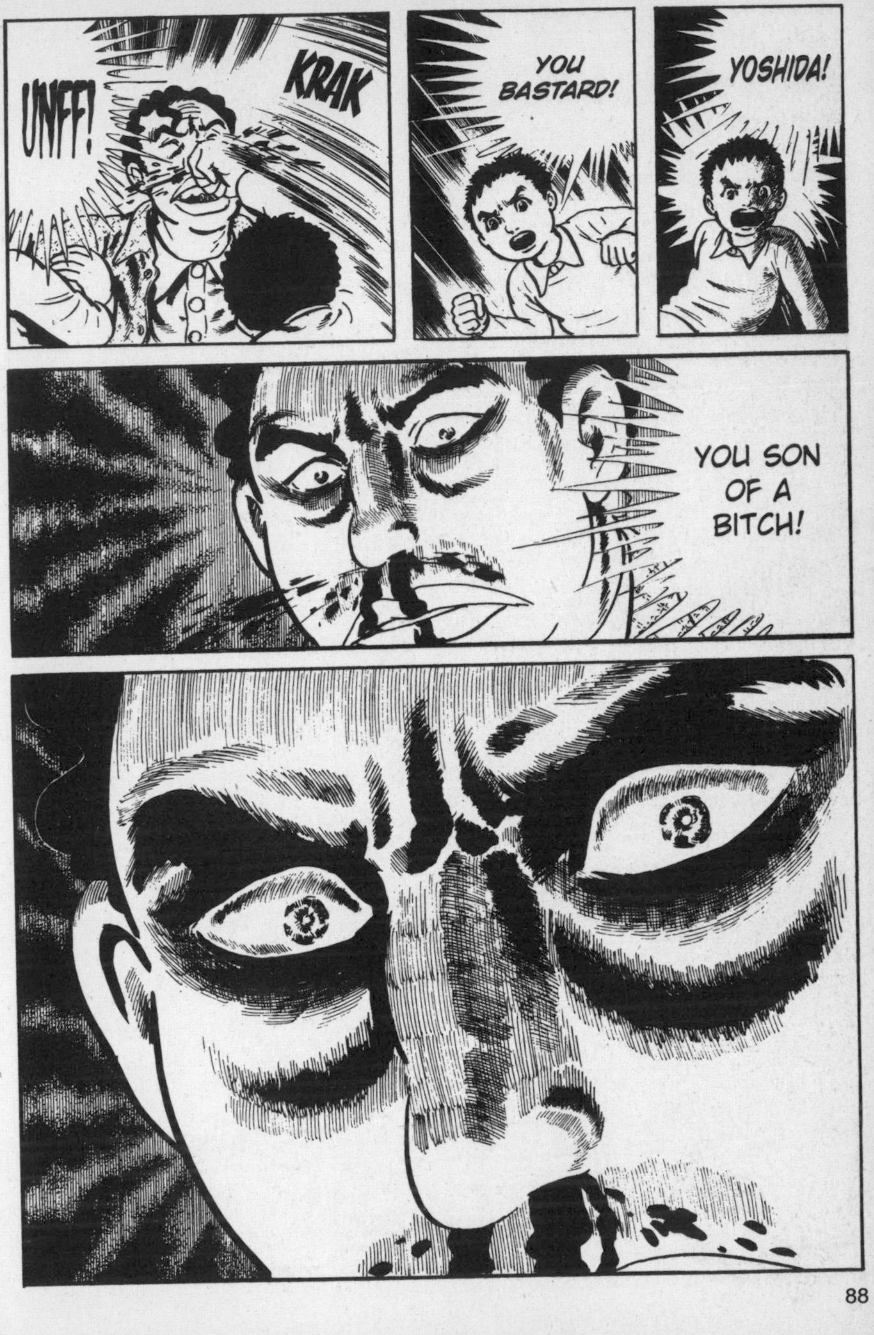
YOSHIDA!
YOU BASTARD!
KRAK
UNFF!
YOU SON OF A BITCH!

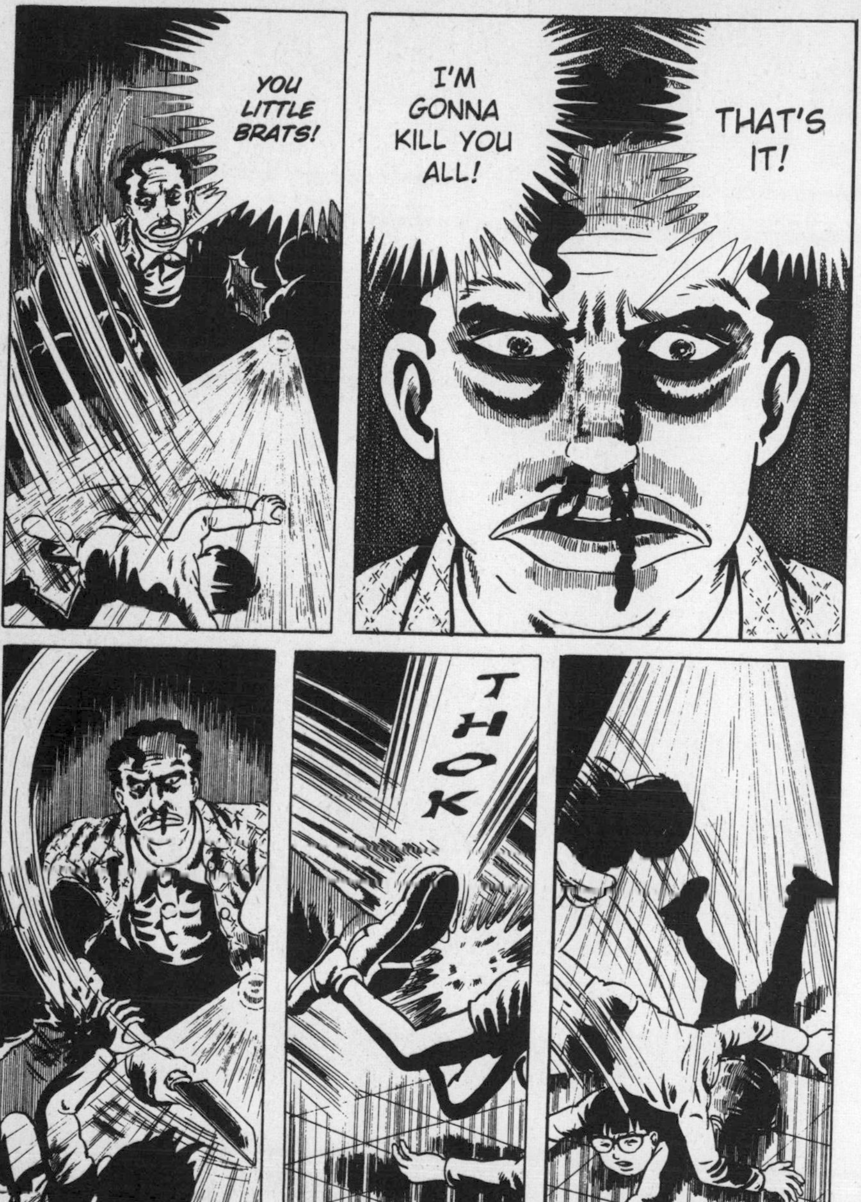
THAT'S IT!
I'M GONNA KILL YOU ALL!
YOU LITTLE BRATS!
THOK

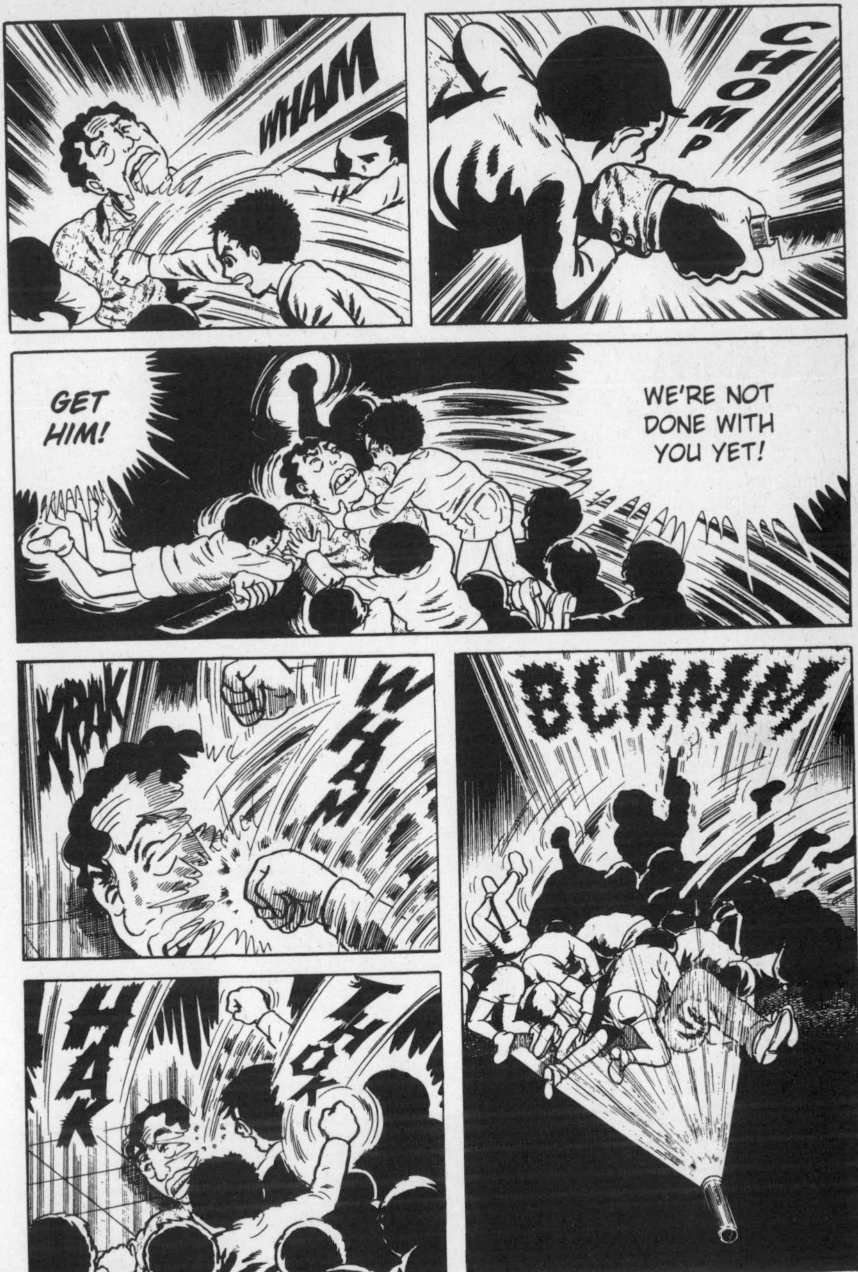
CHOMP
WHAM
WE'RE NOT DONE WITH YOU YET!
GET HIM!
BLAMM
WHAM
KRAK
THOK
HAK

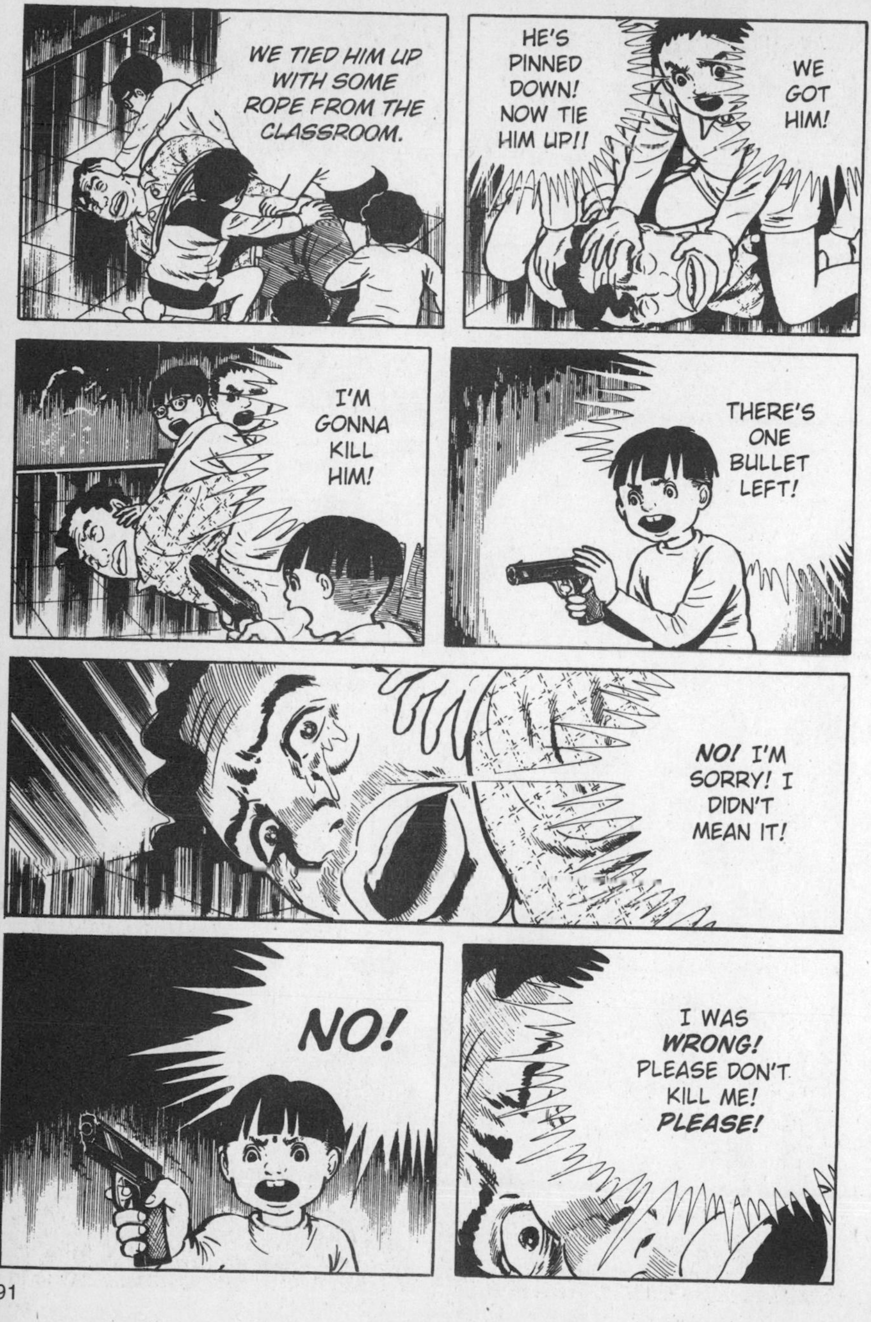
WE GOT HIM!
HE'S PINNED DOWN! NOW TIE HIM UP!!
WE TIED HIM UP WITH SOME ROPE FROM THE CLASSROOM.
THERE'S ONE BULLET LEFT!
I'M GONNA KILL HIM!
NO! I'M SORRY! I DIDN'T MEAN IT!
I WAS WRONG! PLEASE DON'T KILL ME! PLEASE!
NO!

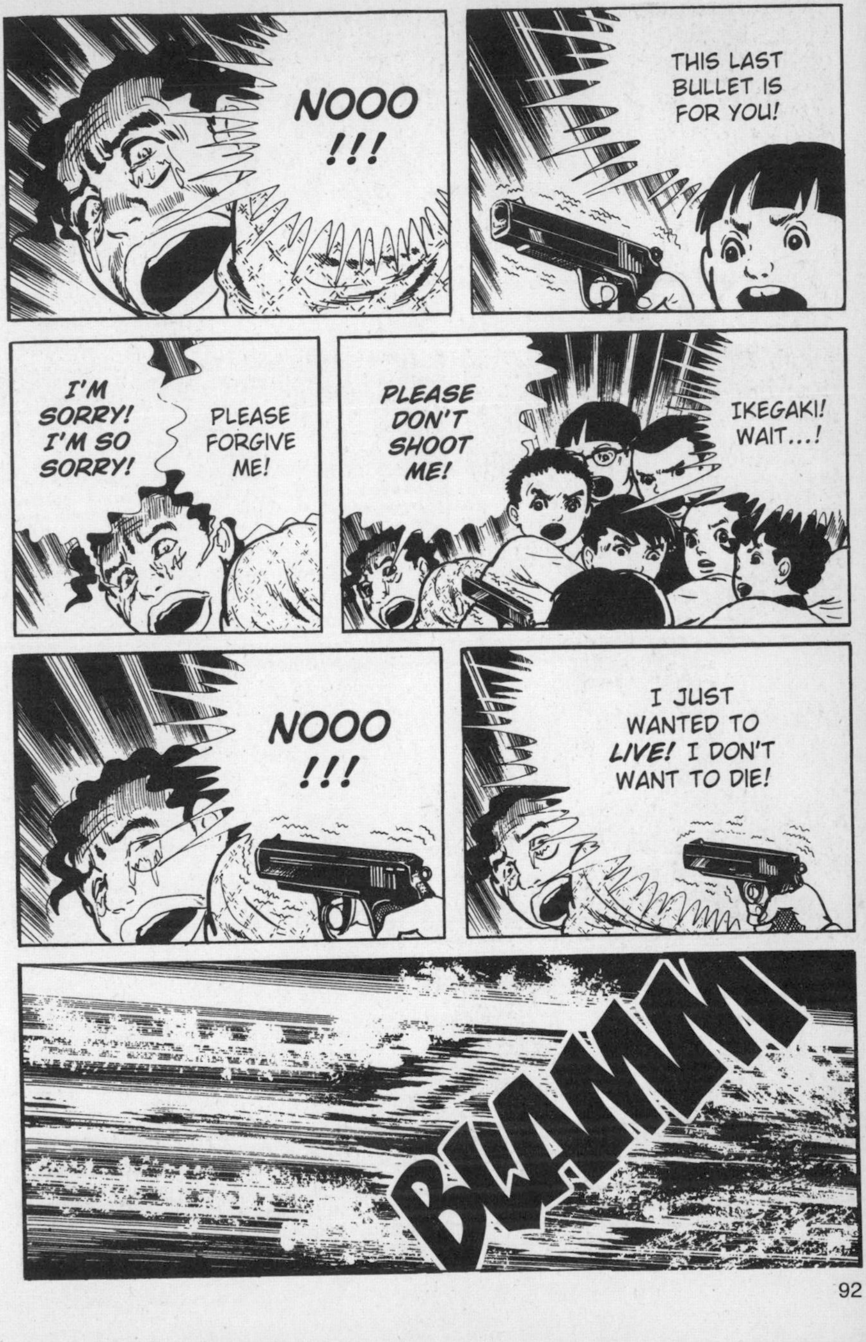
THIS LAST BULLET IS FOR YOU!
NOOO !!!
IKEGAKI! WAIT...!
PLEASE DON'T SHOOT ME!
PLEASE FORGIVE ME!
I'M SORRY! I'M SO SORRY!
I JUST WANTED TO LIVE! I DON'T WANT TO DIE!
NOOO !!!
BLAMM

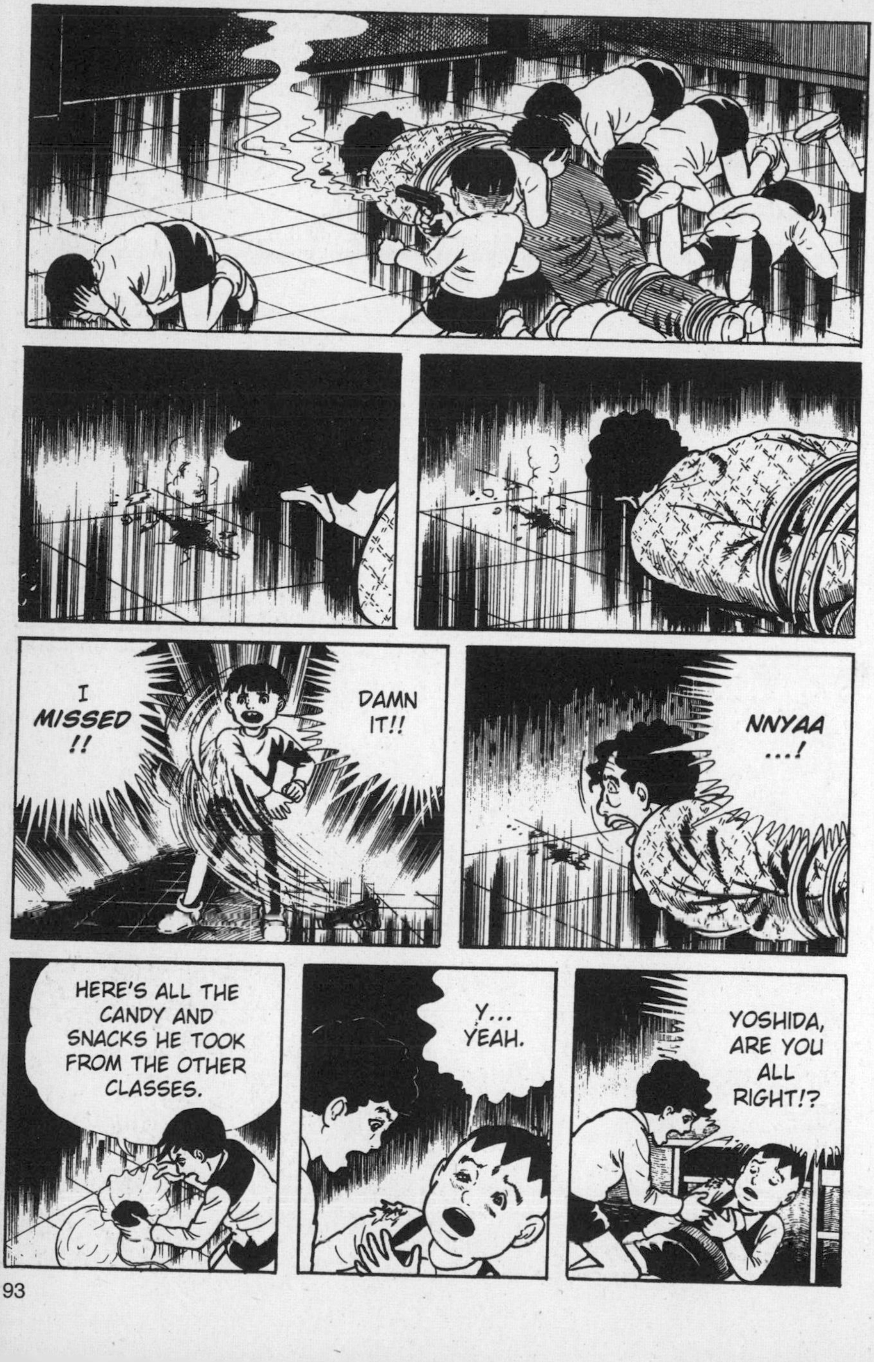
NNYAA ...!
DAMN IT!!
I MISSED !!
YOSHIDA, ARE YOU ALL RIGHT!?
Y... YEAH.
HERE'S ALL THE CANDY AND SNACKS HE TOOK FROM THE OTHER CLASSES.

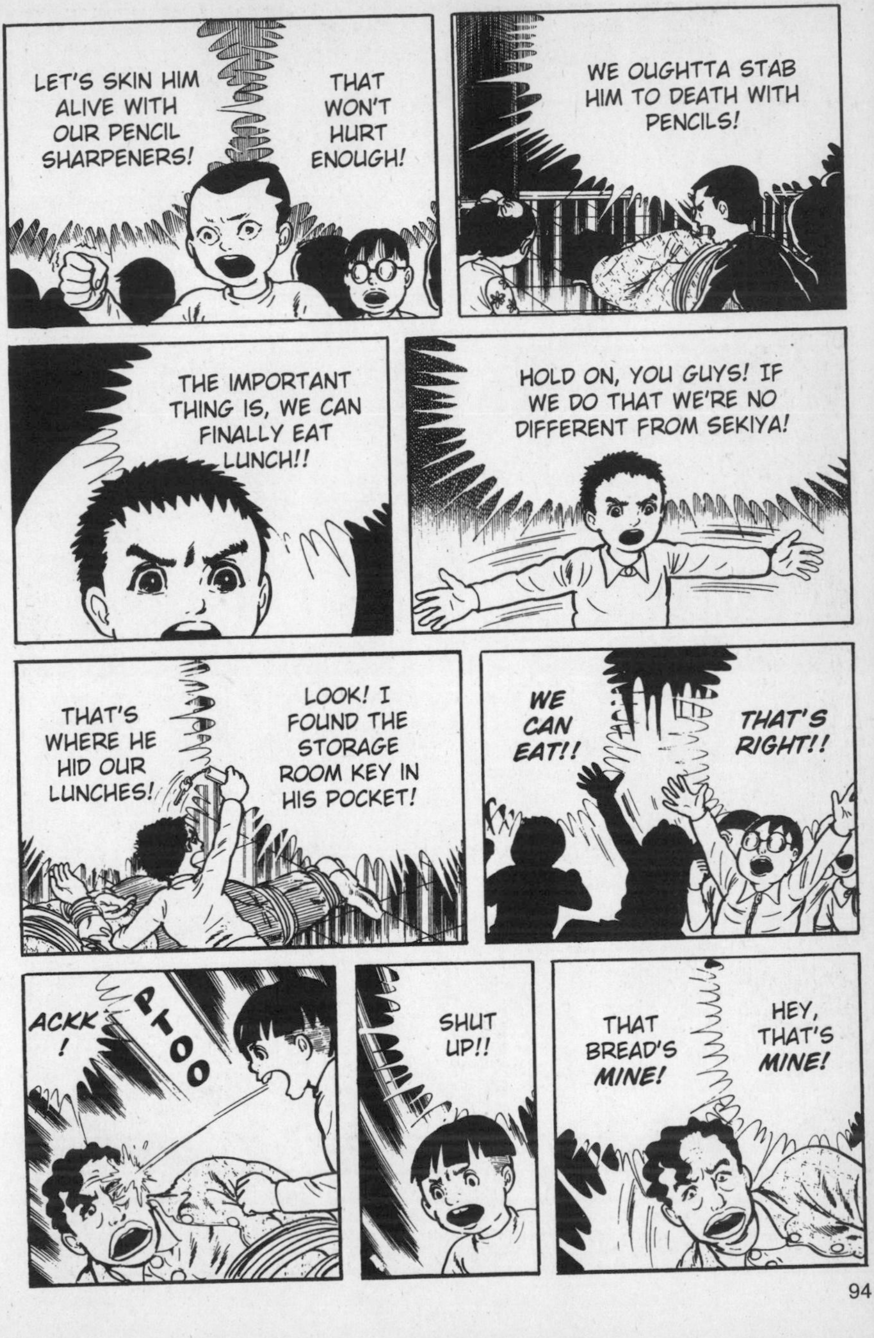
LET'S SKIN HIM ALIVE WITH OUR PENCIL SHARPENERS!
THAT WON'T HURT ENOUGH!
WE OUGHTTA STAB HIM TO DEATH WITH PENCILS!
THE IMPORTANT THING IS, WE CAN FINALLY EAT LUNCH!!
HOLD ON, YOU GUYS! IF WE DO THAT WE'RE NO DIFFERENT FROM SEKIYA!
LOOK! I FOUND THE STORAGE ROOM KEY IN HIS POCKET!
THAT'S WHERE HE HID OUR LUNCHES!
WE CAN EAT!!
THAT'S RIGHT!!
PTOO
ACKK!
SHUT UP!!
HEY, THAT'S MINE!
THAT BREAD'S MINE!

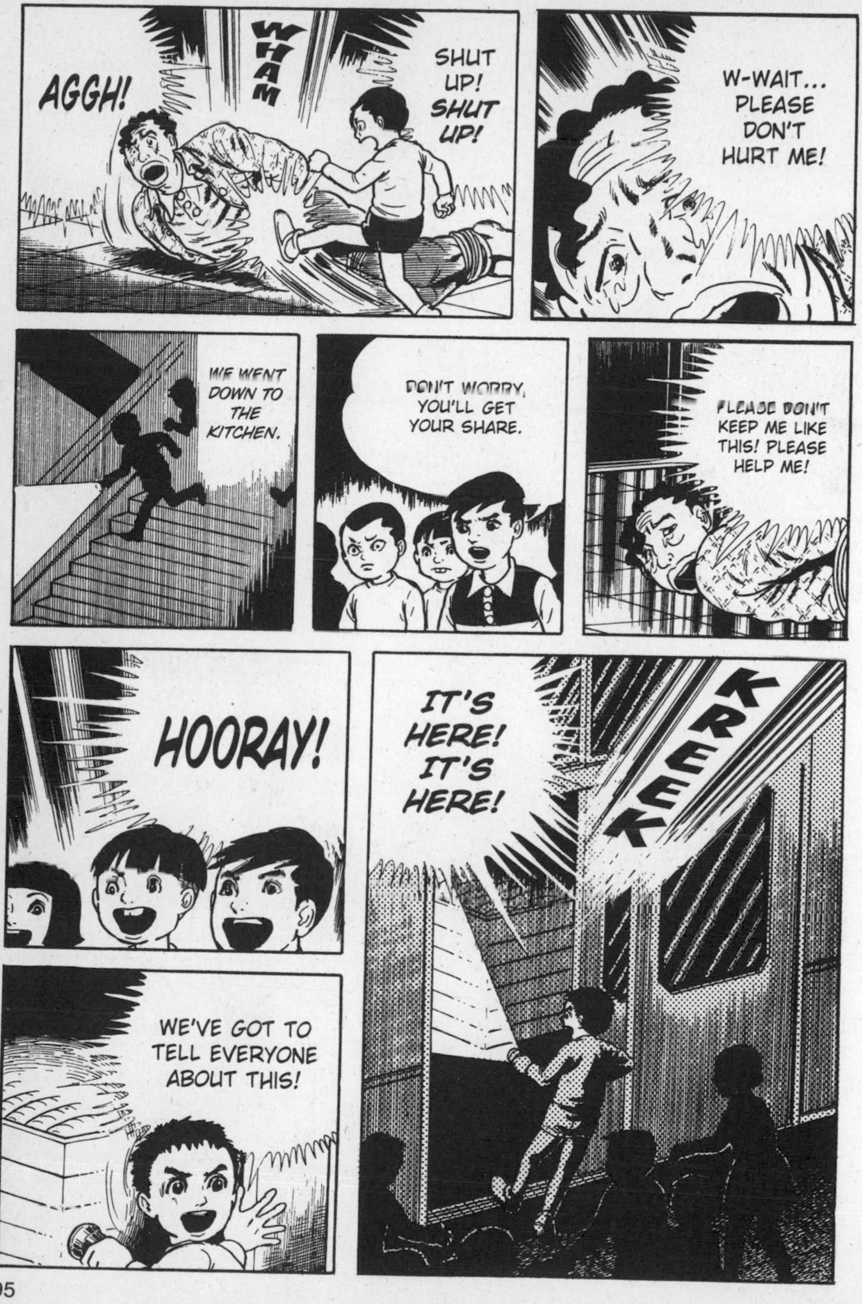
W-WAIT... PLEASE DON'T HURT ME!
SHUT UP! SHUT UP!
WHAM
AGGH!
PLEASE DON'T KEEP ME LIKE THIS! PLEASE HELP ME!
DON'T WORRY, YOU'LL GET YOUR SHARE.
WE WENT DOWN TO THE KITCHEN.
KREEK
IT'S HERE! IT'S HERE!
HOORAY!
WE'VE GOT TO TELL EVERYONE ABOUT THIS!

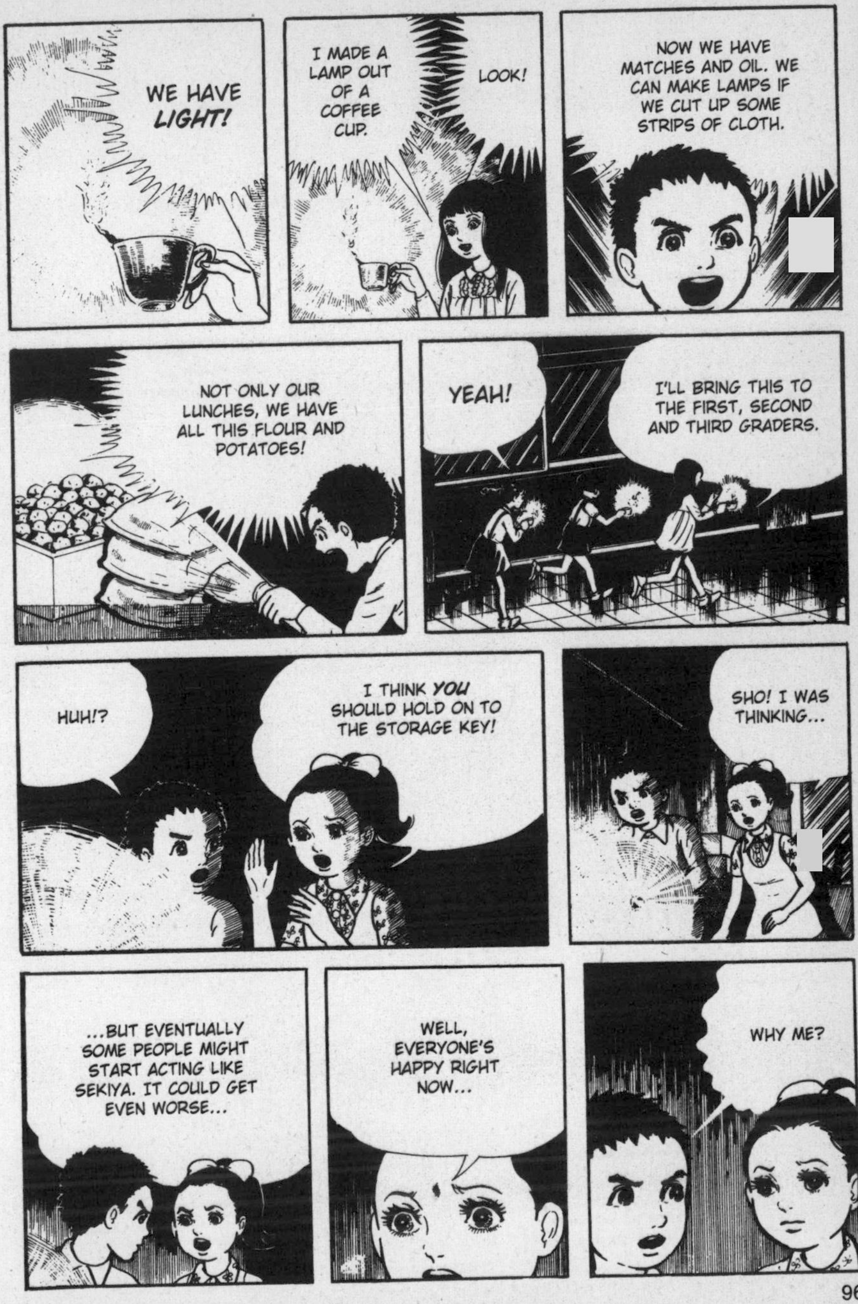
NOW WE HAVE MATCHES AND OIL. WE CAN MAKE LAMPS IF WE CUT UP SOME STRIPS OF CLOTH.
LOOK!
I MADE A LAMP OUT OF A COFFEE CUP.
WE HAVE *LIGHT!*
I'LL BRING THIS TO THE FIRST, SECOND AND THIRD GRADERS.
YEAH!
NOT ONLY OUR LUNCHES, WE HAVE ALL THIS FLOUR AND POTATOES!
SHO! I WAS THINKING...
I THINK *YOU* SHOULD HOLD ON TO THE STORAGE KEY!
HUH!?
WHY ME?
WELL, EVERYONE'S HAPPY RIGHT NOW...
...BUT EVENTUALLY SOME PEOPLE MIGHT START ACTING LIKE SEKIYA. IT COULD GET EVEN WORSE...

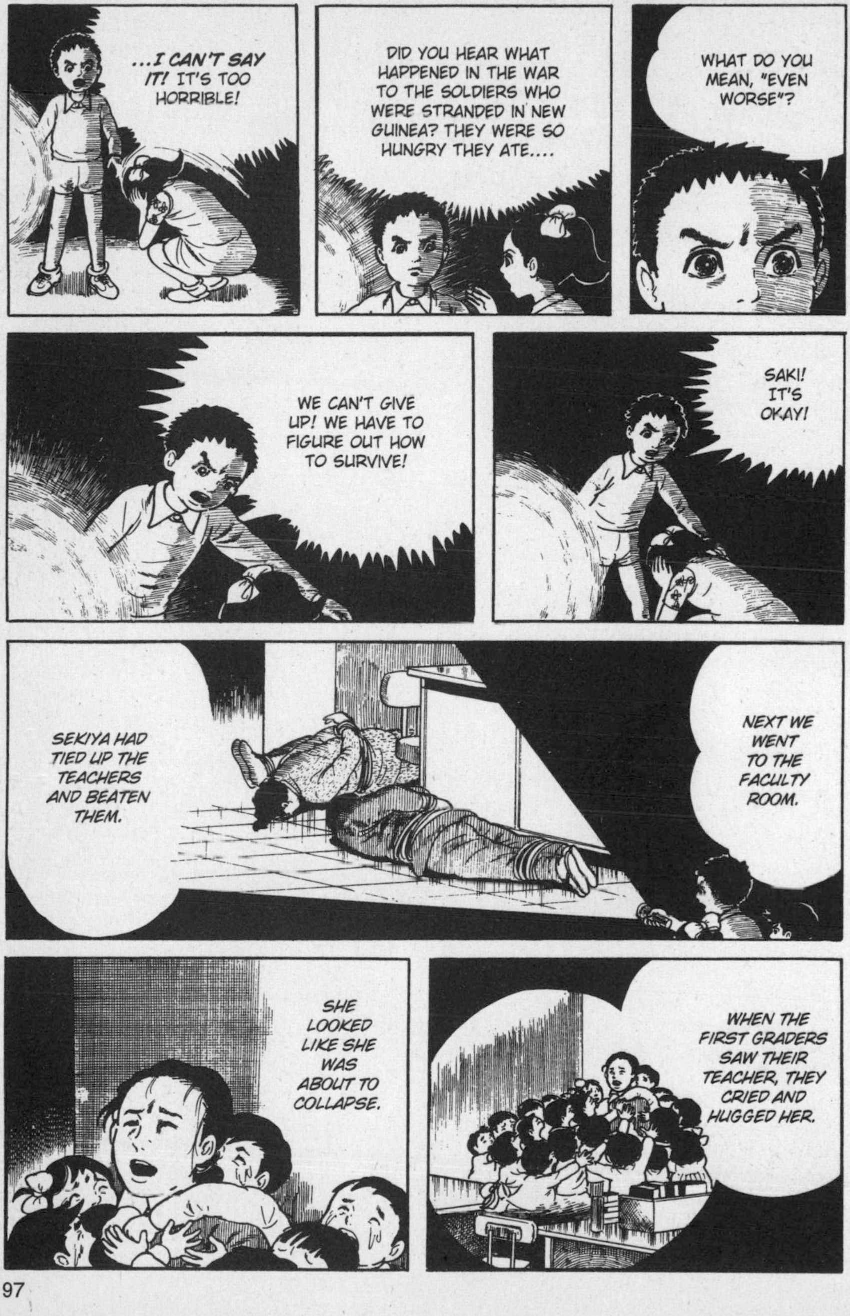
WHAT DO YOU MEAN, "EVEN WORSE"?
DID YOU HEAR WHAT HAPPENED IN THE WAR TO THE SOLDIERS WHO WERE STRANDED IN NEW GUINEA? THEY WERE SO HUNGRY THEY ATE....
...I CAN'T SAY IT! IT'S TOO HORRIBLE!
SAKI! IT'S OKAY!
WE CAN'T GIVE UP! WE HAVE TO FIGURE OUT HOW TO SURVIVE!
NEXT WE WENT TO THE FACULTY ROOM.
SEKIYA HAD TIED UP THE TEACHERS AND BEATEN THEM.
WHEN THE FIRST GRADERS SAW THEIR TEACHER, THEY CRIED AND HUGGED HER.
SHE LOOKED LIKE SHE WAS ABOUT TO COLLAPSE.

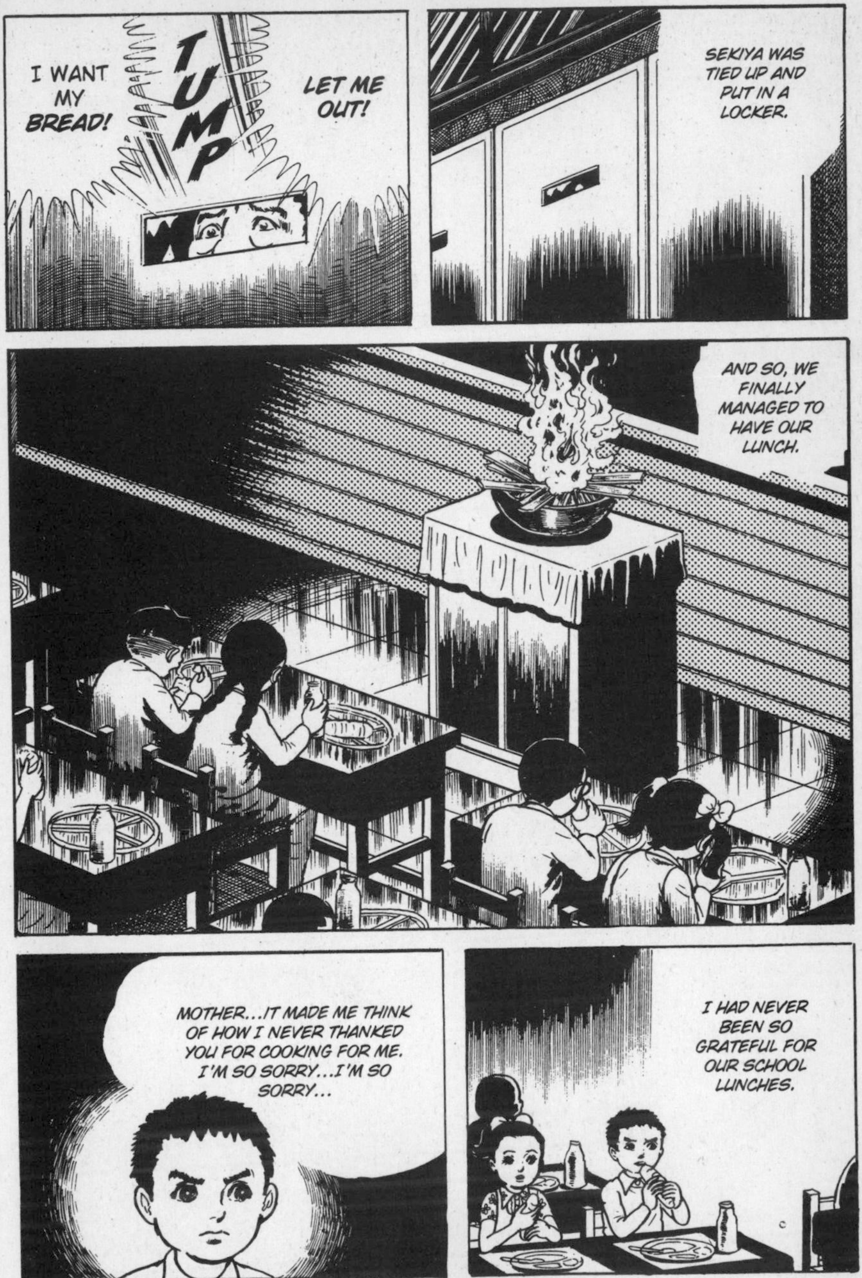
SEKIYA WAS TIED UP AND PUT IN A LOCKER.
LET ME OUT!
TUMP
I WANT MY BREAD!
AND SO, WE FINALLY MANAGED TO HAVE OUR LUNCH.
I HAD NEVER BEEN SO GRATEFUL FOR OUR SCHOOL LUNCHES.
MOTHER...IT MADE ME THINK OF HOW I NEVER THANKED YOU FOR COOKING FOR ME. I'M SO SORRY...I'M SO SORRY...

AFTER I WAS DONE EATING, I FELL ASLEEP RIGHT AWAY.

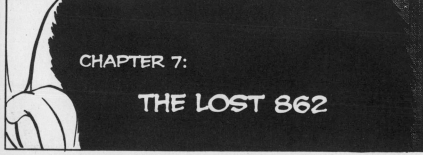

CHAPTER 7:

THE LOST 862

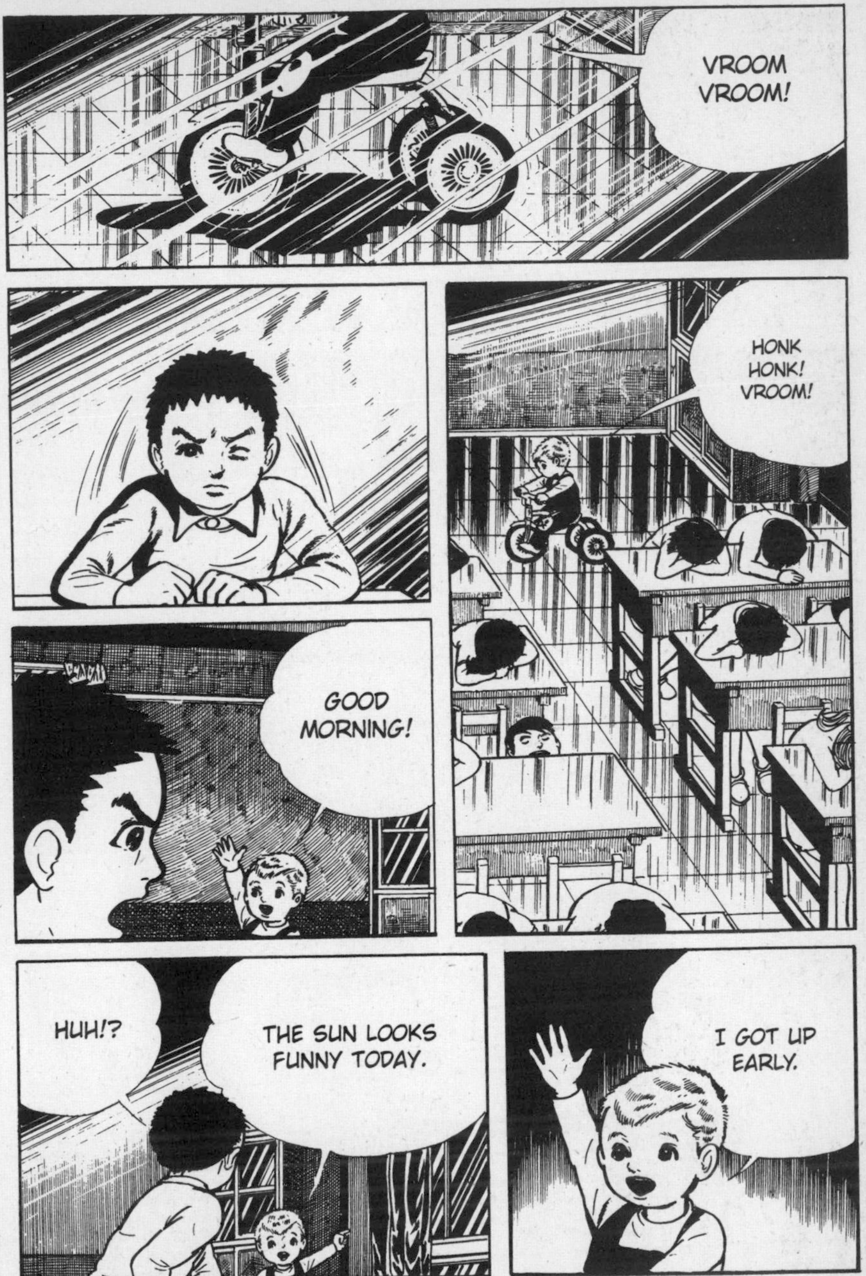
VROOM VROOM!
HONK HONK! VROOM!
GOOD MORNING!
I GOT UP EARLY.
THE SUN LOOKS FUNNY TODAY.
HUH!?

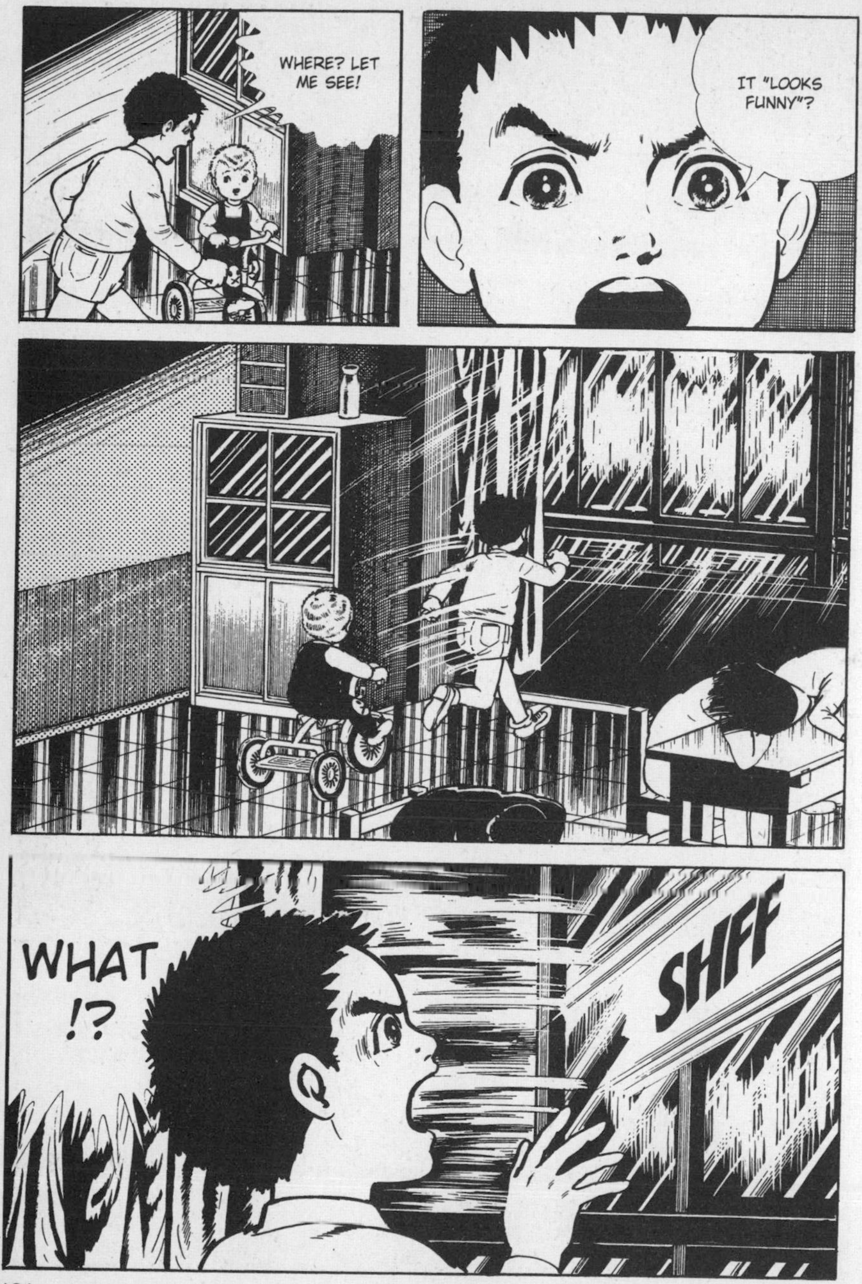
IT "LOOKS FUNNY"?
WHERE? LET ME SEE!
SHFF
WHAT !?

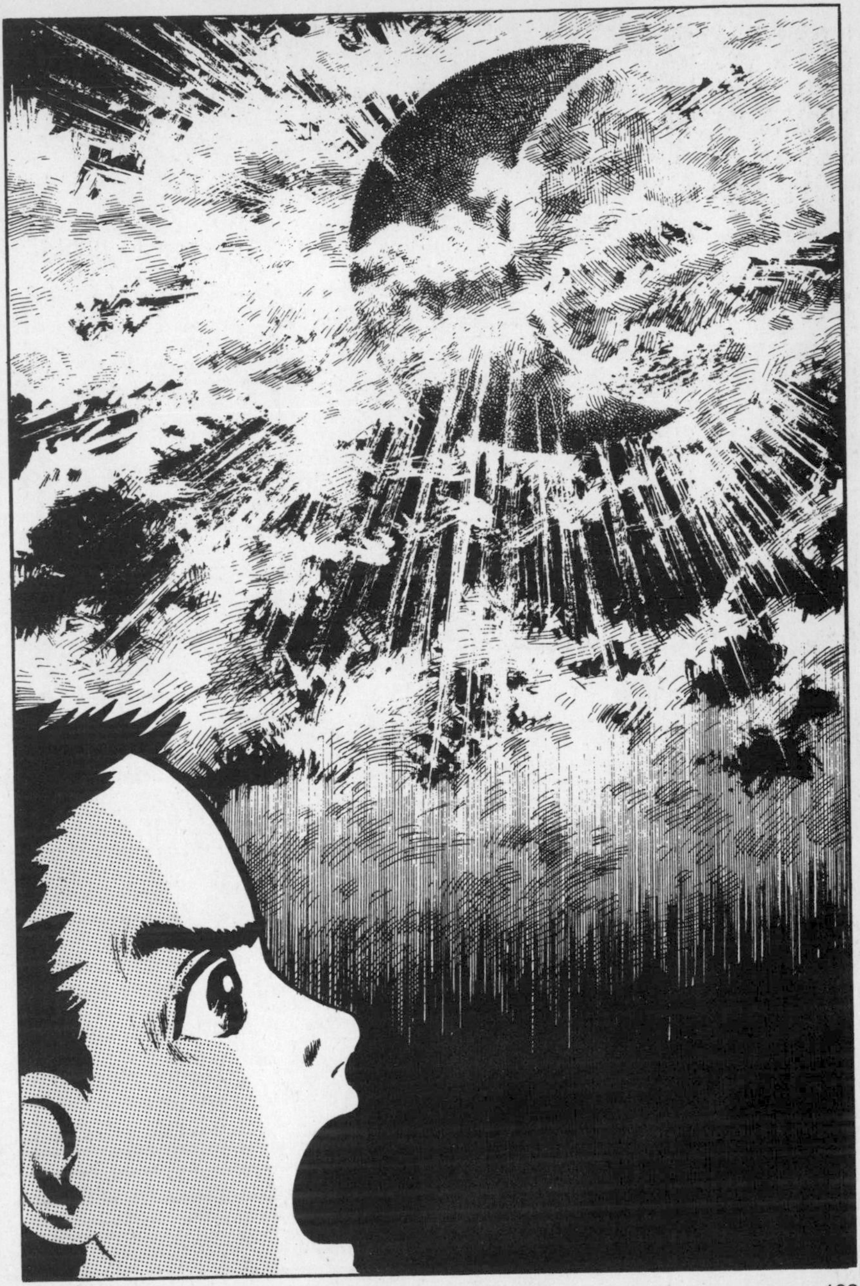

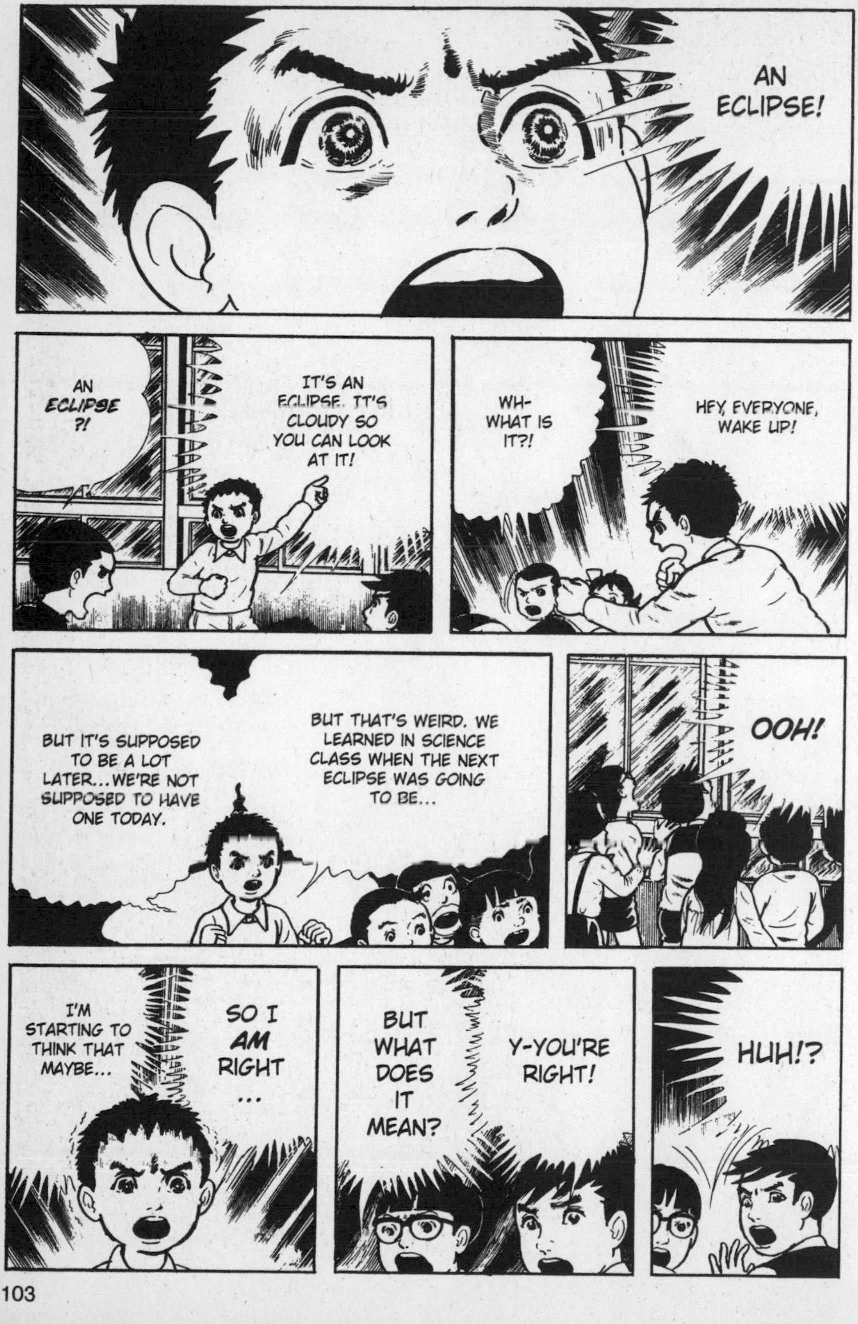
AN ECLIPSE!
HEY, EVERYONE, WAKE UP!
WH- WHAT IS IT?!
IT'S AN ECLIPSE. IT'S CLOUDY SO YOU CAN LOOK AT IT!
AN *ECLIPSE* ?!
OOH!
BUT THAT'S WEIRD. WE LEARNED IN SCIENCE CLASS WHEN THE NEXT ECLIPSE WAS GOING TO BE...
BUT IT'S SUPPOSED TO BE A LOT LATER...WE'RE NOT SUPPOSED TO HAVE ONE TODAY.
HUH!?
Y-YOU'RE RIGHT!
BUT WHAT DOES IT MEAN?
SO I *AM* RIGHT...
I'M STARTING TO THINK THAT MAYBE...

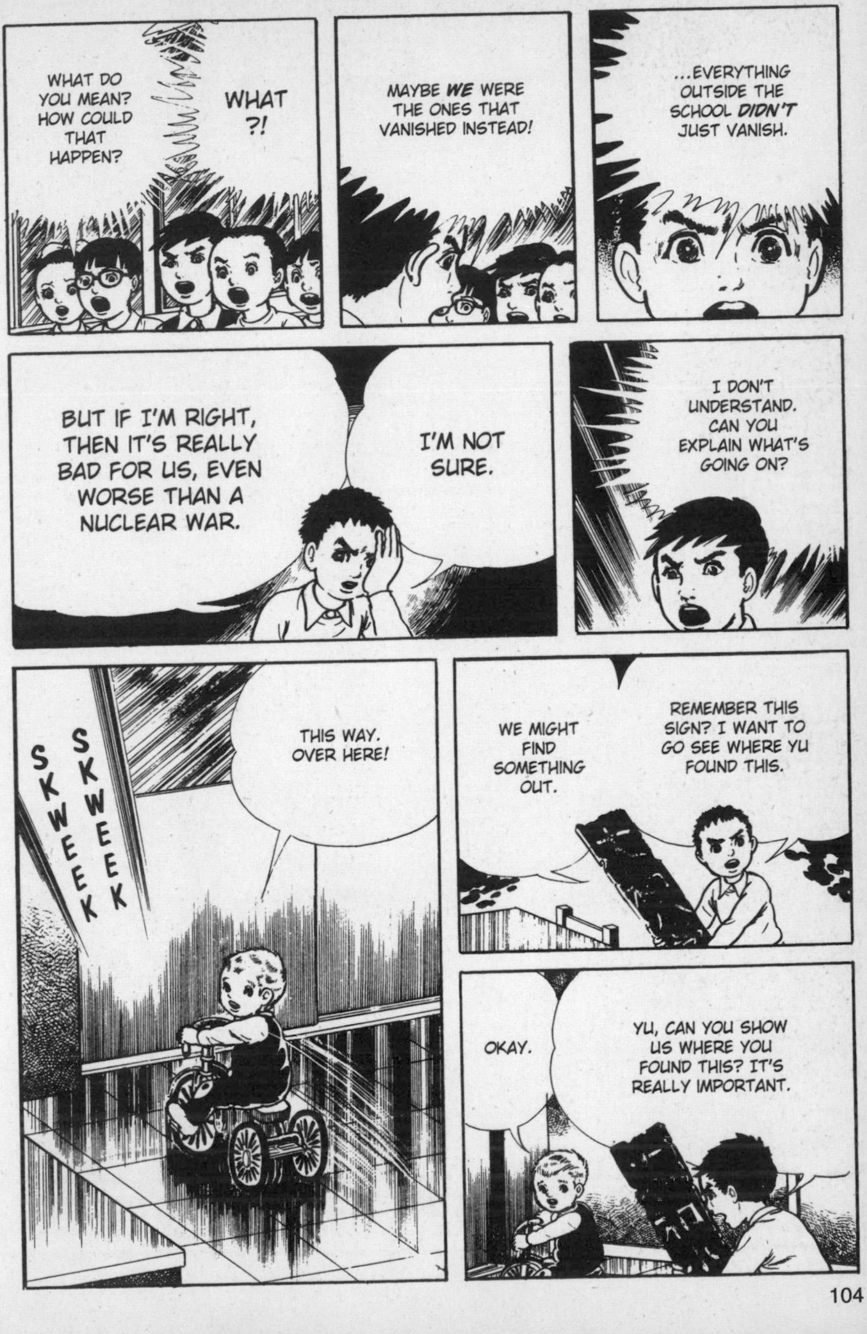
...EVERYTHING OUTSIDE THE SCHOOL ***DIDN'T*** JUST VANISH.
MAYBE ***WE*** WERE THE ONES THAT VANISHED INSTEAD!
WHAT ?!
WHAT DO YOU MEAN? HOW COULD THAT HAPPEN?
I DON'T UNDERSTAND. CAN YOU EXPLAIN WHAT'S GOING ON?
I'M NOT SURE.
BUT IF I'M RIGHT, THEN IT'S REALLY BAD FOR US, EVEN WORSE THAN A NUCLEAR WAR.
REMEMBER THIS SIGN? I WANT TO GO SEE WHERE YU FOUND THIS.
WE MIGHT FIND SOMETHING OUT.
YU, CAN YOU SHOW US WHERE YOU FOUND THIS? IT'S REALLY IMPORTANT.
OKAY.
THIS WAY. OVER HERE!
SKWEEK
SKWEEK

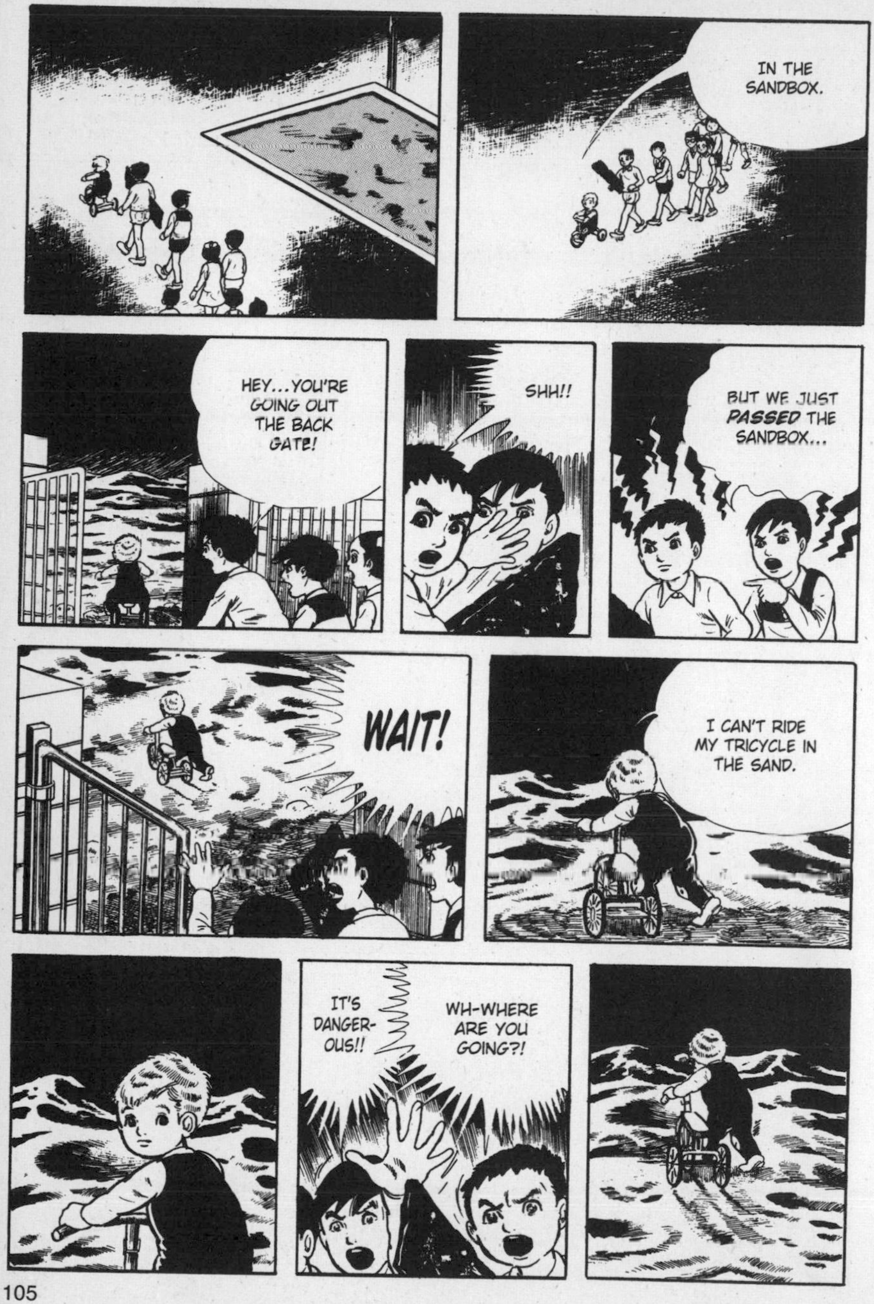
IN THE SANDBOX.
BUT WE JUST PASSED THE SANDBOX...
SHH!!
HEY...YOU'RE GOING OUT THE BACK GATE!
I CAN'T RIDE MY TRICYCLE IN THE SAND.
WAIT!
WH-WHERE ARE YOU GOING?!
IT'S DANGER-OUS!!

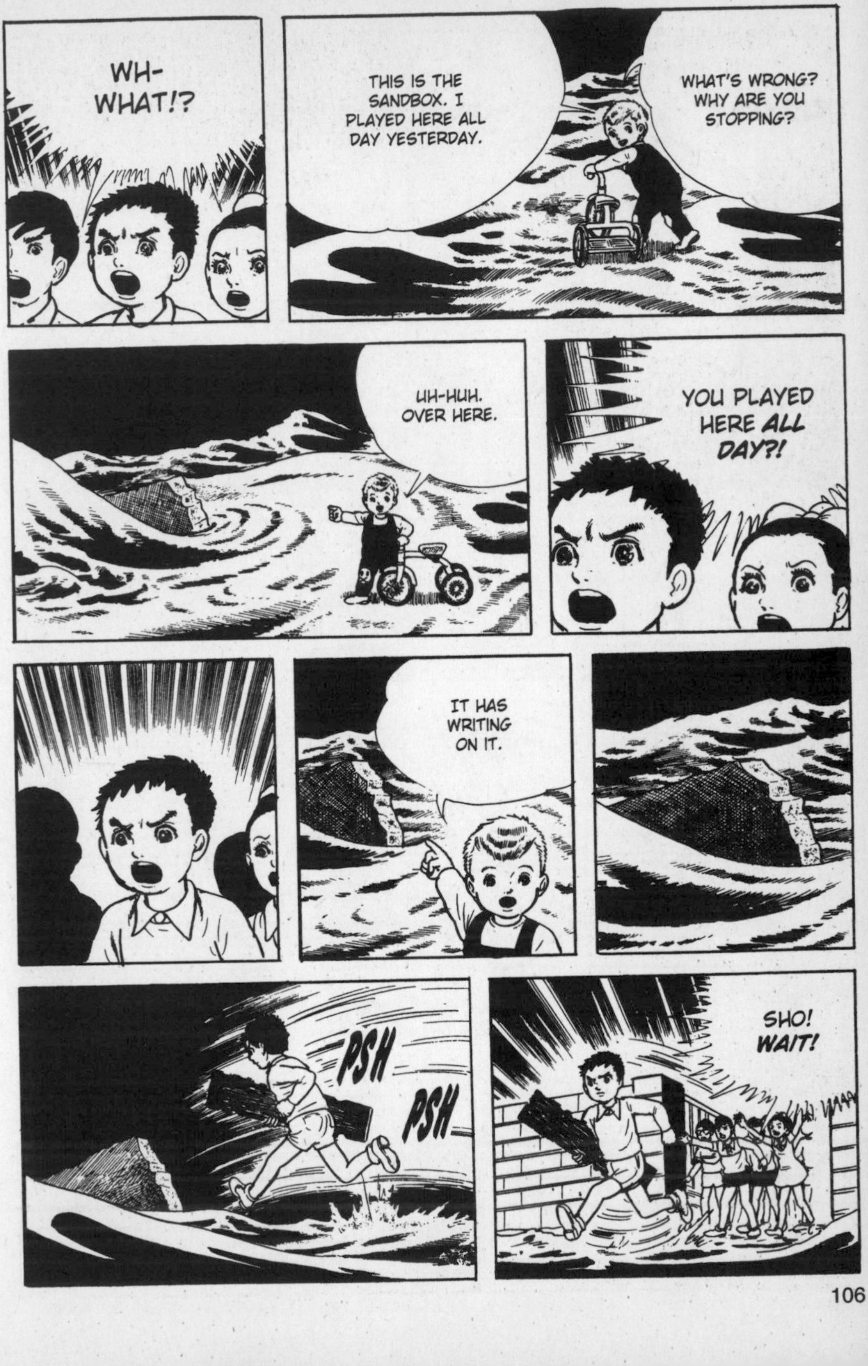
WHAT'S WRONG? WHY ARE YOU STOPPING?
THIS IS THE SANDBOX. I PLAYED HERE ALL DAY YESTERDAY.
WH- WHAT!?
YOU PLAYED HERE ALL DAY?!
UH-HUH. OVER HERE.
IT HAS WRITING ON IT.
SHO! WAIT!
PSH
PSH

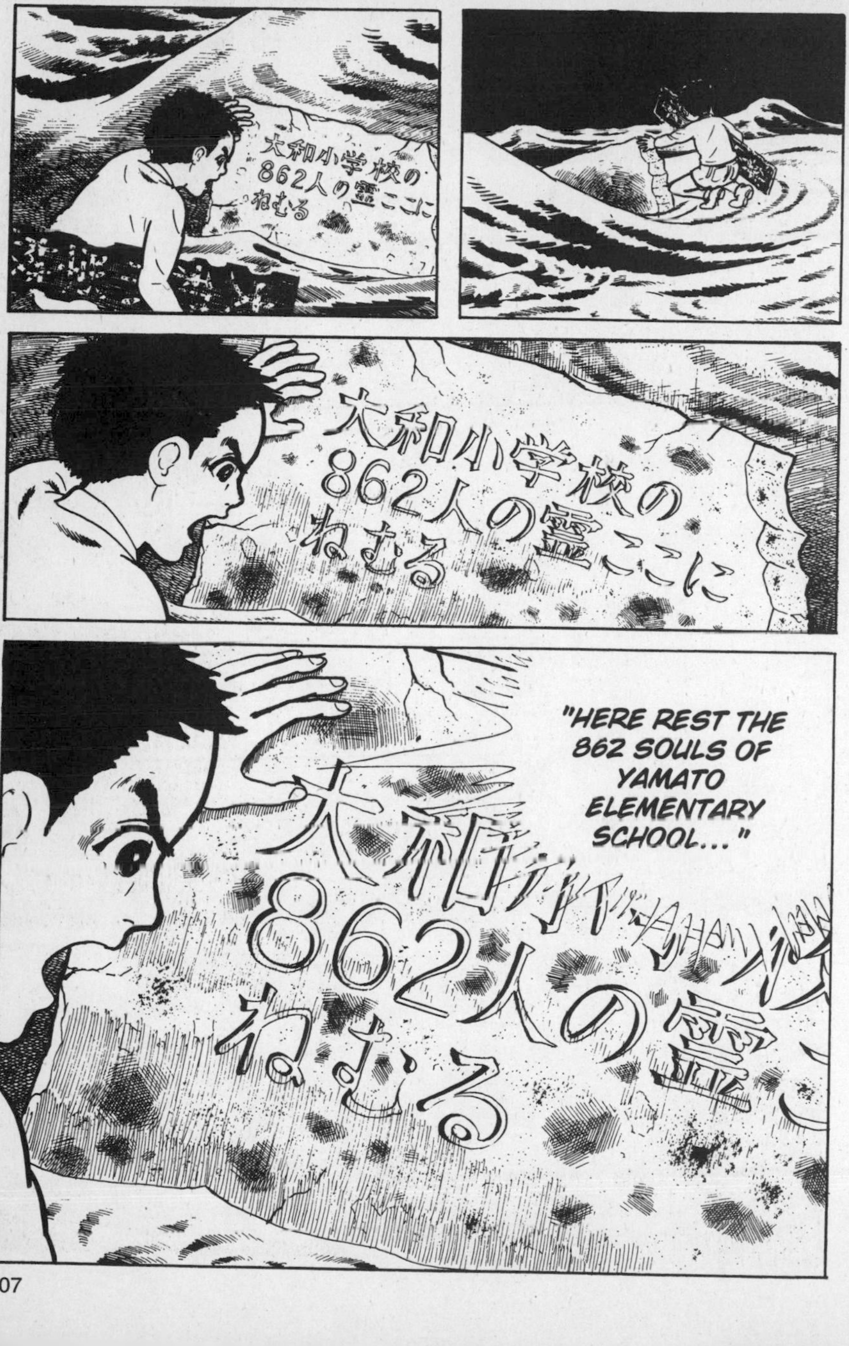
大和小学校の
862人の霊ここに
ねむる
大和小学校の
862人の霊ここに
ねむる
"HERE REST THE 862 SOULS OF YAMATO ELEMENTARY SCHOOL..."
862人の霊
ねむる

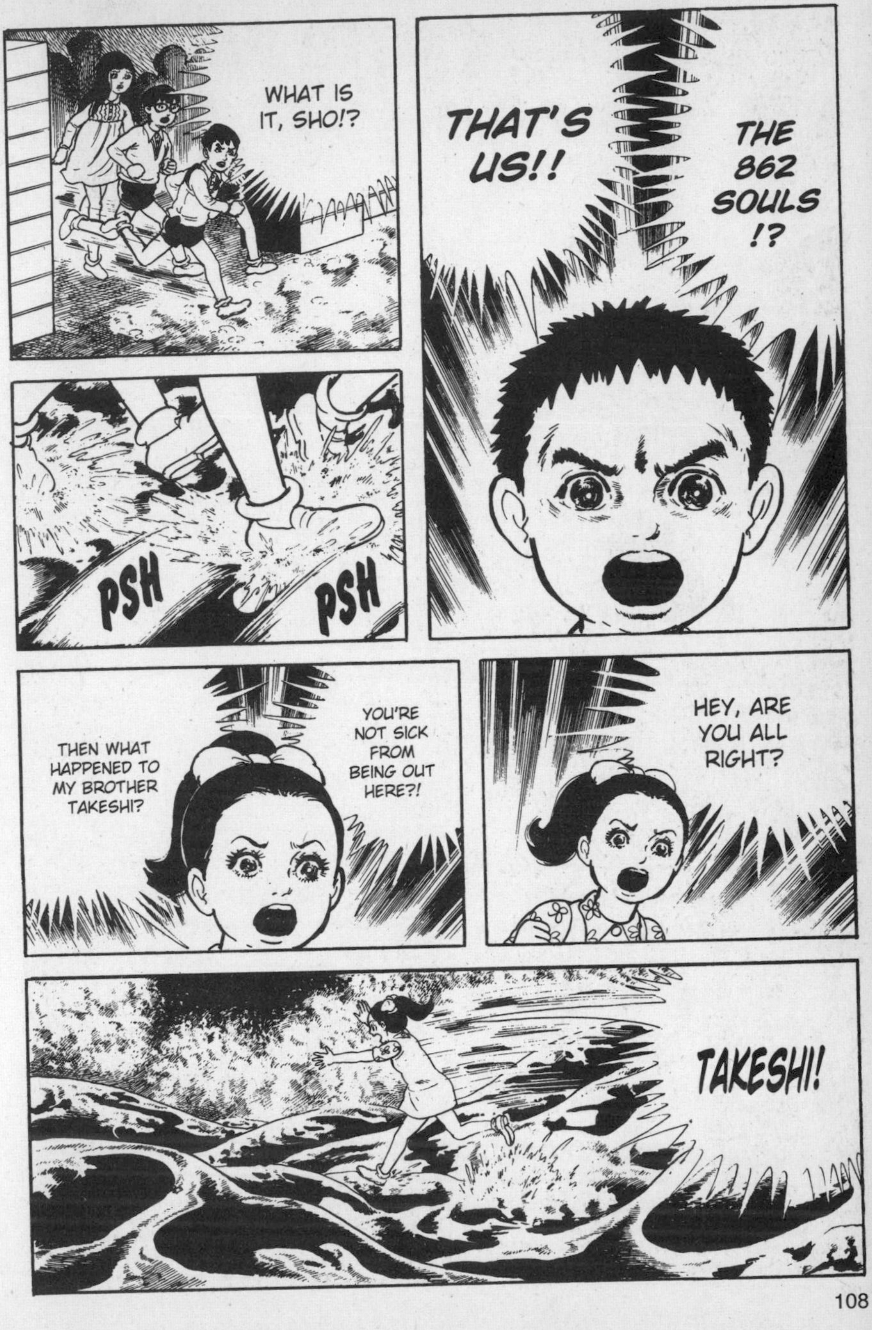
THE 862 SOULS !?
THAT'S US!!
WHAT IS IT, SHO!?
PSH
PSH
HEY, ARE YOU ALL RIGHT?
YOU'RE NOT SICK FROM BEING OUT HERE?!
THEN WHAT HAPPENED TO MY BROTHER TAKESHI?
TAKESHI!

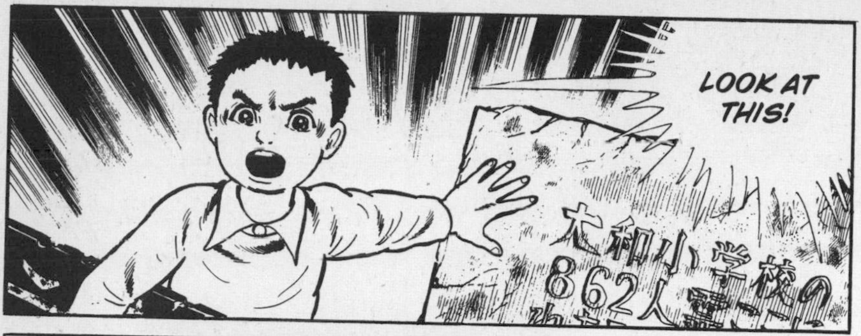
LOOK AT THIS!
大和小学校の
862人

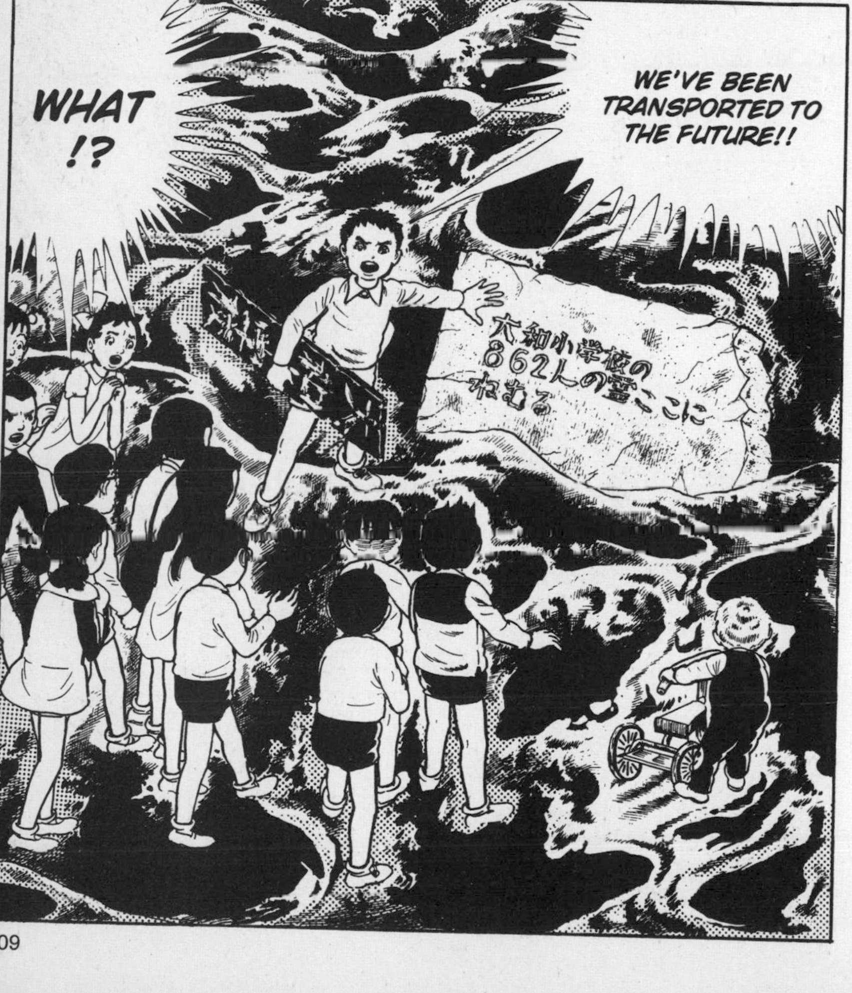
WE'VE BEEN TRANSPORTED TO THE FUTURE!!
大和小学校の
862人の霊ここに
ねむる
WHAT !?

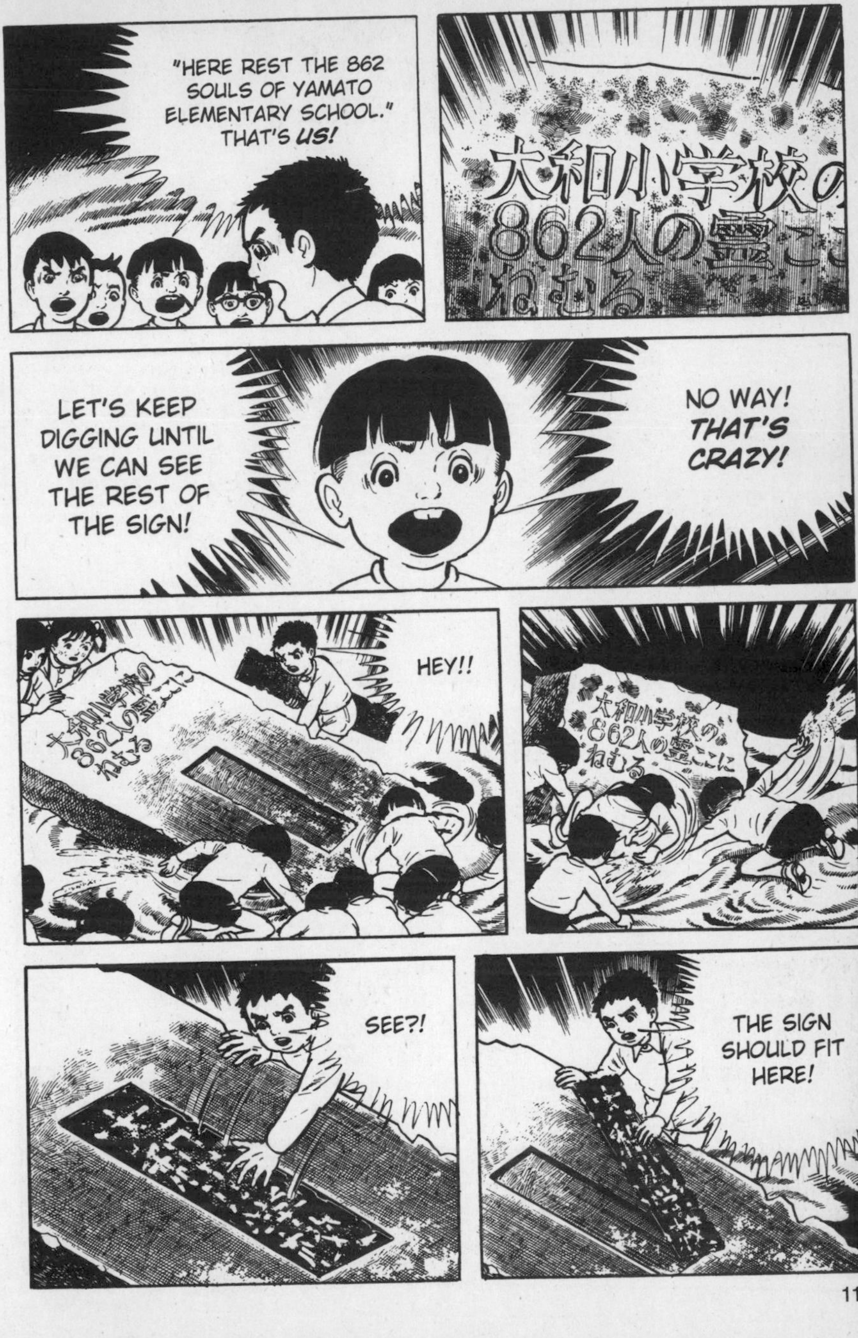
大和小学校の
862人の霊ここ
ねむる
"HERE REST THE 862 SOULS OF YAMATO ELEMENTARY SCHOOL." THAT'S *US!*
NO WAY! *THAT'S CRAZY!*
LET'S KEEP DIGGING UNTIL WE CAN SEE THE REST OF THE SIGN!
大和小学校の
862人の霊ここに
ねむる
HEY!!
大和小学校の
862人の霊ここに
ねむる
THE SIGN SHOULD FIT HERE!
SEE?!

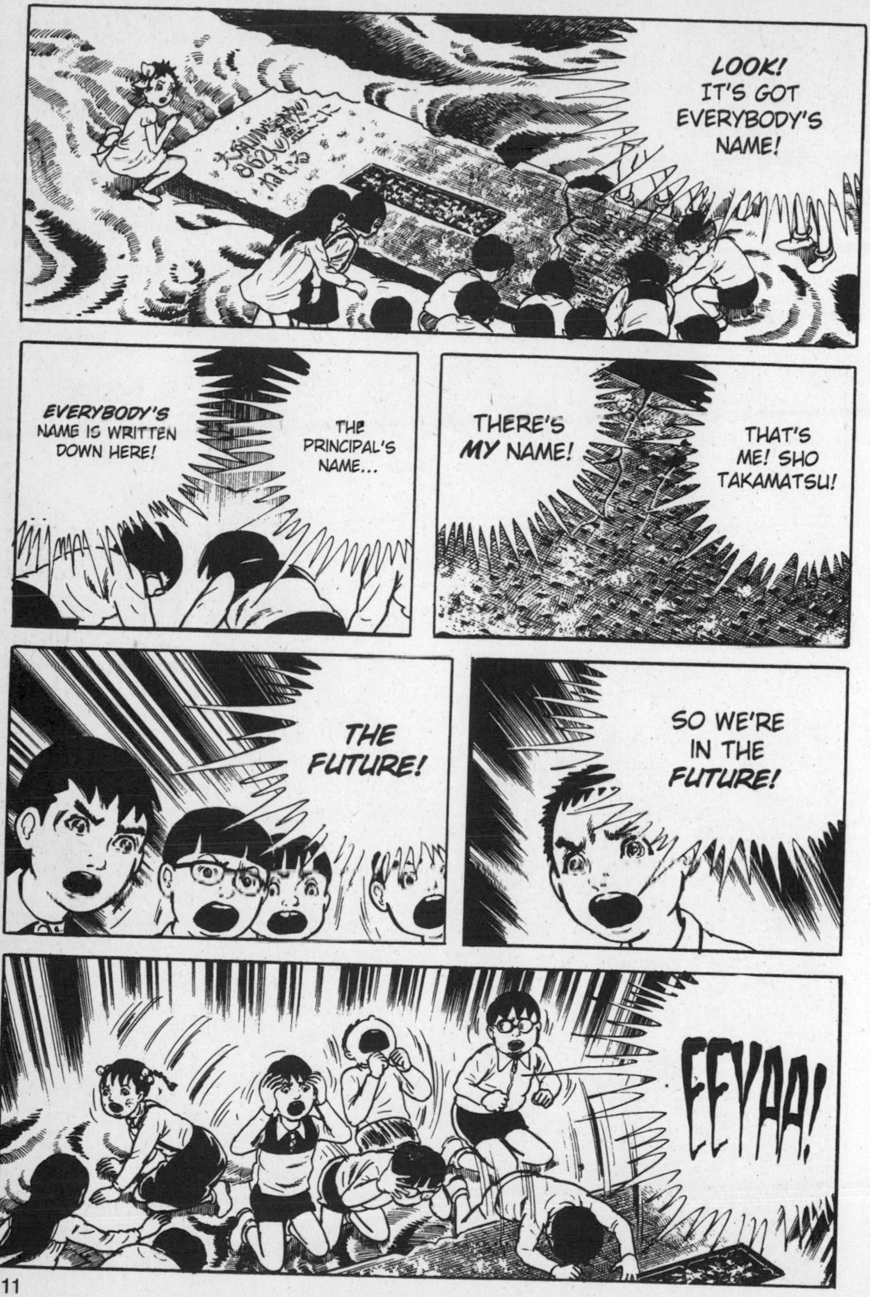
LOOK! IT'S GOT EVERYBODY'S NAME!
THAT'S ME! SHO TAKAMATSU!
THERE'S MY NAME!
THE PRINCIPAL'S NAME...
EVERYBODY'S NAME IS WRITTEN DOWN HERE!
SO WE'RE IN THE FUTURE!
THE FUTURE!
EEYAA!

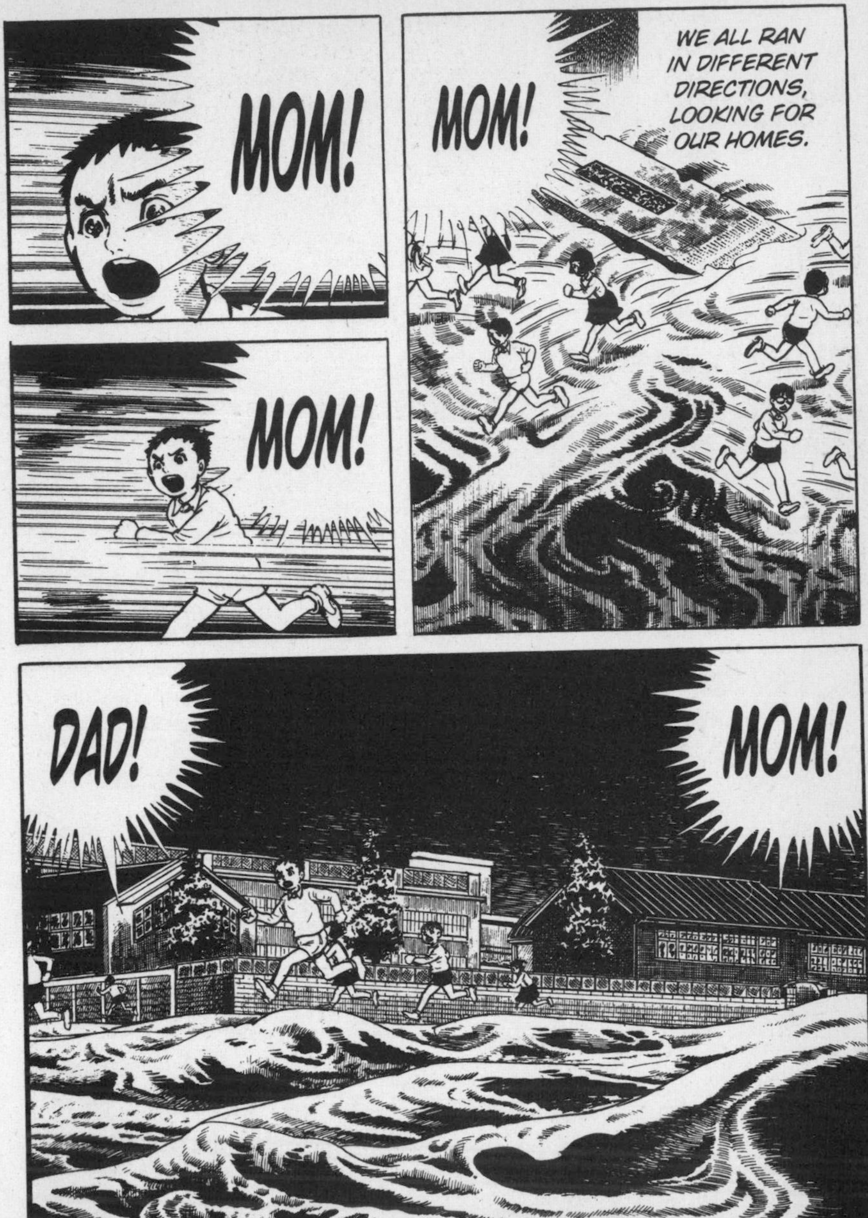
WE ALL RAN IN DIFFERENT DIRECTIONS, LOOKING FOR OUR HOMES.
MOM!
MOM!
MOM!
MOM!
DAD!

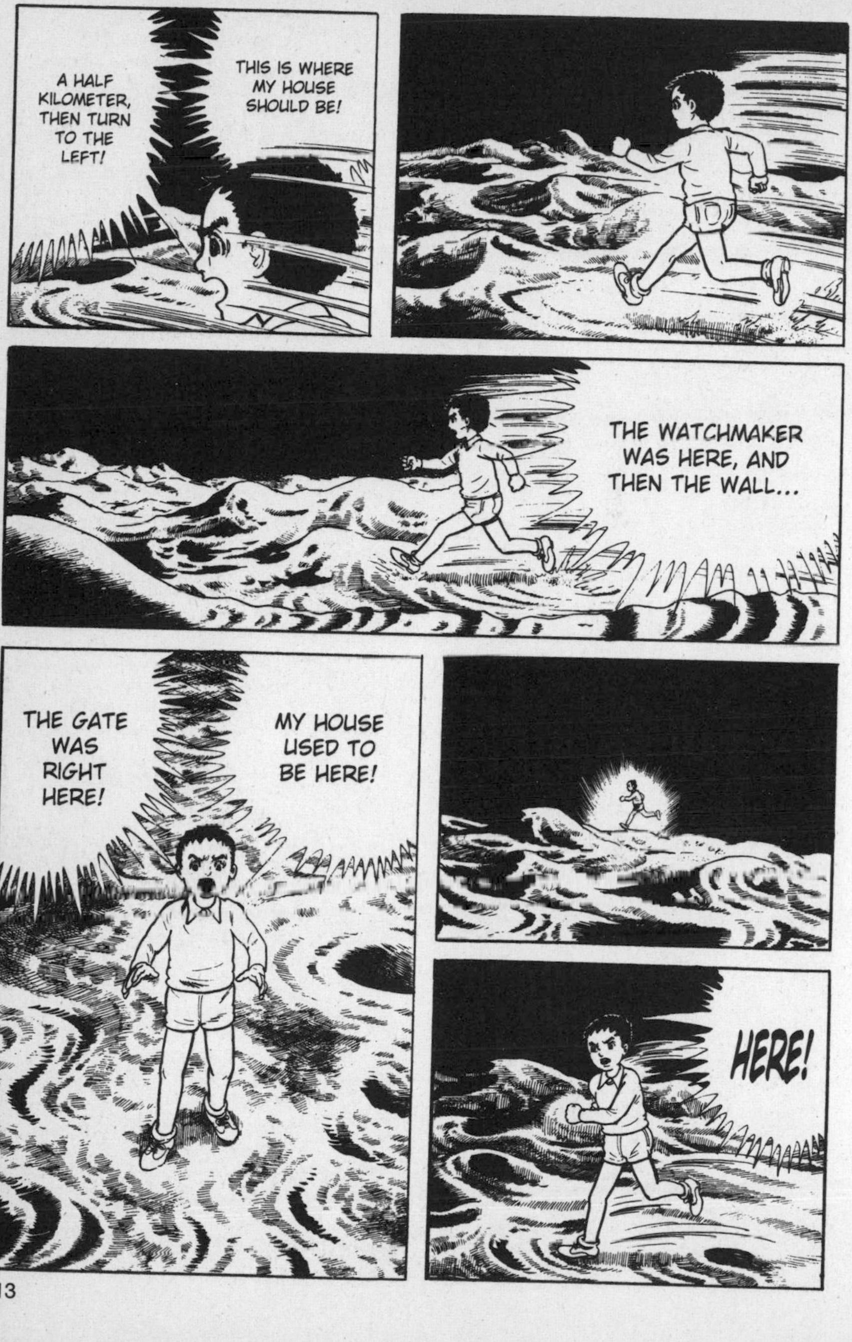
THIS IS WHERE MY HOUSE SHOULD BE!
A HALF KILOMETER, THEN TURN TO THE LEFT!
THE WATCHMAKER WAS HERE, AND THEN THE WALL...
HERE!
MY HOUSE USED TO BE HERE!
THE GATE WAS RIGHT HERE!

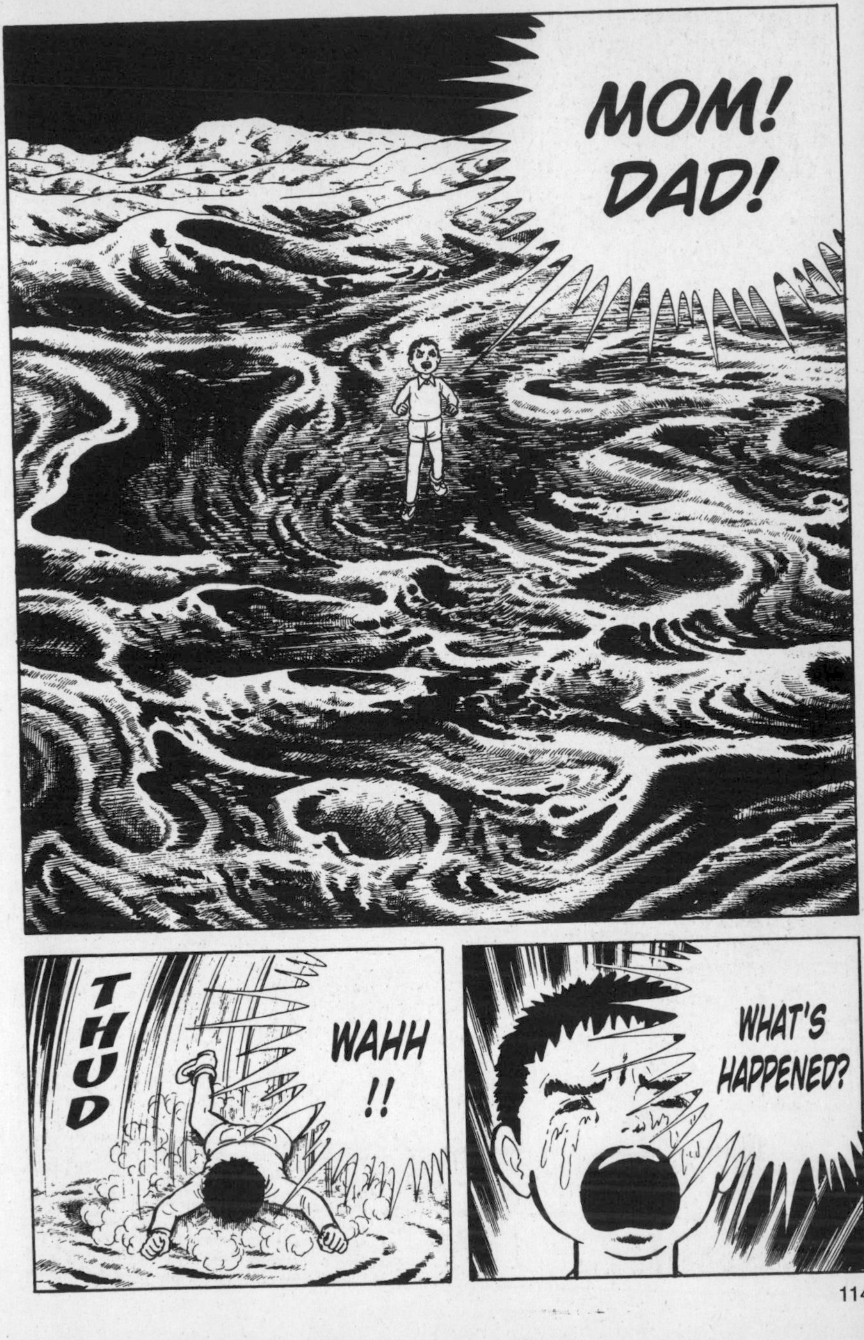
MOM! DAD!
WHAT'S HAPPENED?
THUD
WAHH !!

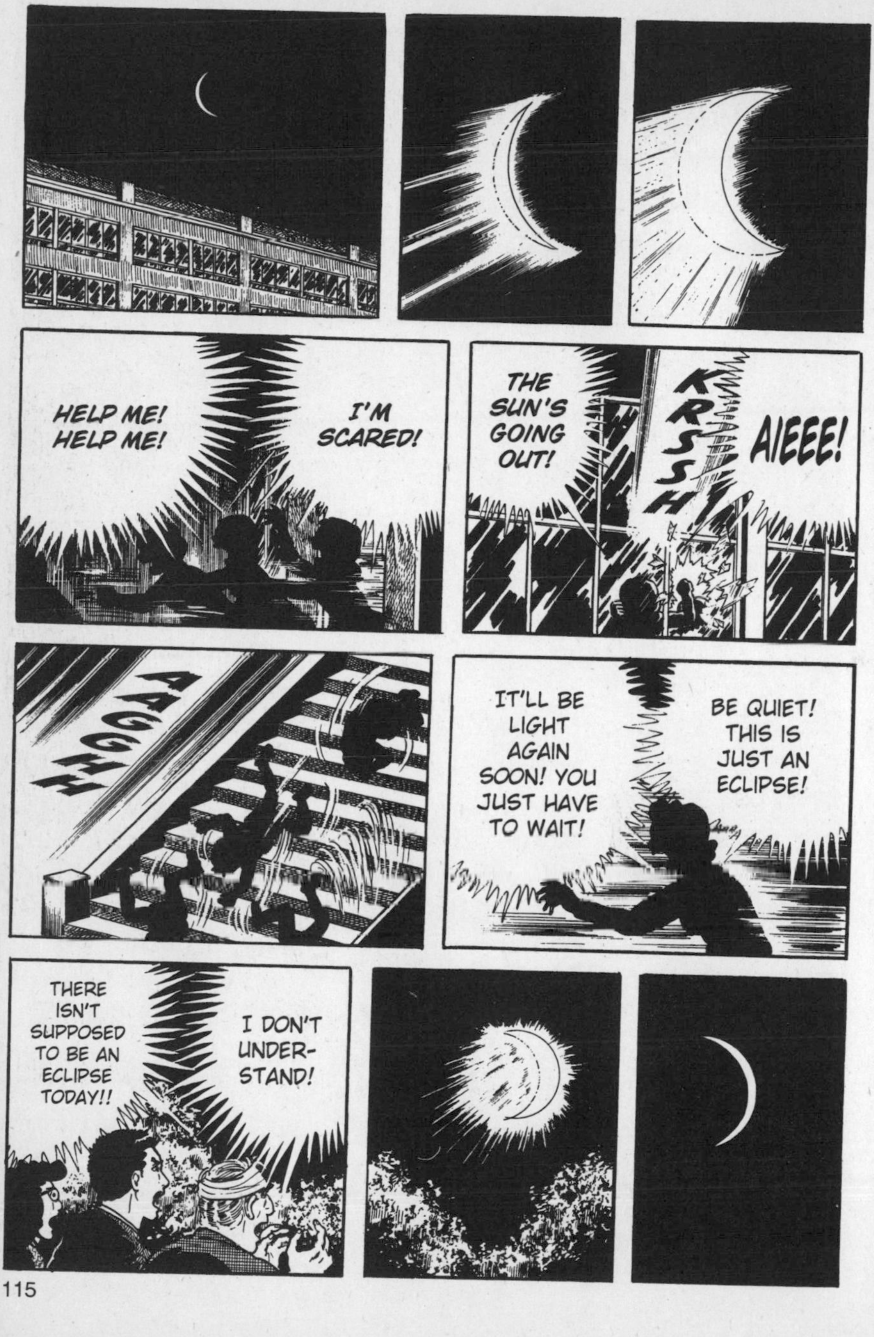
AIEEE!
KRSSH
THE SUN'S GOING OUT!
I'M SCARED!
HELP ME! HELP ME!
BE QUIET! THIS IS JUST AN ECLIPSE!
IT'LL BE LIGHT AGAIN SOON! YOU JUST HAVE TO WAIT!
AAGGH
I DON'T UNDER-STAND!
THERE ISN'T SUPPOSED TO BE AN ECLIPSE TODAY!!

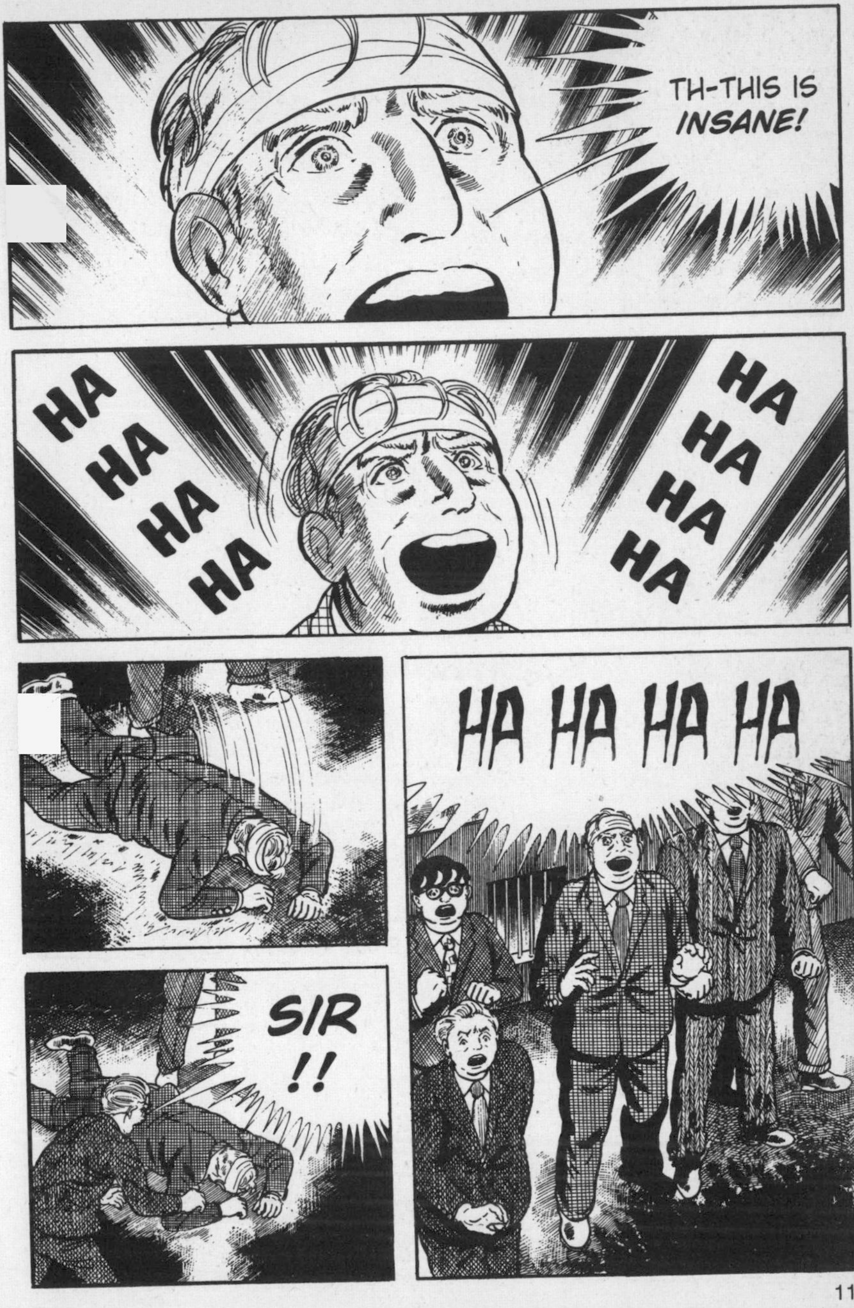
TH-THIS IS *INSANE!*
HA HA HA HA HA
HA HA HA HA
HA HA HA HA
SIR !!

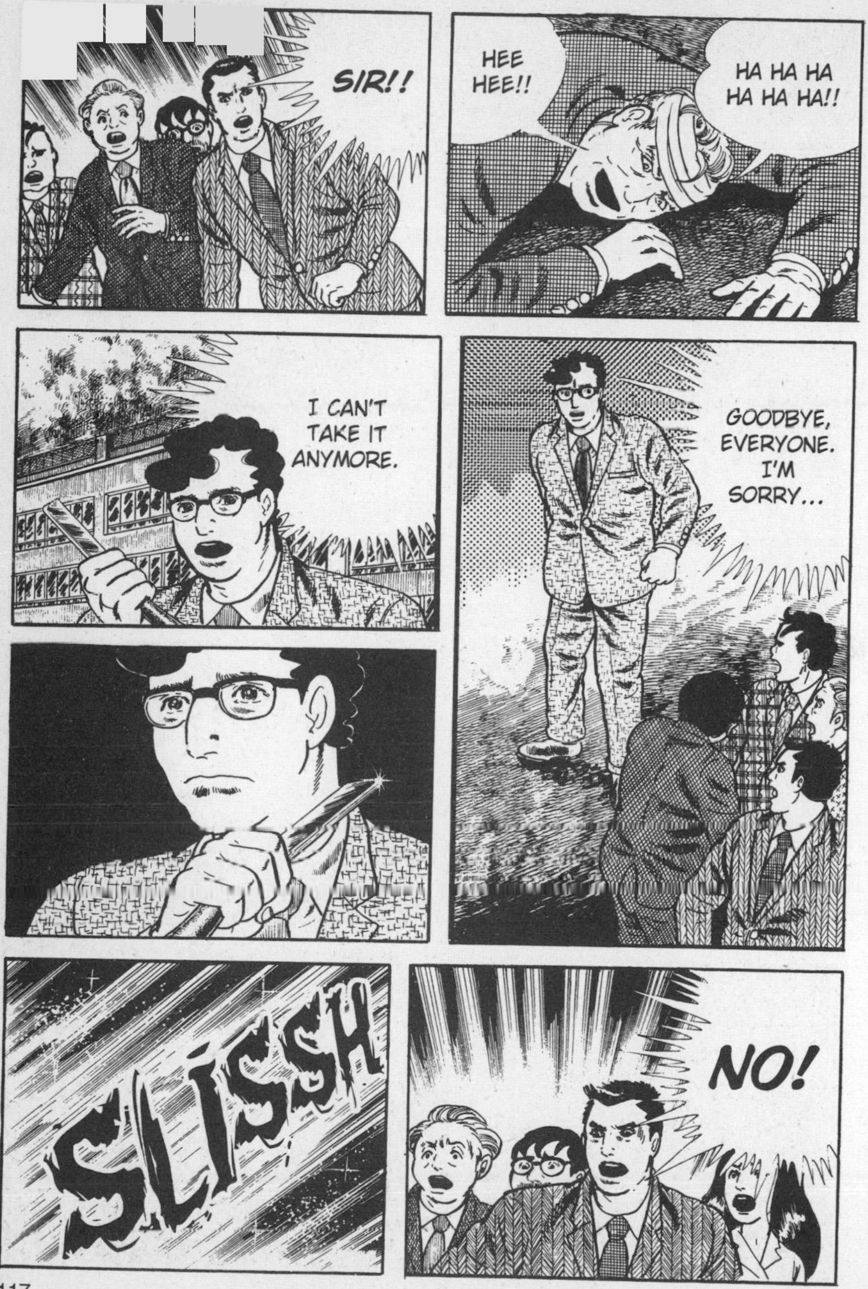
HA HA HA
HA HA HA!!
HEE
HEE!!
SIR!!
GOODBYE, EVERYONE. I'M SORRY...
I CAN'T TAKE IT ANYMORE.
NO!
SLISSH

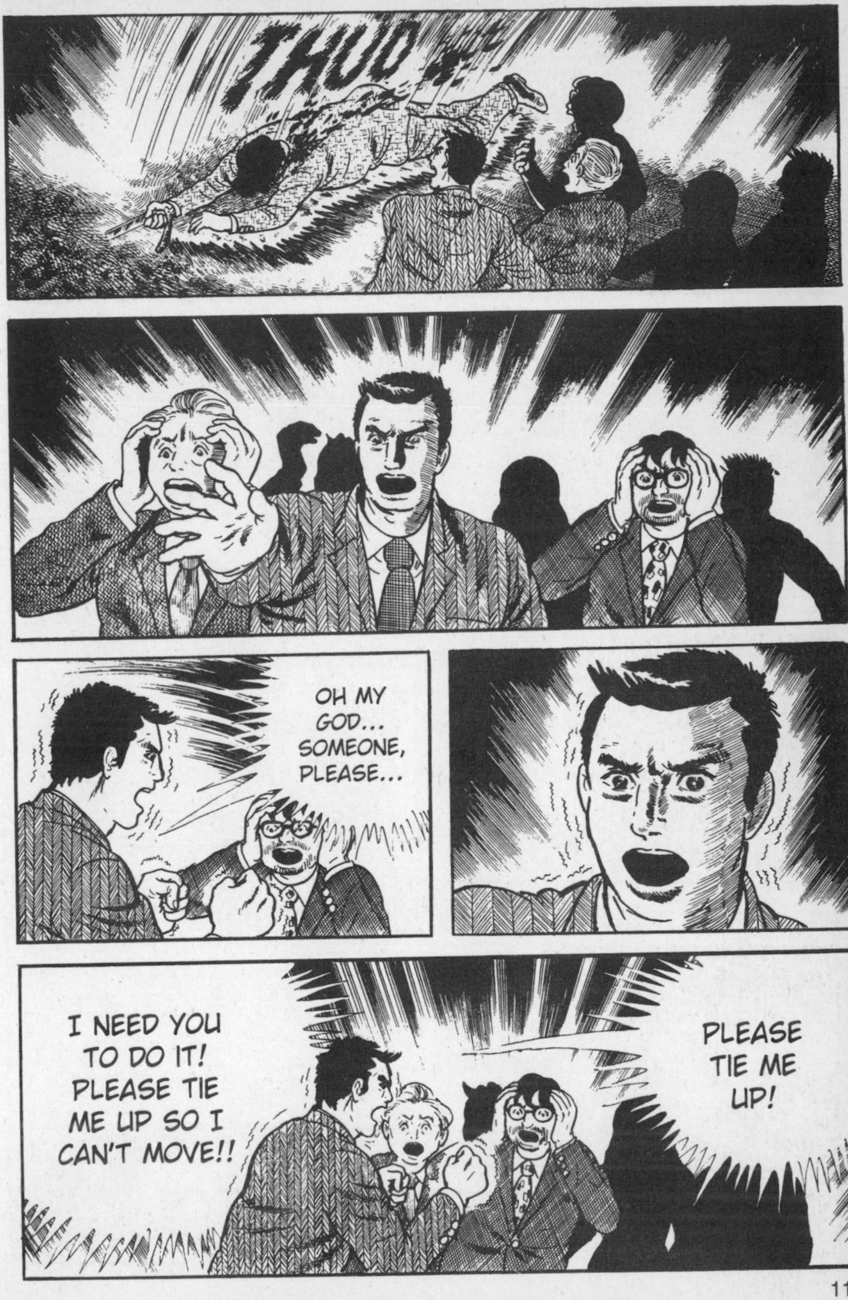
THUD
OH MY GOD... SOMEONE, PLEASE...
PLEASE TIE ME UP!
I NEED YOU TO DO IT! PLEASE TIE ME UP SO I CAN'T MOVE!!

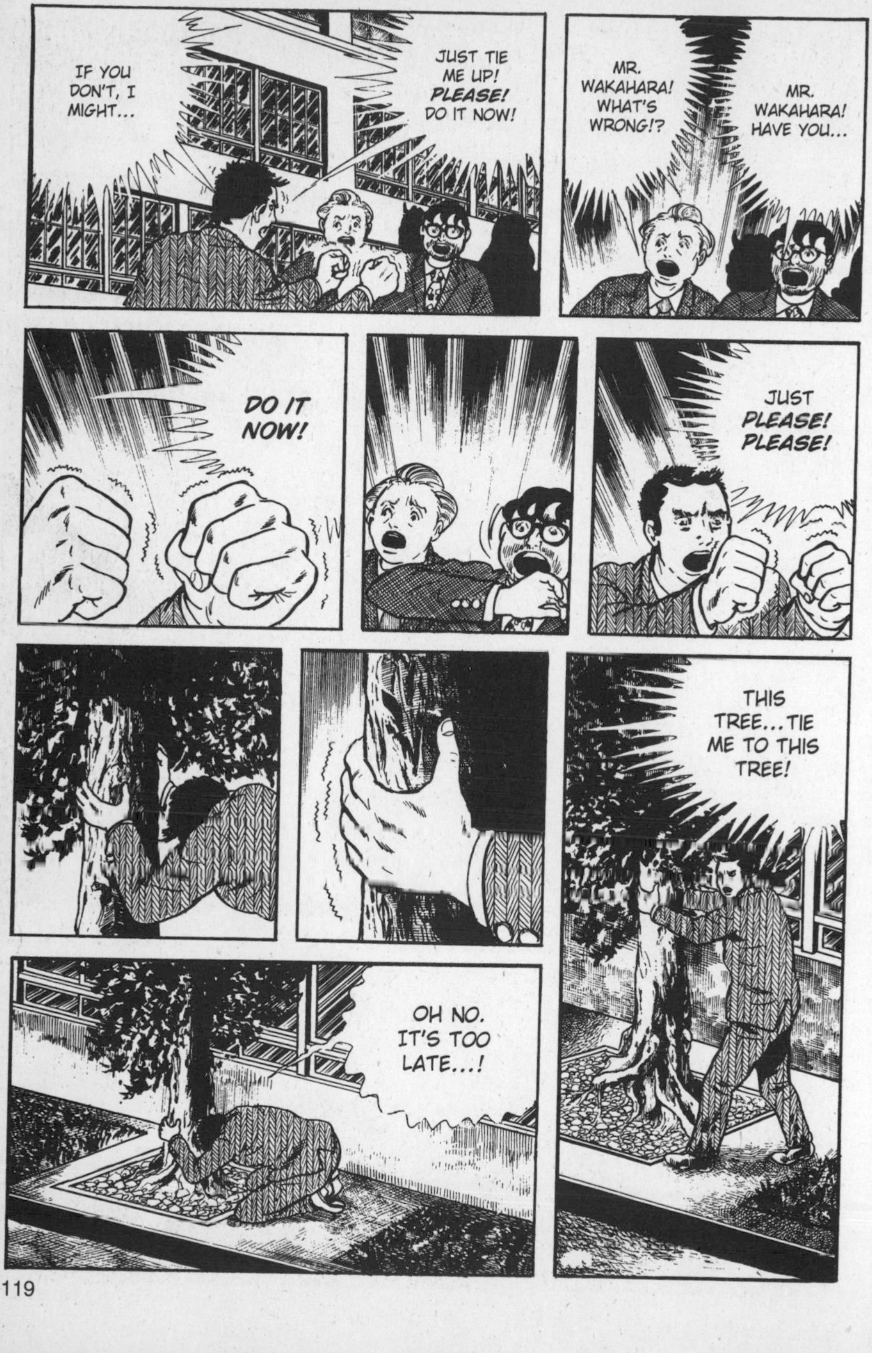
MR. WAKAHARA! HAVE YOU...
MR. WAKAHARA! WHAT'S WRONG!?
JUST TIE ME UP! **PLEASE!** DO IT NOW!
IF YOU DON'T, I MIGHT...
JUST **PLEASE! PLEASE!**
DO IT NOW!
THIS TREE... TIE ME TO THIS TREE!
OH NO. IT'S TOO LATE...!

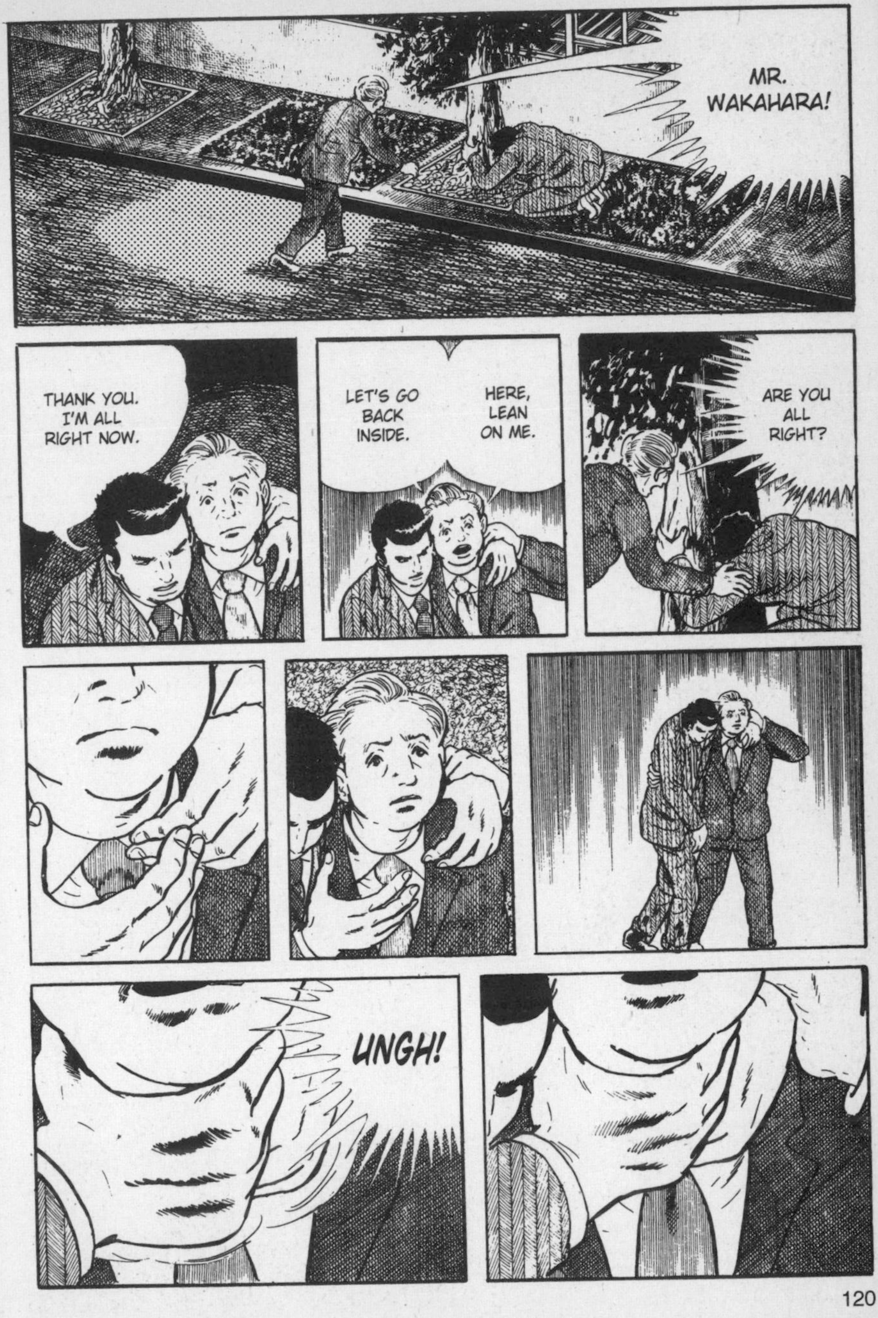
MR. WAKAHARA!
ARE YOU ALL RIGHT?
HERE, LEAN ON ME.
LET'S GO BACK INSIDE.
THANK YOU. I'M ALL RIGHT NOW.
UNGH!

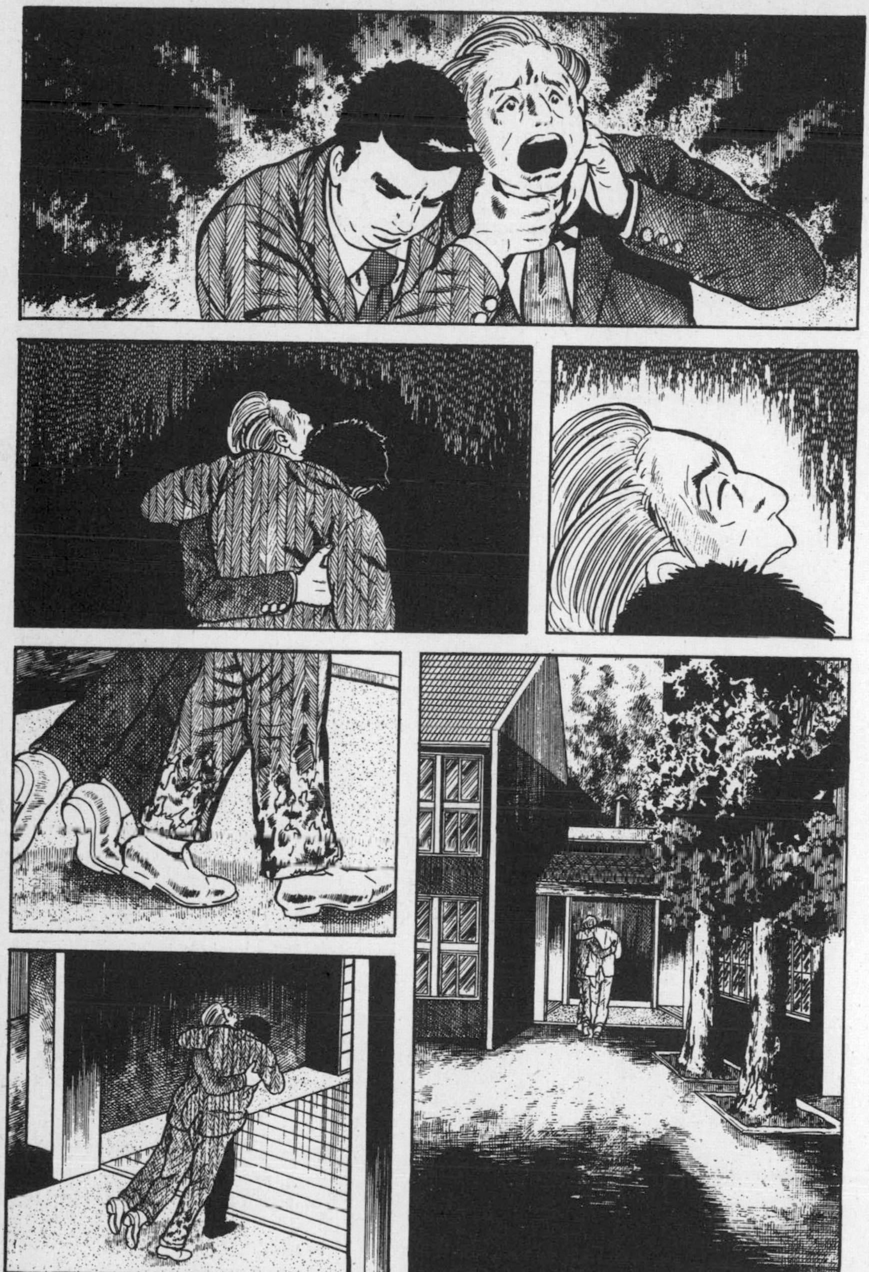

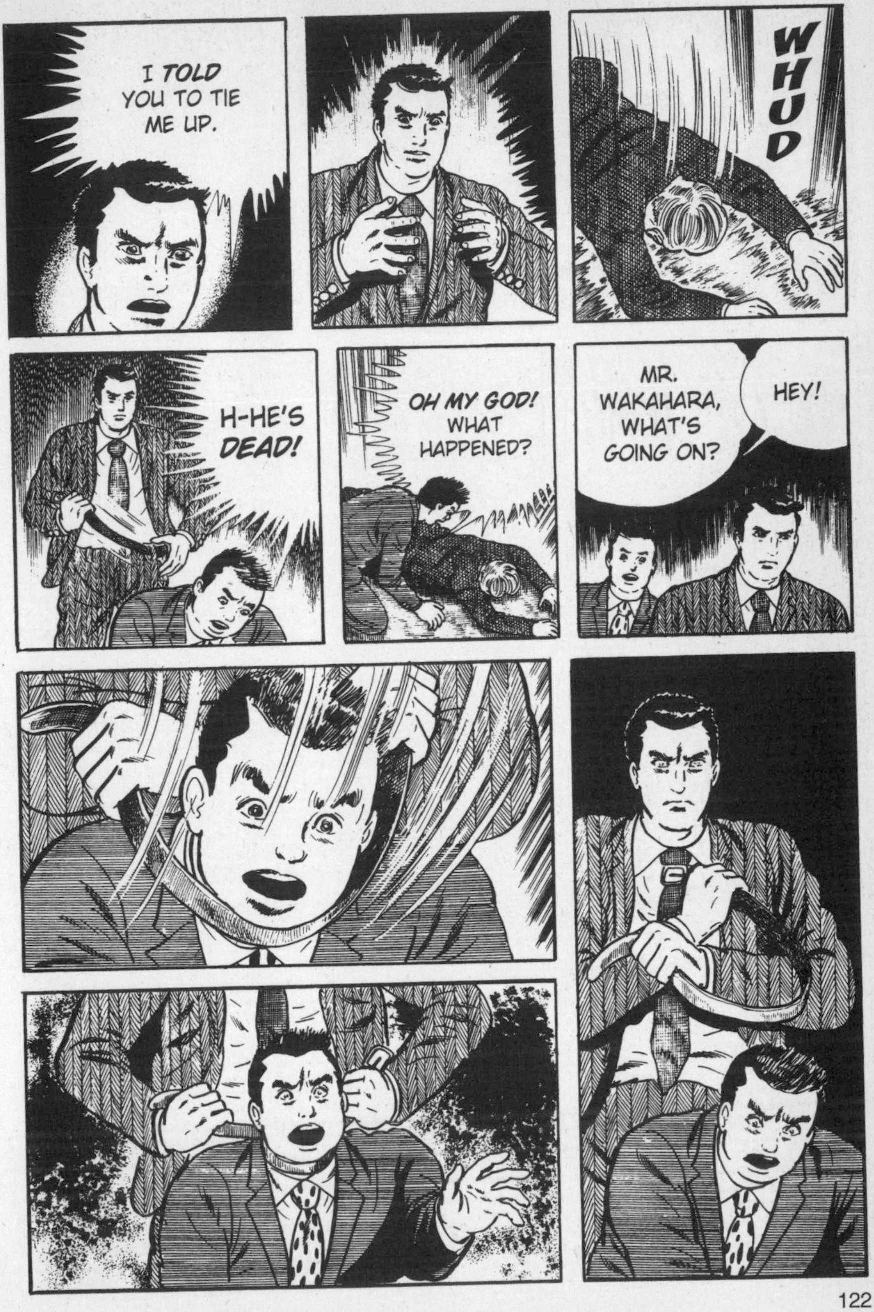
WHUD
I TOLD YOU TO TIE ME UP.
HEY!
MR. WAKAHARA, WHAT'S GOING ON?
OH MY GOD! WHAT HAPPENED?
H-HE'S DEAD!

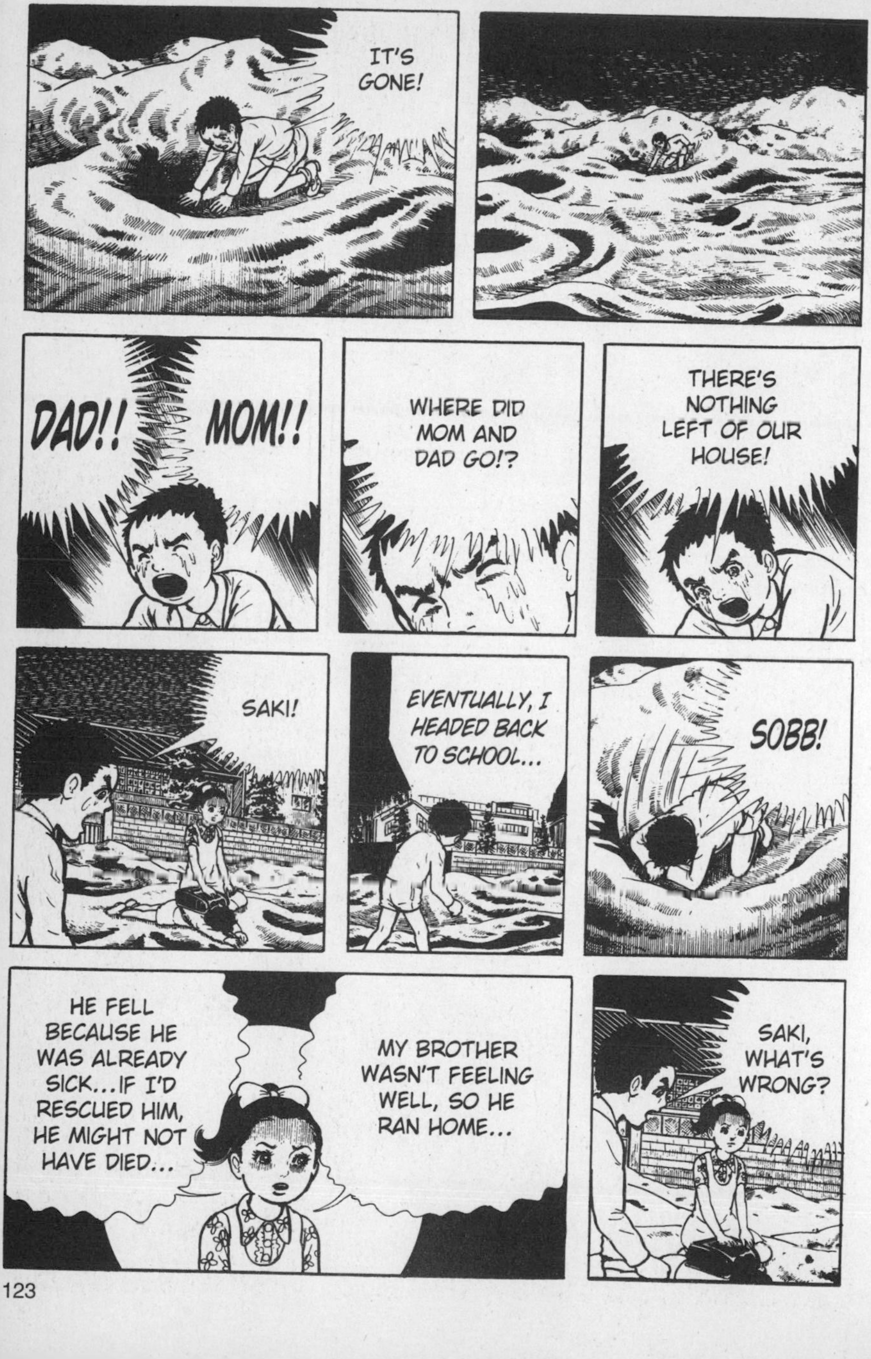
IT'S GONE!
THERE'S NOTHING LEFT OF OUR HOUSE!
WHERE DID MOM AND DAD GO!?
MOM!!
DAD!!
SOBB!
EVENTUALLY, I HEADED BACK TO SCHOOL...
SAKI!
SAKI, WHAT'S WRONG?
MY BROTHER WASN'T FEELING WELL, SO HE RAN HOME...
HE FELL BECAUSE HE WAS ALREADY SICK...IF I'D RESCUED HIM, HE MIGHT NOT HAVE DIED...

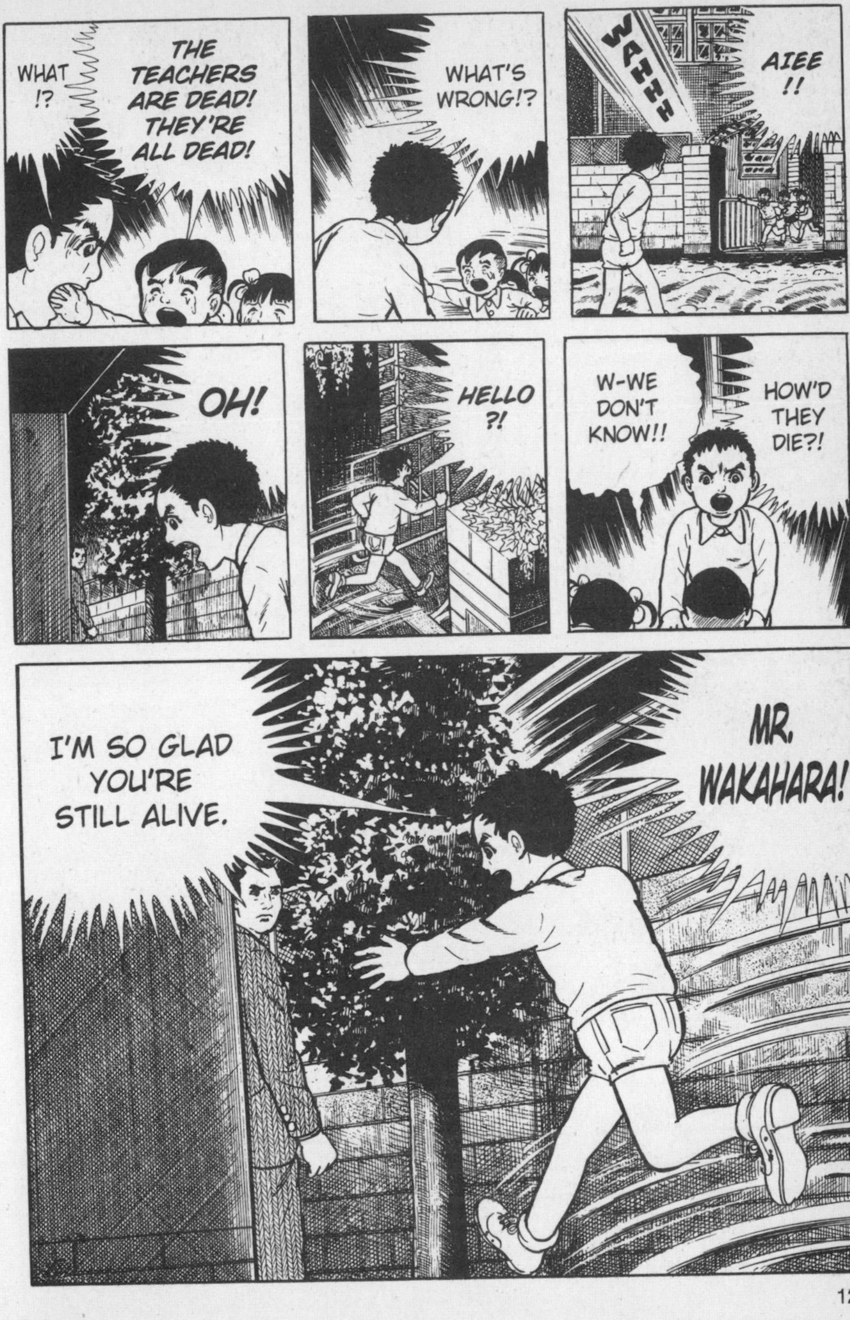
WAHHH
AIEE !!
WHAT'S WRONG!?
THE TEACHERS ARE DEAD! THEY'RE ALL DEAD!
WHAT !?
HOW'D THEY DIE?!
W-WE DON'T KNOW!!
HELLO ?!
OH!
MR. WAKAHARA!
I'M SO GLAD YOU'RE STILL ALIVE.

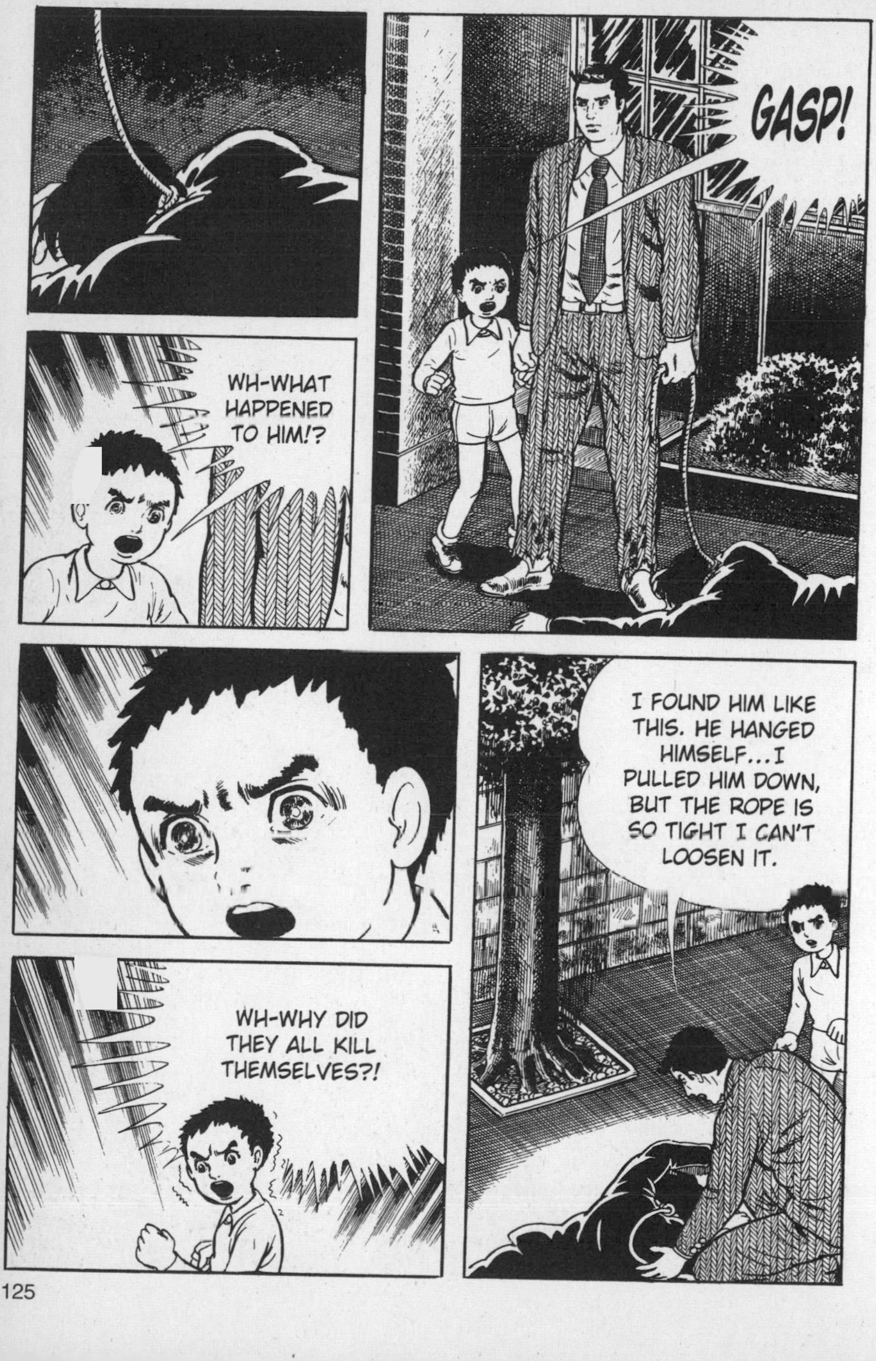
GASP!
WH-WHAT HAPPENED TO HIM!?
I FOUND HIM LIKE THIS. HE HANGED HIMSELF...I PULLED HIM DOWN, BUT THE ROPE IS SO TIGHT I CAN'T LOOSEN IT.
WH-WHY DID THEY ALL KILL THEMSELVES?!

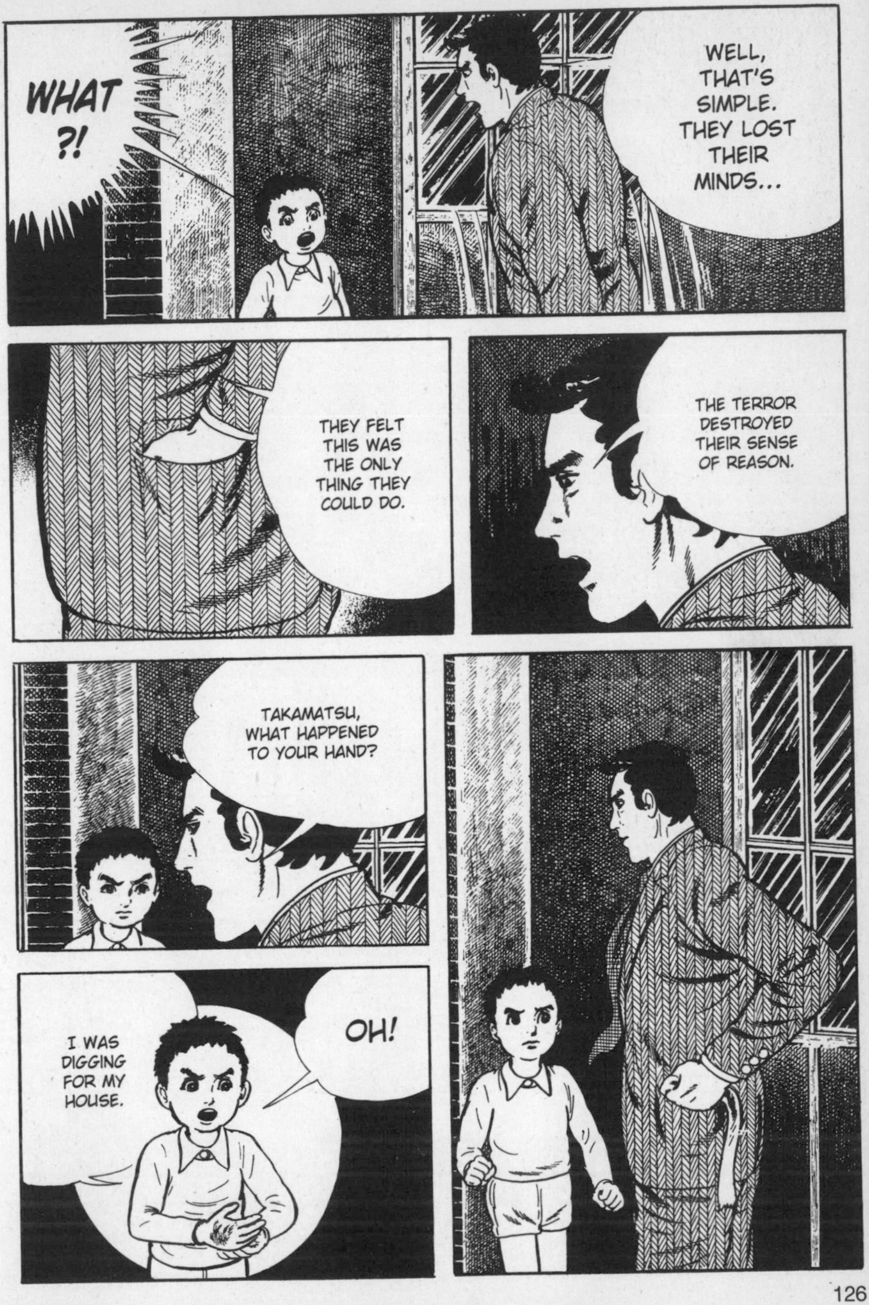
WELL, THAT'S SIMPLE. THEY LOST THEIR MINDS...
WHAT ?!
THE TERROR DESTROYED THEIR SENSE OF REASON.
THEY FELT THIS WAS THE ONLY THING THEY COULD DO.
TAKAMATSU, WHAT HAPPENED TO YOUR HAND?
OH!
I WAS DIGGING FOR MY HOUSE.

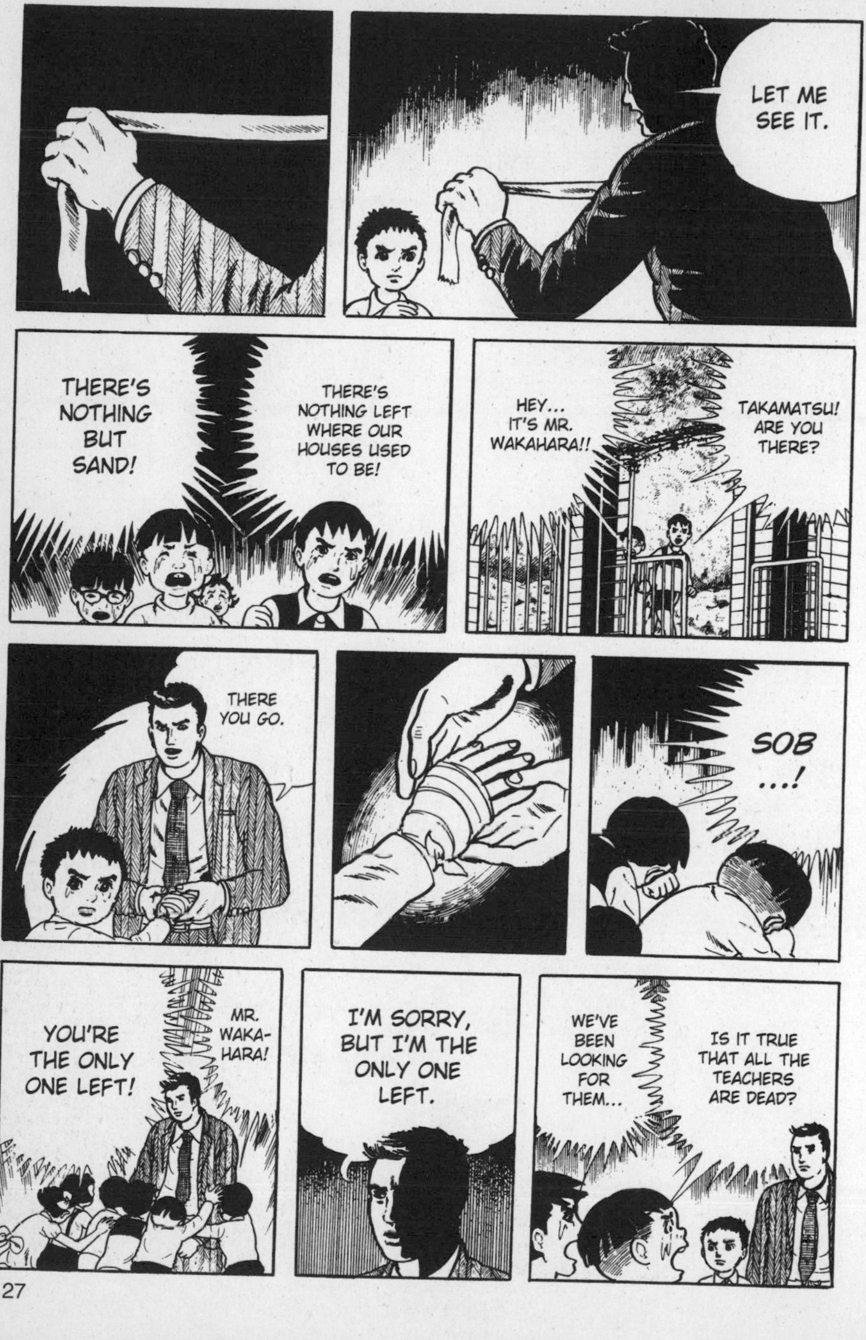
LET ME SEE IT.
TAKAMATSU! ARE YOU THERE?
HEY... IT'S MR. WAKAHARA!!
THERE'S NOTHING LEFT WHERE OUR HOUSES USED TO BE!
THERE'S NOTHING BUT SAND!
SOB ...!
THERE YOU GO.
IS IT TRUE THAT ALL THE TEACHERS ARE DEAD?
WE'VE BEEN LOOKING FOR THEM...
I'M SORRY, BUT I'M THE ONLY ONE LEFT.
MR. WAKA-HARA!
YOU'RE THE ONLY ONE LEFT!

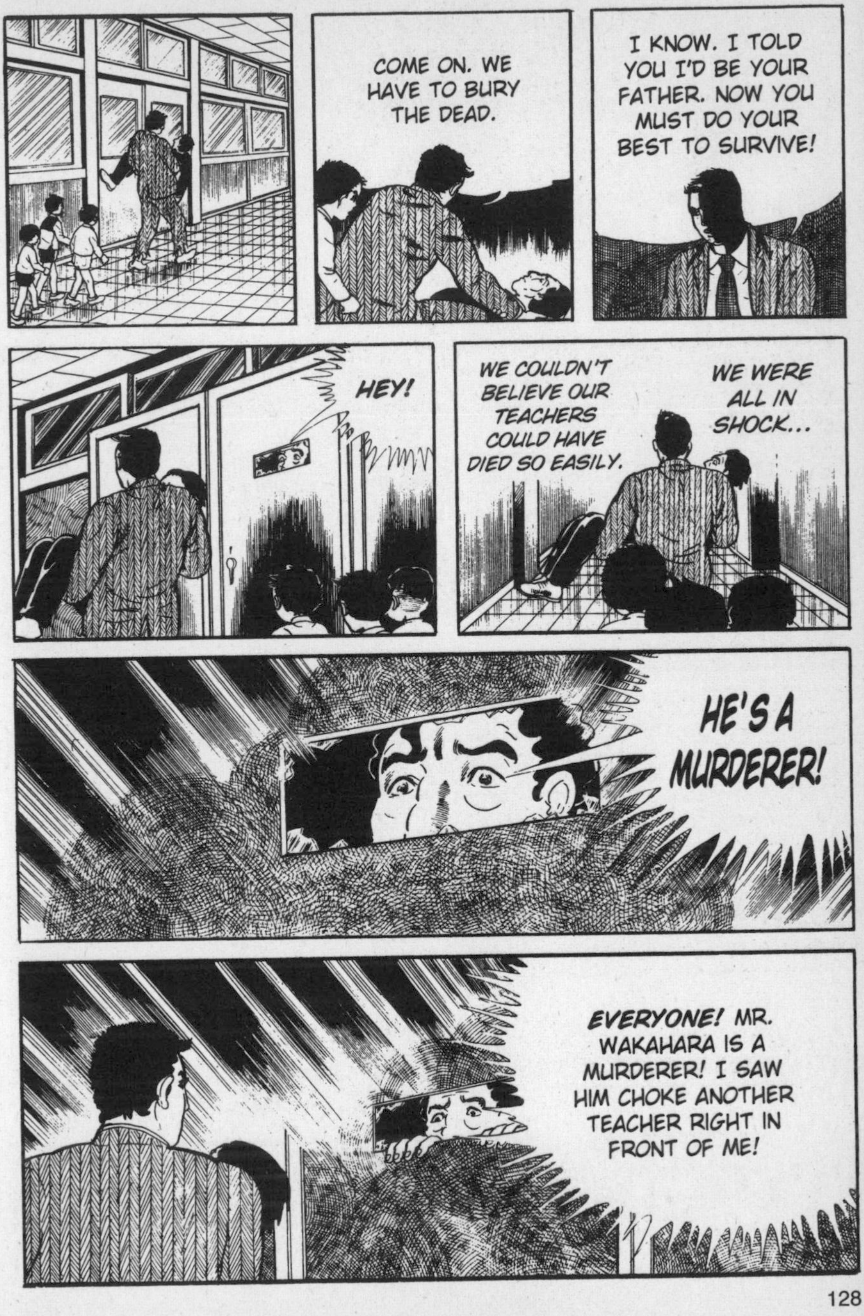
I KNOW. I TOLD YOU I'D BE YOUR FATHER. NOW YOU MUST DO YOUR BEST TO SURVIVE!
COME ON. WE HAVE TO BURY THE DEAD.
WE WERE ALL IN SHOCK...
WE COULDN'T BELIEVE OUR TEACHERS COULD HAVE DIED SO EASILY.
HEY!
HE'S A MURDERER!
EVERYONE! MR. WAKAHARA IS A MURDERER! I SAW HIM CHOKE ANOTHER TEACHER RIGHT IN FRONT OF ME!

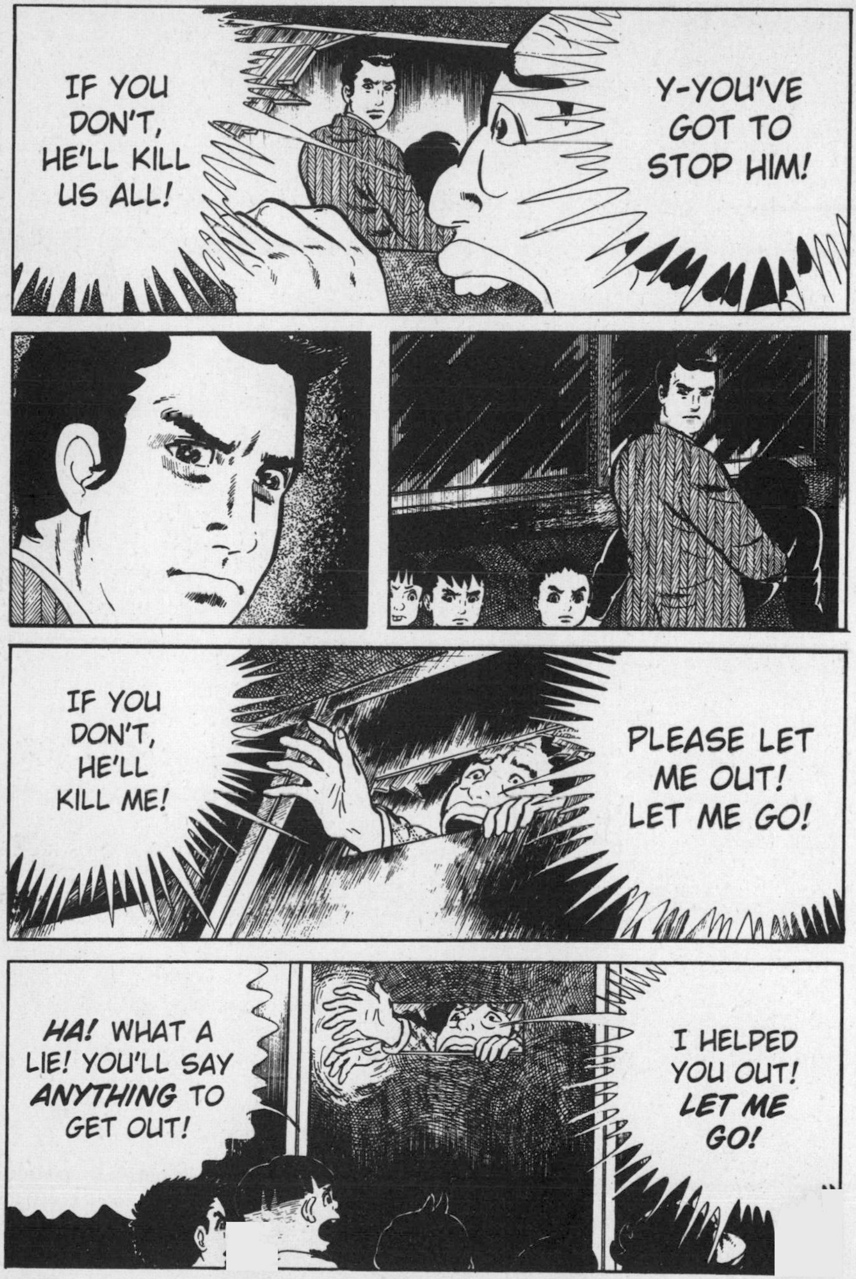
Y-YOU'VE GOT TO STOP HIM!
IF YOU DON'T, HE'LL KILL US ALL!
PLEASE LET ME OUT! LET ME GO!
IF YOU DON'T, HE'LL KILL ME!
I HELPED YOU OUT! *LET ME GO!*
HA! WHAT A LIE! YOU'LL SAY *ANYTHING* TO GET OUT!

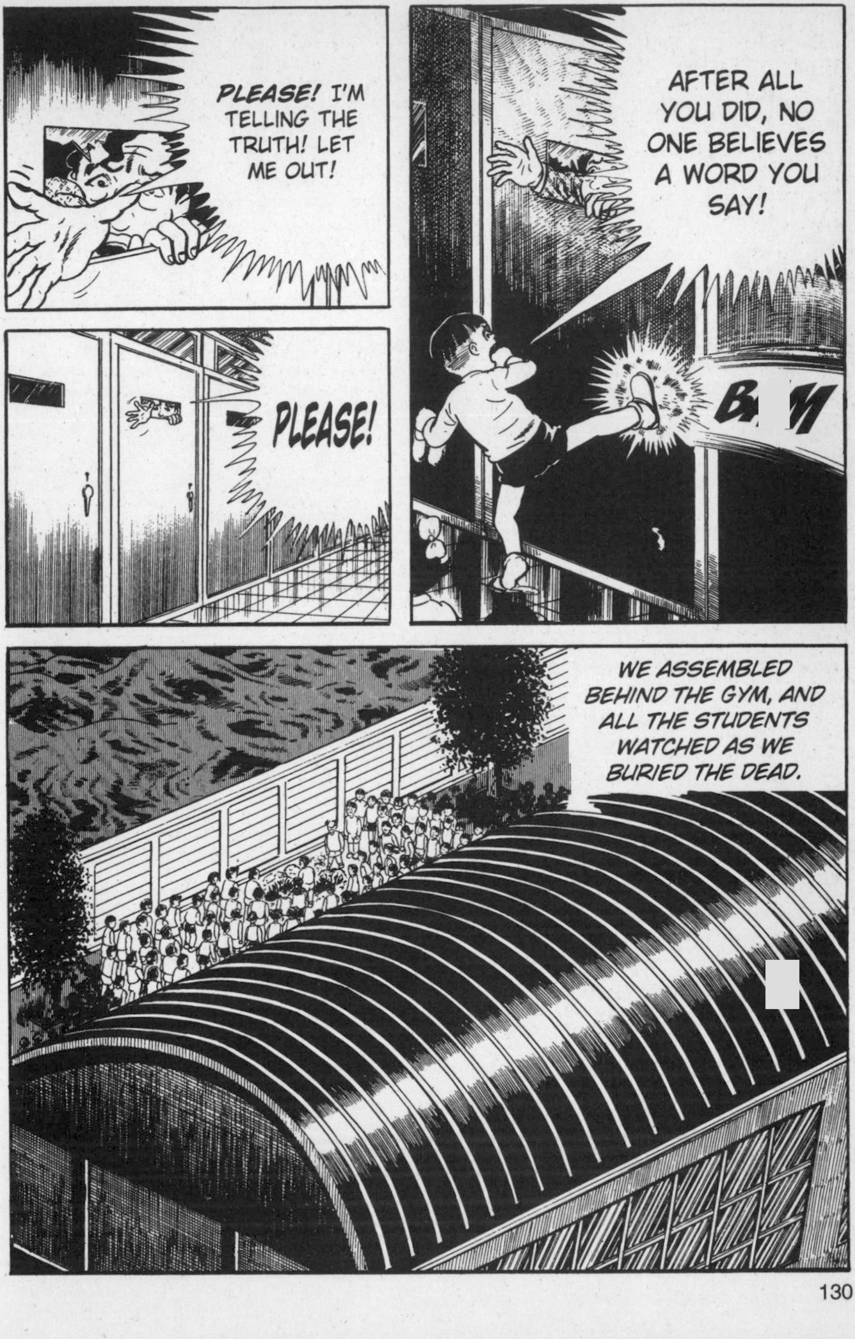
AFTER ALL YOU DID, NO ONE BELIEVES A WORD YOU SAY!
PLEASE! I'M TELLING THE TRUTH! LET ME OUT!
PLEASE!
WE ASSEMBLED BEHIND THE GYM, AND ALL THE STUDENTS WATCHED AS WE BURIED THE DEAD.

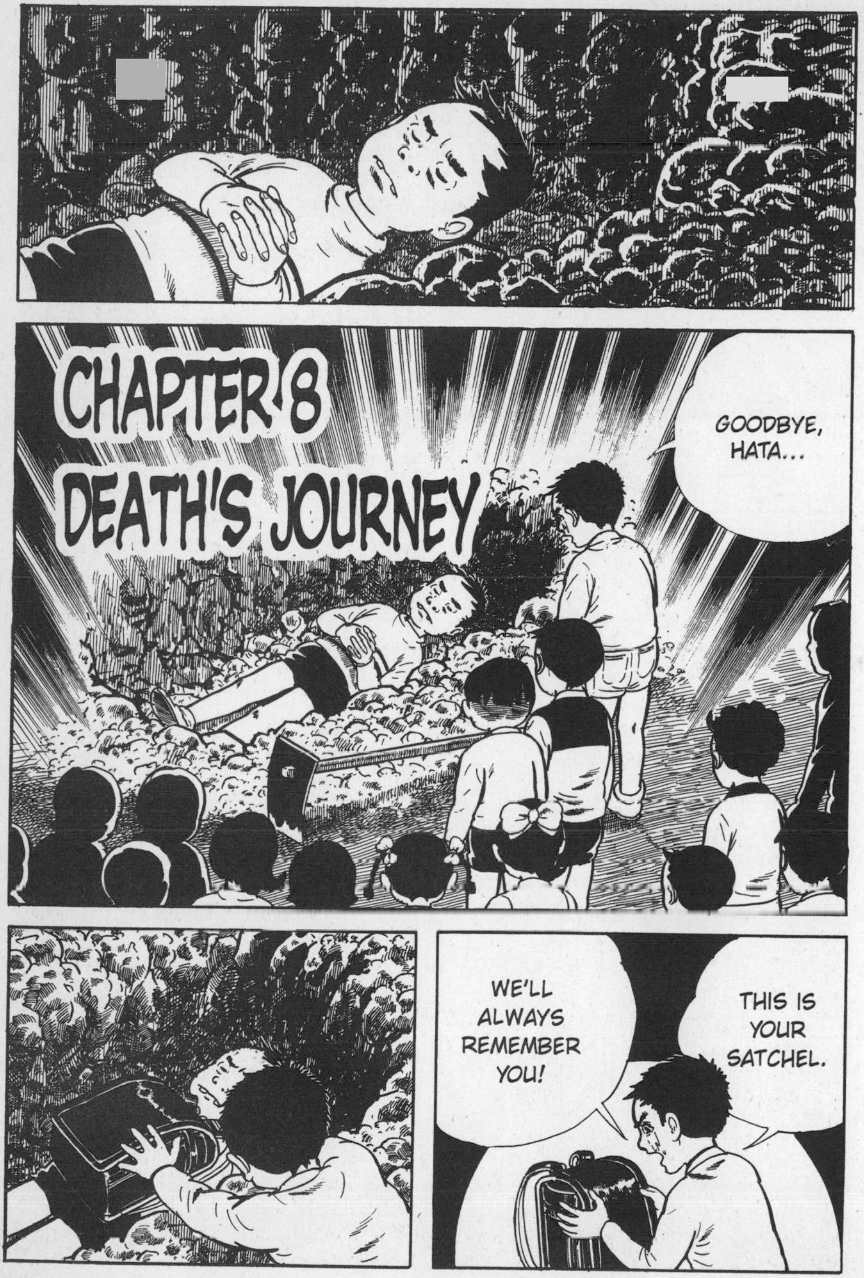
CHAPTER 8
DEATH'S JOURNEY
GOODBYE, HATA...
THIS IS YOUR SATCHEL.
WE'LL ALWAYS REMEMBER YOU!

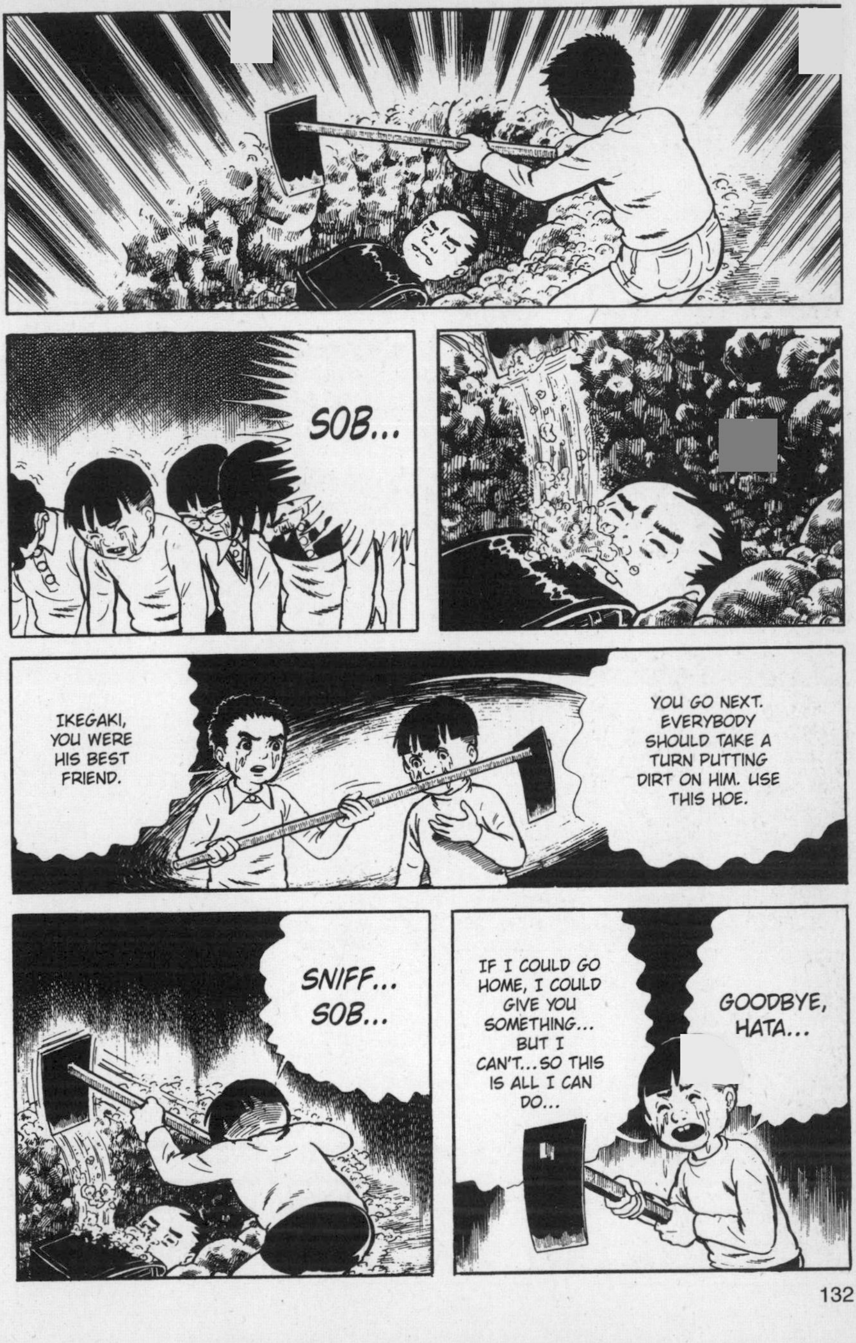
SOB...
YOU GO NEXT. EVERYBODY SHOULD TAKE A TURN PUTTING DIRT ON HIM. USE THIS HOE.
IKEGAKI, YOU WERE HIS BEST FRIEND.
GOODBYE, HATA...
IF I COULD GO HOME, I COULD GIVE YOU SOMETHING... BUT I CAN'T...SO THIS IS ALL I CAN DO...
SNIFF... SOB...

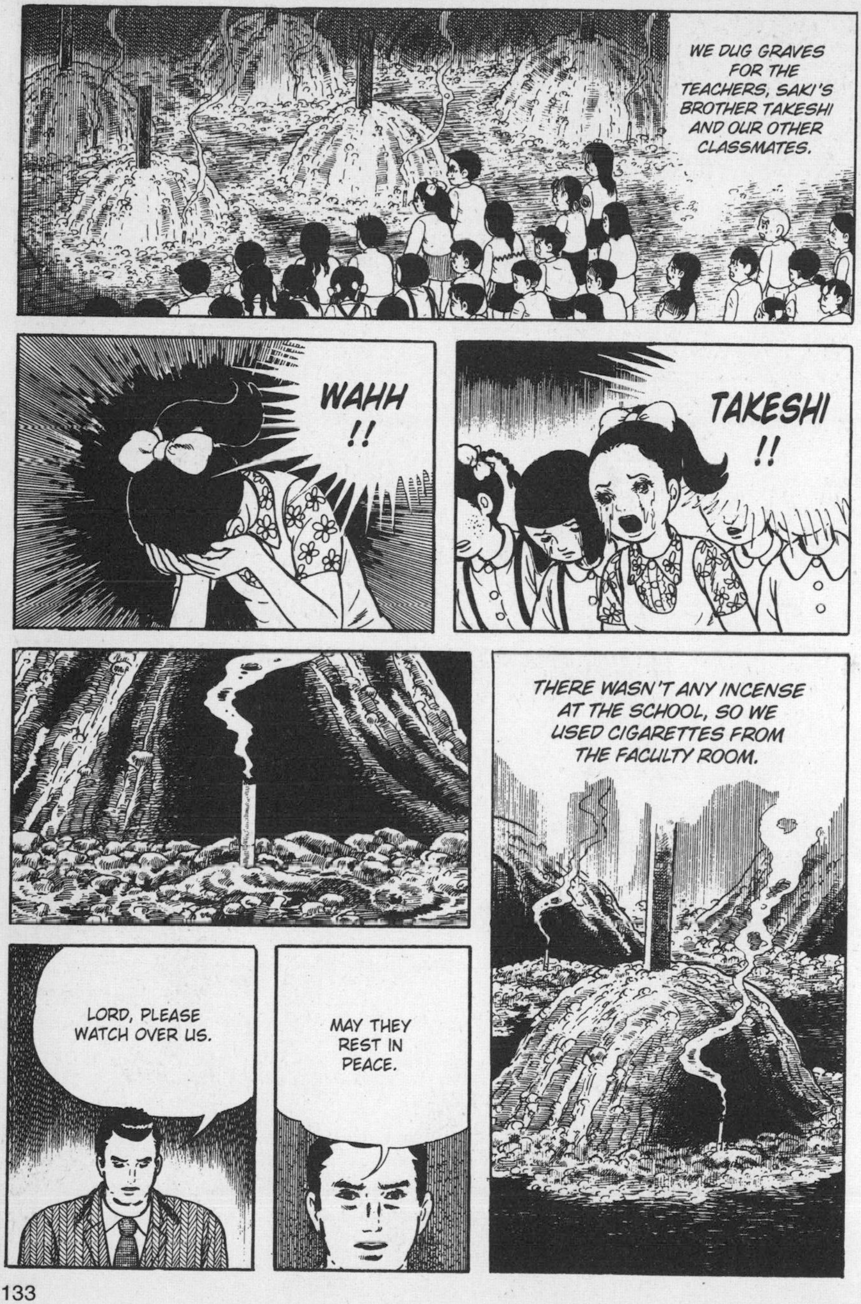
WE DUG GRAVES FOR THE TEACHERS, SAKI'S BROTHER TAKESHI AND OUR OTHER CLASSMATES.
TAKESHI !!
WAHH !!
THERE WASN'T ANY INCENSE AT THE SCHOOL, SO WE USED CIGARETTES FROM THE FACULTY ROOM.
MAY THEY REST IN PEACE.
LORD, PLEASE WATCH OVER US.

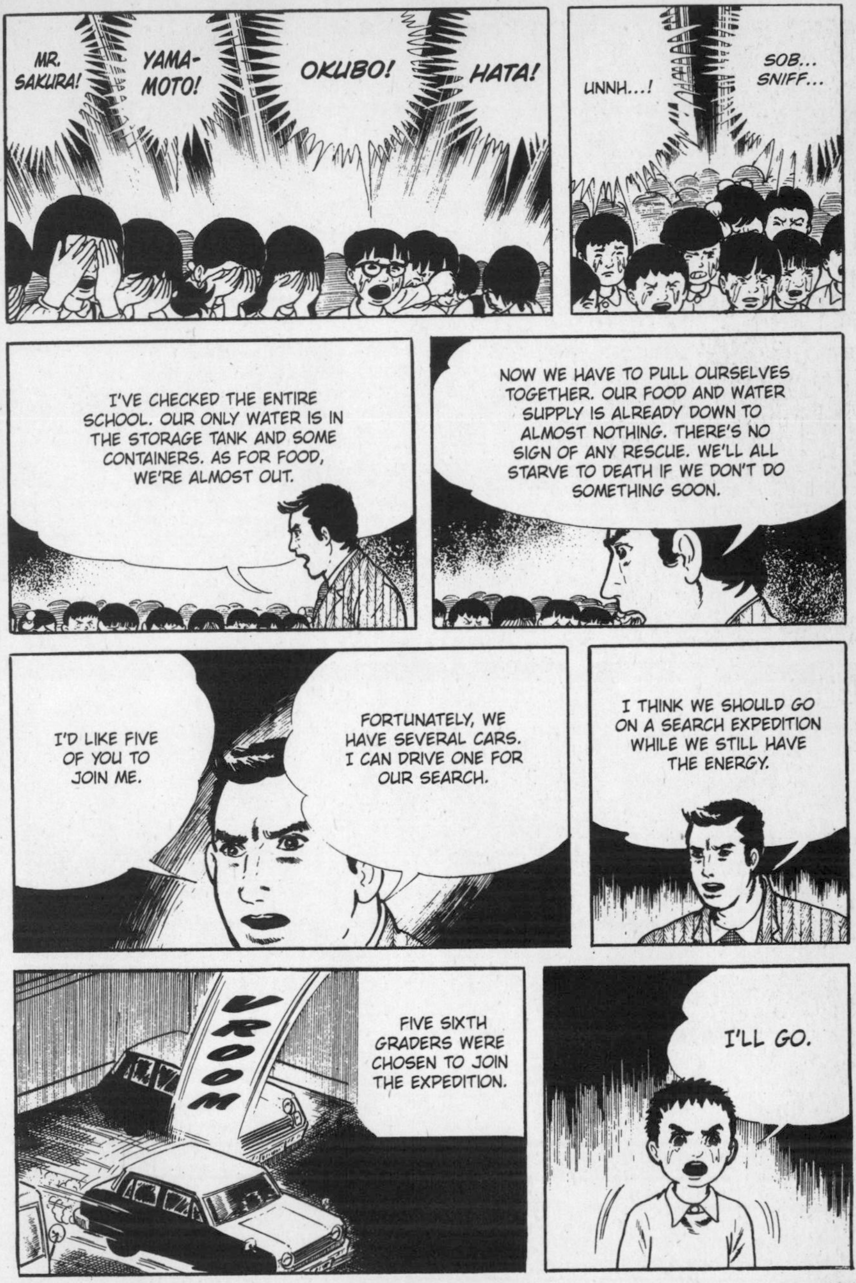
SOB... SNIFF...
UNNH...!
HATA!
OKUBO!
YAMA-MOTO!
MR. SAKURA!
NOW WE HAVE TO PULL OURSELVES TOGETHER. OUR FOOD AND WATER SUPPLY IS ALREADY DOWN TO ALMOST NOTHING. THERE'S NO SIGN OF ANY RESCUE. WE'LL ALL STARVE TO DEATH IF WE DON'T DO SOMETHING SOON.
I'VE CHECKED THE ENTIRE SCHOOL. OUR ONLY WATER IS IN THE STORAGE TANK AND SOME CONTAINERS. AS FOR FOOD, WE'RE ALMOST OUT.
I THINK WE SHOULD GO ON A SEARCH EXPEDITION WHILE WE STILL HAVE THE ENERGY.
FORTUNATELY, WE HAVE SEVERAL CARS. I CAN DRIVE ONE FOR OUR SEARCH.
I'D LIKE FIVE OF YOU TO JOIN ME.
I'LL GO.
FIVE SIXTH GRADERS WERE CHOSEN TO JOIN THE EXPEDITION.
VROOOM

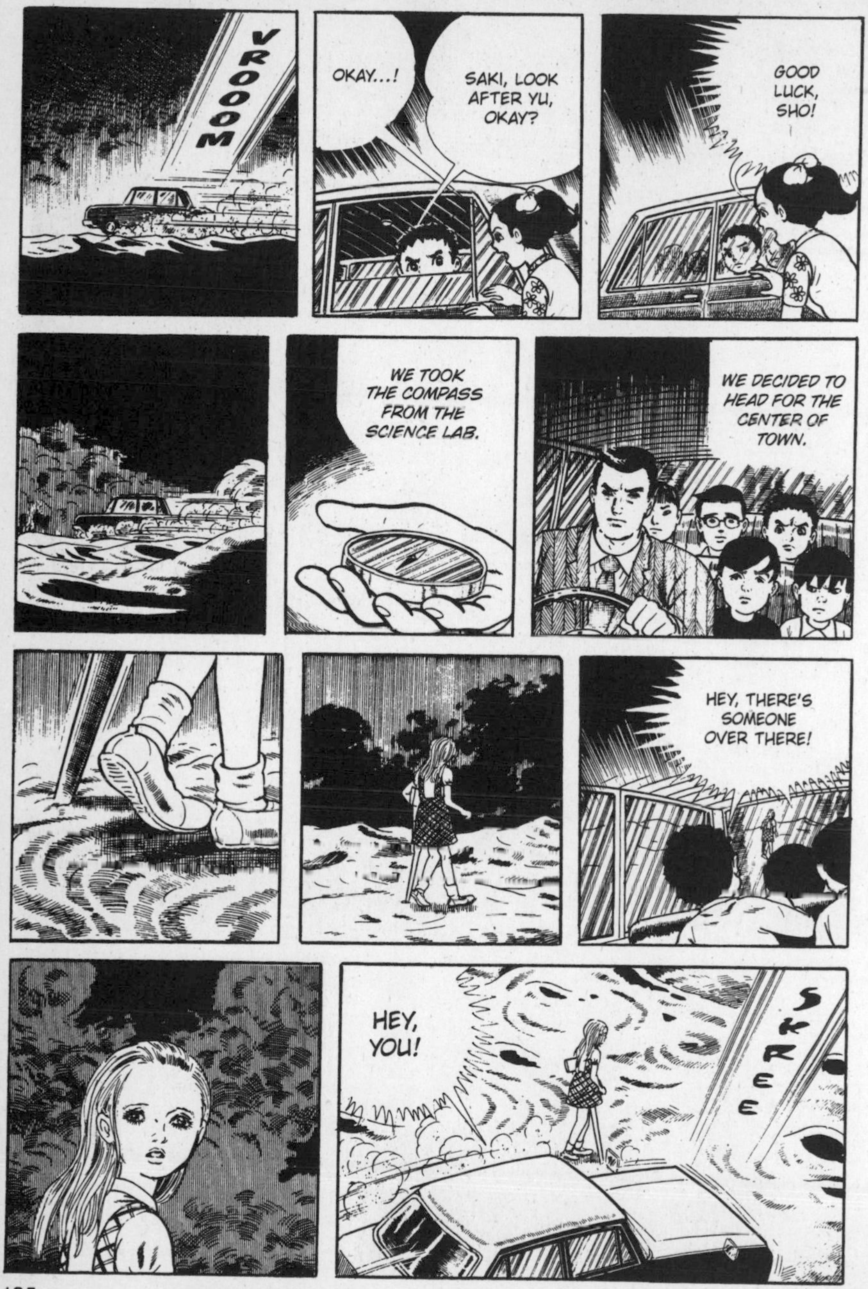
GOOD LUCK, SHO!
SAKI, LOOK AFTER YU, OKAY?
OKAY...!
VROOOM
WE DECIDED TO HEAD FOR THE CENTER OF TOWN.
WE TOOK THE COMPASS FROM THE SCIENCE LAB.
HEY, THERE'S SOMEONE OVER THERE!
SKREE
HEY, YOU!

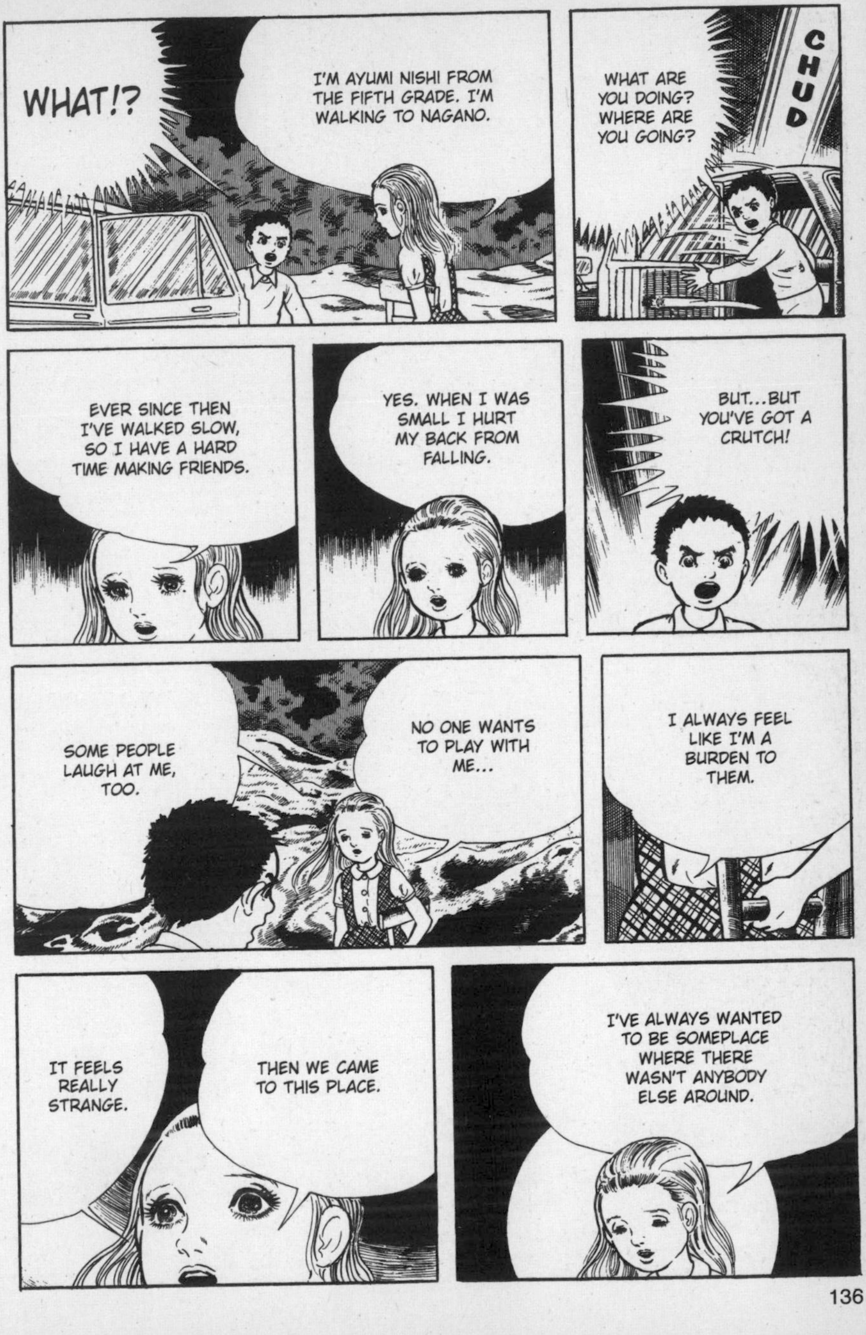
CHUD
WHAT ARE YOU DOING? WHERE ARE YOU GOING?
I'M AYUMI NISHI FROM THE FIFTH GRADE. I'M WALKING TO NAGANO.
WHAT!?
BUT...BUT YOU'VE GOT A CRUTCH!
YES. WHEN I WAS SMALL I HURT MY BACK FROM FALLING.
EVER SINCE THEN I'VE WALKED SLOW, SO I HAVE A HARD TIME MAKING FRIENDS.
I ALWAYS FEEL LIKE I'M A BURDEN TO THEM.
NO ONE WANTS TO PLAY WITH ME...
SOME PEOPLE LAUGH AT ME, TOO.
I'VE ALWAYS WANTED TO BE SOMEPLACE WHERE THERE WASN'T ANYBODY ELSE AROUND.
THEN WE CAME TO THIS PLACE.
IT FEELS REALLY STRANGE.

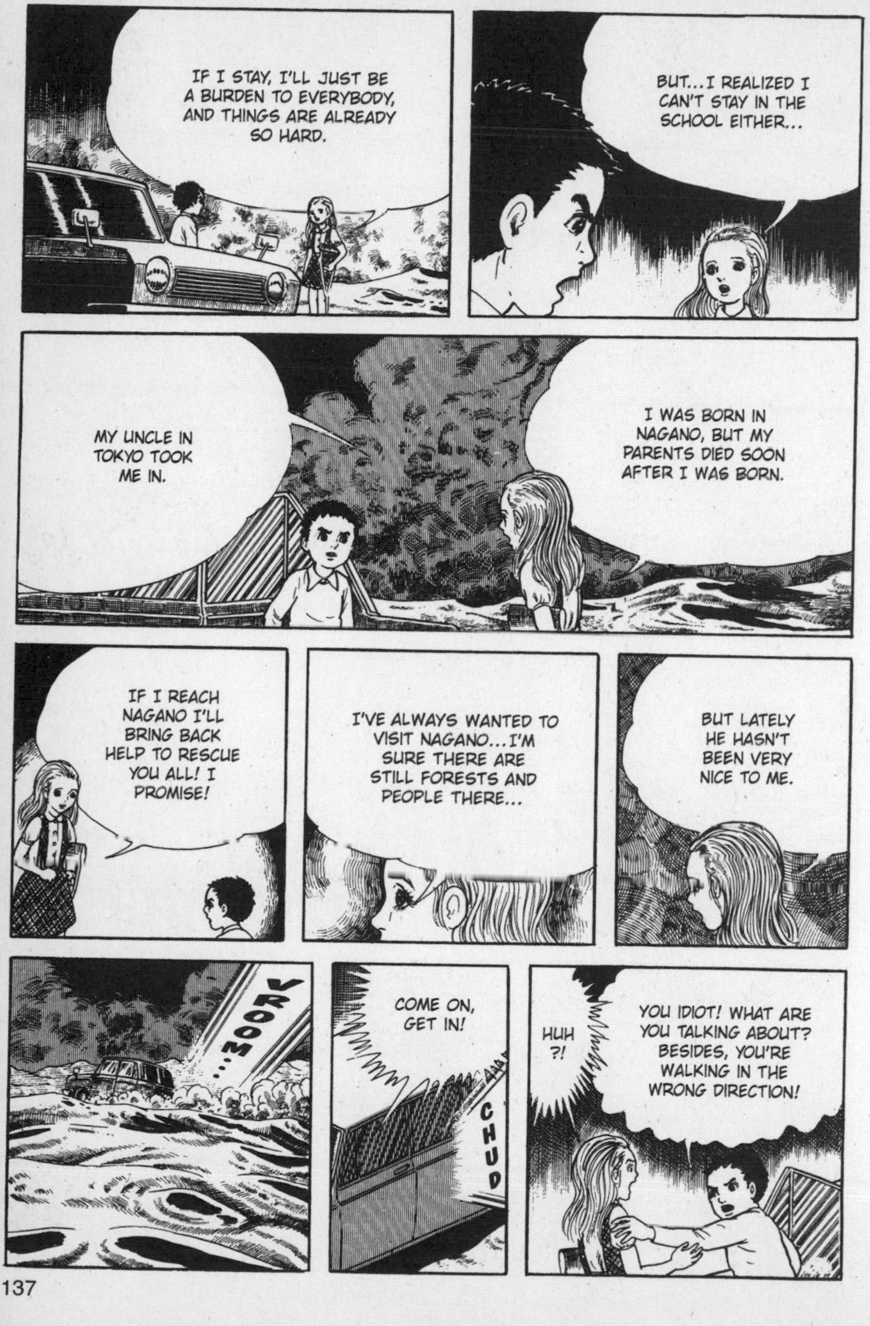
BUT...I REALIZED I CAN'T STAY IN THE SCHOOL EITHER...
IF I STAY, I'LL JUST BE A BURDEN TO EVERYBODY, AND THINGS ARE ALREADY SO HARD.
I WAS BORN IN NAGANO, BUT MY PARENTS DIED SOON AFTER I WAS BORN.
MY UNCLE IN TOKYO TOOK ME IN.
BUT LATELY HE HASN'T BEEN VERY NICE TO ME.
I'VE ALWAYS WANTED TO VISIT NAGANO...I'M SURE THERE ARE STILL FORESTS AND PEOPLE THERE...
IF I REACH NAGANO I'LL BRING BACK HELP TO RESCUE YOU ALL! I PROMISE!
YOU IDIOT! WHAT ARE YOU TALKING ABOUT? BESIDES, YOU'RE WALKING IN THE WRONG DIRECTION!
HUH ?!
COME ON, GET IN!
CHUD
VROOOM...

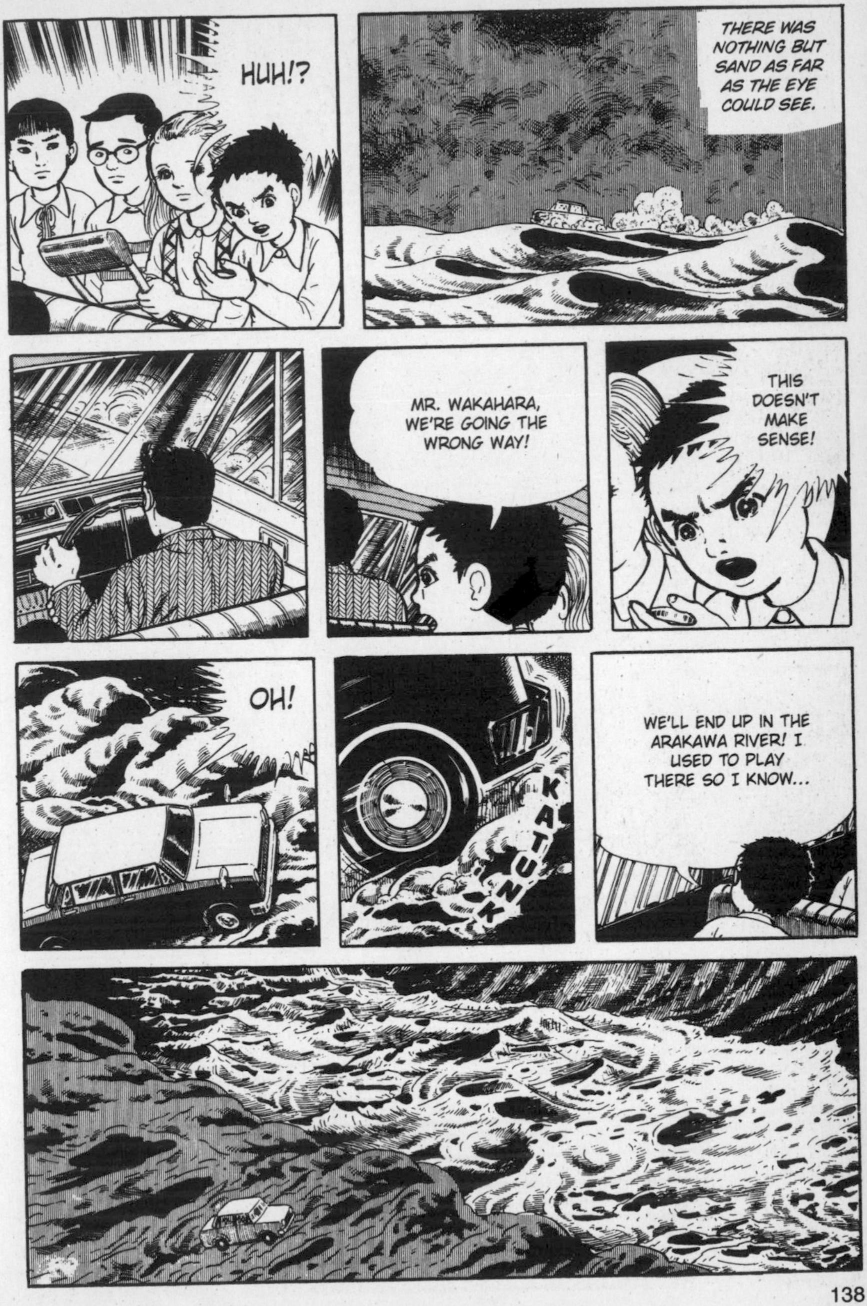
THERE WAS NOTHING BUT SAND AS FAR AS THE EYE COULD SEE.
HUH!?
THIS DOESN'T MAKE SENSE!
MR. WAKAHARA, WE'RE GOING THE WRONG WAY!
WE'LL END UP IN THE ARAKAWA RIVER! I USED TO PLAY THERE SO I KNOW...
KATUNK
OH!

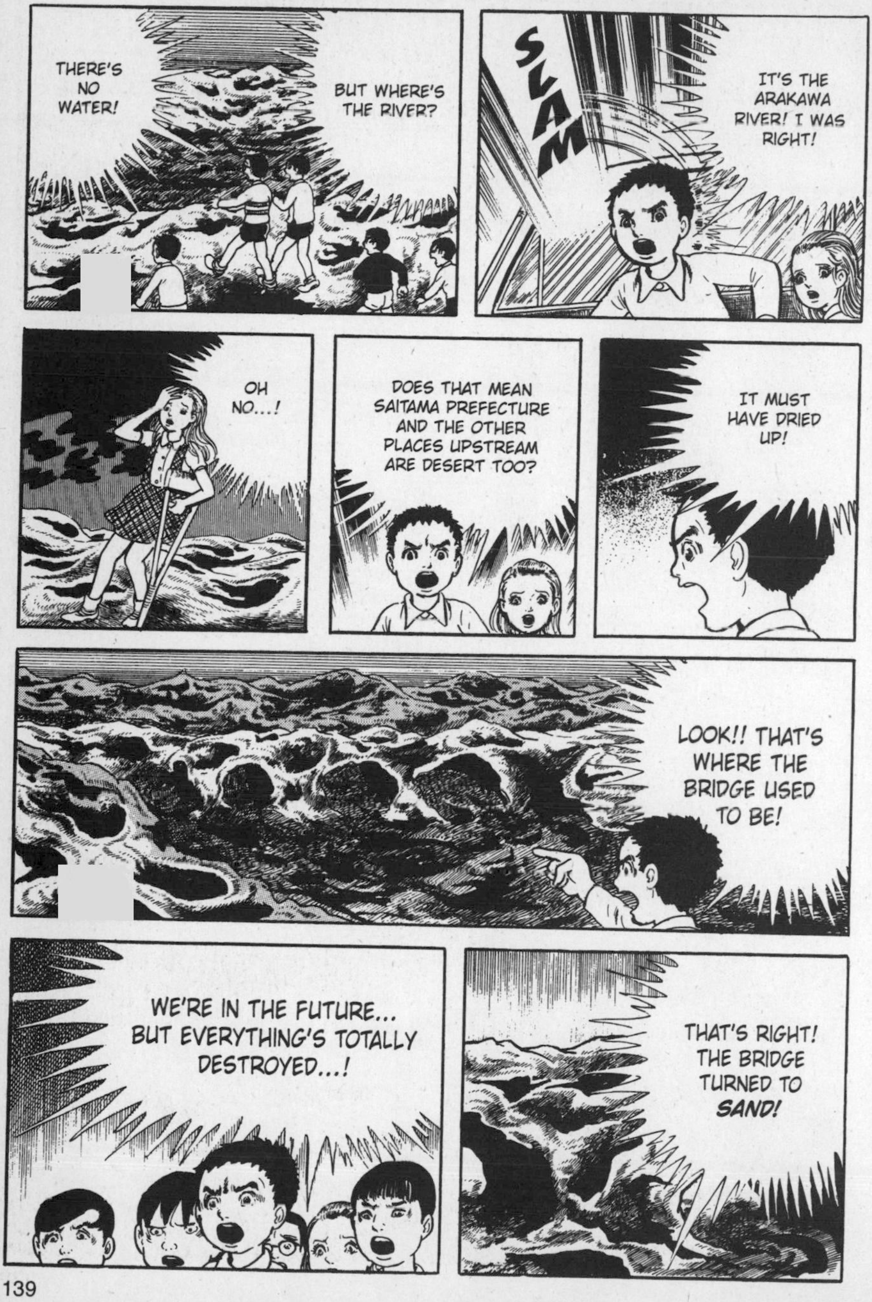
SLAM
IT'S THE ARAKAWA RIVER! I WAS RIGHT!
BUT WHERE'S THE RIVER?
THERE'S NO WATER!
IT MUST HAVE DRIED UP!
DOES THAT MEAN SAITAMA PREFECTURE AND THE OTHER PLACES UPSTREAM ARE DESERT TOO?
OH NO...!
LOOK!! THAT'S WHERE THE BRIDGE USED TO BE!
THAT'S RIGHT! THE BRIDGE TURNED TO *SAND!*
WE'RE IN THE FUTURE... BUT EVERYTHING'S TOTALLY DESTROYED...!

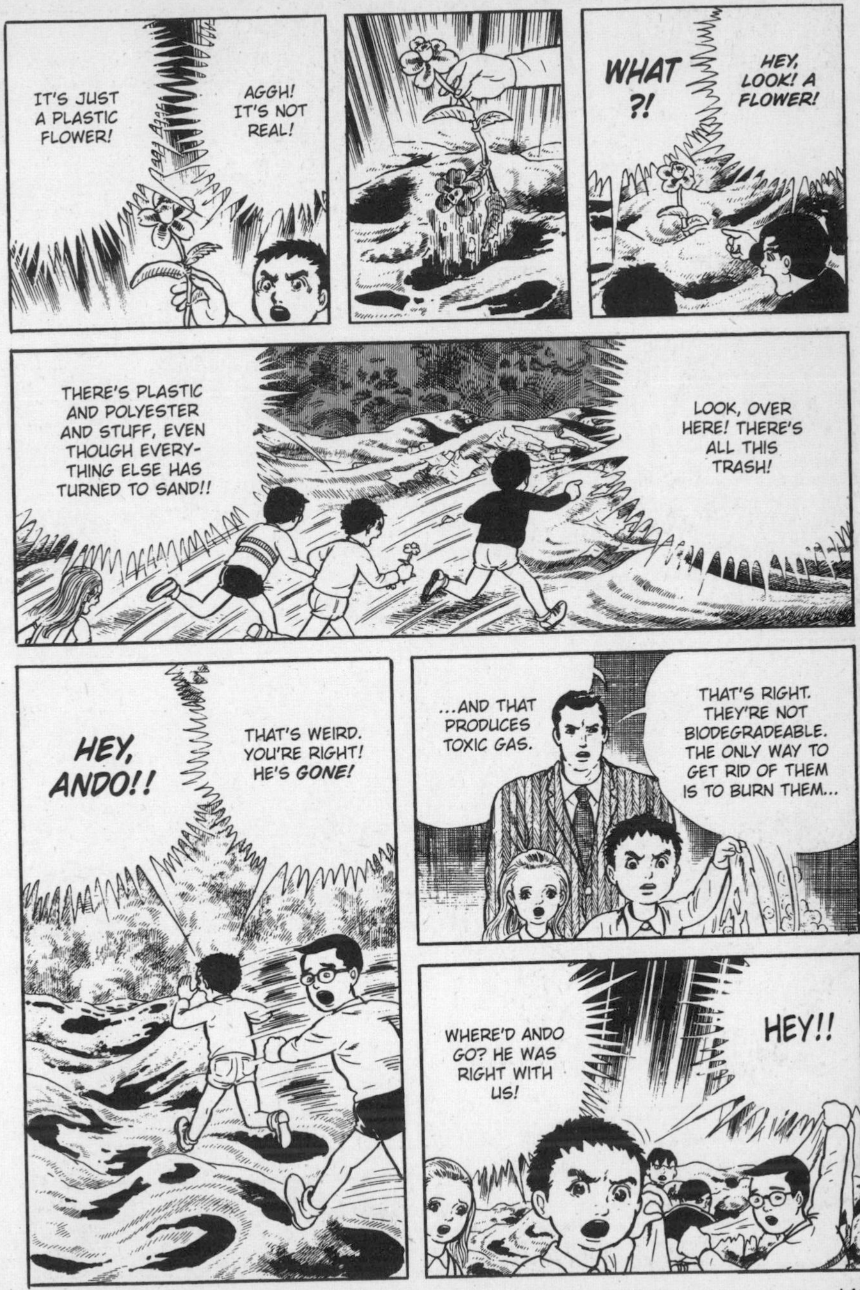
HEY, LOOK! A FLOWER!
WHAT ?!
AGGH! IT'S NOT REAL!
IT'S JUST A PLASTIC FLOWER!
LOOK, OVER HERE! THERE'S ALL THIS TRASH!
THERE'S PLASTIC AND POLYESTER AND STUFF, EVEN THOUGH EVERY-THING ELSE HAS TURNED TO SAND!!
THAT'S RIGHT. THEY'RE NOT BIODEGRADEABLE. THE ONLY WAY TO GET RID OF THEM IS TO BURN THEM...
...AND THAT PRODUCES TOXIC GAS.
HEY!!
WHERE'D ANDO GO? HE WAS RIGHT WITH US!
THAT'S WEIRD. YOU'RE RIGHT! HE'S *GONE!*
HEY, ANDO!!

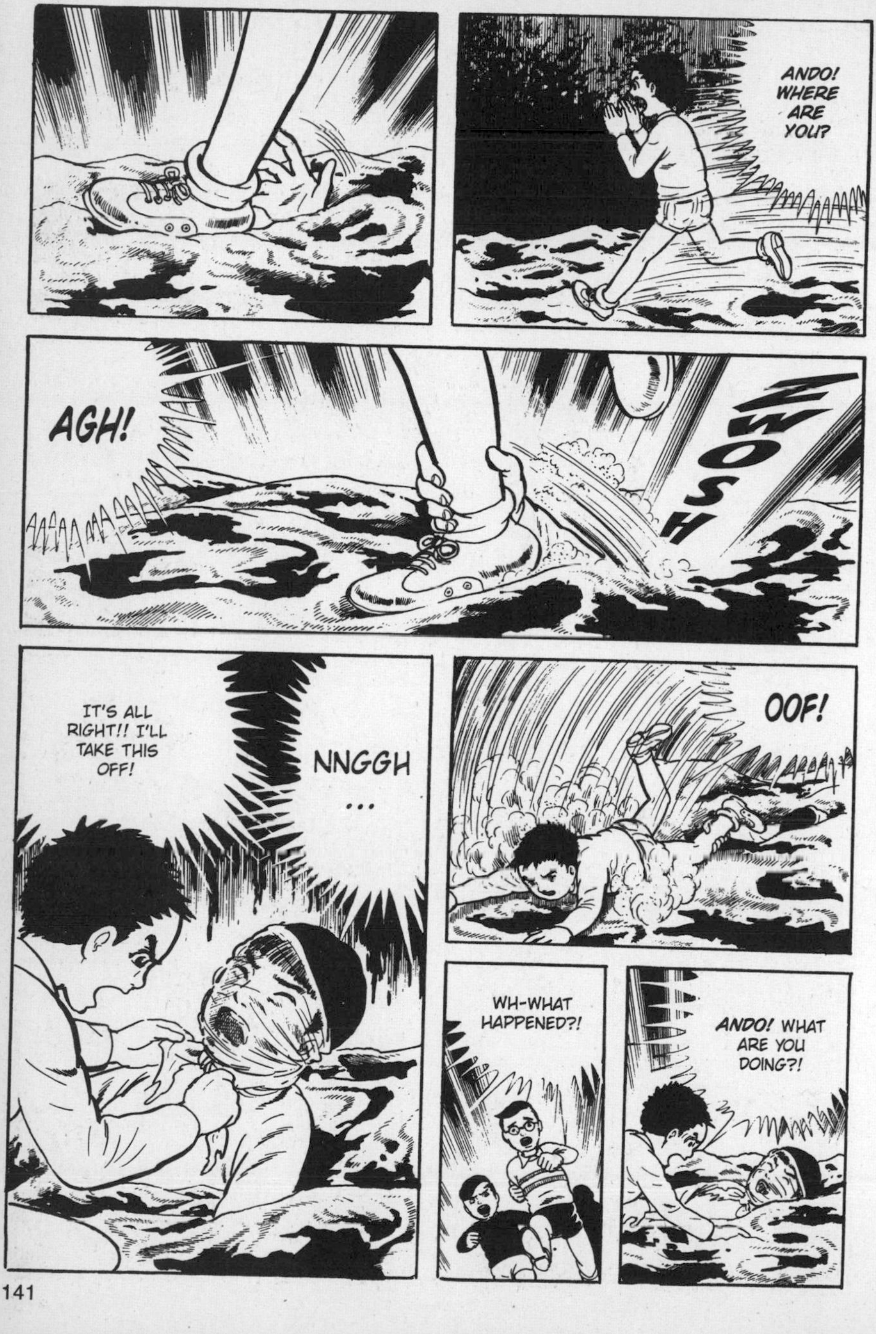
ANDO! WHERE ARE YOU?
WWOSH
AGH!
OOF!
ANDO! WHAT ARE YOU DOING?!
WH-WHAT HAPPENED?!
NNGGH ...
IT'S ALL RIGHT!! I'LL TAKE THIS OFF!

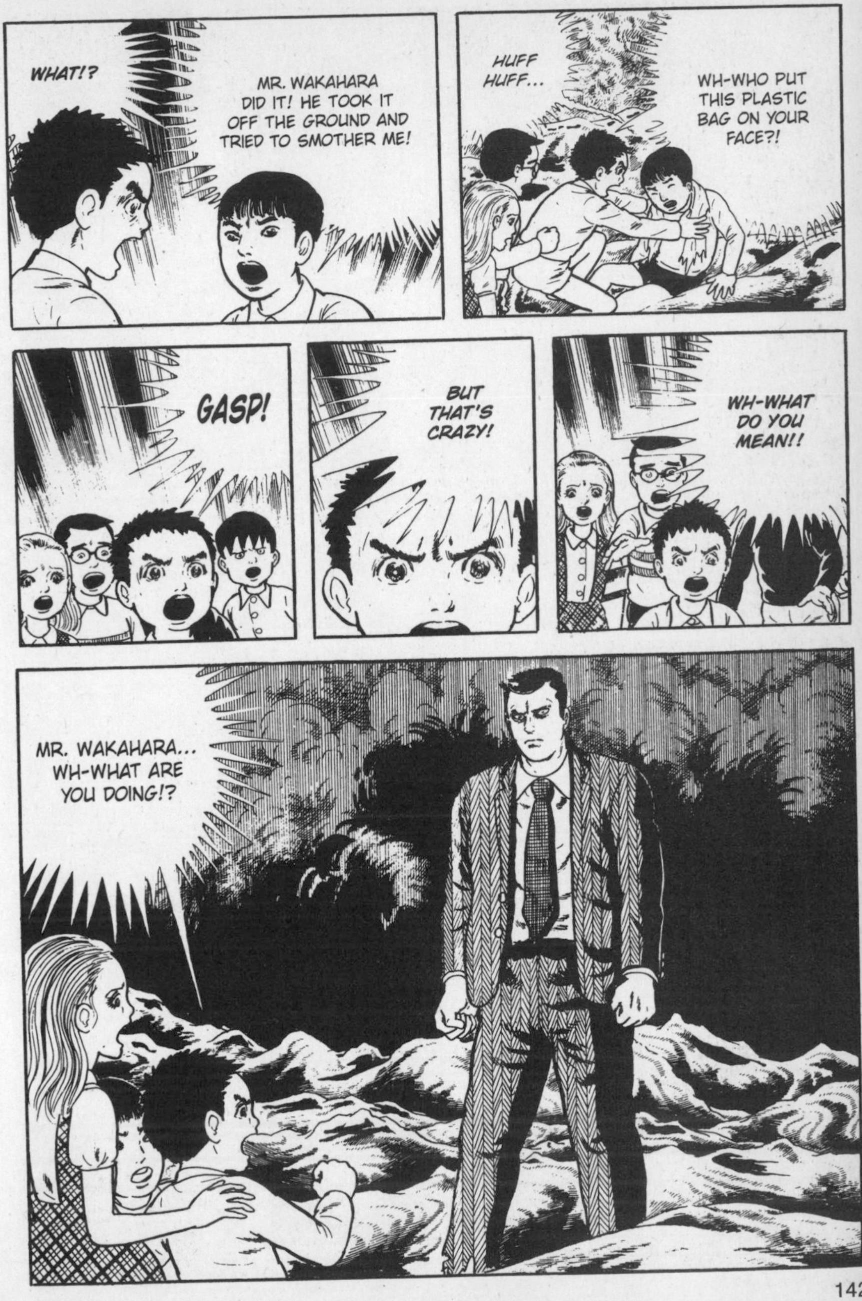
WH-WHO PUT THIS PLASTIC BAG ON YOUR FACE?!
HUFF HUFF...
MR. WAKAHARA DID IT! HE TOOK IT OFF THE GROUND AND TRIED TO SMOTHER ME!
WHAT!?
WH-WHAT DO YOU MEAN!!
BUT THAT'S CRAZY!
GASP!
MR. WAKAHARA... WH-WHAT ARE YOU DOING!?

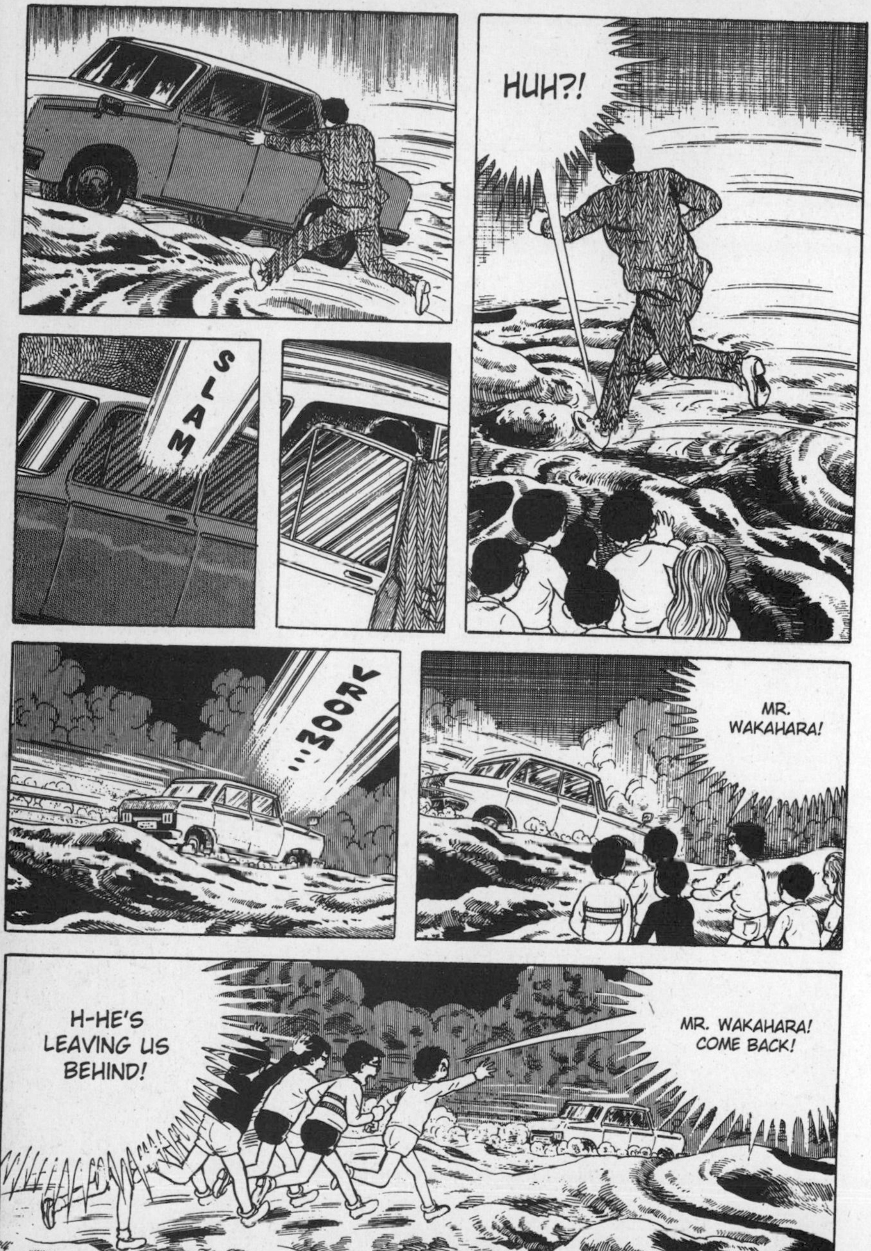
HUH?!
SLAM
MR. WAKAHARA!
VROOM...
MR. WAKAHARA! COME BACK!
H-HE'S LEAVING US BEHIND!

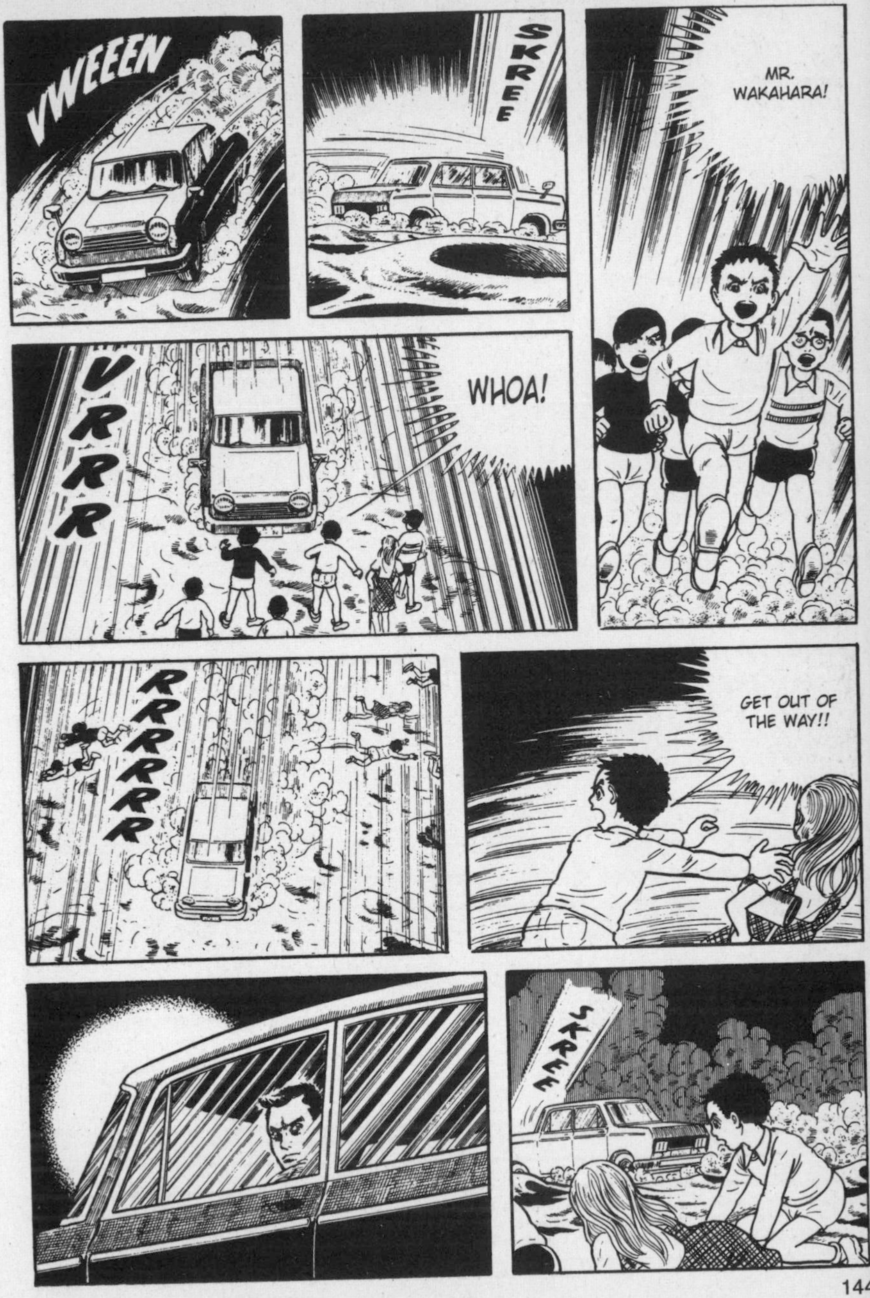
MR. WAKAHARA!
SKREE
VWEEEN
WHOA!
VRRRR
GET OUT OF THE WAY!!
RRRRRRR
SKREE

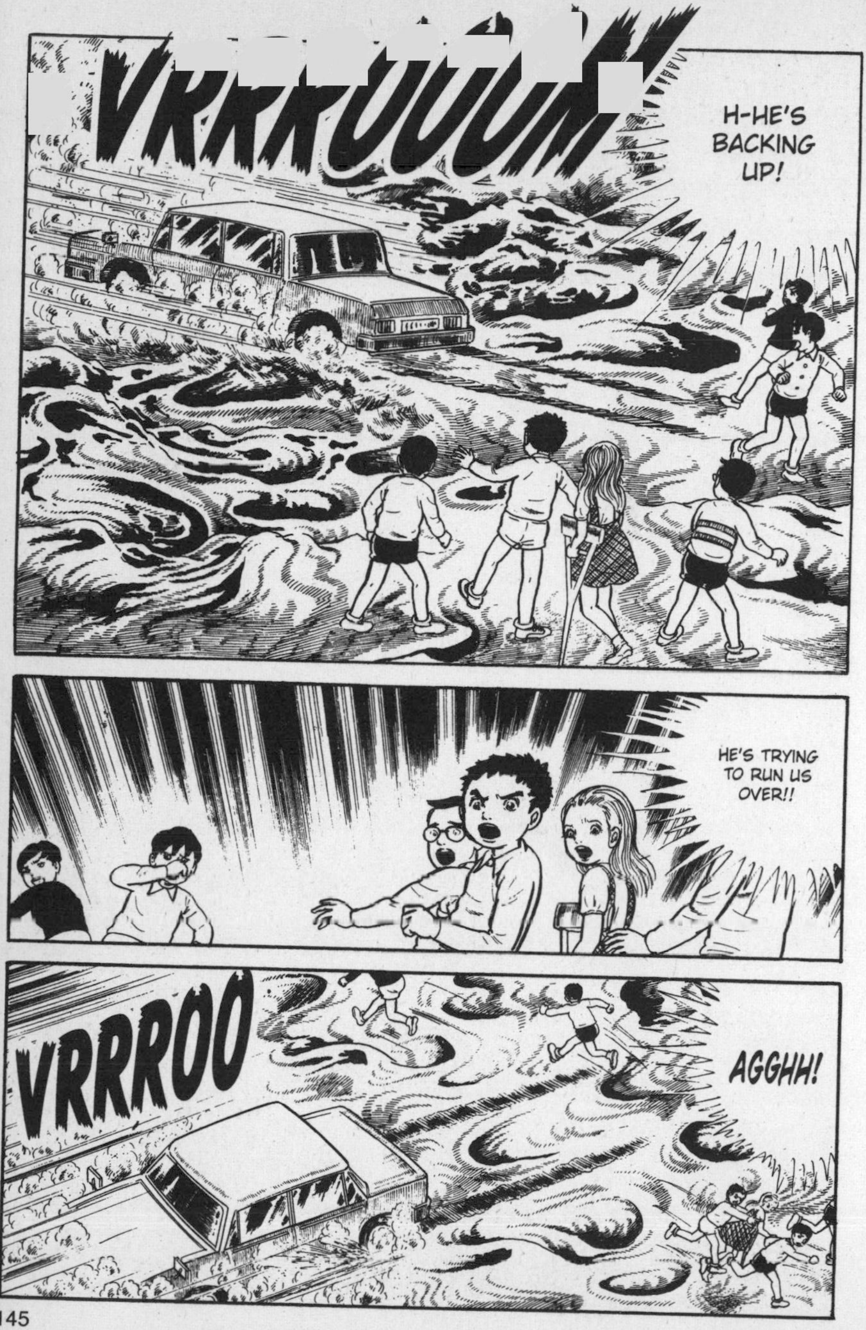
VRRROOOM!
H-HE'S BACKING UP!
HE'S TRYING TO RUN US OVER!!
AGGHH!
VRRROO

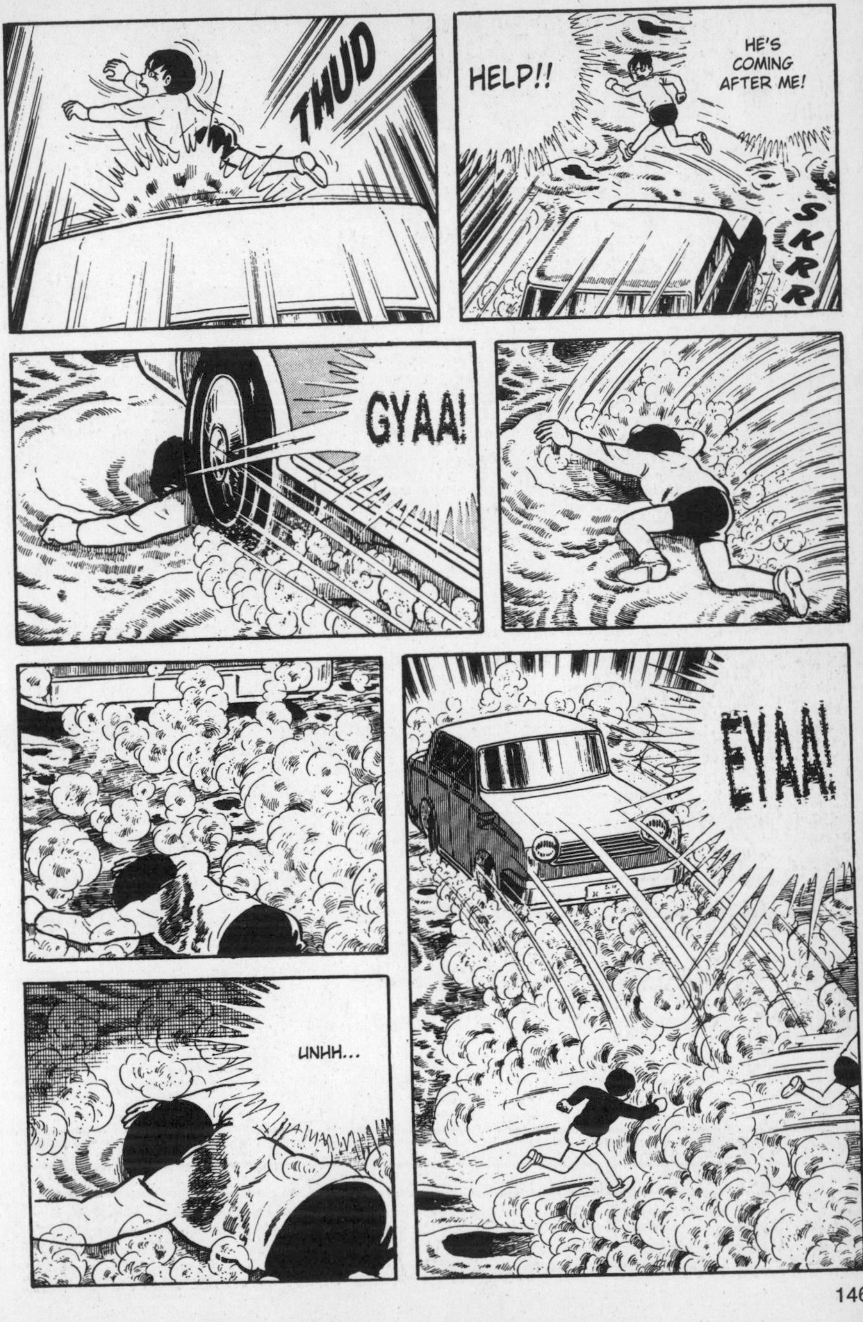
HE'S COMING AFTER ME!
HELP!!
SKRR
THUD
GYAA!
EYAA!
UNHH...

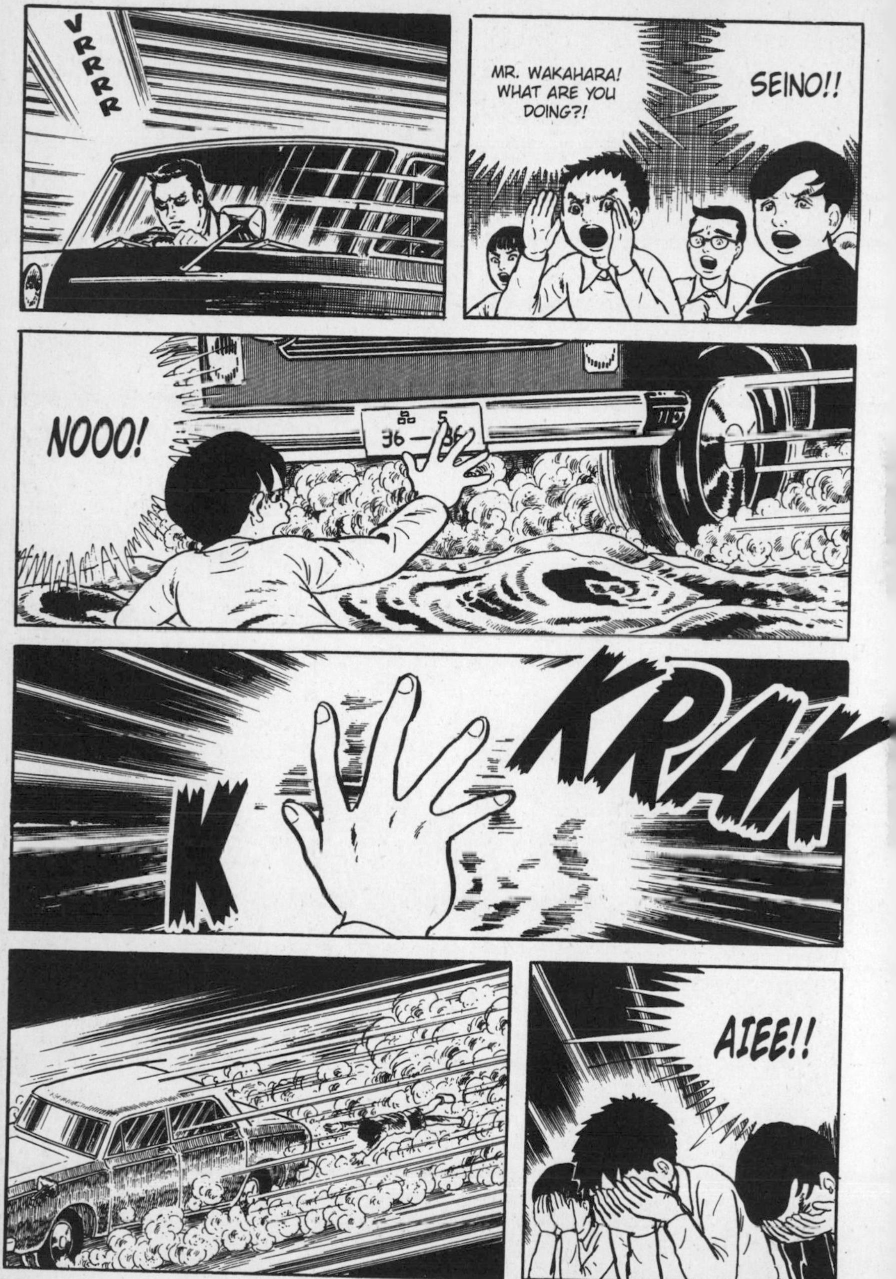
SEINO!!
MR. WAKAHARA! WHAT ARE YOU DOING?!
VRRRR
NOOO!
KRAK
K
AIEE!!

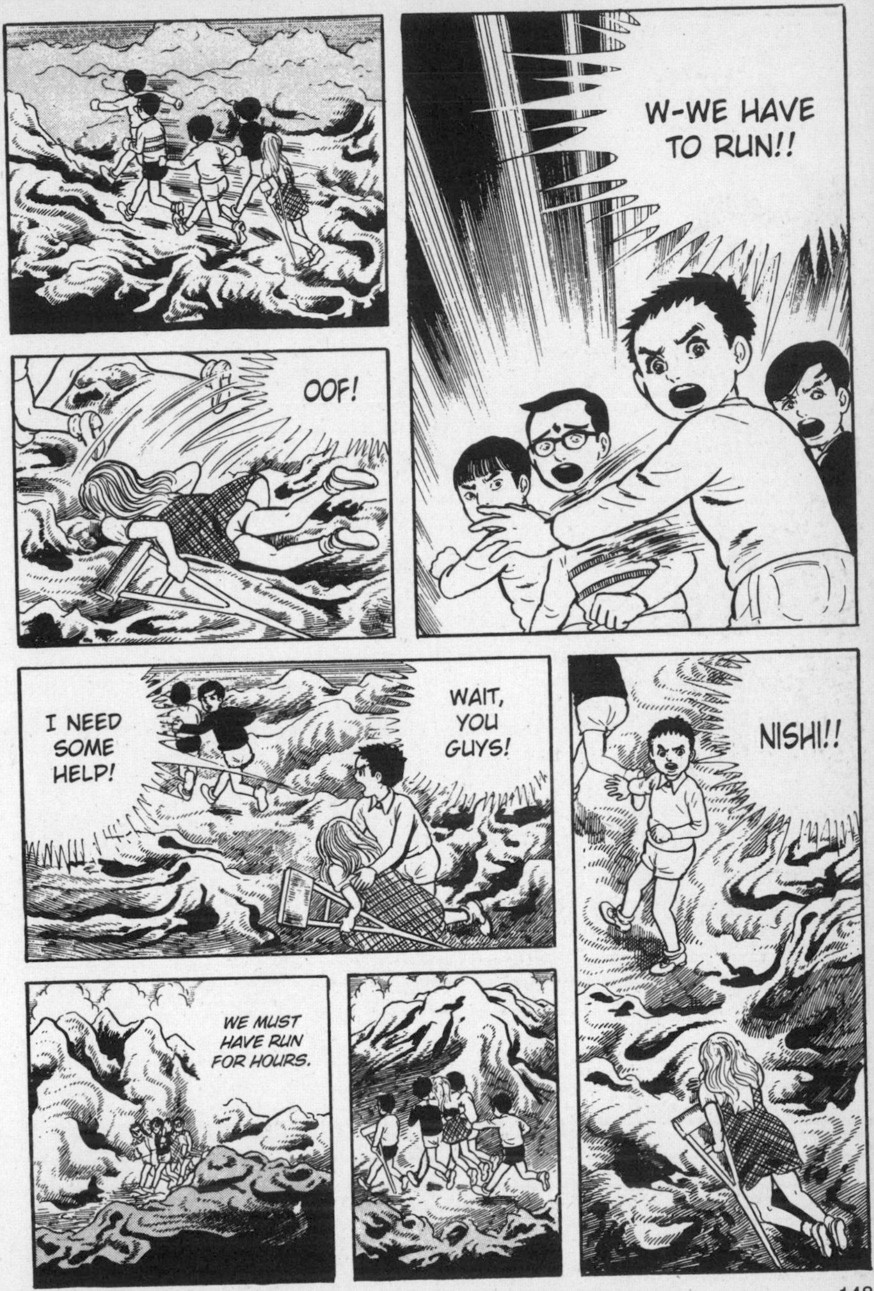
W-WE HAVE TO RUN!!
OOF!
NISHI!!
WAIT, YOU GUYS!
I NEED SOME HELP!
WE MUST HAVE RUN FOR HOURS.

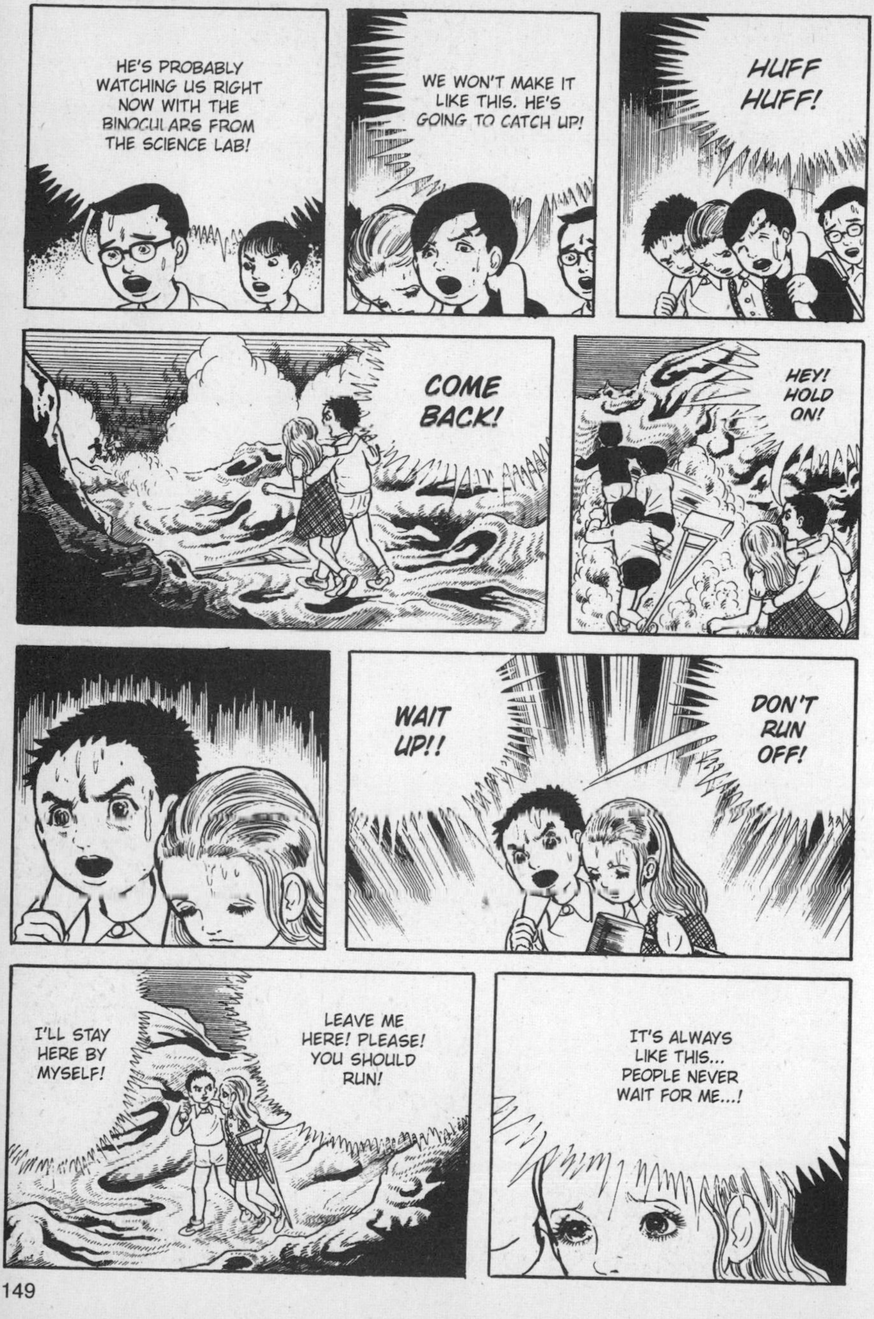
HUFF HUFF!
WE WON'T MAKE IT LIKE THIS. HE'S GOING TO CATCH UP!
HE'S PROBABLY WATCHING US RIGHT NOW WITH THE BINOCULARS FROM THE SCIENCE LAB!
HEY! HOLD ON!
COME BACK!
DON'T RUN OFF!
WAIT UP!!
IT'S ALWAYS LIKE THIS... PEOPLE NEVER WAIT FOR ME...!
LEAVE ME HERE! PLEASE! YOU SHOULD RUN!
I'LL STAY HERE BY MYSELF!

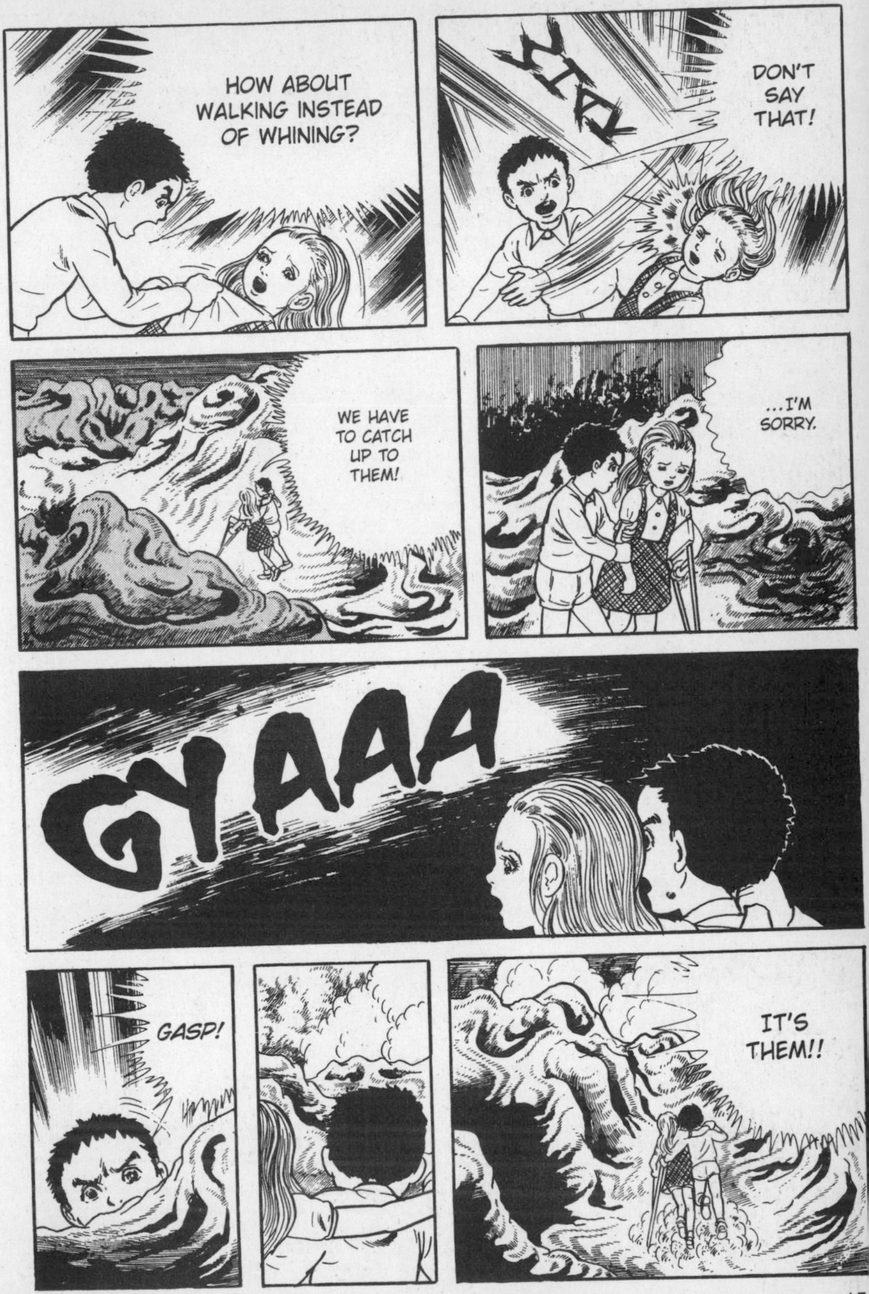
DON'T SAY THAT!
HOW ABOUT WALKING INSTEAD OF WHINING?
...I'M SORRY.
WE HAVE TO CATCH UP TO THEM!
GYAAA
IT'S THEM!!
GASP!

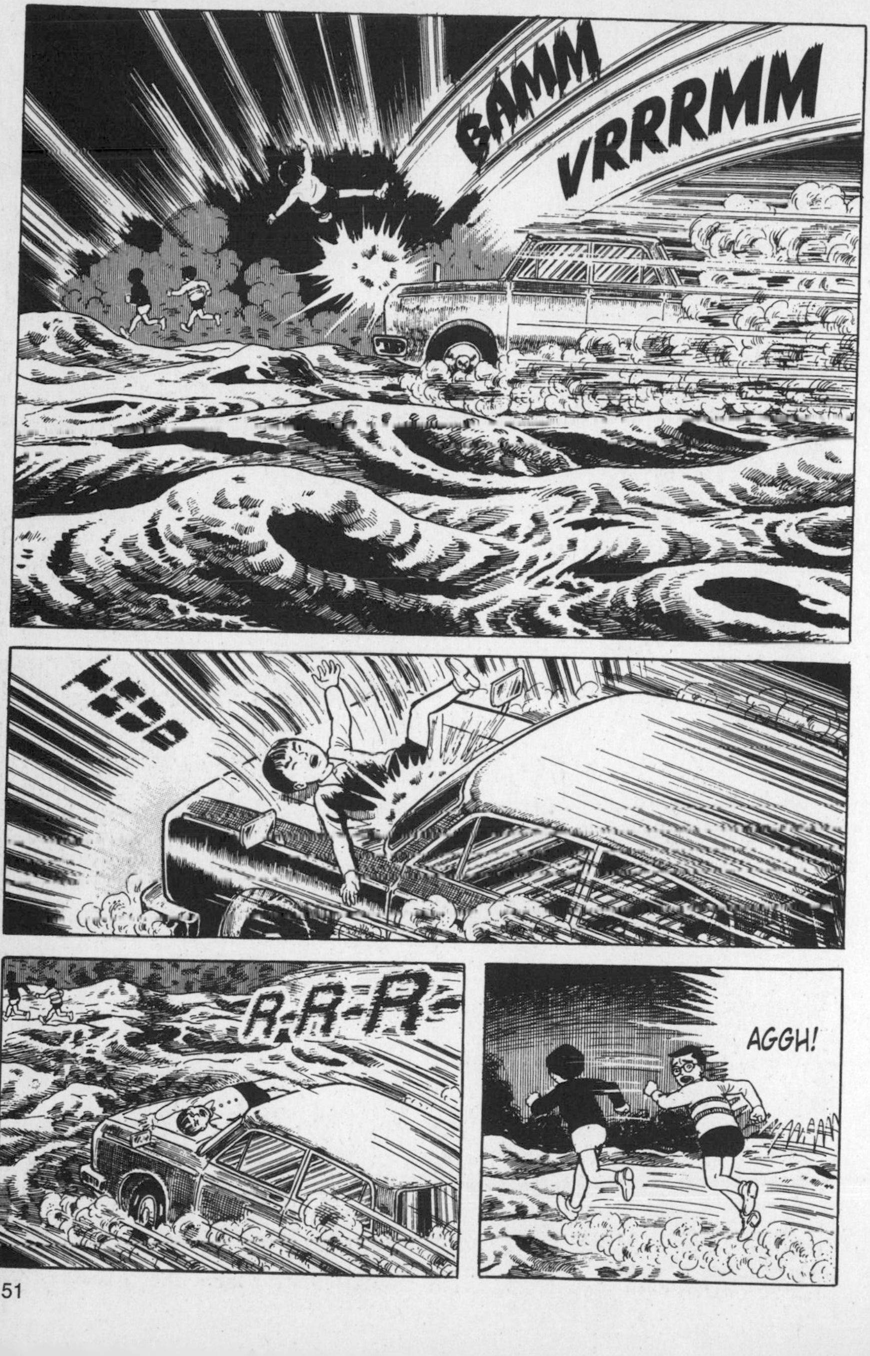
BAMM
VRRRMM
THUD
AGGH!
R-R-R

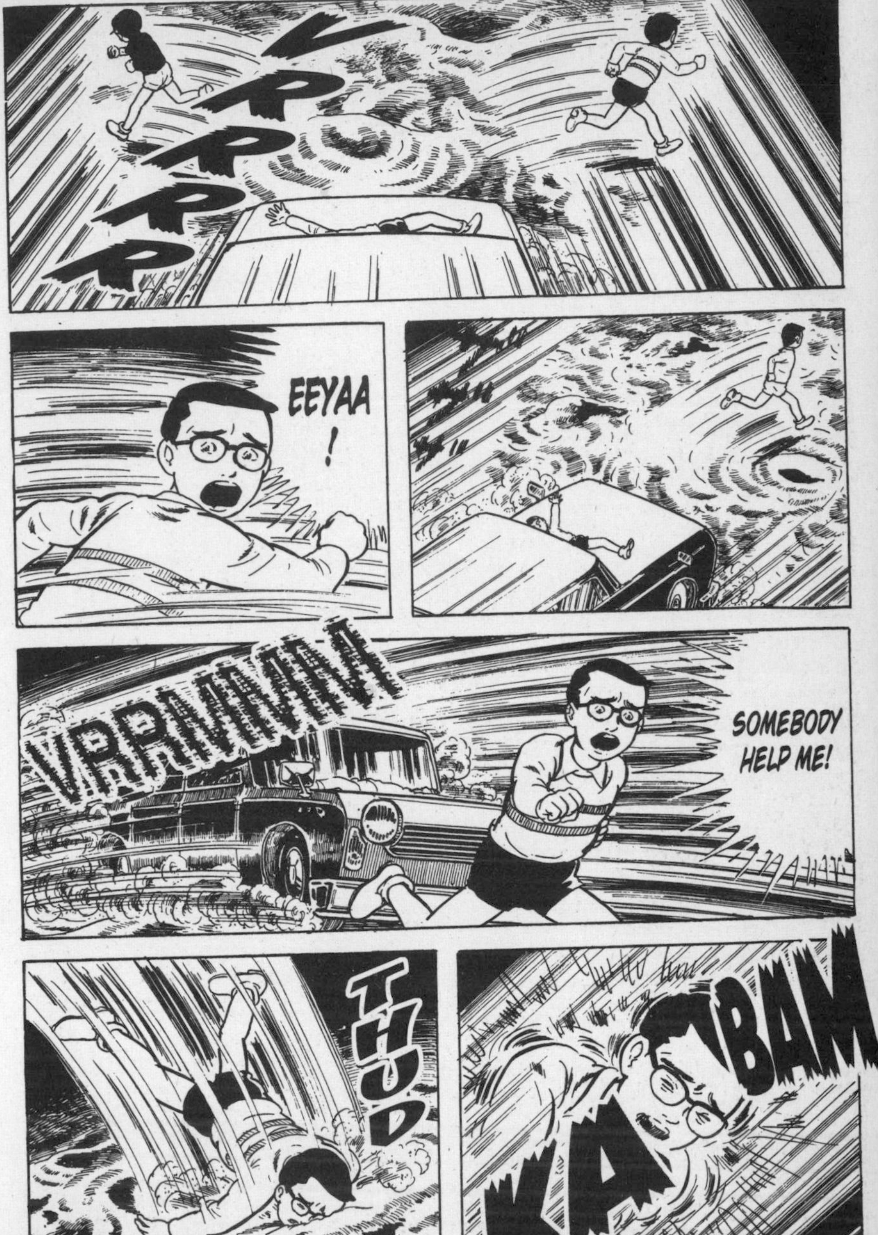
VRRRR
EEYAA !
SOMEBODY HELP ME!
VRRMMMMM
KA-BAM
THUD

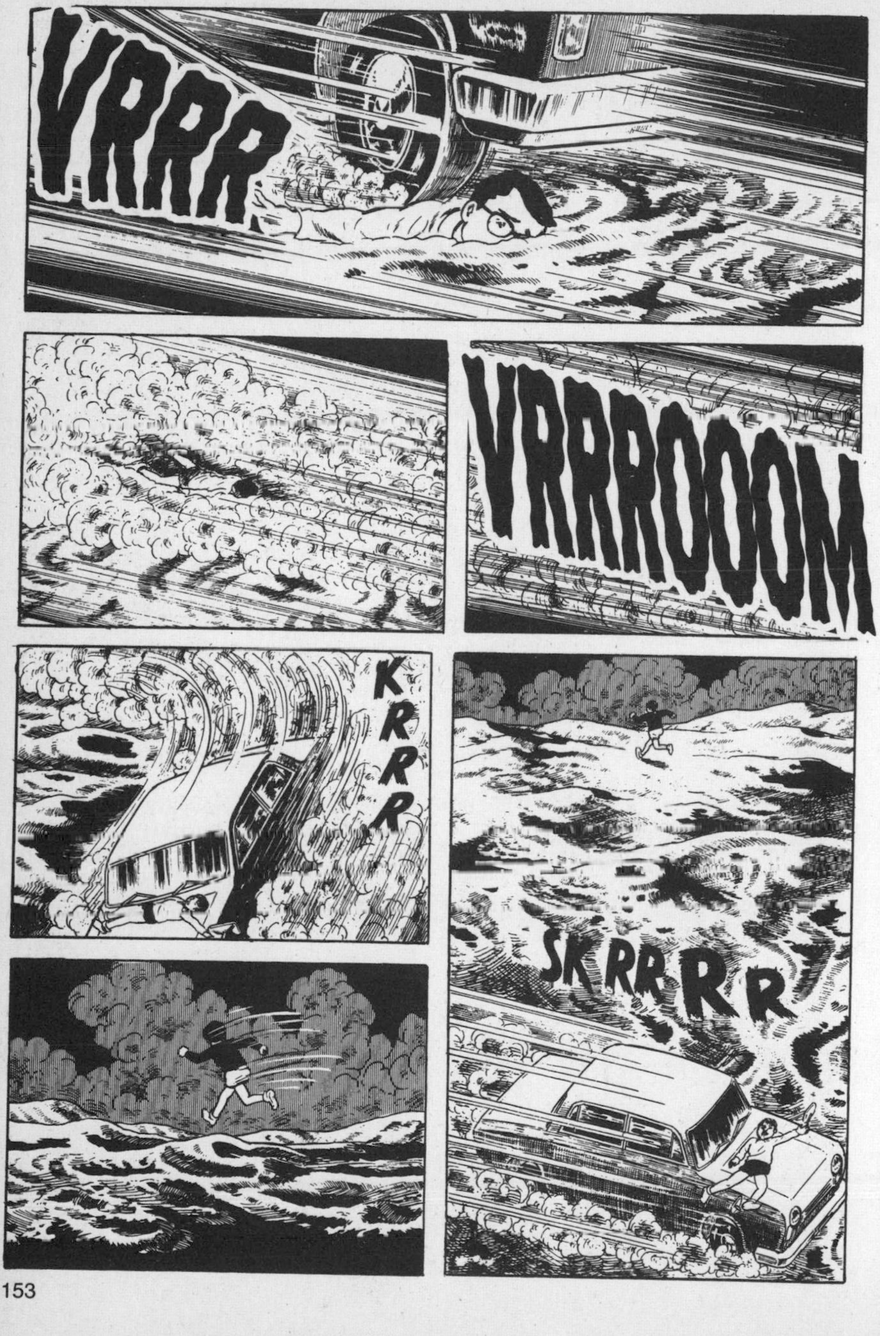
VRRR
VRRROOOM
SKRRRR
KRRR

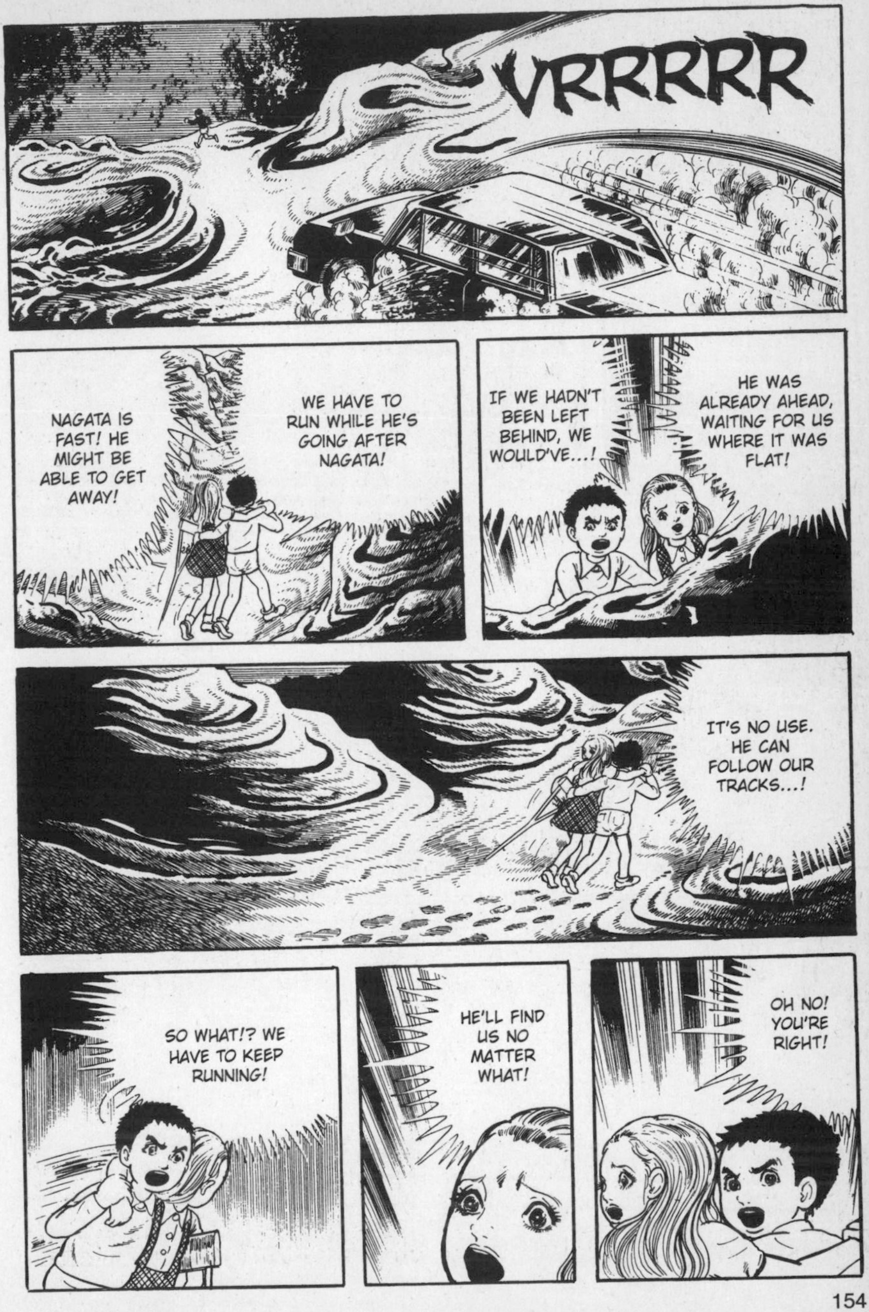
VRRRRR
HE WAS ALREADY AHEAD, WAITING FOR US WHERE IT WAS FLAT!
IF WE HADN'T BEEN LEFT BEHIND, WE WOULD'VE...!
WE HAVE TO RUN WHILE HE'S GOING AFTER NAGATA!
NAGATA IS FAST! HE MIGHT BE ABLE TO GET AWAY!
IT'S NO USE. HE CAN FOLLOW OUR TRACKS...!
OH NO! YOU'RE RIGHT!
HE'LL FIND US NO MATTER WHAT!
SO WHAT!? WE HAVE TO KEEP RUNNING!

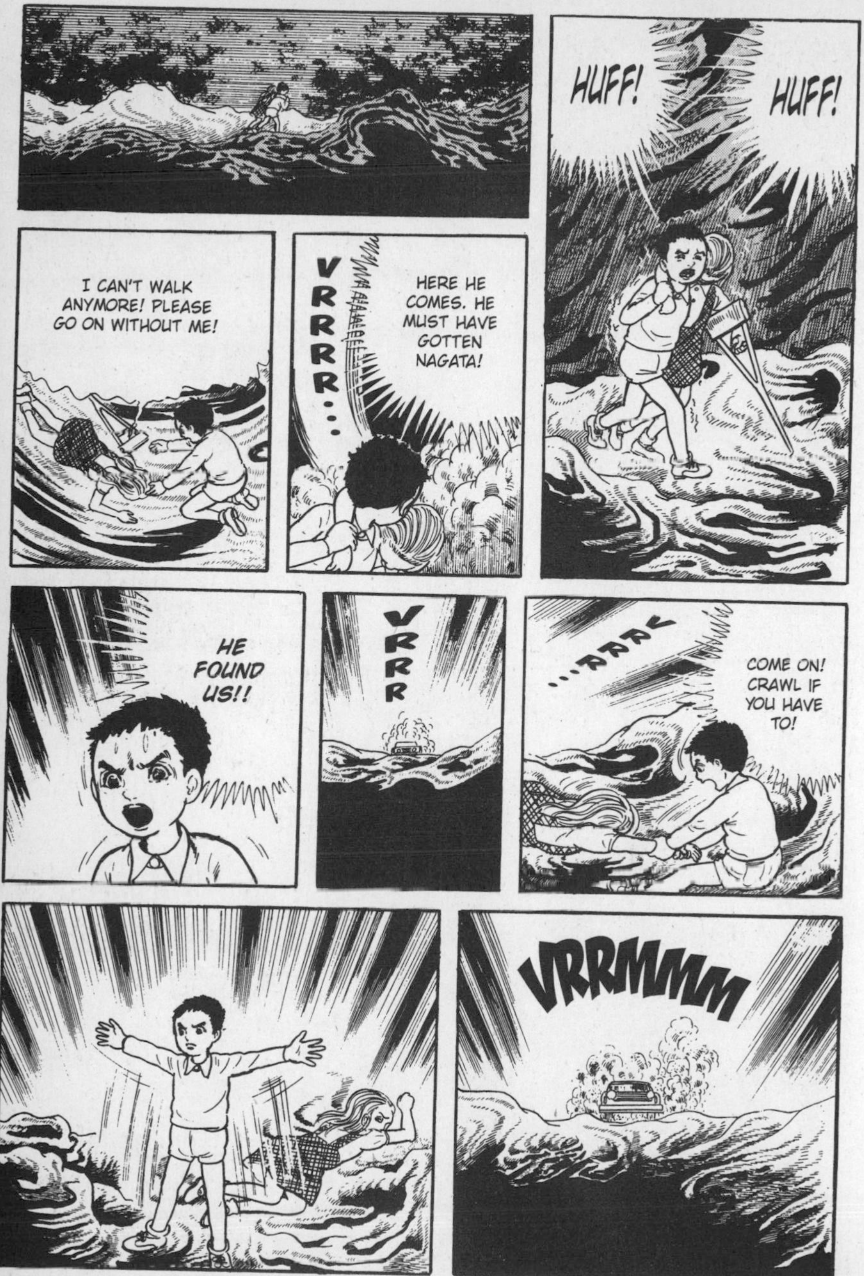
HUFF!
HUFF!
VRRRR...
HERE HE COMES. HE MUST HAVE GOTTEN NAGATA!
I CAN'T WALK ANYMORE! PLEASE GO ON WITHOUT ME!
...RRRV
COME ON! CRAWL IF YOU HAVE TO!
VRRR
HE FOUND US!!
VRRMMMM

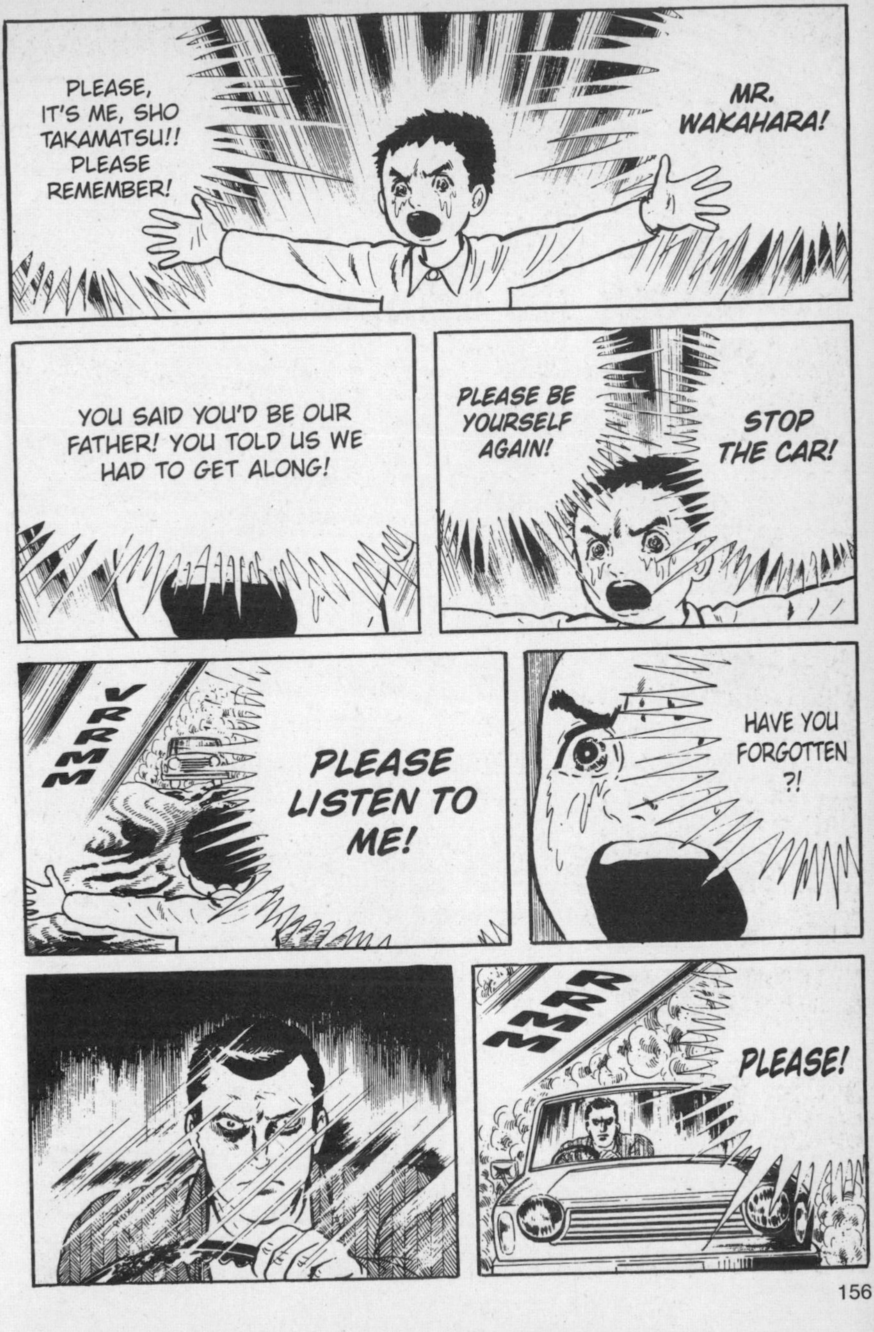
MR. WAKAHARA!
PLEASE, IT'S ME, SHO TAKAMATSU!! PLEASE REMEMBER!
STOP THE CAR!
PLEASE BE YOURSELF AGAIN!
YOU SAID YOU'D BE OUR FATHER! YOU TOLD US WE HAD TO GET ALONG!
HAVE YOU FORGOTTEN ?!
VRRMM
PLEASE LISTEN TO ME!
RRMM
PLEASE!

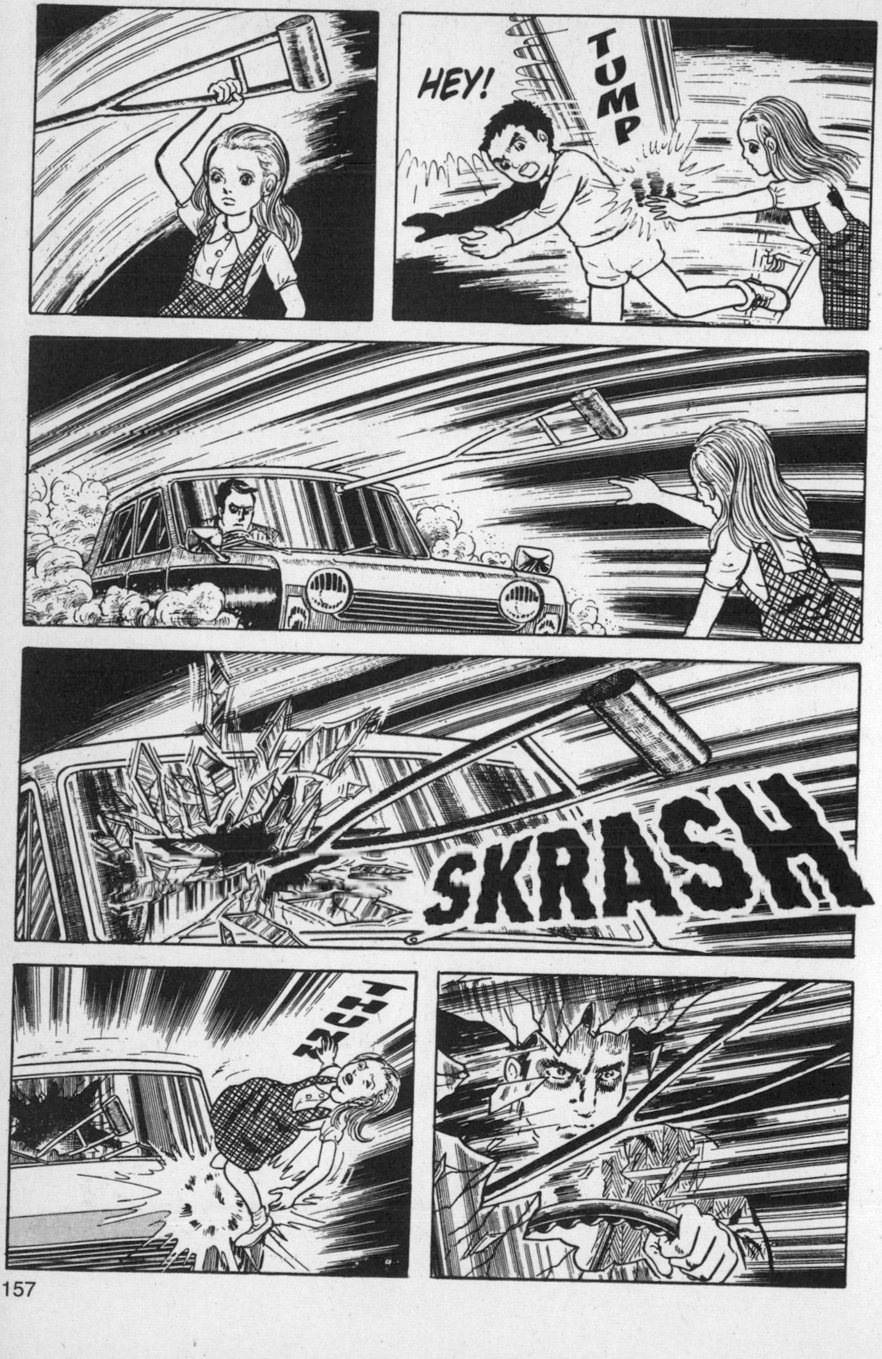
HEY!
TUMP
SKRASH
THUK

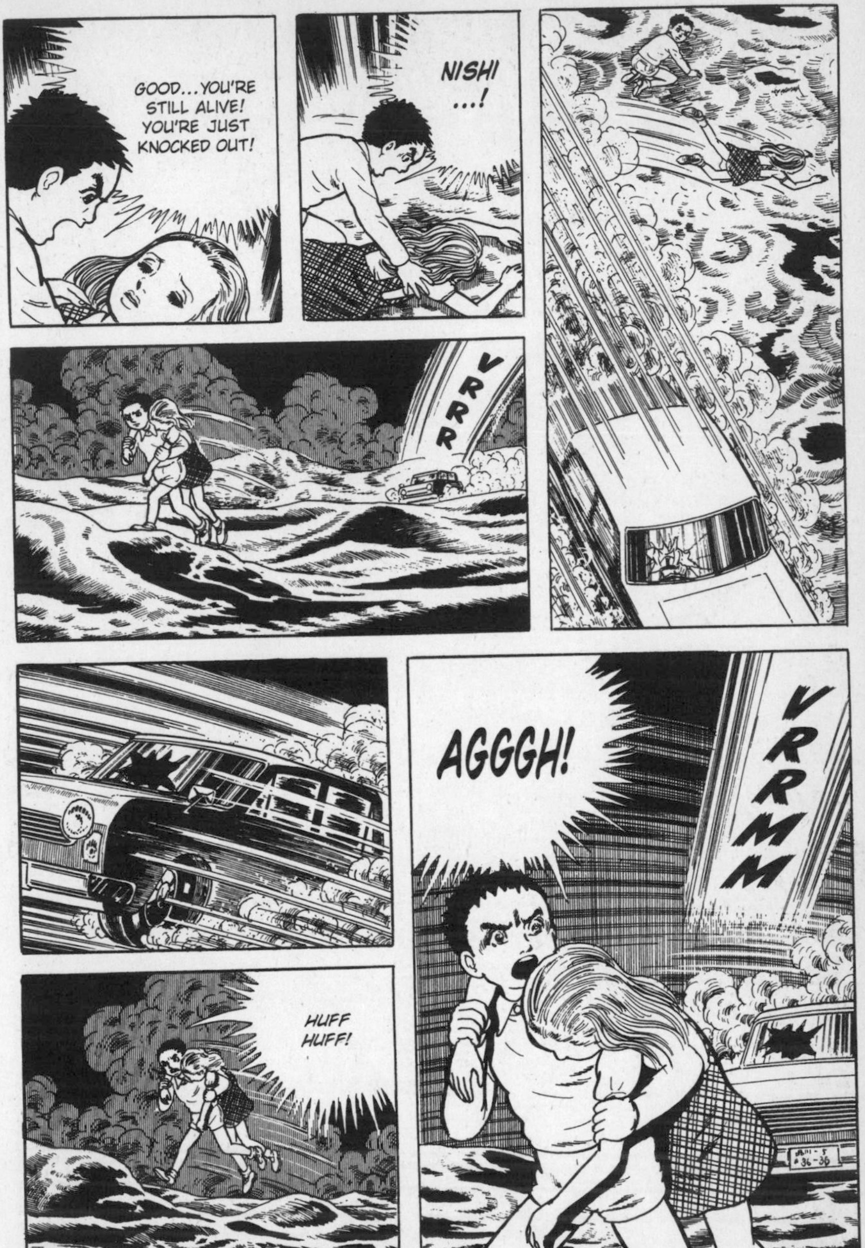
NISHI ...!
GOOD...YOU'RE STILL ALIVE! YOU'RE JUST KNOCKED OUT!
VRRR
VRRMM
AGGGH!
HUFF HUFF!

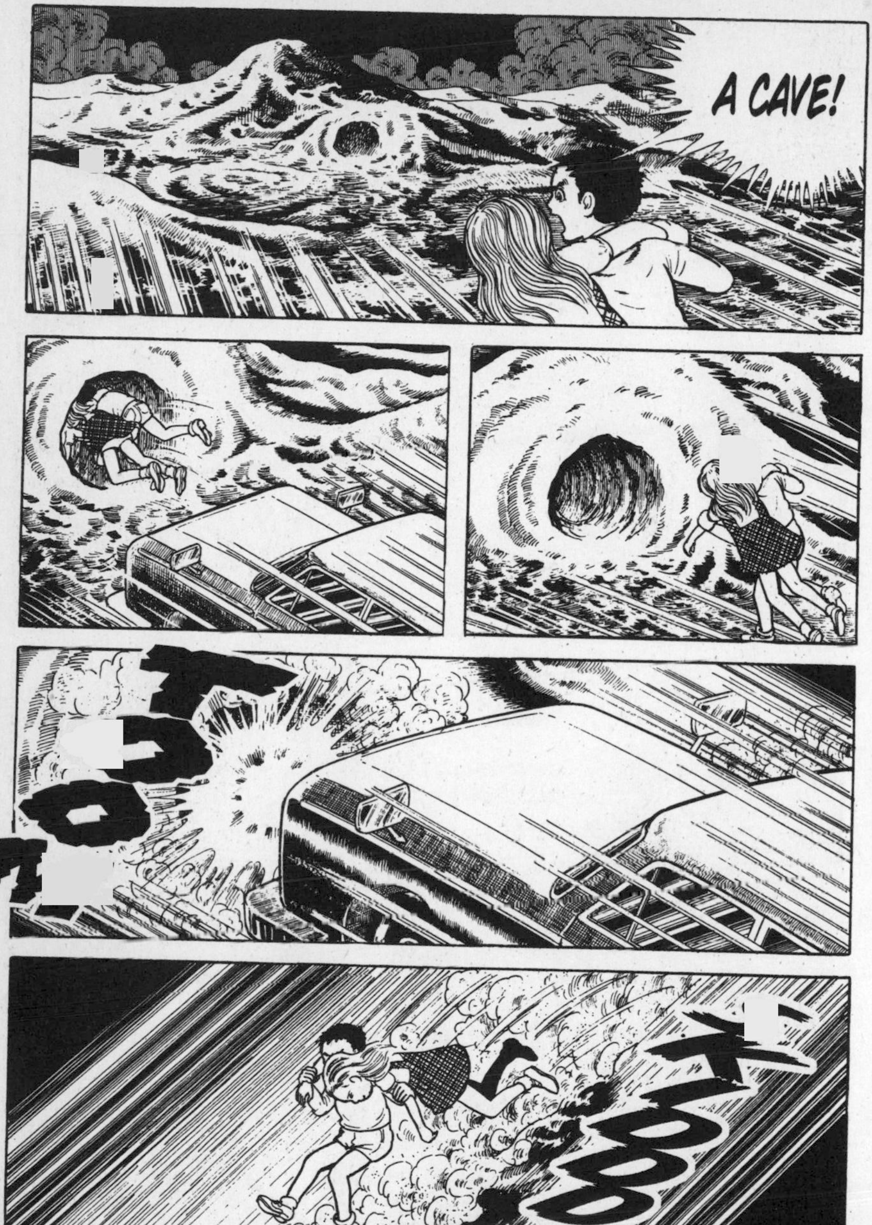
A CAVE!

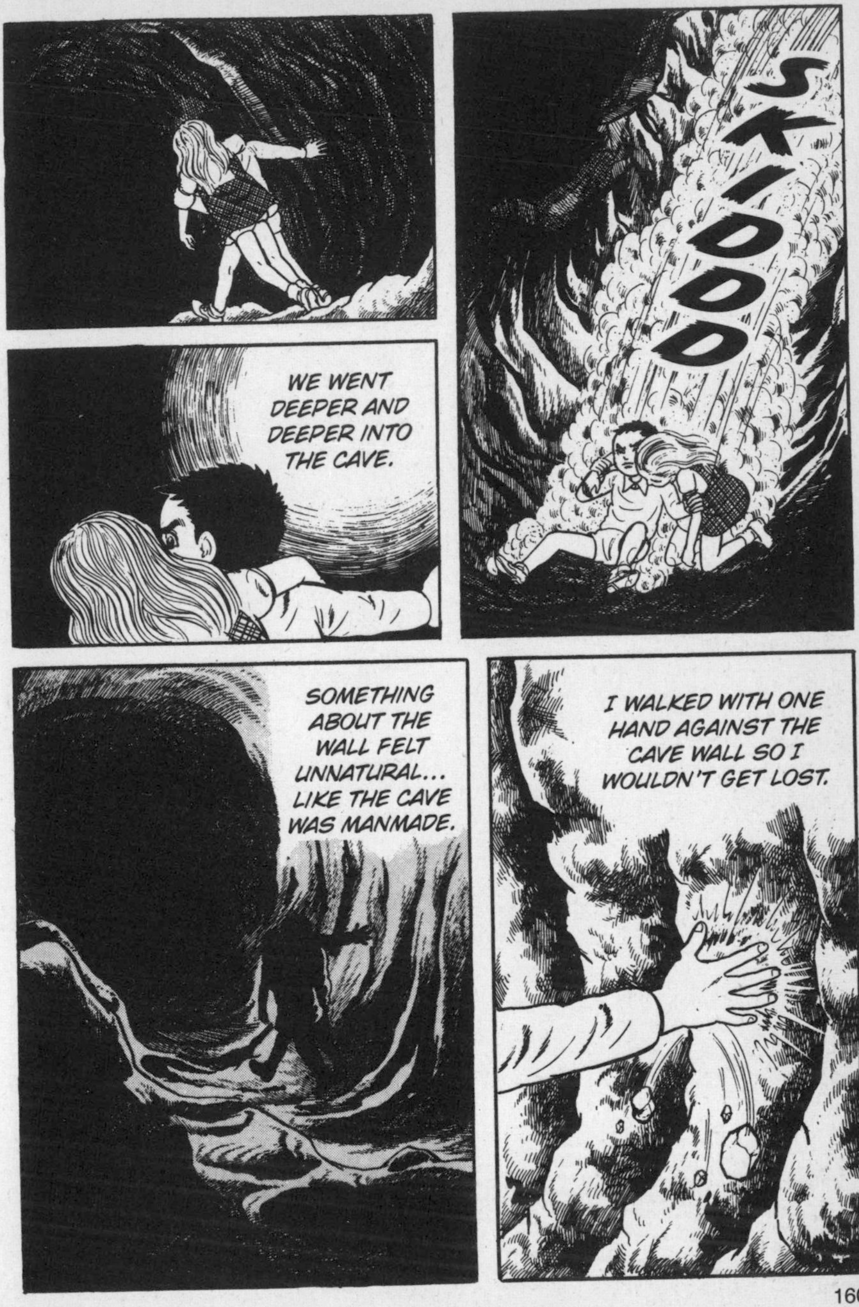
SKIDDD
WE WENT DEEPER AND DEEPER INTO THE CAVE.
I WALKED WITH ONE HAND AGAINST THE CAVE WALL SO I WOULDN'T GET LOST.
SOMETHING ABOUT THE WALL FELT UNNATURAL... LIKE THE CAVE WAS MANMADE.

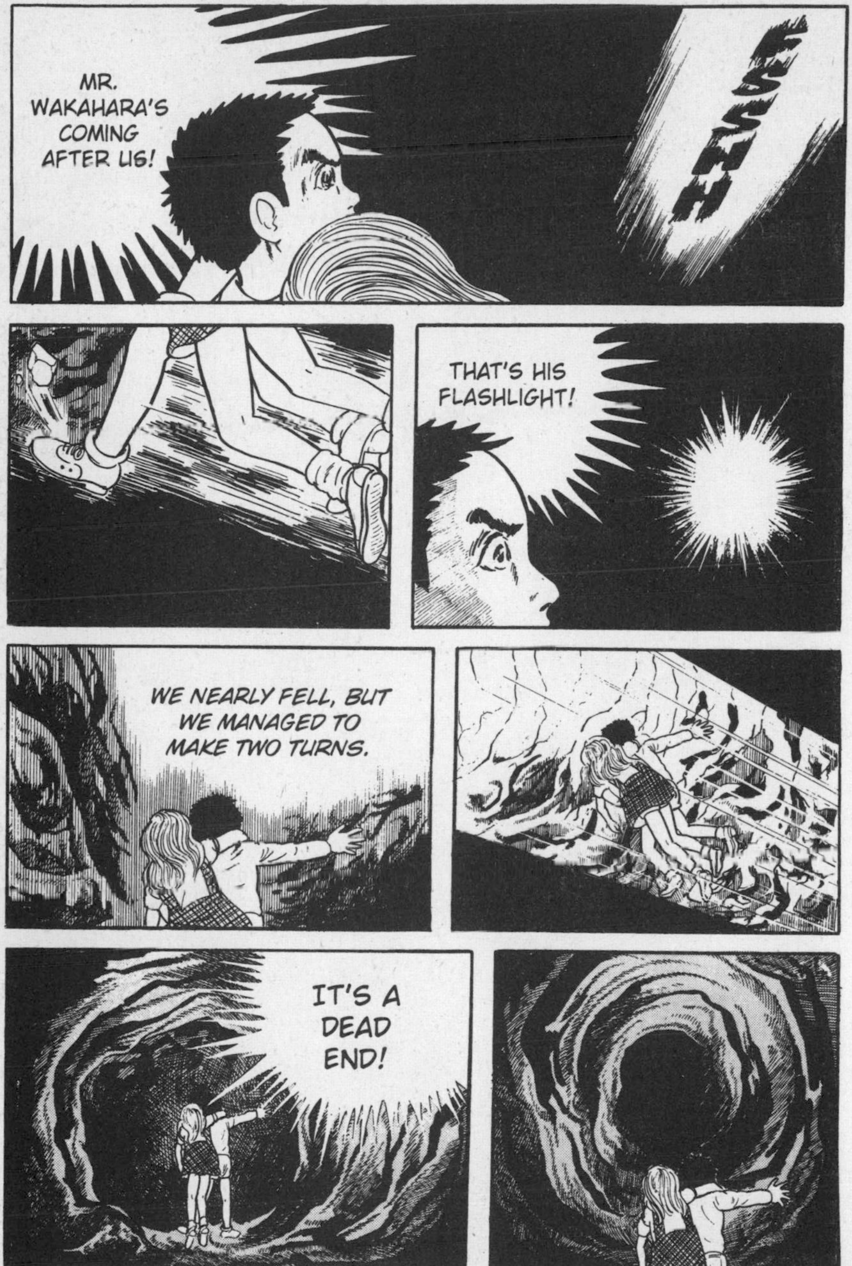
FSSHH
MR. WAKAHARA'S COMING AFTER US!
THAT'S HIS FLASHLIGHT!
WE NEARLY FELL, BUT WE MANAGED TO MAKE TWO TURNS.
IT'S A DEAD END!

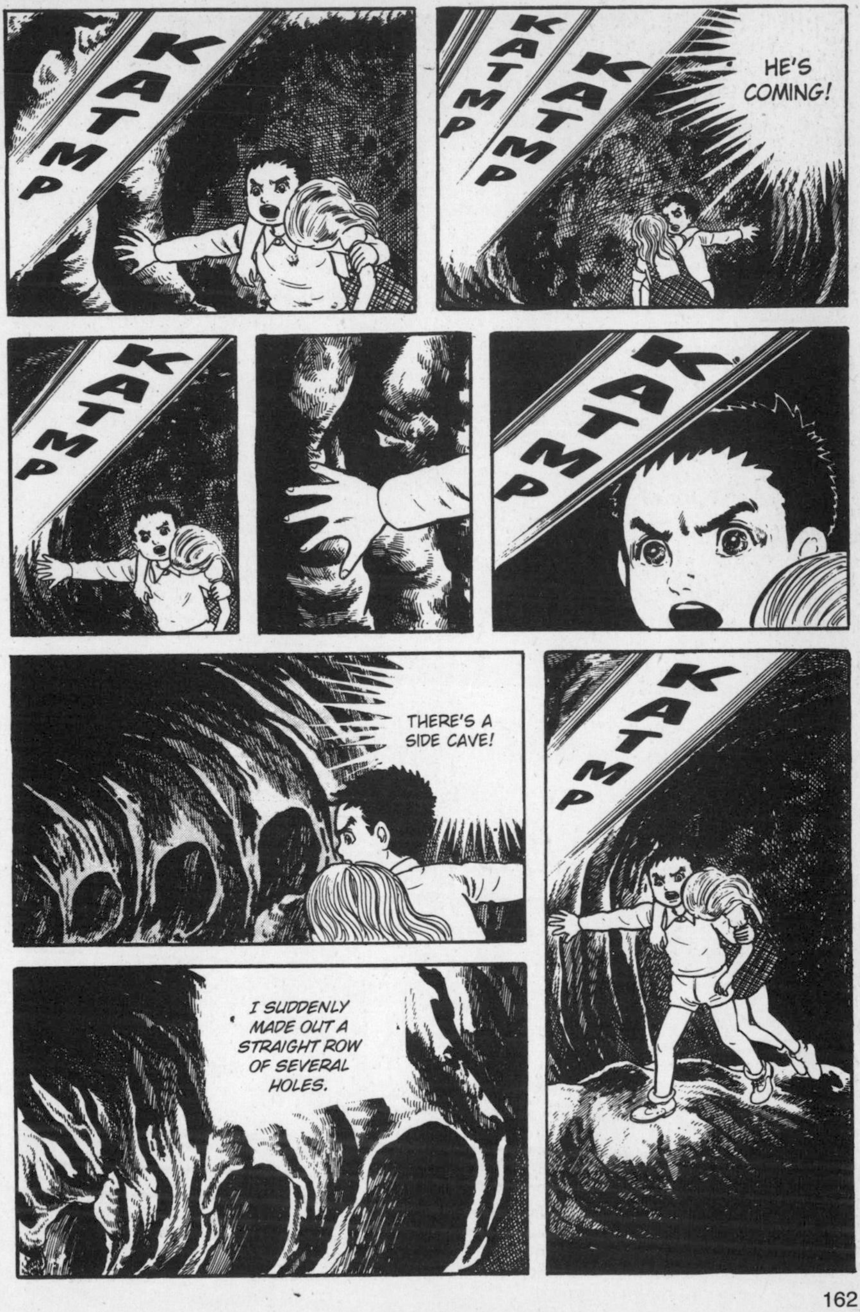
KATMP
KATMP
HE'S COMING!
KATMP
KATMP
KATMP
KATMP
THERE'S A SIDE CAVE!
I SUDDENLY MADE OUT A STRAIGHT ROW OF SEVERAL HOLES.

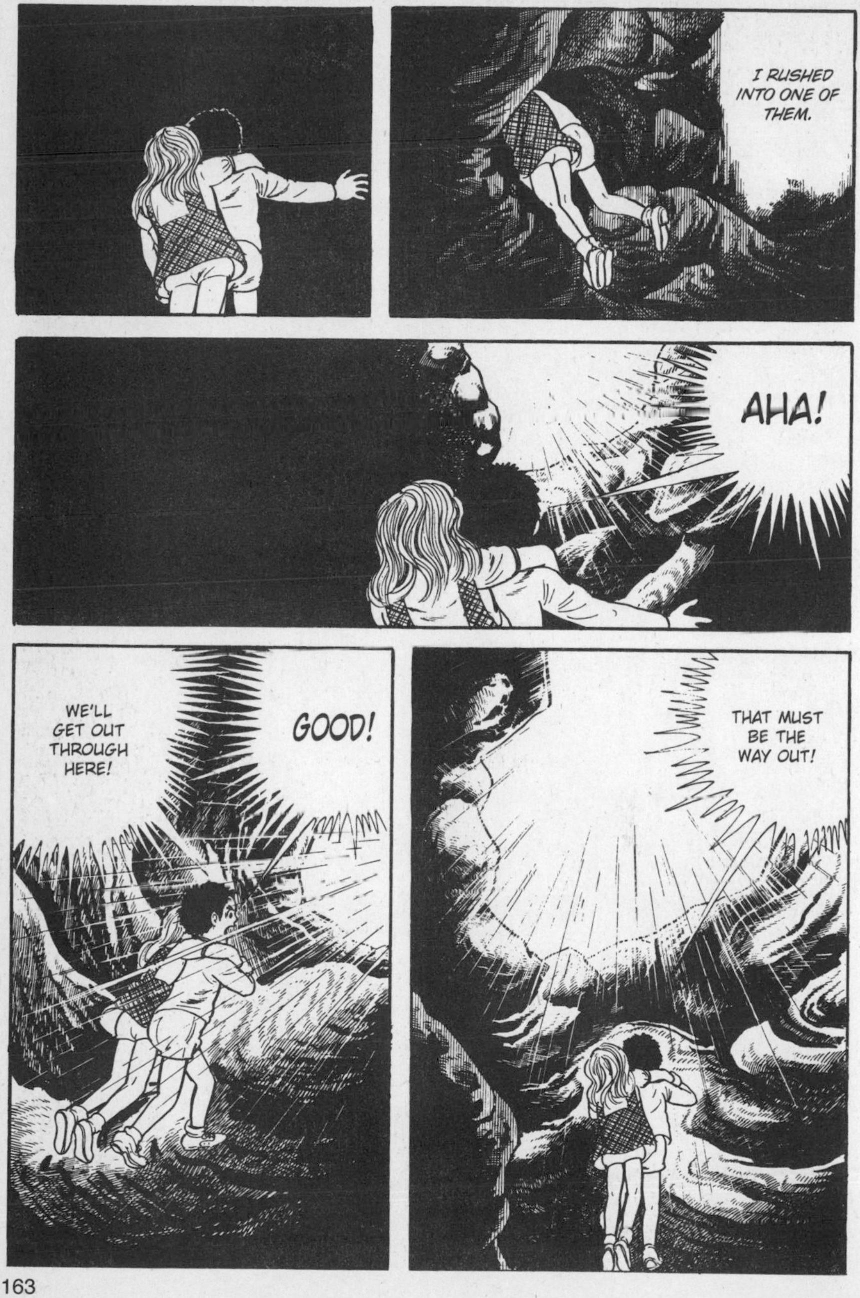
I RUSHED INTO ONE OF THEM.
AHA!
THAT MUST BE THE WAY OUT!
GOOD!
WE'LL GET OUT THROUGH HERE!

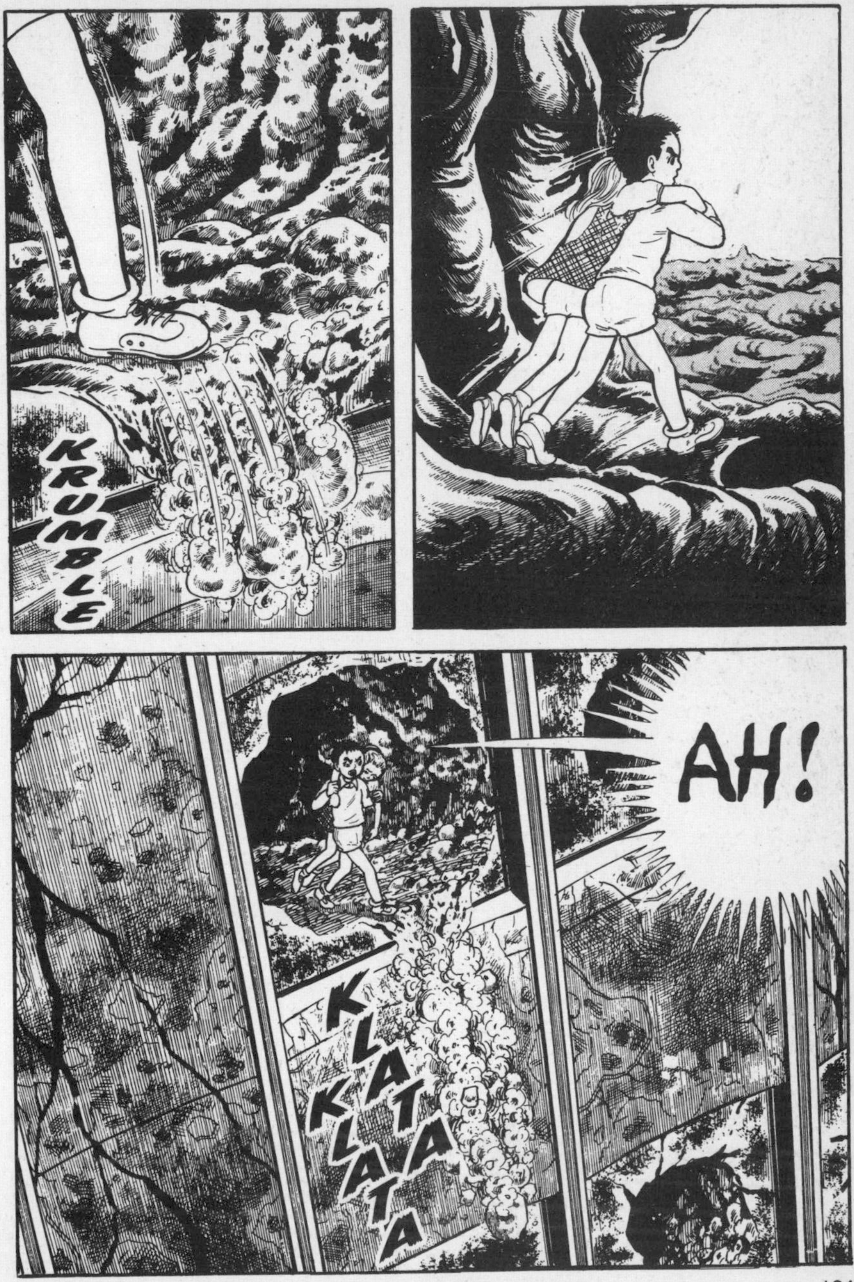
KRUMBLE
AH!
KLATA KLATA

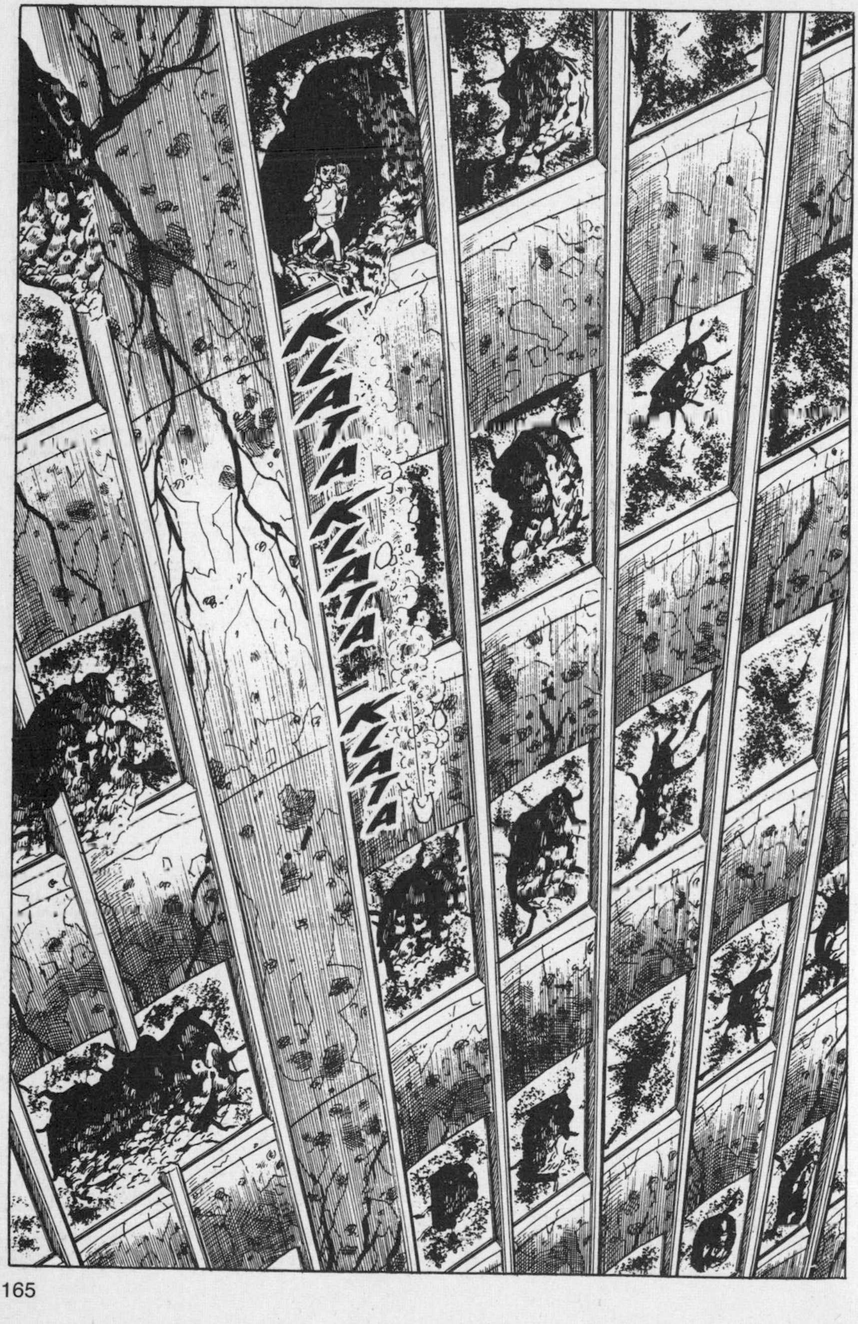
KLATA KLATA KLATA KLATA

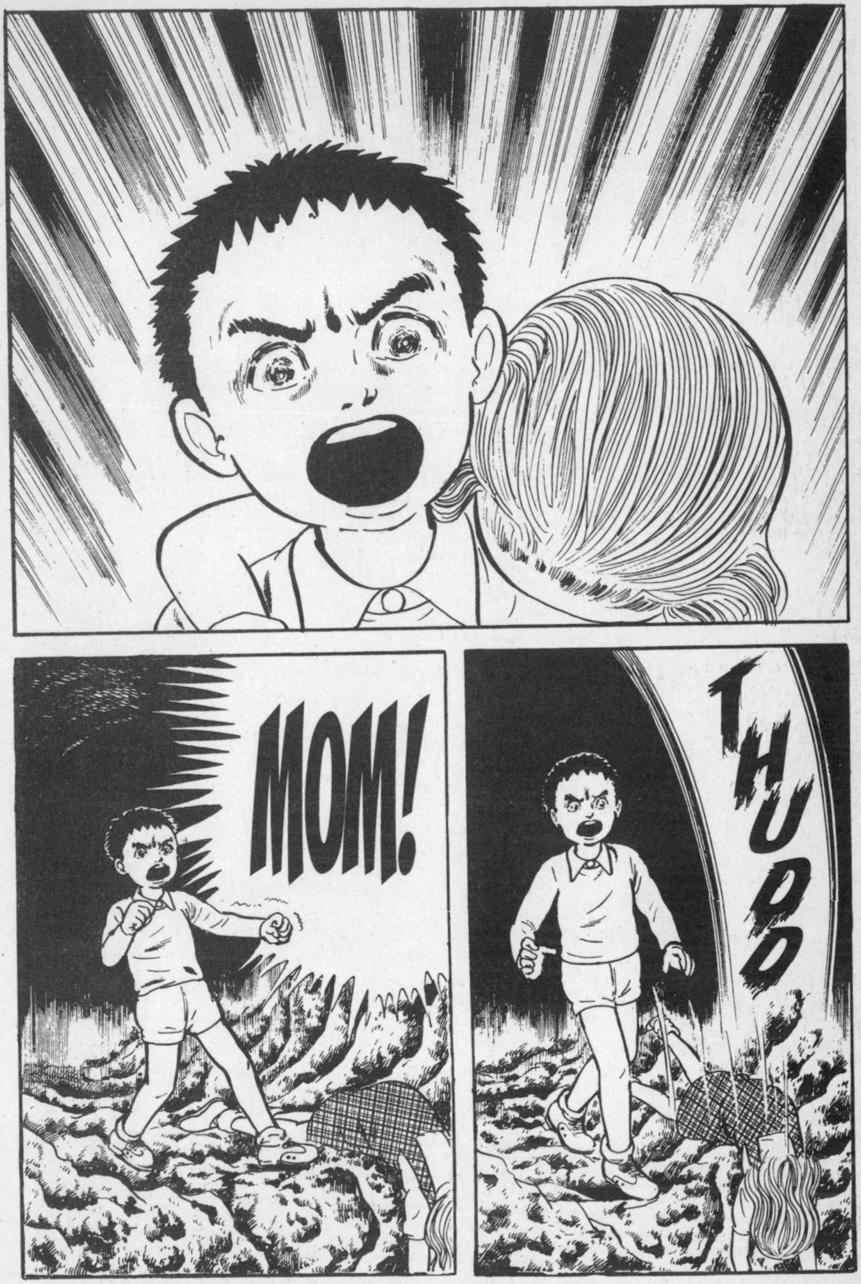
THUD
MOM!

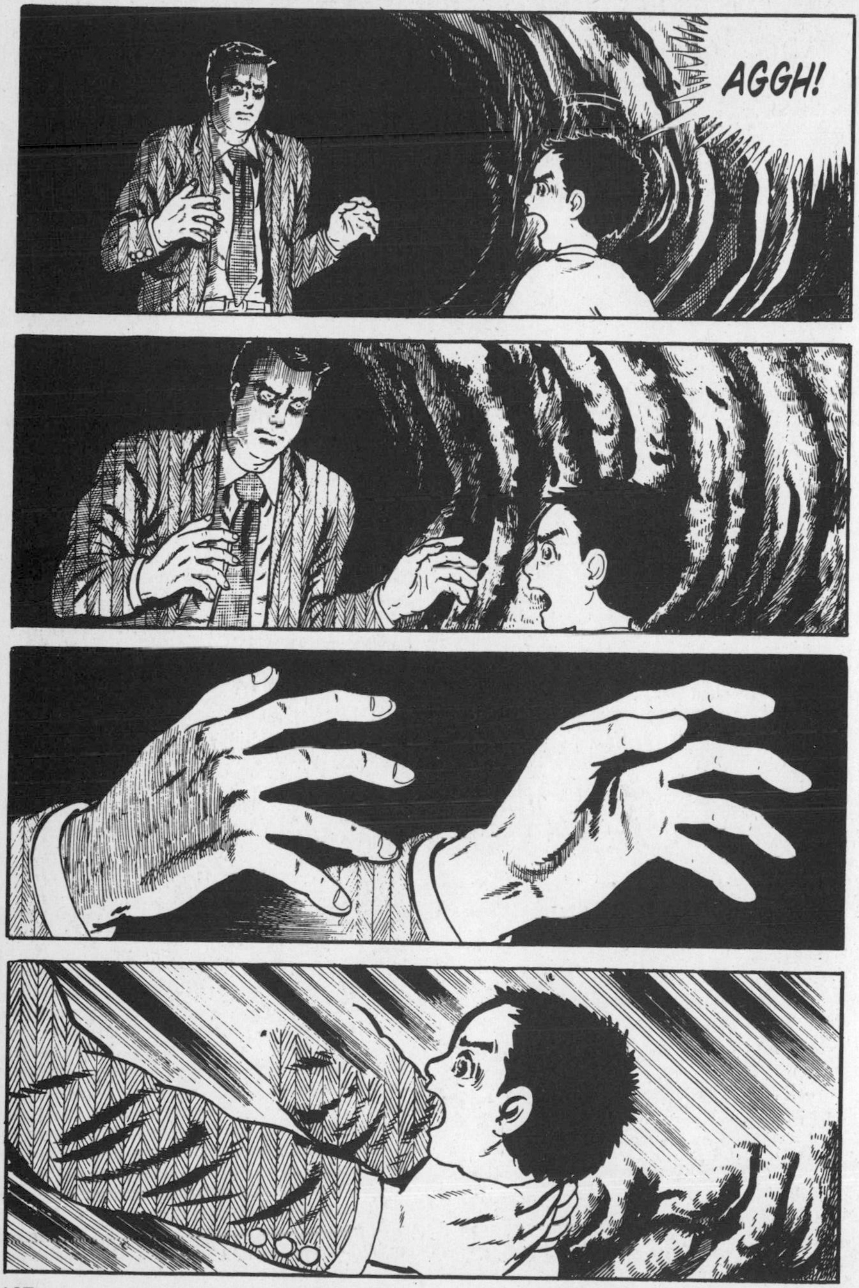
AGGH!

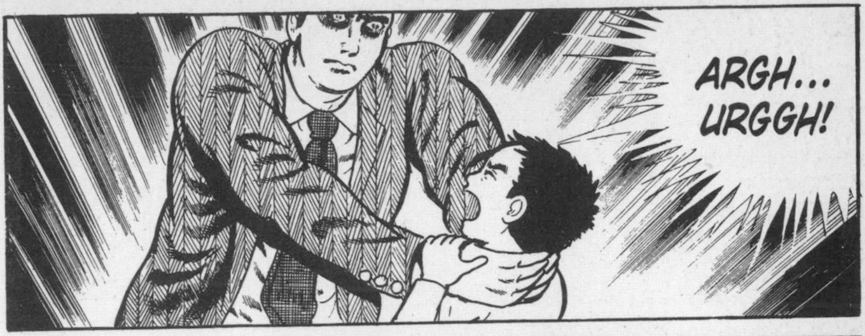
ARGH... URGGH!

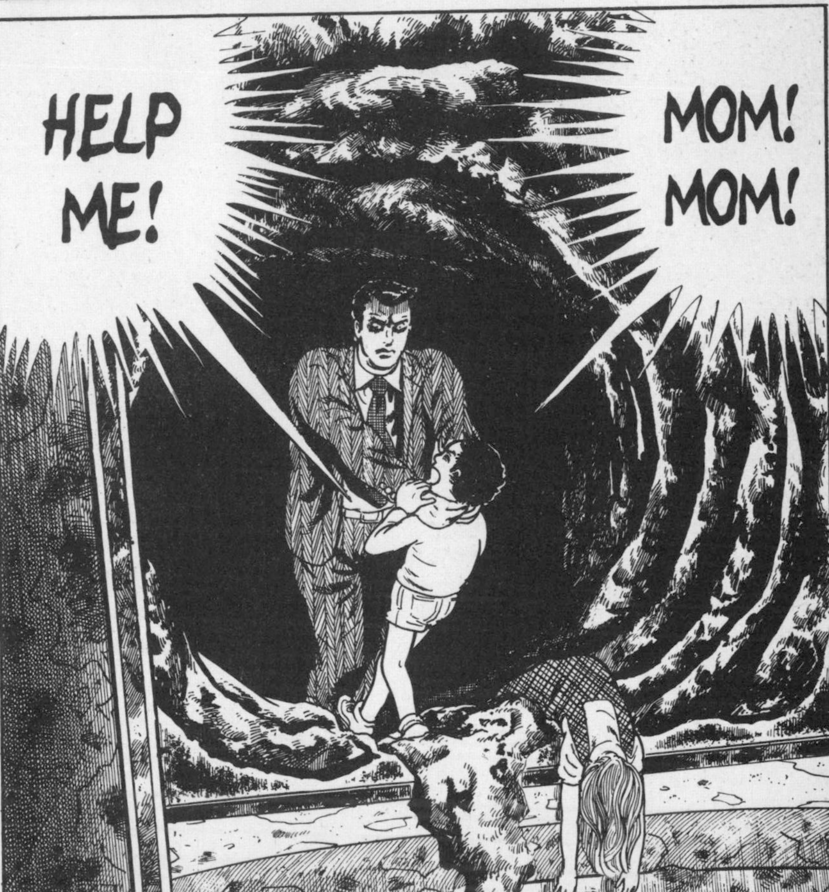
MOM! MOM!
HELP ME!

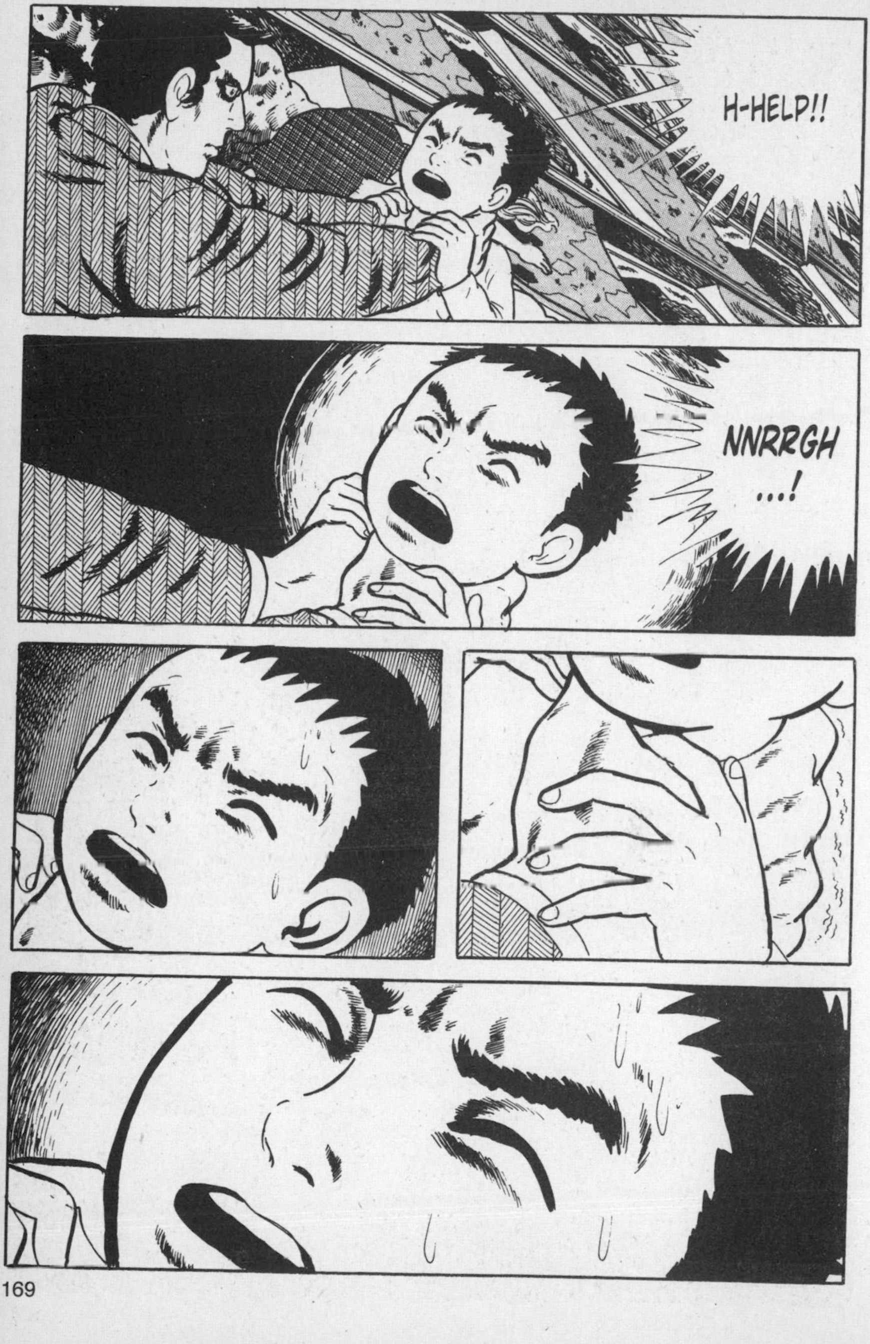
H-HELP!!
NNRRGH
...!

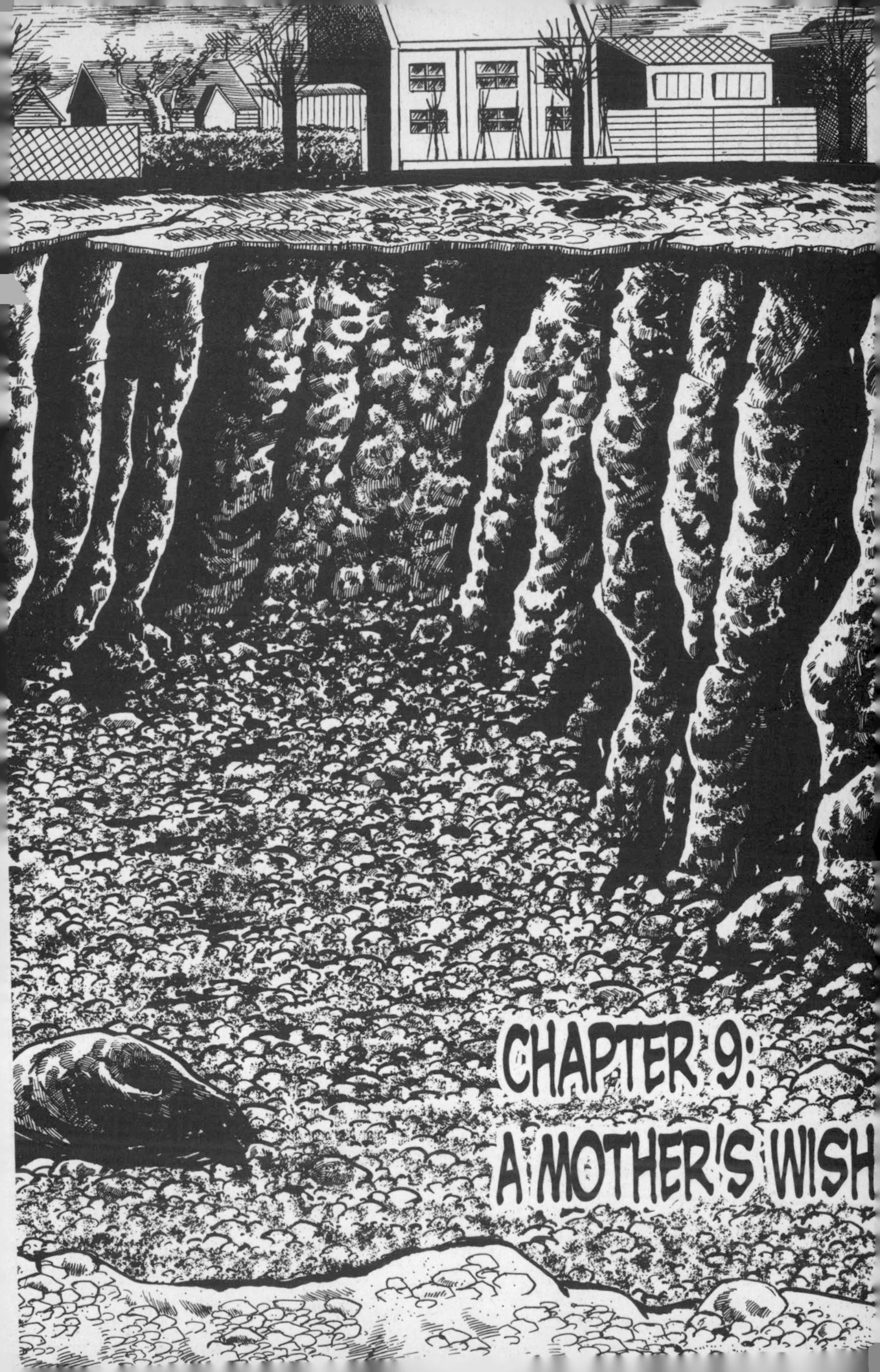
CHAPTER 9:
A MOTHER'S WISH

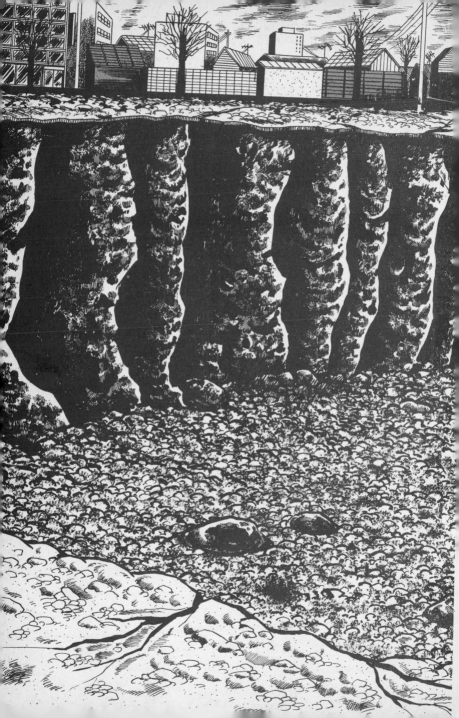

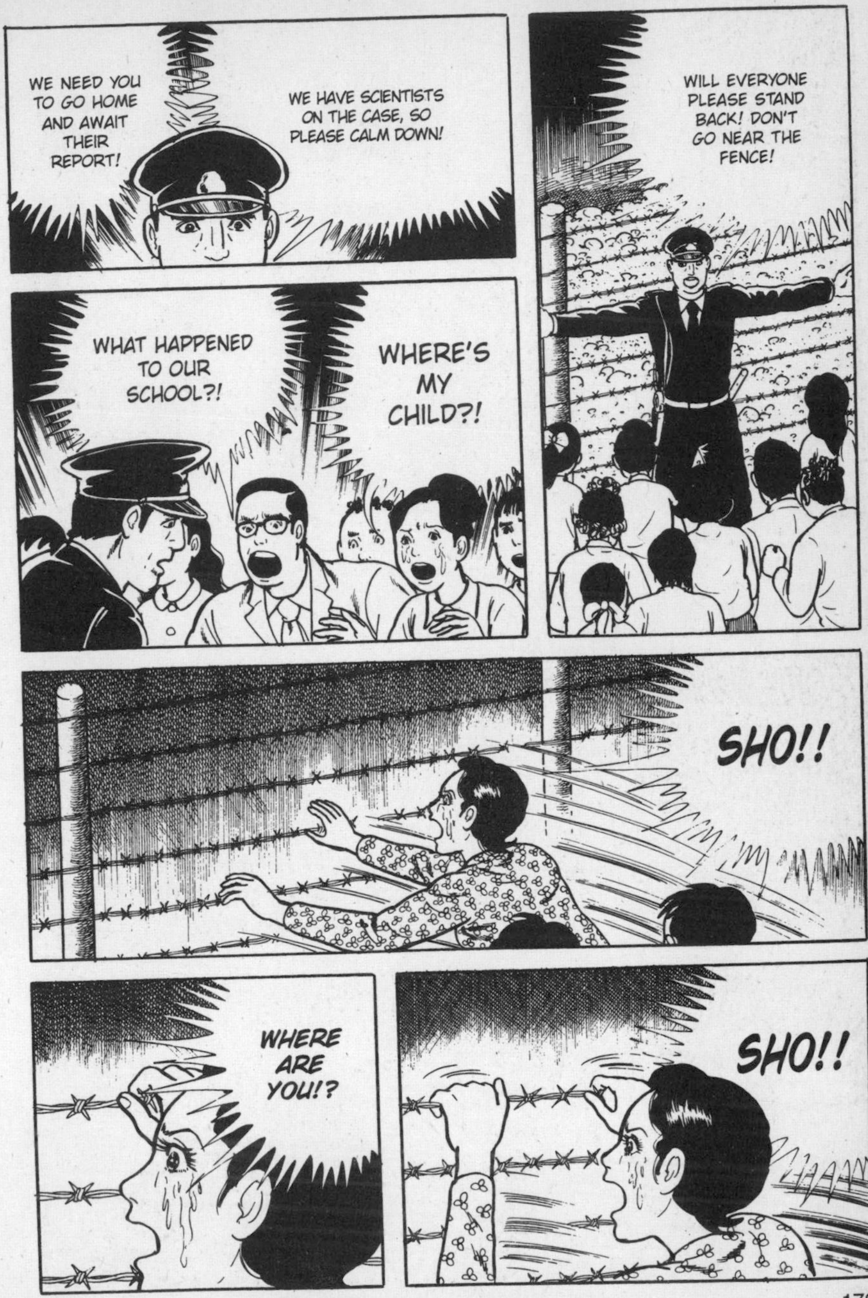
WILL EVERYONE PLEASE STAND BACK! DON'T GO NEAR THE FENCE!
WE HAVE SCIENTISTS ON THE CASE, SO PLEASE CALM DOWN!
WE NEED YOU TO GO HOME AND AWAIT THEIR REPORT!
WHERE'S MY CHILD?!
WHAT HAPPENED TO OUR SCHOOL?!
SHO!!
SHO!!
WHERE ARE YOU!?

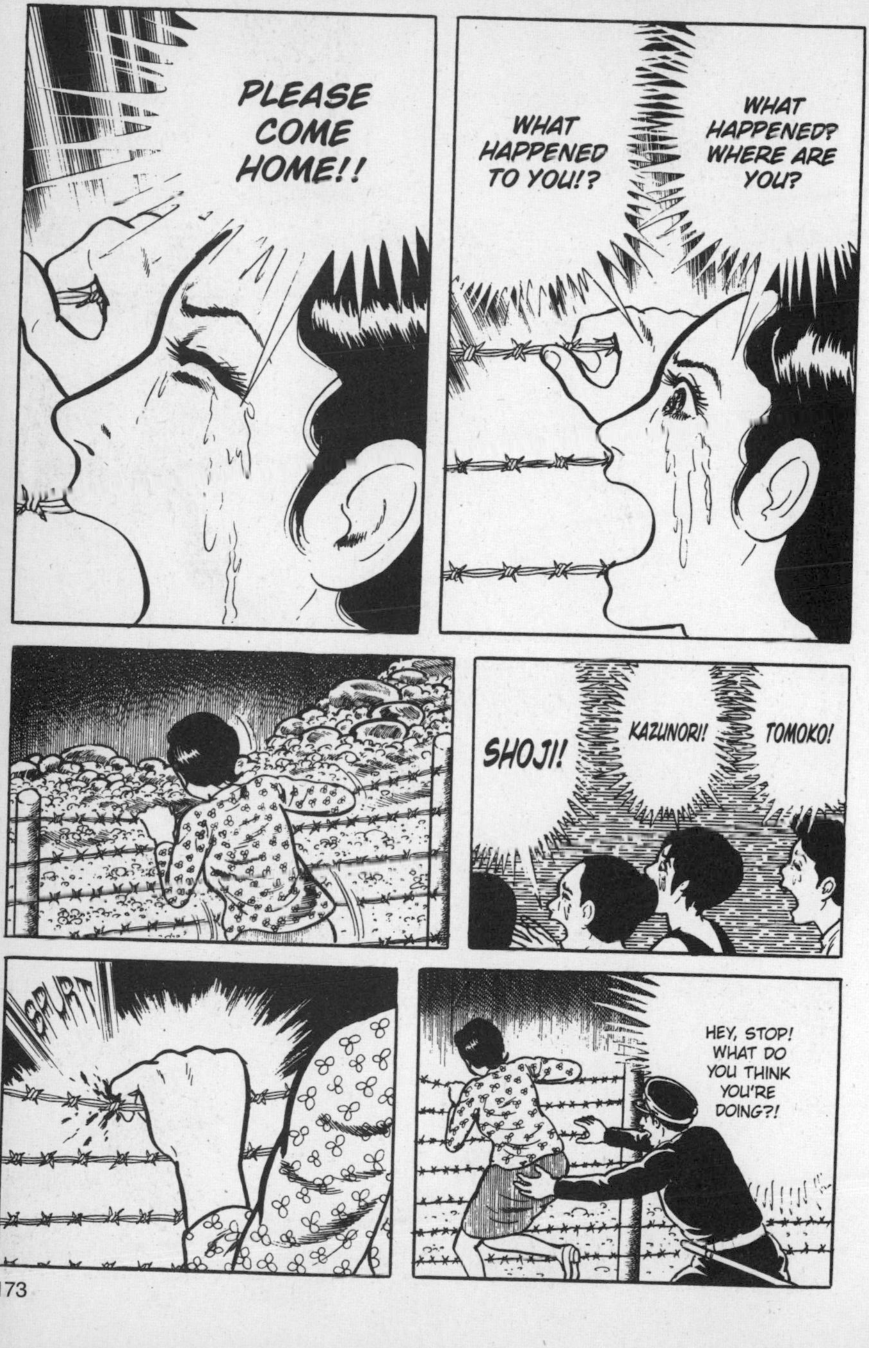
WHAT HAPPENED? WHERE ARE YOU?
WHAT HAPPENED TO YOU!?
PLEASE COME HOME!!
TOMOKO!
KAZUNORI!
SHOJI!
HEY, STOP! WHAT DO YOU THINK YOU'RE DOING?!
SPURT

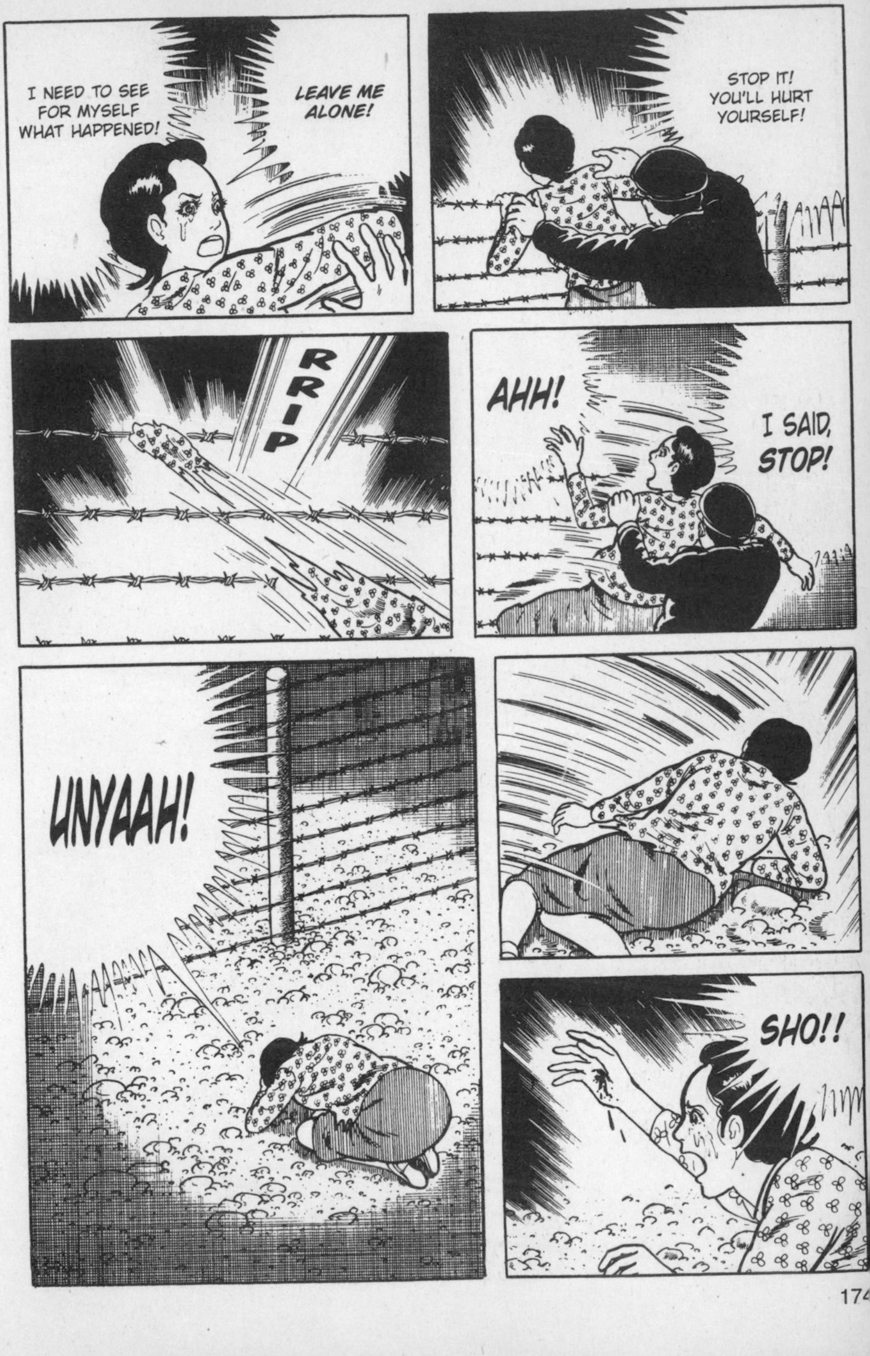
STOP IT! YOU'LL HURT YOURSELF!
LEAVE ME ALONE!
I NEED TO SEE FOR MYSELF WHAT HAPPENED!
I SAID, STOP!
AHH!
RRIP
SHO!!
UNYAAH!

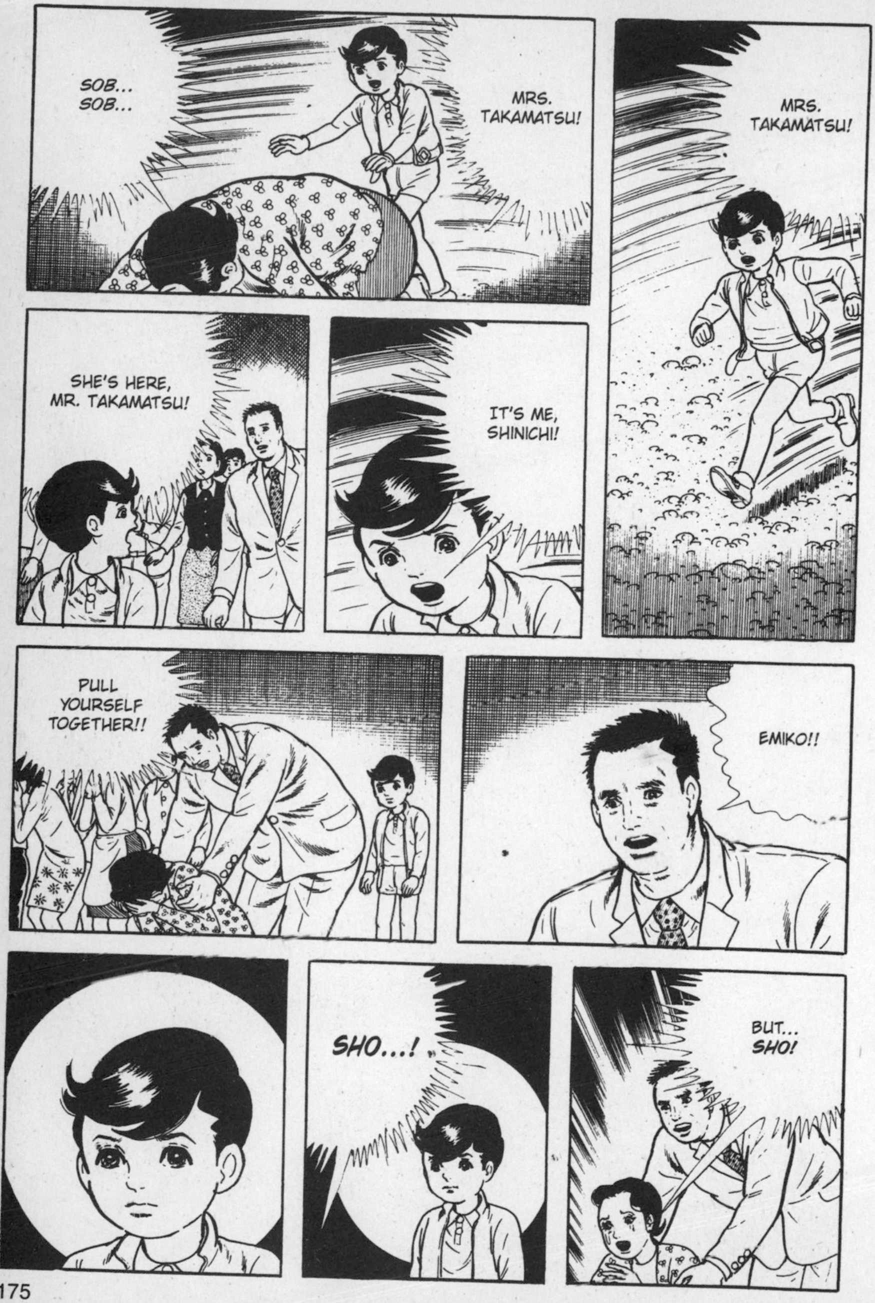
MRS. TAKAMATSU!
MRS. TAKAMATSU!
SOB... SOB...
IT'S ME, SHINICHI!
SHE'S HERE, MR. TAKAMATSU!
EMIKO!!
PULL YOURSELF TOGETHER!!
BUT... SHO!
SHO...!

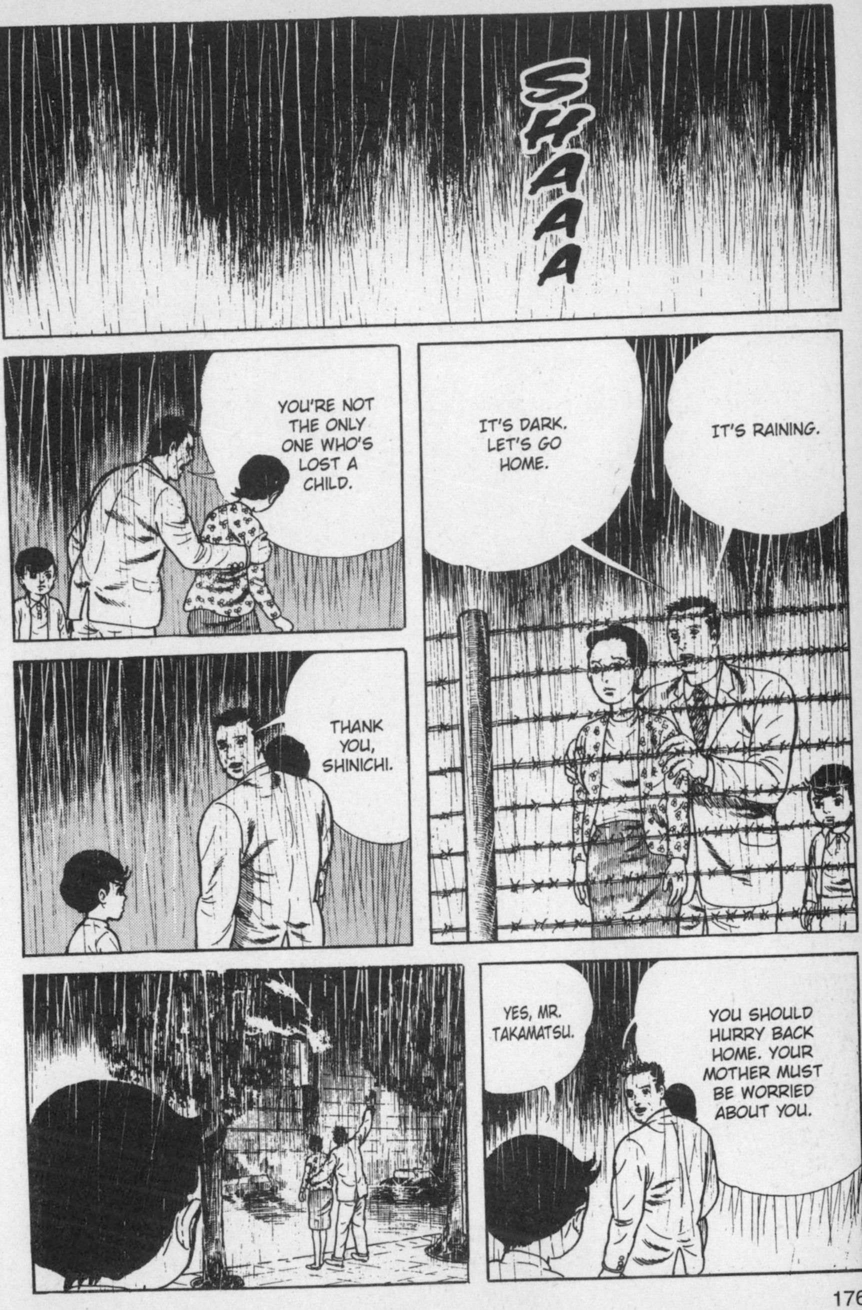
SHAAA
IT'S RAINING.
IT'S DARK. LET'S GO HOME.
YOU'RE NOT THE ONLY ONE WHO'S LOST A CHILD.
THANK YOU, SHINICHI.
YOU SHOULD HURRY BACK HOME. YOUR MOTHER MUST BE WORRIED ABOUT YOU.
YES, MR. TAKAMATSU.

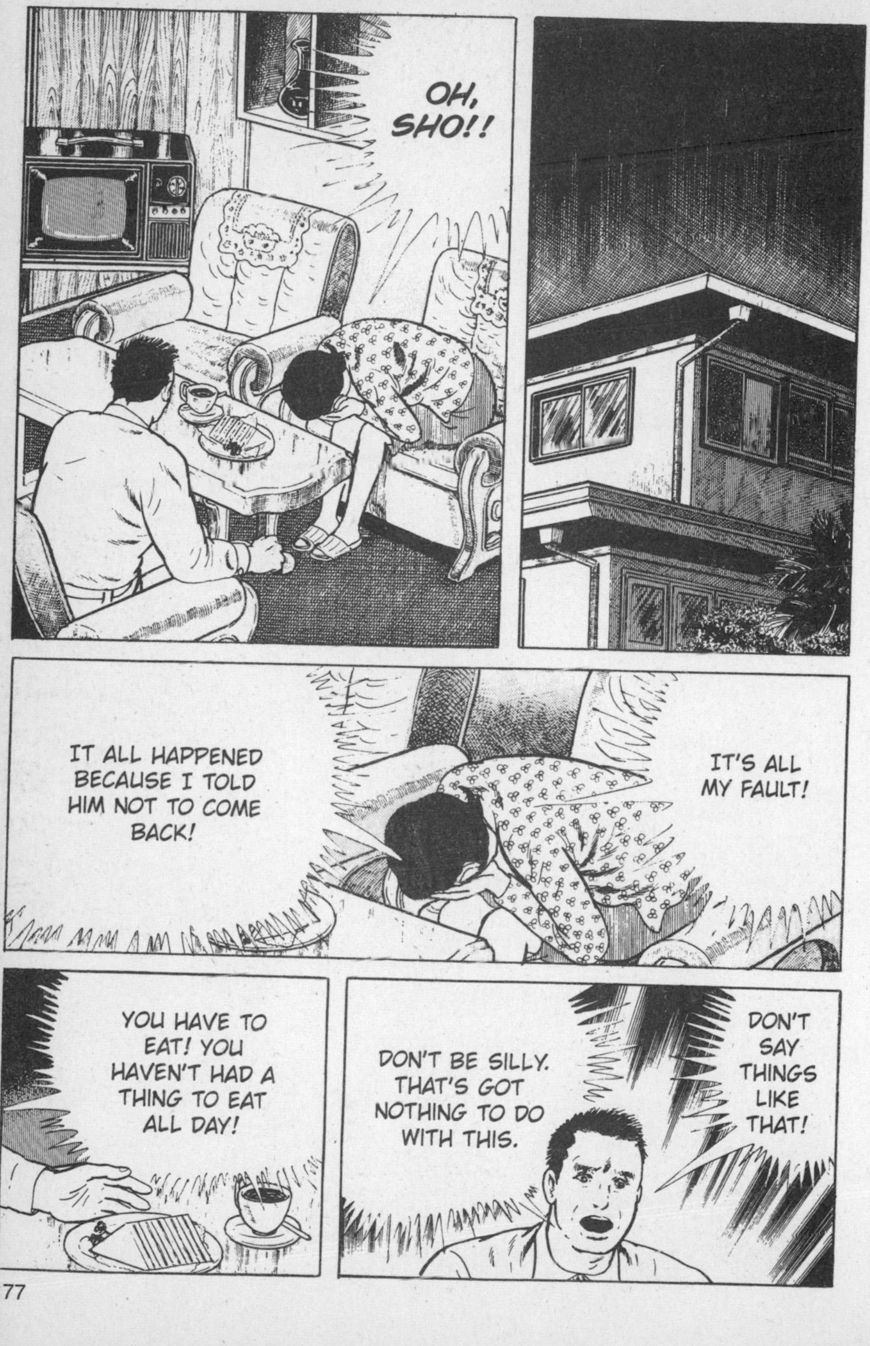
OH, SHO!!
IT'S ALL MY FAULT!
IT ALL HAPPENED BECAUSE I TOLD HIM NOT TO COME BACK!
DON'T SAY THINGS LIKE THAT!
DON'T BE SILLY. THAT'S GOT NOTHING TO DO WITH THIS.
YOU HAVE TO EAT! YOU HAVEN'T HAD A THING TO EAT ALL DAY!

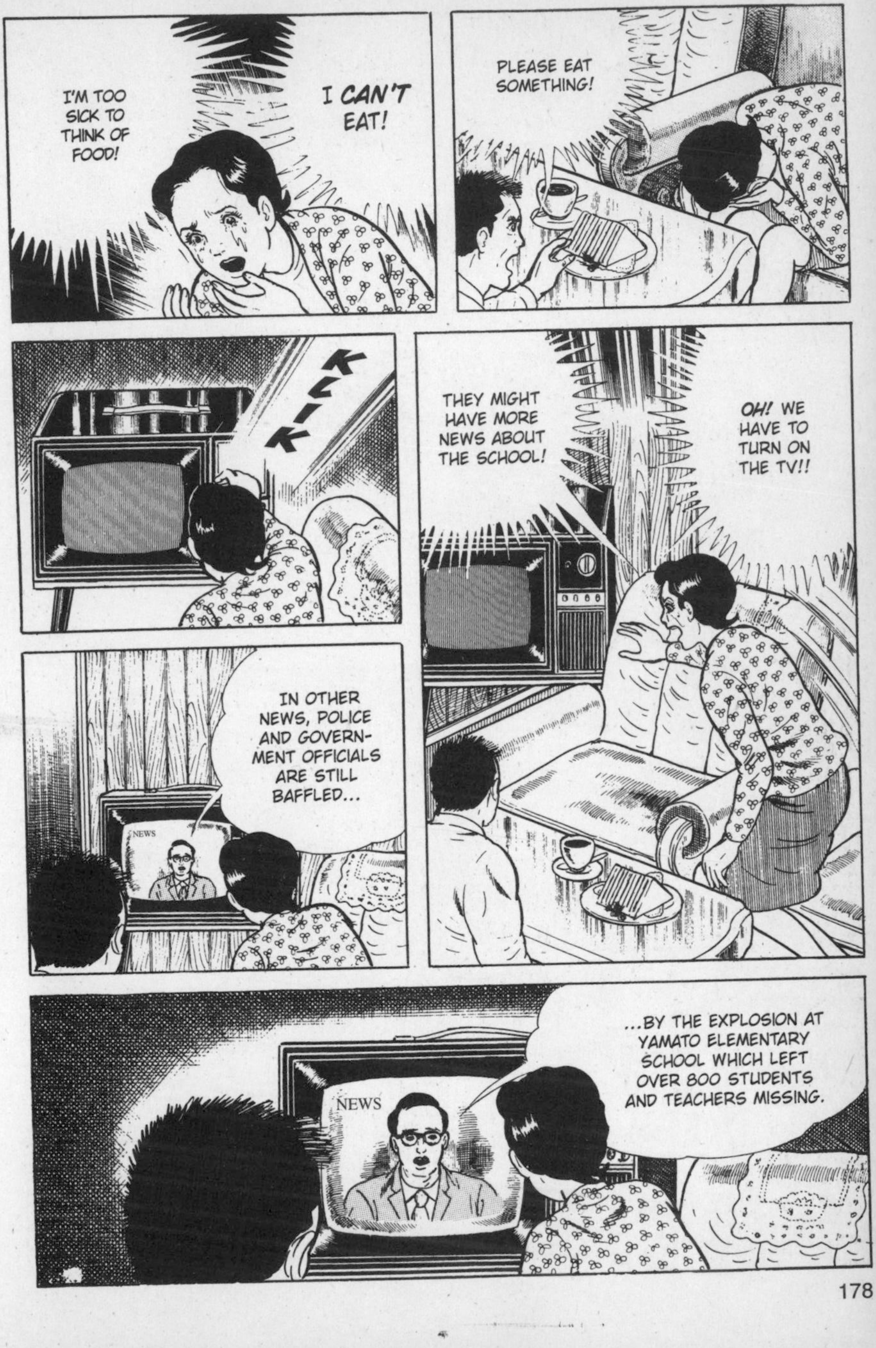
PLEASE EAT SOMETHING!
I CAN'T EAT!
I'M TOO SICK TO THINK OF FOOD!
OH! WE HAVE TO TURN ON THE TV!!
THEY MIGHT HAVE MORE NEWS ABOUT THE SCHOOL!
KLIK
IN OTHER NEWS, POLICE AND GOVERNMENT OFFICIALS ARE STILL BAFFLED...
NEWS
...BY THE EXPLOSION AT YAMATO ELEMENTARY SCHOOL WHICH LEFT OVER 800 STUDENTS AND TEACHERS MISSING.
NEWS

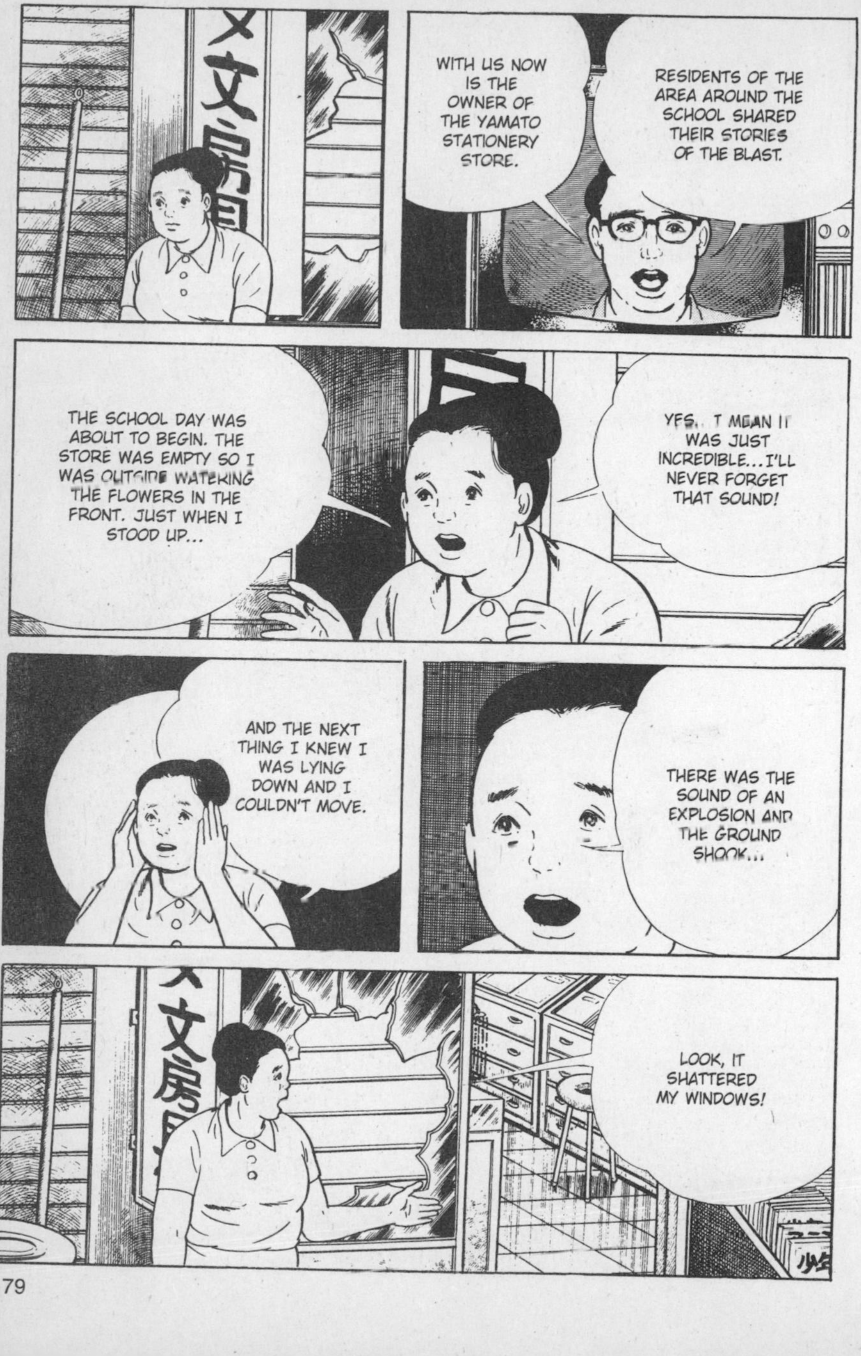
RESIDENTS OF THE AREA AROUND THE SCHOOL SHARED THEIR STORIES OF THE BLAST.
WITH US NOW IS THE OWNER OF THE YAMATO STATIONERY STORE.
YES... I MEAN IT WAS JUST INCREDIBLE...I'LL NEVER FORGET THAT SOUND!
THE SCHOOL DAY WAS ABOUT TO BEGIN. THE STORE WAS EMPTY SO I WAS OUTSIDE WATERING THE FLOWERS IN THE FRONT. JUST WHEN I STOOD UP...
THERE WAS THE SOUND OF AN EXPLOSION AND THE GROUND SHOOK...
AND THE NEXT THING I KNEW I WAS LYING DOWN AND I COULDN'T MOVE.
LOOK, IT SHATTERED MY WINDOWS!

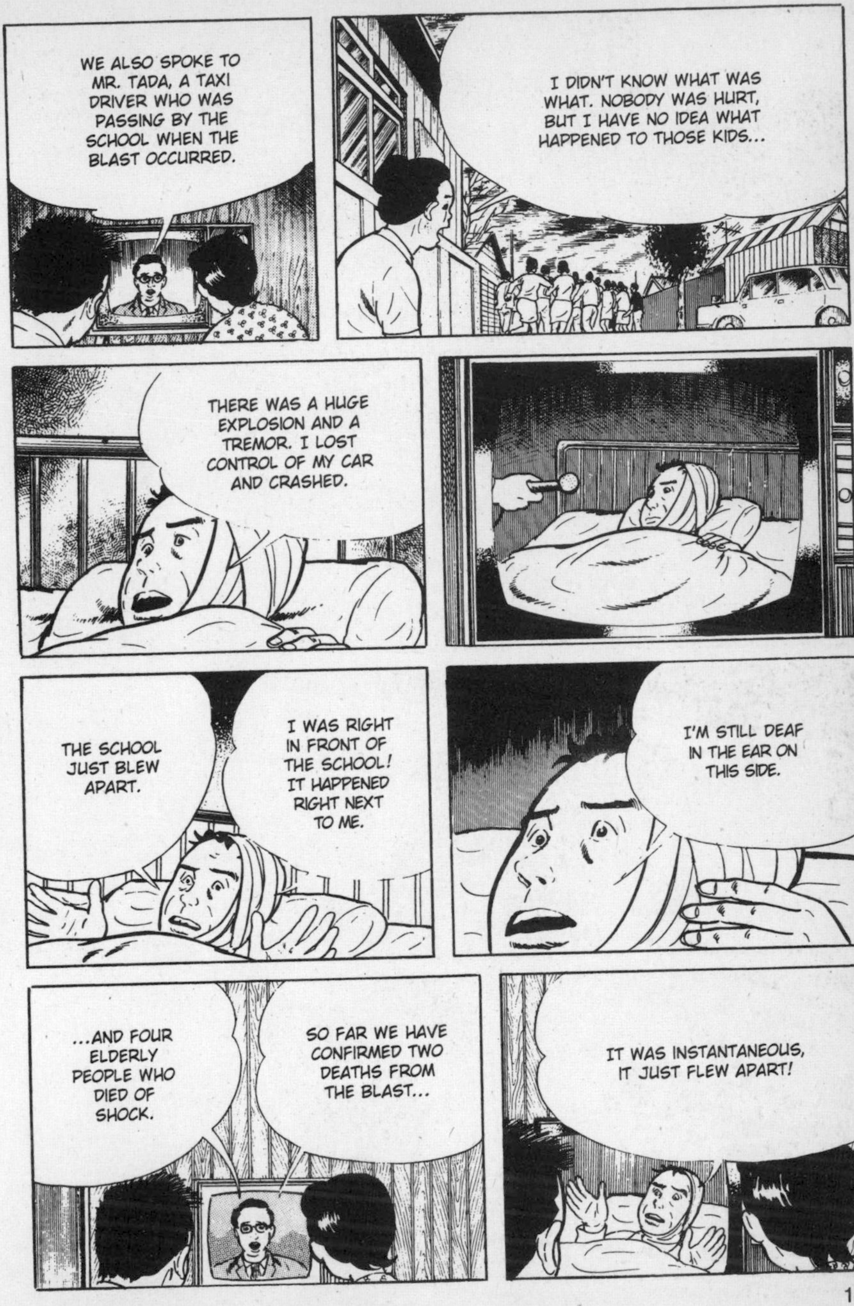
I DIDN'T KNOW WHAT WAS WHAT. NOBODY WAS HURT, BUT I HAVE NO IDEA WHAT HAPPENED TO THOSE KIDS...
WE ALSO SPOKE TO MR. TADA, A TAXI DRIVER WHO WAS PASSING BY THE SCHOOL WHEN THE BLAST OCCURRED.
THERE WAS A HUGE EXPLOSION AND A TREMOR. I LOST CONTROL OF MY CAR AND CRASHED.
I'M STILL DEAF IN THE EAR ON THIS SIDE.
I WAS RIGHT IN FRONT OF THE SCHOOL! IT HAPPENED RIGHT NEXT TO ME.
THE SCHOOL JUST BLEW APART.
IT WAS INSTANTANEOUS, IT JUST FLEW APART!
SO FAR WE HAVE CONFIRMED TWO DEATHS FROM THE BLAST...
...AND FOUR ELDERLY PEOPLE WHO DIED OF SHOCK.

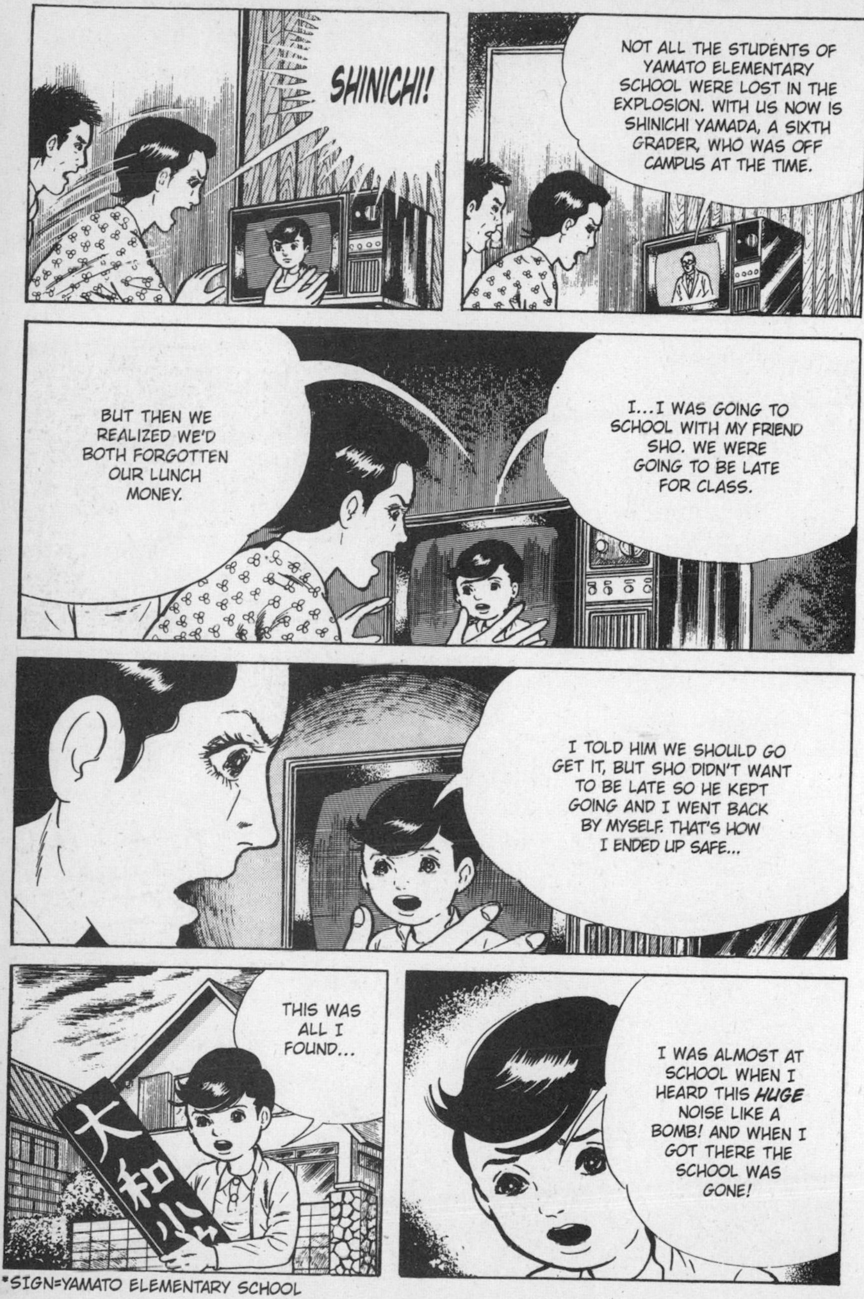
NOT ALL THE STUDENTS OF YAMATO ELEMENTARY SCHOOL WERE LOST IN THE EXPLOSION. WITH US NOW IS SHINICHI YAMADA, A SIXTH GRADER, WHO WAS OFF CAMPUS AT THE TIME.
SHINICHI!
I...I WAS GOING TO SCHOOL WITH MY FRIEND SHO. WE WERE GOING TO BE LATE FOR CLASS.
BUT THEN WE REALIZED WE'D BOTH FORGOTTEN OUR LUNCH MONEY.
I TOLD HIM WE SHOULD GO GET IT, BUT SHO DIDN'T WANT TO BE LATE SO HE KEPT GOING AND I WENT BACK BY MYSELF. THAT'S HOW I ENDED UP SAFE...
I WAS ALMOST AT SCHOOL WHEN I HEARD THIS *HUGE* NOISE LIKE A BOMB! AND WHEN I GOT THERE THE SCHOOL WAS GONE!
THIS WAS ALL I FOUND...
大和小

*SIGN=YAMATO ELEMENTARY SCHOOL

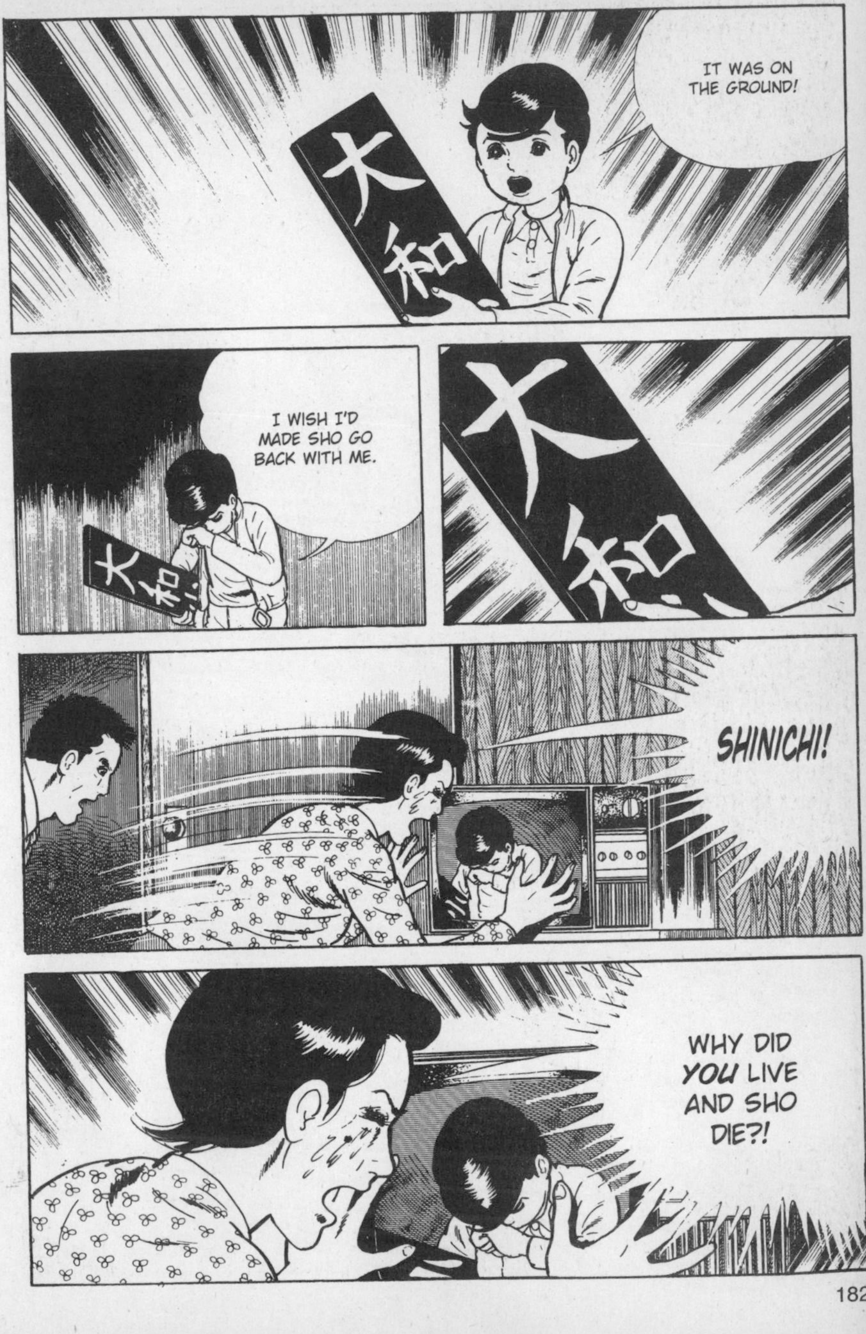
IT WAS ON THE GROUND!
大和
大和
I WISH I'D MADE SHO GO BACK WITH ME.
大和
SHINICHI!
WHY DID *YOU* LIVE AND SHO DIE?!

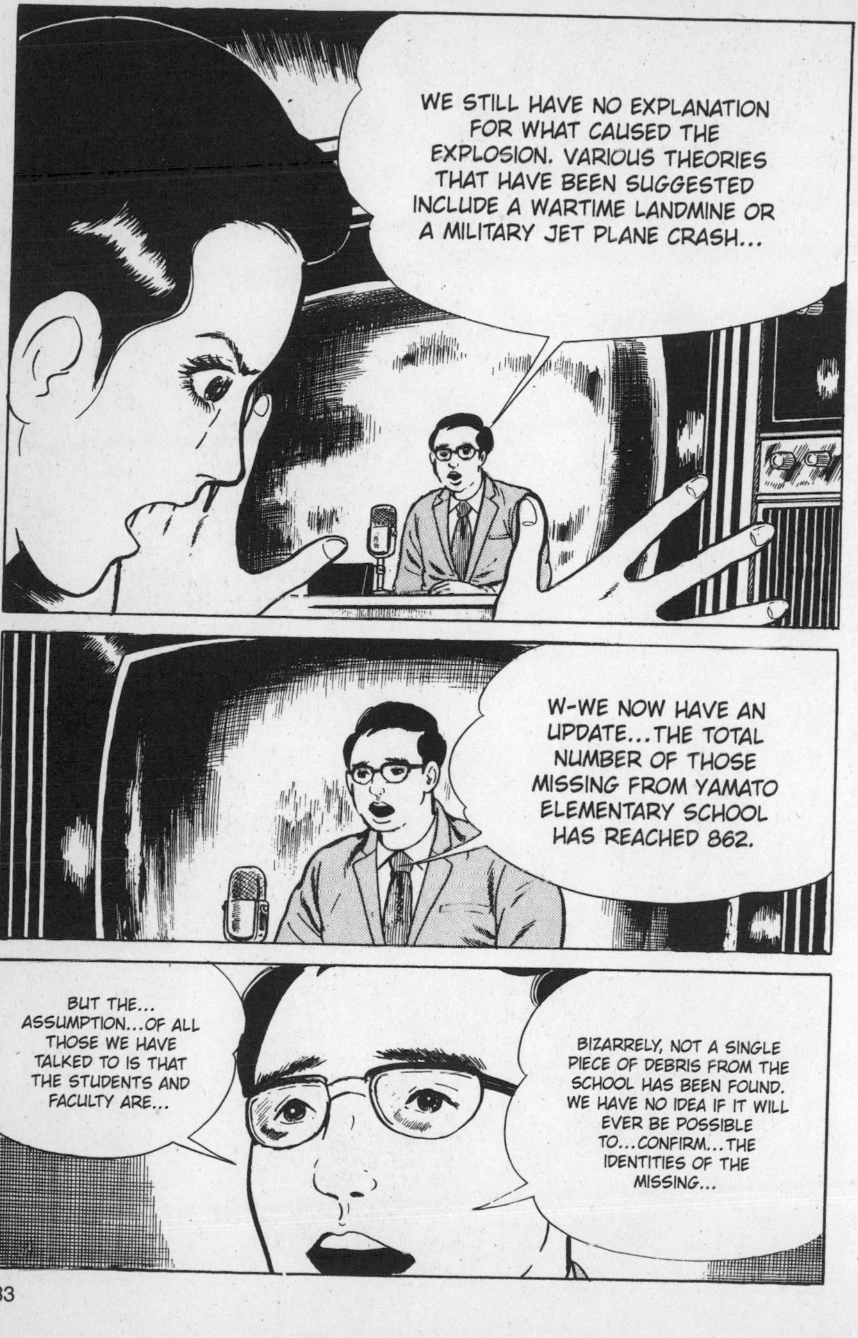
WE STILL HAVE NO EXPLANATION FOR WHAT CAUSED THE EXPLOSION. VARIOUS THEORIES THAT HAVE BEEN SUGGESTED INCLUDE A WARTIME LANDMINE OR A MILITARY JET PLANE CRASH...
W-WE NOW HAVE AN UPDATE...THE TOTAL NUMBER OF THOSE MISSING FROM YAMATO ELEMENTARY SCHOOL HAS REACHED 862.
BIZARRELY, NOT A SINGLE PIECE OF DEBRIS FROM THE SCHOOL HAS BEEN FOUND. WE HAVE NO IDEA IF IT WILL EVER BE POSSIBLE TO...CONFIRM...THE IDENTITIES OF THE MISSING...
BUT THE... ASSUMPTION...OF ALL THOSE WE HAVE TALKED TO IS THAT THE STUDENTS AND FACULTY ARE...

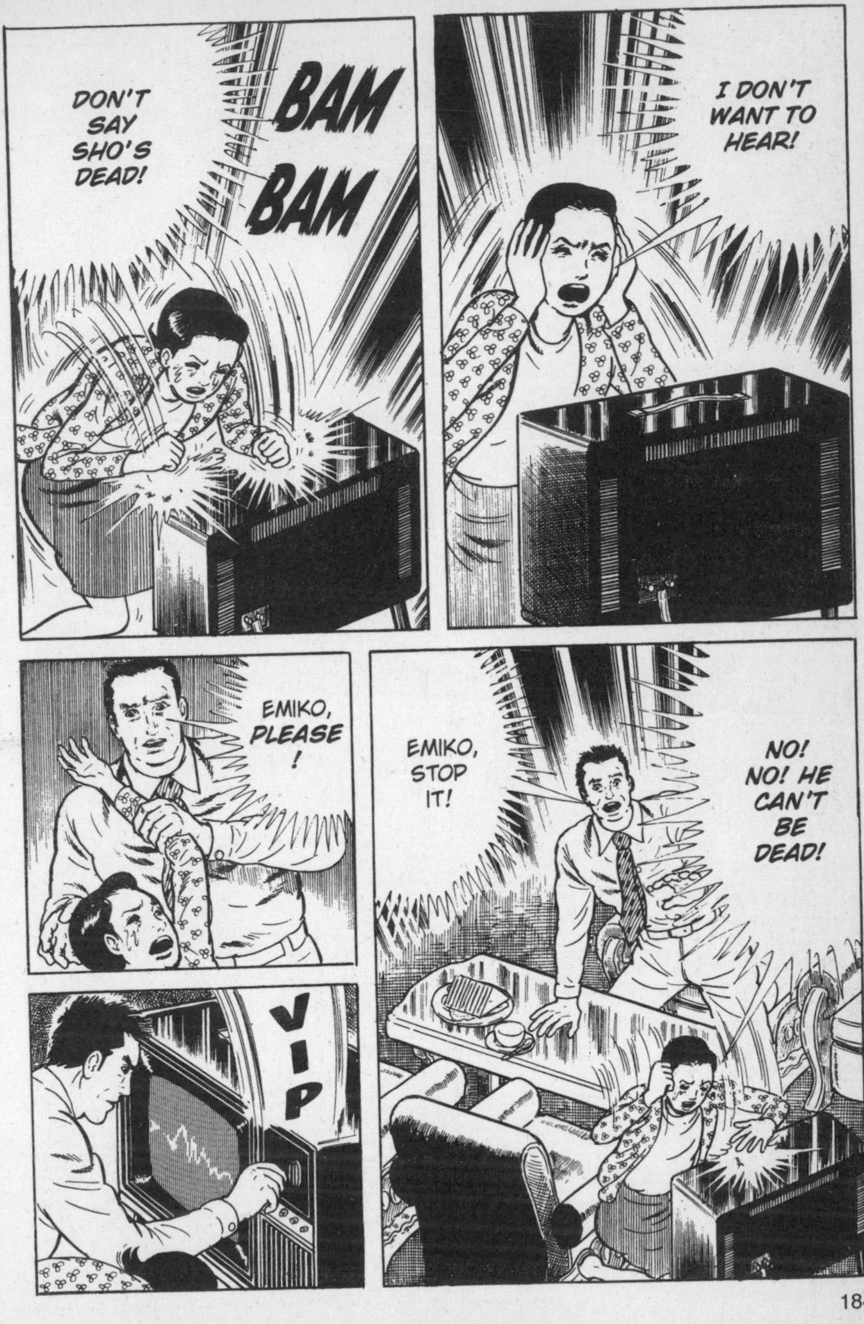
I DON'T WANT TO HEAR!
DON'T SAY SHO'S DEAD!
BAM
BAM
NO! NO! HE CAN'T BE DEAD!
EMIKO, STOP IT!
EMIKO, PLEASE!
VIP

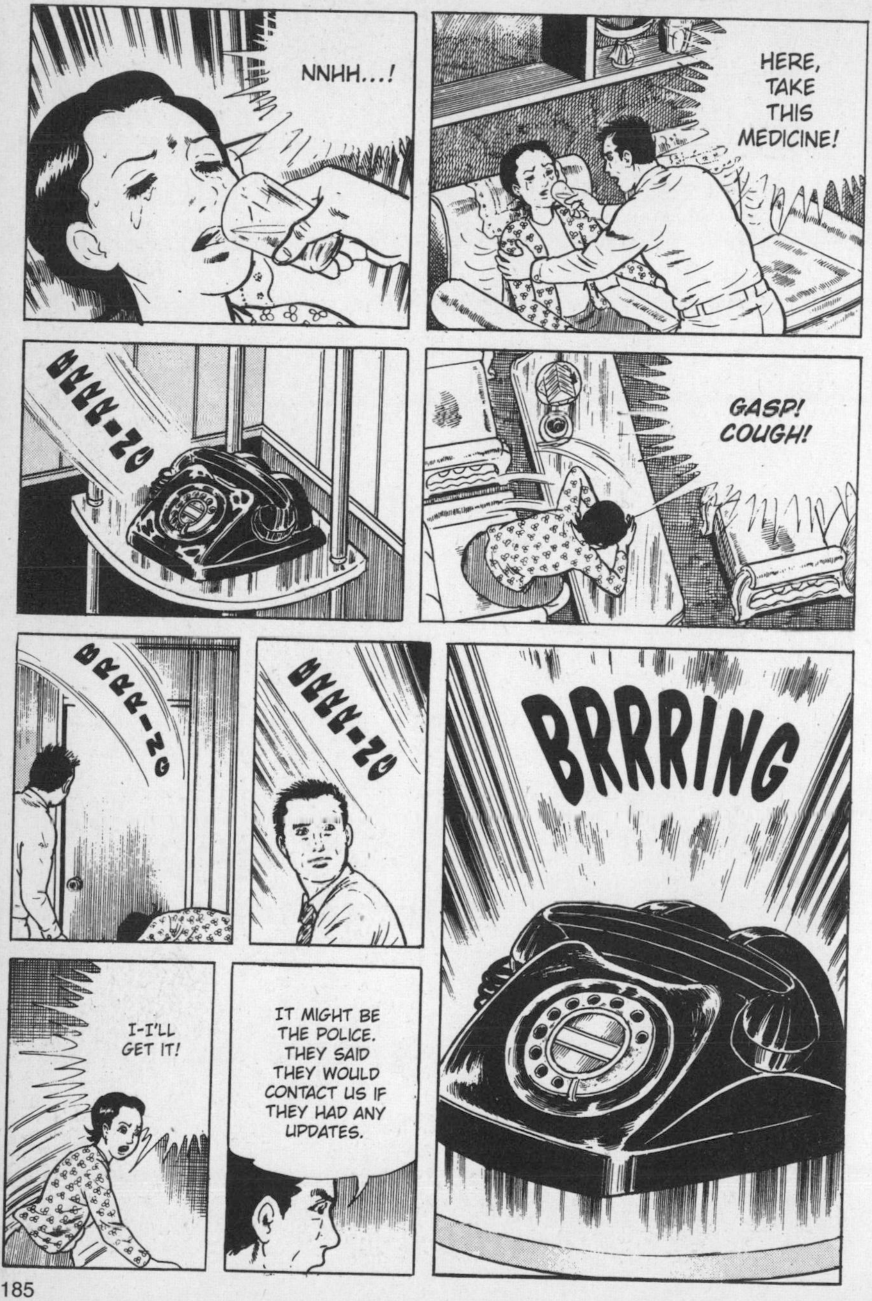
HERE, TAKE THIS MEDICINE!
NNHH...!
GASP! COUGH!
BRRRING
BRRRING
BRRRING
BRRRING
IT MIGHT BE THE POLICE. THEY SAID THEY WOULD CONTACT US IF THEY HAD ANY UPDATES.
I-I'LL GET IT!

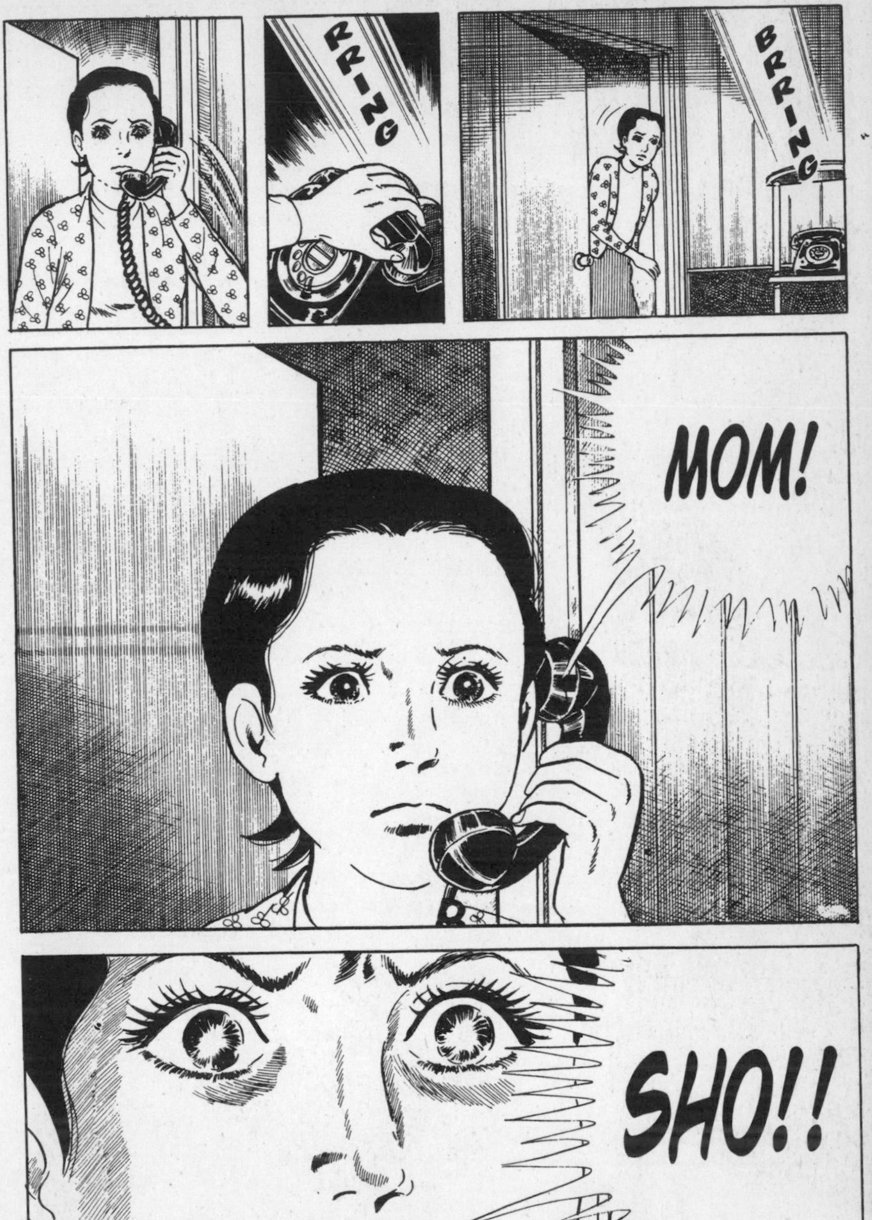
BRRING
RRING
MOM!
SHO!!

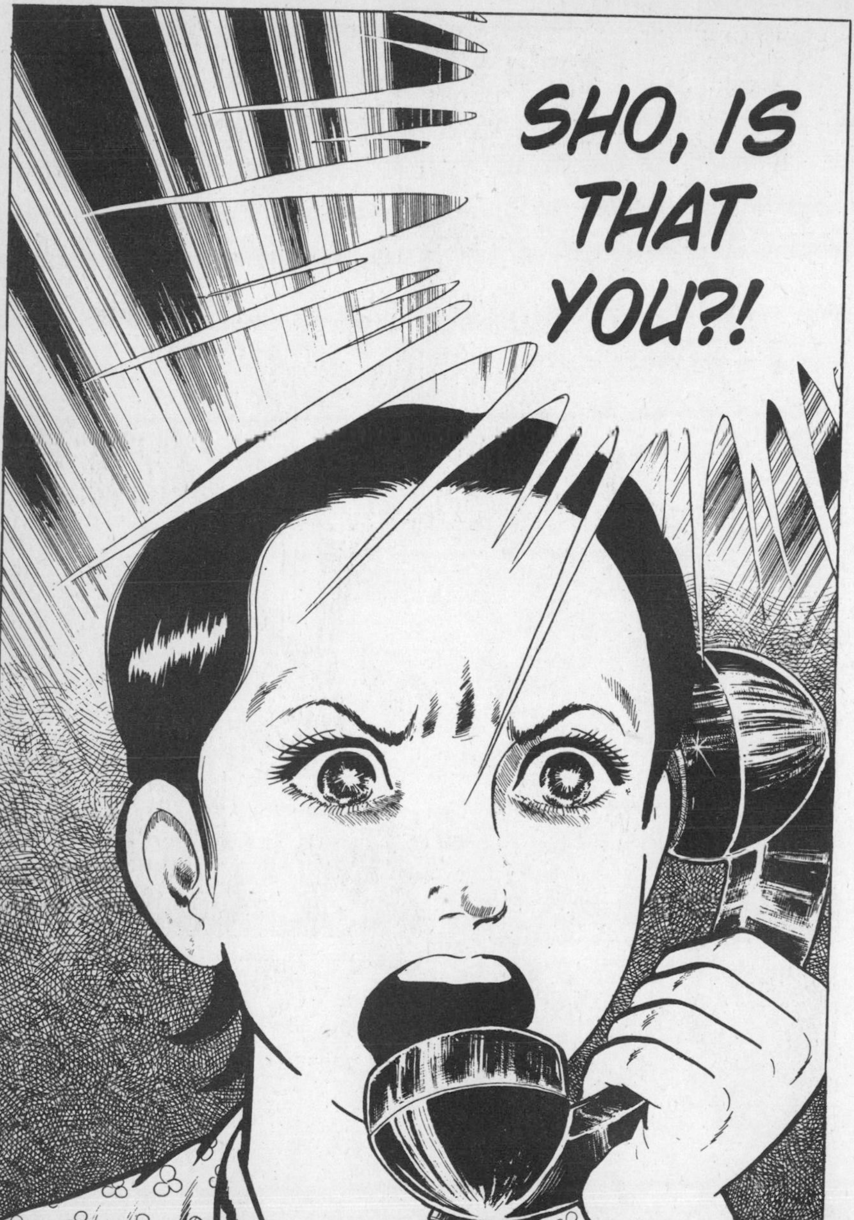
SHO, IS THAT YOU?!

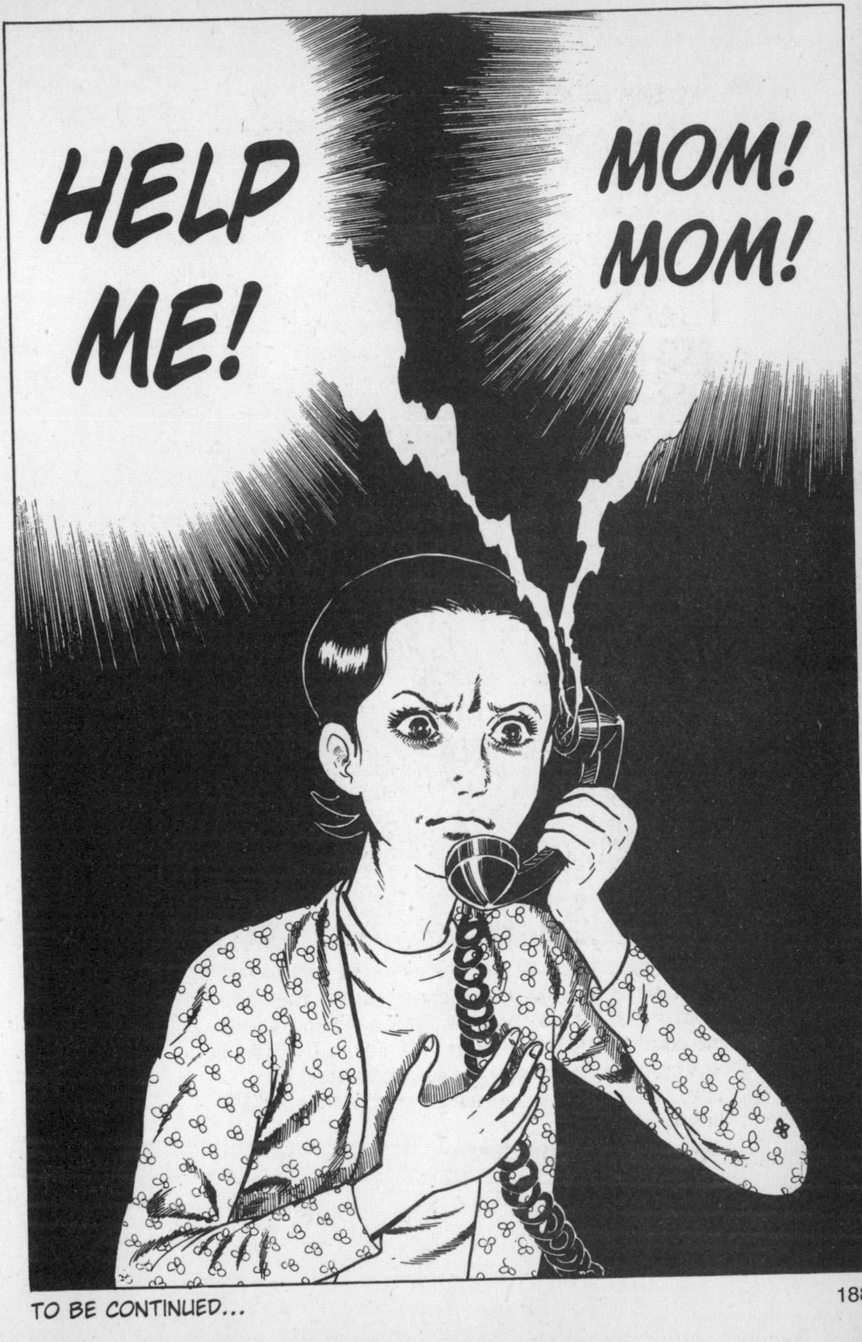
MOM! MOM!
HELP ME!

TO BE CONTINUED...

IN THE NEXT VOLUME...

As Sho fights for his life in the buried city that once was Tokyo, his cries for help travel across time and reach the ears of his mother in the distant past. But how can she save her son now? Back at the school, as their resources dwindle, the students revert to savagery and despair. But suicide, starvation and madness are not the most horrible things in their new world...

AVAILABLE DECEMBER 2006!

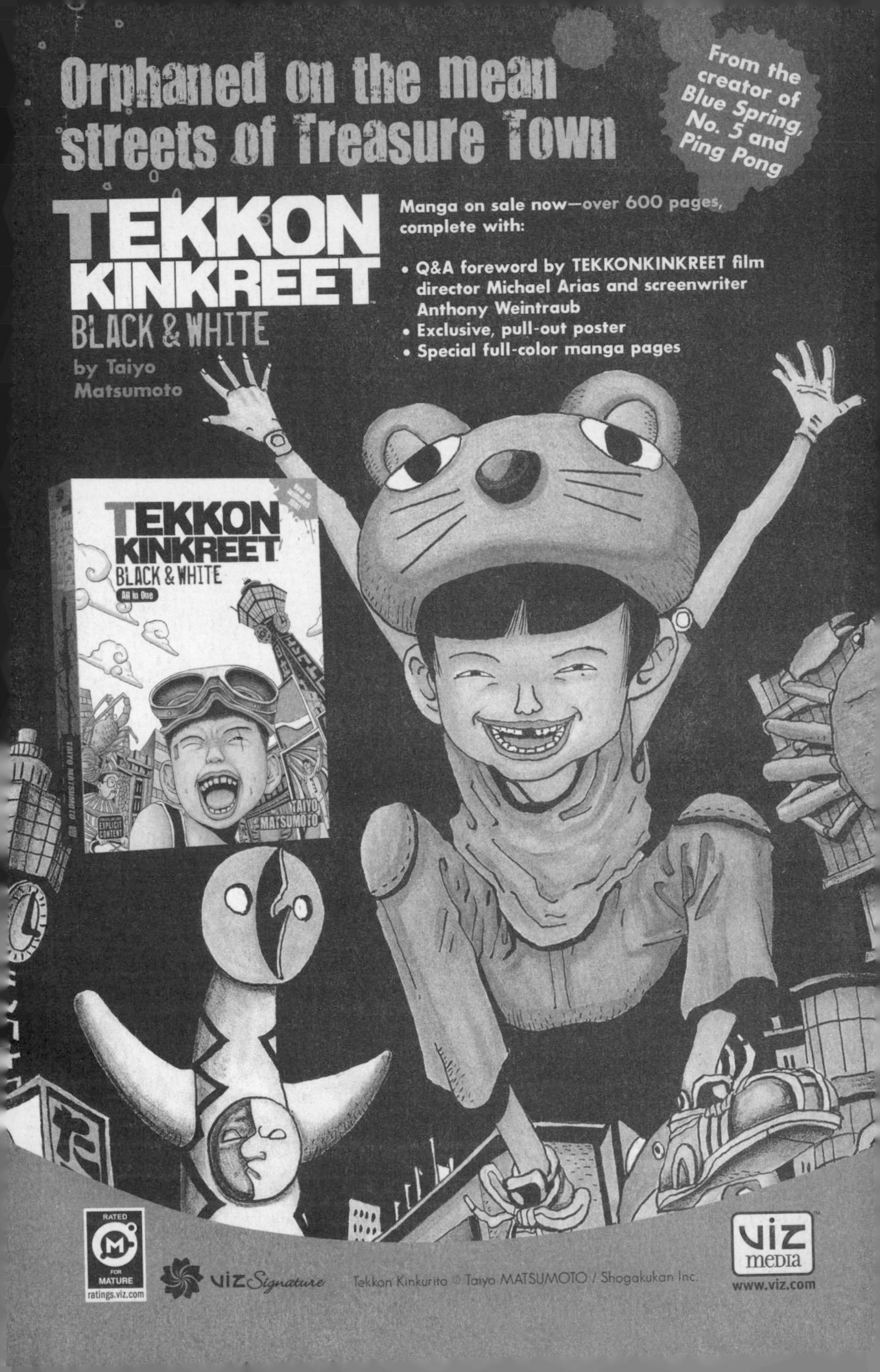
Orphaned on the mean streets of Treasure Town
From the creator of Blue Spring, No. 5 and Ping Pong
TEKKON KINKREET BLACK & WHITE
by Taiyo Matsumoto
Manga on sale now—over 600 pages, complete with:
• Q&A foreword by TEKKONKINKREET film director Michael Arias and screenwriter Anthony Weintraub
• Exclusive, pull-out poster
• Special full-color manga pages
TEKKON KINKREET BLACK & WHITE
All in One
TAIYO MATSUMOTO
EXPLICIT CONTENT
RATED M FOR MATURE
ratings.viz.com
VIZ Signature
Tekkon Kinkurito © Taiyo MATSUMOTO / Shogakukan Inc.
VIZ media
www.viz.com

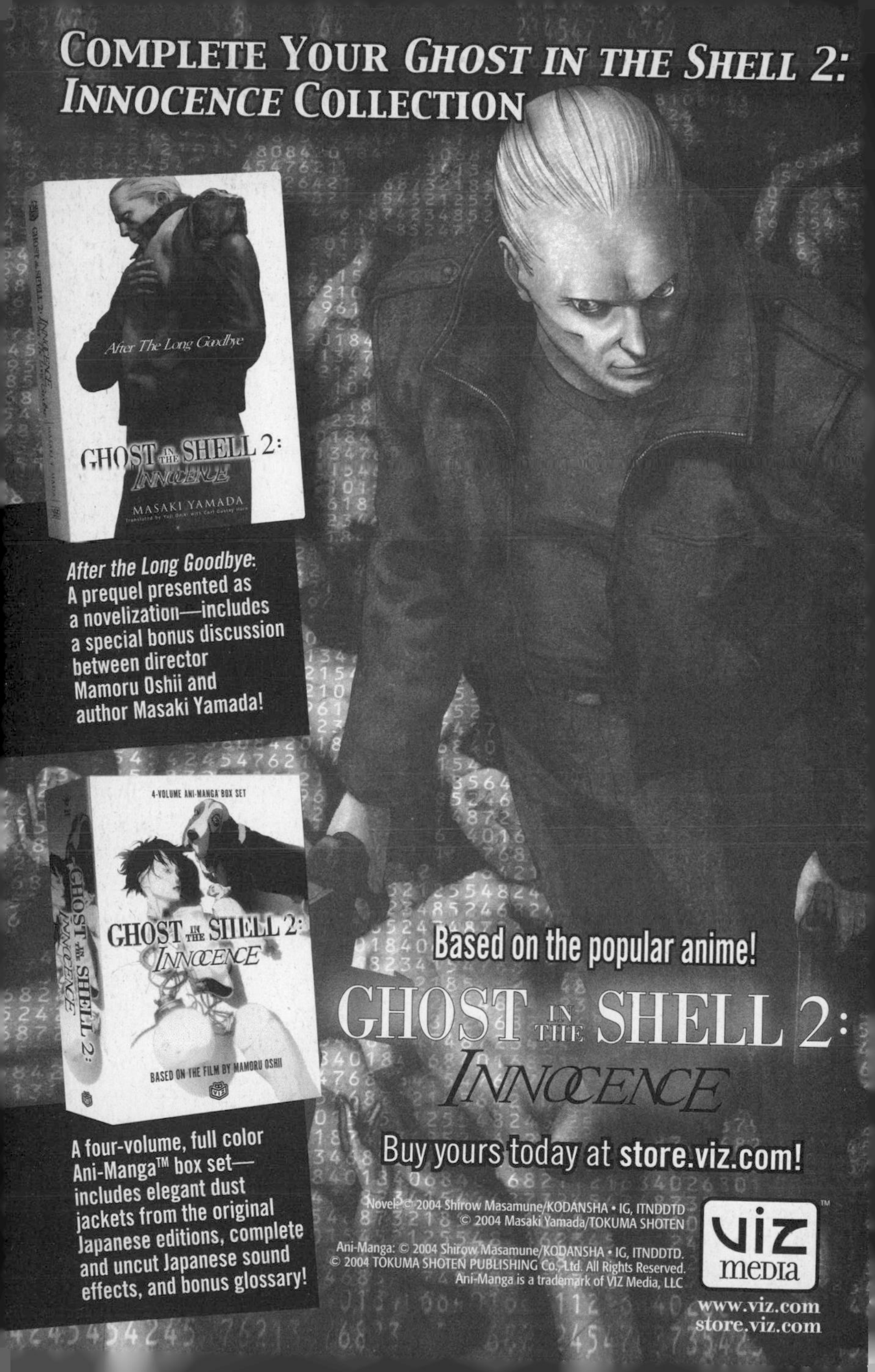
COMPLETE YOUR GHOST IN THE SHELL 2: INNOCENCE COLLECTION
After The Long Goodbye
GHOST IN THE SHELL 2: INNOCENCE
MASAKI YAMADA
After the Long Goodbye: A prequel presented as a novelization—includes a special bonus discussion between director Mamoru Oshii and author Masaki Yamada!
4-VOLUME ANI-MANGA BOX SET
GHOST IN THE SHELL 2: INNOCENCE
BASED ON THE FILM BY MAMORU OSHII
A four-volume, full color Ani-Manga™ box set—includes elegant dust jackets from the original Japanese editions, complete and uncut Japanese sound effects, and bonus glossary!
Based on the popular anime!
GHOST IN THE SHELL 2: INNOCENCE
Buy yours today at store.viz.com!
Novel: © 2004 Shirow Masamune/KODANSHA • IG, ITNDDTD
© 2004 Masaki Yamada/TOKUMA SHOTEN
Ani-Manga: © 2004 Shirow Masamune/KODANSHA • IG, ITNDDTD.
© 2004 TOKUMA SHOTEN PUBLISHING Co., Ltd. All Rights Reserved.
Ani-Manga is a trademark of VIZ Media, LLC
viz media
www.viz.com
store.viz.com

LOVE MANGA?
LET U… HINK!

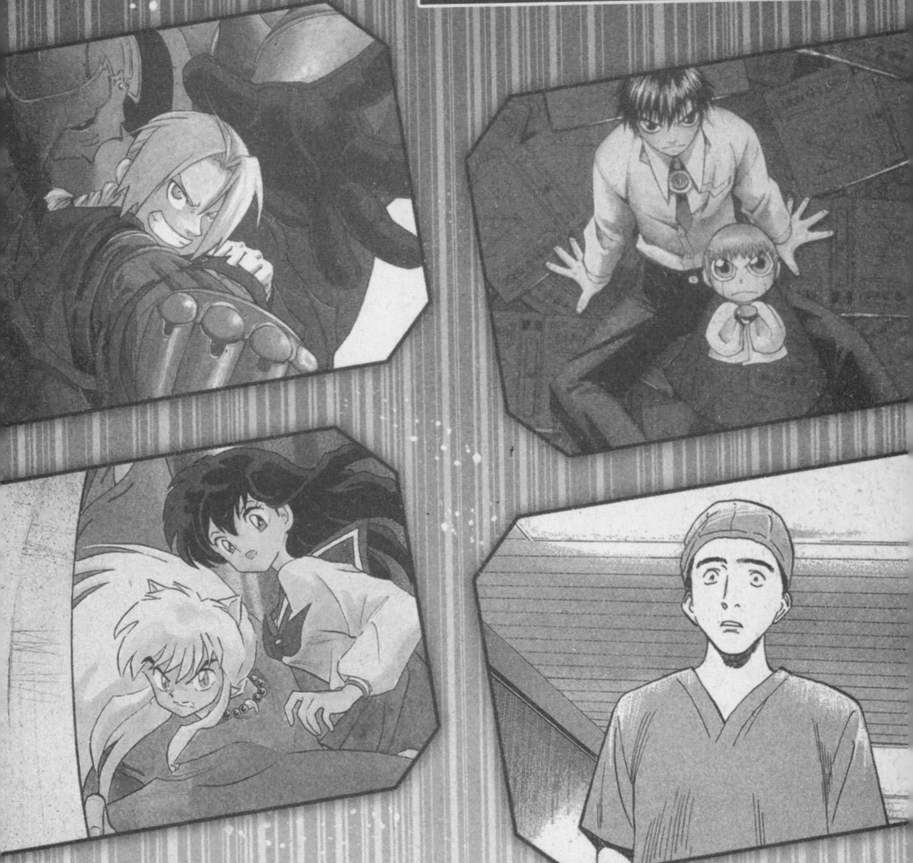